The Public Image

THE PUBLIC IMAGE

PHOTOGRAPHY AND CIVIC SPECTATORSHIP

Robert Hariman and
John Louis Lucaites

The University of Chicago Press
Chicago and London

ROBERT HARIMAN is professor of communication studies at Northwestern University. JOHN LOUIS LUCAITES is associate dean of arts and humanities and Provost Professor of Rhetoric and Public Culture at Indiana University. They are the authors of *No Caption Needed: Iconic Photographs, Public Culture, and Liberal Democracy*.

The University of Chicago Press, Chicago 60637
The University of Chicago Press, Ltd., London

Printed in China

25 24 23 22 21 20 19 18 17 16   1 2 3 4 5

ISBN-13: 978-0-226-34293-1 (cloth)
ISBN-13: 978-0-226-34309-9 (e-book)
DOI: 10.7208/chicago/9780226343099.001.0001

Publication of this book has been aided by a grant from the Neil Harris Endowment Fund, which honors the innovative scholarship of Neil Harris, the Preston and Sterling Morton Professor Emeritus of History at the University of Chicago. The Fund is supported by contributions from the students, colleagues, and friends of Neil Harris.

Library of Congress Cataloging-in-Publication Data

Names: Hariman, Robert, author. | Lucaites, John Louis, author.
Title: The public image : photography and civic spectatorship / Robert Hariman and John Louis Lucaites.
Description: Chicago ; London : The Univesity of Chicago Press, 2016. | Includes bibliographical references and index.
Identifiers: LCCN 2016001195 | ISBN 9780226342931 (cloth : alk. paper) | ISBN 9780226343099 (e-book)
Subjects: LCSH: Photography—Social aspects. | Visual communication.
Classification: LCC TR183 .H375 2016 | DDC 770—dc23 LC record available at http://lccn.loc.gov/2016001195

♾ This paper meets the requirements of ANSI/NISO Z39.48-1992 (Permanence of Paper).

You are an instrument of visible music, Camera, a focused mind
In love with witness.

TERRANCE HAYES, *"Self-Portrait as the Mind of a Camera"*

CONTENTS

ACKNOWLEDGMENTS

First of all, we want to thank the photographers. Every claim we make on behalf of the significance of the public image depends on their skill, intelligence, courage, and persistence. Every day they provide the public with the images that are needed to both sustain a civil society and reflect on its limitations. Nothing in this book is said to suggest that they should do anything differently. Instead, we aspire to help spectators think about what is there to be seen.

We also have been inspired by our fellow bloggers: Michael Shaw, Jim Johnson, Jörg Colberg, Pete Brook, and David Campbell not least among them. The golden age of blogging was a brief one, but it nurtured a way of writing about and with images that is the raison d'être of this book. That engagement was created by our readers as well, especially those who commented at our blog and in other forums on our work. We don't know what the future of nocaptionneeded.com will be, but our years of posting there were the incubator for the arguments set forth here, which in turn are backed (we believe) by the many hundreds of photographs that we featured and the thousands more that could have been included.

Our work also has benefited immensely from the critical engagement it has received in scholarly forums. These include numerous presentations at academic conferences in the United States, as well as invited presentations in Athens (GA), Beijing, Bergen, Bloomington (IN), Chicago, Copenhagen, Crawfordsville, Dublin, Durham (UK), Evanston, Heidelberg, Leeds, Lincoln, Linfield, Los Angeles, Luxembourg, Montreal, New York, Norman, Örebro, Paris, Pittsburgh, Södertörn, Tel Aviv, Uppsala, and Wassenaar. We are grateful for the candid criticisms and generous encouragement that we have encountered in each of these settings. These qualities also were evident in the reviews and editorial work for the scholarly publications that have been folded into this text. These include "Bad Image, Good Art: Thinking through Banality," *Flow* 15, no. 2 (2011); "The Banality of Violence," *Flow* 15, no. 5 (2012); "On the Surface," *Flow* 15, no. 10 (2012); "Seeing the Stranger in the Mirror: Everyday Life in Magnum's Public World," in *Reading Magnum: A Visual Archive of the Modern World*, ed. Steven Hoelscher (Austin: University of Texas Press, 2013), 246–65; "Watching War Evolve: Photojournalism and New Forms of Violence," in *The Violence of the Image: Photography and International Conflict*, ed. Liam Kennedy and Caitlin Patrick (London: I. B. Tauris, 2014), 139–63; "Icons, Iconicity, and Cultural Critique," *Sociologica*, no. 1 (2015), 1–32; and "Photography: The Abundant Art," *Photography and Culture* 9 (2016). As this volume came together, it also drew on the skills and dedication of four outstanding research assistants: Amina Asim, E. Cram, Chris Gilbert, and Saul Kutnicki. We anticipate hearing much more about them in the future.

We especially want to thank those colleagues who took time from their busy schedules to read one or more chapter drafts: David Campbell, Ralph Cintron, Jörg Colberg, Dilip Gaonkar, Liam Kennedy, Wendy Kozol, Mark Reinhardt, and Vanessa Schwartz. They were there when the work was at once too long and not developed enough, and their criticisms and suggestions were enormously helpful.

The students in our graduate seminars at Northwestern and Indiana Universities read the entire manuscript in draft form, and their insightful comments made many direct contributions to the book. Thanks go to Lauren DeLaCruz, Eddie Gamboa, Gabby Garcia, Harriette Kevill-Davies, Evelyn Kreutzer, Zach Mills, Liam Olson-Mayes, Lital Pascar, Tatiana Poddubnykh, Jiajin Tu, Catalina Uribe, LaCharles Ward, and Yanhong Yang, and to Kathleen de Onís, Beth Kaszynski, Saul Kutnicki, Katie Lind, Norma Musih, and Philip Perdue.

Our home institutions have also played a key role, providing us with the time and resources necessary for such an undertaking. At Northwestern University we would especially like to thank Department Chair Ellen Wartella and the Department of Communication Studies for the generous research funding they provided. At Indiana University we would like to thank Greg Waller and Jane Goodman, who chaired the Department of Communication and Culture and provided support at vital junctures of the project; Executive Dean Larry Singell of the College of Arts and Sciences, who has never let the thin air of administration compromise his commitment to scholarship; the College of Arts and Humanities Institute, which supported the project in its embryonic stages; and the Office of the Vice Provost for Research for a research grant-in-aid.

Once again, we are indebted to the suggestions of the external reviewers for the University of Chicago Press and to Doug Mitchell for his exemplary editorial stewardship. Thanks also to Kyle Wagner for sweating the details as we moved the manuscript through to publication. Because of Doug and those he includes in the work, we consider our relationship with the press to be one of the treasures of academic life.

As always, our work depends most profoundly on the support of our families and friends. Thanks especially to Yogi for saying exactly the right thing at the right time, and to Jane and Ginny for being there always.

CHAPTER ONE

CLIMBING OUT OF PLATO'S CAVE

While children fear monsters lurking in the dark, adults are told to beware of phantoms of light. Images are deceptive, we are reminded again and again—and photographic images are especially beguiling because they conform so closely to reality. They stand in for reality, but they are not real.

So what are they, and what do they do? The answers, it seems, bring more bad news. Photographs are inchoate fragments of the events they purport to record, essentially meaningless without verbal contextualization. They depict only the surface features of the world, its sheer particularity, rather than structure, complexity, or depth. They activate merely emotional reactions that short-circuit deliberative thought, and even the better emotions such as compassion soon are exhausted by excessive exposure. Most tellingly, they "aestheticize reality," putting a smile on anything to evoke reactions of pleasure, including guilty pleasures such as voyeurism, nostalgia, and other fantasies. Such tendencies are easily put to worse use, as photographs become means of mass manipulation and political domination: the result is a society of spectacles and scopic regimes where citizens are converted into both passive spectators and objects of surveillance. The large-scale consequences are already before us: celebrity culture metastasizes across all media, advertising images cover every nook and cranny of the lifeworld, the press publishes ever more images of the same abject bodies to elicit only token responses, and the planet veers toward environmental catastrophe driven by forces that elude visualization.[1]

Susan Sontag's 1977 pronouncement seems prophetic: "Humankind lingers unregenerately in Plato's cave, still reveling, its age-old habit, in mere images of the truth."[2] We are not so modern after all;

or, more to the point, modern technologies such as photography have only made our benighted habits more dangerous. And it may be too late to change. We can climb out of the cave today only to step into "the world as picture," as human consciousness, our inherent capacity for knowing the world, has already been transformed by media technologies to make knowledge itself compromised by its entanglement with the image.[3] If enlightenment is possible, it seems that it will have to include a resolute critique of how visual media are instruments of distraction, deception, and dependency. In modern societies, both individual and collective freedoms require breaking the thralldom of the image world.

You can have a good academic career doing just that. And you can get a lot of points at the bar or the coffee shop or the blog. And you can do a lot of good: let's not forget for a minute that there are staggering amounts of delusion, denial, and dangerous nonsense sloshing around in any modern society. Even if we have passed through the looking glass into a culture of "enlightened false consciousness" that makes irony ubiquitous while disabling critique, justice still can depend on drawing a line between truth and illusion, image and reality.[4] If the alarm has been sounded from Plato to Sontag and beyond, surely the danger is ever present.

And so it is, but . . . compared to what? Is photography really that one-sided? Is politics really that simple? Has nothing really changed? In this book we don't deny that human beings are easily misled by images of their own making, but we do insist that credulity is only part of the story. We recognize that photography has been adopted for every kind of human viciousness, but we also believe that it is a boon for human understanding and solidarity. We grant that photography often is conventional, sentimental, and otherwise compromised, but we also believe that it is a vital technology of democratic citizenship.[5] And we believe that the critique of photography suffers from a number of errors—errors due to mistaken assumptions, biased comparisons, and failure to observe significant changes in society and politics. Although these errors were recognized along the way, dissenting arguments are only now accumulating to the point that, along with many other changes in communication technologies, institutions, and practices, a paradigm shift is becoming possible.

We are not interested merely in setting the record straight. At the least, that would be simplistic, as some of these disputes are perennial controversies about essentially contested concepts or structural tensions: "reality" is thinkable, in part, through the contrast with "illusion," while visual meaning, like all meaning, exceeds any one standpoint or perspective. Other differences are due to imbalances in power that may or may not change but in every case require thoughtful and courageous response: human rights may be advancing in one area through acts of social recognition and declining in another due to willful blindness. Philosophical debates must go on, just as stupidity and exploitation must be resisted again and again. What can be overlooked across the board, however, are the possibilities for a more transformative conception of photography as a mode of experience, a medium for social thought, and a public art.

The purpose of this book is to demonstrate how photography and particularly photojournalism provide vital resources for thinking about the problems of collective living. As will be clear, "thinking" here includes feeling, talking, and acting in response to those problems. Even so, we are not interested in determining when and how specific photographs or photographic techniques are influential. Despite the incessant demand for such knowledge, it is exceedingly hard to come by—and not just for photographs. Words, it should be widely acknowledged, have the same problem: speeches, news reports, editorial commentary, government reports, histories, novels, and all other texts typically have only minuscule effects on collective behavior; in almost every case, continual repetition and other forms of social investment are required to effect real change. What remains underappreciated is how words and images alike are used all along the way as "equipment for living"—that is, as means for continually making sense of the world and for adjusting one's place in it in relation to others.[6] As C. Wright Mills observed, thinking involves the selection and manipulation of available symbolic materials.[7] The phrasing reflects the instrumental tone of his social scientific context, but the point remains sound: we think with many "things," including words, numbers, sounds, objects—and images. Photography has provided modern societies with an enormous and continually expanding archive of images, and many of them were created for the purpose of communicating with other people in order to live together more richly.

What has been lacking is an adequate discourse for public discussion of those images seen in common. Sontag observed that "the language in which photographs are generally evaluated is extremely meager," and she found the fault to be "something inherent in photography itself, whenever it is viewed as an art."[8] Unfortunately, that is right where Sontag's aesthetic judgments kept it. As she became the central author of a twentieth-century discourse on photography, the misrecognition continued—that is, photography was systematically interpreted in a manner to maintain privileged conceptions of the fine arts and the critic's own medium of well-wrought prose.[9] As Susie Linfield has documented, the only variation, also following Sontag, was to supplement the aesthetic disregard with scathing critique of its social functions and political effects: spectators could be bourgeois "tourists" or dupes of the ruling class but hardly citizens.[10]

A richer understanding of photography requires a different attitude. Photography has been from the start a democratic medium—one addressed to, used by, and even constitutionally chartered for the public.[11] News and documentary photography have been developed to serve this public trust most directly.[12] The question of what a public art is, however, has been vexing since the first attempt at definition, which was when oratory became an object of philosophical and practical discussion in Greek antiquity.[13] Many of the issues remain the same: Is the speech/photograph a matter of truth or opinion? Is it rational or emotional? Authentic or crafted? Beautiful or effective? As judged by the audience or an expert? Many other questions reflect the complications of our current media environment, including the different forms of news, advocacy, advertising, art, and entertainment and their continual intertwining; the ongoing transformations wrought by digitization, a technological innovation comparable to the printing press or photography itself; the economic, political, and cultural forces testing democratic institutions and complicating democratization; and the fraught relationship between progress and catastrophe exposed by global modernization. Obviously, neither the perennial nor the more pressing questions can be answered once and for all, but perhaps they can be brought together to develop a new discourse on photography as a public art for the twenty-first century.

By focusing on photography's capacity as public art, we are concerned primarily with photojournalism—news photography, documentary photography, and similar practices of production and circulation. Whatever the label, these are the photographs that are presented in the news media—and also in related sites for advocacy, commentary, and education—about the events, conflicts, customs, and other subjects that are of common concern or interest. To do justice to these images, however, one has to take up questions about both the relatively narrow (but still capacious) ambit of the news and photography in general. One reason for this double focus is that the critical discourse on photography has been characterized by frequent conflations of the wider and narrower practices, and usually to the detriment of both. More recently, there is no doubt that whatever lines existed in the past have become increasingly blurred by technological and cultural change. In this environment, "photography" is too broad and "photojournalism" is too narrow a label for the public image, but no better terms are yet widely recognized. Thus some of the time this book discusses the medium of photography as a whole, but always on behalf of understanding those images that are found regularly in the news media and in other sites oriented toward public discussion. This perspective is neither a definitional exercise nor an attempt to deflect attention away from the astonishing range of photography; it is an argument for more robust forms of civic spectatorship.

What is crucial is that the public image not be seen as a poor substitute for a work of art, verbal statement, or reality. It is a work of public art, not a fine art; an image, not a text; a real artifact, not a fabricated reality. Thus one task is to consider what it can do on its own terms, that is, as a means for communicating with others about common concerns. And ironically, by giving up on the higher functions of language, art, and culture, we can discern how the photograph can be capable of speaking, and of disturbing perception toward profundity, and of becoming a worthwhile second nature.

Changing Paradigms in the Digital Stream

We are not alone in attempting to see photography anew. Photography theory today is in a state of flux; we could say that it is tending in the direction we are taking, but time will have to tell. What can be said is that a shift in the interpretive community is beginning to emerge. The older paradigm was defined on several sides by the Frankfurt School media theorists (e.g., Siegfried Kracauer, Walter Benjamin, Bertolt Brecht, Theodor Adorno, Max Horkheimer);[14] by Sontag and others channeling an iconoclastic critical attitude (e.g., Roland Barthes, Guy Debord, Allan Sekula, John Berger, John Tagg, Victor Burgin, Rosalind Krauss, Abigail Solomon-Godeau, Martha Rosler, Carol Squiers, and the thousands of scholars who extended the work of the Birmingham School of Cultural Studies);[15] and, indirectly, by the scholars and practitioners maintaining the professional norms of photojournalism, who too often limit the legitimate function of the news image to the transfer of information. There were, of course, considerable differences among these writers, just as there are within the loosely defined interpretive community that is emerging today.[16] The more recent community, which itself will continue to evolve, includes historians, critics, and theorists such as Dora Apel, Ariella Azoulay, Geoffrey Batchen, Susan Buck-Morss, David Campbell, Lilie Chouliaraki, Geoff Dyer, Jae Emerling, Cara Finnegan, Liam Kennedy, Wendy Kozol, Susie Linfield, Nicholas Mirzoeff, W. J. T. Mitchell, Margaret Olin, Griselda Pollock, Jacques Rancière, Mark Reinhardt, Fred Ritchin, John Roberts, Vanessa Schwartz, Sharon Sliwinski, Shawn Michelle Smith, David Levi Strauss, Barbie Zelizer, and ourselves, among many others.[17] We do not claim to speak for any of these other writers, and we have learned a great deal from all of those listed on each side. We do hope to suggest how photographs can be analyzed and valued as resources for thinking seriously about the public world of society, politics, and culture.

The change that we see in contemporary photographic theory is akin to the "paradigm shift" ascribed to scientific communities by Thomas Kuhn and subsequently applied to a broad array of professional practices.[18] Any program of collaborative learning depends on a shared conception of the object and method of study, a common set of problems to be solved, and assumptions about what needs to be said and what need not be said. As time passes, however, there arise significant irregularities and incongruities that cannot be accounted for adequately within the standard model. Eventually a shift occurs in the attention space and conceptual vocabulary defining the field: new theories emerge that don't solve earlier problems so much as subsume them under different questions representing a new configuration of ideas, methods, and other factors such as changes in technology and social context. A successful shift will answer some questions, new and old, to advance knowledge and professional practice; as it does so, it solidifies into a "normal science" like the consensus that it had displaced, and thus eventually becomes susceptible to the same fate.

Paradigm shifts do not take place overnight—they are more evolutionary than revolutionary—and it is not uncommon to see advocates for the older way of thinking attempt to adapt even as they are trapped by the language and assumptions engrained in the conventional framework.[19] One example of this dilemma can be seen in watching Sontag struggle to move beyond the strong iconoclasm of *On Photography*, written in the mid-1970s, in her post-9/11 book *Regarding the Pain of Others*.

Sontag is not the most nuanced, rigorous, or original of the authors of the late-twentieth-century paradigm, but she almost singlehandedly moved photography from the margins to a position of cultural significance. She took photography very seriously, and she remains the leading influence on thinking about photography in the United States and the only American writer on photography to acquire the status of a public intellectual.[20] *On Photography* "became, almost instantly, a bible": it has been selling briskly since 1977 and has been translated into at least fifteen languages.[21] *Regarding the Pain of Others* also does well, while being lauded as a powerful reconsideration of photography's ethical and political limitations. Both books are regularly assigned in college courses across a number of disciplines. Most notably, Sontag is a forceful writer. There is no lack of intensity in her relationship with her subject, and she is not shy about stating her opinion.

Unfortunately, Sontag continues to stand in the way of moving beyond the old paradigm. Because she repudiated or modified a few of the more extreme claims of *On Photography* on behalf of a more considered acceptance of the medium's capacity for moral witness, many readers do not ask if she went far enough to provide a sufficient basis for understanding the public image.[22] *Regarding the Pain of Others* does offer a partial retraction: Sontag now questions the idea that "our culture of spectatorship neutralizes the moral force of photographs of atrocities."[23] This is progress, as are her acknowledgments that photography lends itself to a range of responses and that aesthetics and morality can work together in the photographic statement. The fact that Susan Sontag came to challenge some of the conventional wisdom is reason enough to assume that a paradigm shift is needed and well under way.

Even so, *Regarding the Pain of Others* also reaffirms too many of the conventional assumptions about photography that were set out in *On Photography* and that continue to have considerable influence today. These notions limit understanding of photography, the public, and moral response.

Photographs are "a species of rhetoric" that "simplify," "agitate," and create the "illusion of consensus"; they are "totems" and "tokens" rather than adequate representations, and also like "sound bites" and "postage stamps"; they "objectify" and yet also are a form of "alchemy" that either beautify and thereby can "bleach out a moral response," or uglify and thereby can at most be provocative; they require no artistic training and so have led to "permissive" standards for visual eloquence; they depend on a "sleight of hand" and a "surrealist" aesthetic that with the ascendancy of capitalist values is thought to be realism; they compare unfavorably with or have an unfair advantage over other arts, especially writing; they depend absolutely on written captions for their meaning, and while they can shock, "they are not much help if the task is to understand," something that can only come from narrative exposition.[24]

The public that consumes these images has matching characteristics. They take for granted their privilege, safety, and distance from the events being reported; they are alternately "voyeurs" or "cowards" and also "literalist(s)," while the "indecency" of spectatorship is of a piece with viewing lynching photographs or images of "colonized human beings" from Africa and Asia; they are being corrupted by television and are prone to remember only images, not the stories that could provide complexity and understanding; they rely instead on photojournalists, who are "professional, specialized tourists," some of whom become celebrities whose pronouncements can be so much "humbug."[25]

Moral response to a photograph is acknowledged to be possible, even after repeated exposure to images of violence, but also severely limited. Photographs serve the public by shocking the viewer, but they leave "opinions, prejudices, fantasies, misinformation untouched"; they also can go too far, making suffering "abstract" and thus fostering cynicism and fatalism; even when the emotions of compassion or sympathy are elicited, they are "unstable," tend toward "mystification of our real relations of power," and are "impertinent"; in any case, they "cannot dictate a course of action" and instead "supply only an initial spark."[26]

In short, a photograph's moral content can at best provide only a surge of raw emotional energy that is devoid of the rational capabilities necessary for ethical relationships. The public is locked into passive spectatorship rather than authentic participation and thereby is given only poor or worse options for ethical living. Photography may be put to better or worse uses but remains a profoundly suspect medium of representation, indeed one that is inherently fraudulent because the image can never provide the adequate knowledge of reality that is promised. Thus Sontag's reconsideration of photography remains locked into the same modernist binaries that need to be challenged.[27]

This summary does not pretend to do justice to the breadth of Sontag's thinking, but we do want to suggest that her second thoughts remain all too consistent with her early and still highly influential discourse. Sontag sensed that her original discourse led to some seriously mistaken conclusions, yet she could not scrap it entirely. Thus her work acquired a high degree of internal inconsistency—like the habitus of photography today. Whatever else might be happening, too often critical commentary remains beholden to a vocabulary and set of assumptions that need to be reexamined. They never were entirely accurate, but at one time they were sharp enough to mount a progressive critique of an important medium of mass communication.[28] They are not now wholly inaccurate—far from it, as they identify deep risks of media dependency—but they do not provide the conceptual resources that are needed to understand the many roles that photography can play as a public art.[29]

This book is one attempt to start over. We have not set out to dismantle the conventional approach, nor can we provide anything like a comprehensive account of what photography is today. Indeed, we are indebted to those we criticize, and we are striving to extend lines of cultural critique and themes of progressive thought that they made part of the public conversation. In place of comprehensiveness, we offer a blend of theory and practice that we hope can be taken further by others: an account of how photojournalism creates a distinctive and valuable way of understanding the modern world, and examples of how the public spectator can think about and with photographs in order to develop that understanding. These interpretations of specific images surely are partial and fallible, but they are offered as a basis for discussion. Whatever the limitations of this volume, we are confident that such discussion can reveal photography's contribution to the richness of public culture and demonstrate the extent to which democratic spectatorship can be an experience of both plurality and community.

Sontag's reconsideration was driven by the events following 9/11, which brought more attention to photojournalism, and politics and photojournalism remain vital interests for many of those who are challenging the aging paradigm. That conventional discourse is coming apart for other reasons as well, most notably the comprehensive changes produced by digitization and globalization. As Trevor Paglen has stated, the traditional debates about photography "have become largely exhausted. Simply put, there is probably not much more to say about such problems as 'indexicality,' 'truth claims,' 'the rhetoric of the image,' and other touchstones of classical photography theory. And what remains to be said about these photographic 'problems' seems increasingly extraneous to the larger photographic landscape that we inhabit."[30]

One result is that it appears increasingly preposterous to make any claim about photography in general.[31] How can "photography" make sense in a high-tech, multimedia, multiplatform environment that includes everything from images of individual atoms to a constant stream of infotainment? Where exactly is the image that is taken by multiple cameras, relayed across a dizzying array of servers, networks, and personal devices, and archived, altered, or transferred to other media? What is the news image when news sources include cell phones, surveillance cameras, and professional photographers who may work for both news media and advocacy organizations? What is a media effect when many images circulate globally across hundreds of different cultures even as most images are salient within only a few, relatively local networks while unseen elsewhere?

Obviously, one response to these predicaments is to tailor research according to precisely defined technologies, media, genres, contexts, political interests, and so forth. That important work in media studies will continue under its own steam, while we will attempt to outline a shift in attitude that can run along or aslant specific research projects. Our more general approach does *not* mean that we are attempting to catalog the range of photographic practices. That would be a staggering project, and one that could come to mirror virtually all forms of human activity. Nor are we trying to position our work as directly representative of the current state of technological development and global circulation. Instead, what we find most intriguing about the new media environment and globalization is how they highlight what have long been central tensions within photography and especially within photojournalism. Contemporary photographic practices resist many of the underlying assumptions of the older paradigm, but it is our contention that the same was true of the older practices. The critical discourse on photography never had it entirely right, never was comprehensive, never accounted for all that people do with photographs, and certainly didn't appreciate photography's affordances to the degree that it faulted the medium's constraints. We cannot be comprehensive either, but perhaps now it is becoming easier to see some things anew, particularly as they relate to fundamental tensions of modern public culture—not least those tensions between appearance and reality, the individual and society, violence and civilization, and progress and catastrophe.

Small Art, Big Audience

Instead of comprehensiveness, this book sets out a modest definition of photography in order to equip spectators to better develop the richness of the medium as a resource for public life. Thus, photography is a small language about vernacular life in a public world. Each of these three elements is an artistic limitation, and in many photographs energy is diffused rather than concentrated along one or more of these vectors. Nonetheless, often the camera does produce a moment of visual acuity precisely because these three foci intersect to provide both an intensification of experience and a moment for reflection.

Photography works like a small language because the image is minute, fragmentary, cheap, highly repetitive, having only the most rudimentary syntax, and otherwise lacking most of the semantic and artistic resources of literature and other arts. Moreover, it is small in another sense, for it is used much of the time on behalf of familiar, all-too-ordinary pursuits: pictures of the birthday party for the family album, advertisements selling anything and everything, news stories filed no matter how little there is to report. And photography is made smaller yet when it is subordinated within the status hierarchies of print media and the fine arts as merely a mode of illustration rather than a bearer of culture.

Yet in the right hands these supposed deficits become a compact and powerful instrument for illuminating vernacular life. The vernacular dimension refers to where life is lived most of the time: not standing on top of Mt. Everest or in the crucible of history or holding the levers of power, but packed like sardines on a Coney Island beach or standing in a checkout line or waiting to be asked to dance. It is the lifeworld of most people most of the time, a democracy of recognizable habits and familiar frustrations. Equally important, the quality of life in that quotidian world has become one of the defining features of the modern age: modernization is seen to be legitimate as it improves the everyday experience of ordinary people, and flawed as it fails to do so or creates new conditions of servitude or want.

Some ordinary experience occurs indoors, out of view and encapsulated in the relationships of family life. What occurs in public, however, becomes crucial to living well anywhere. The public sphere is not only a fundamental institution of modern politics but also the space in which all aspects of society can be represented and framed for judgment in respect to a just and sustainable social contract. Modern societies are defined by norms of personal liberty, equality before the law, institutional transparency, civility, and other values that depend on seeing and being seen in public. Images that appear in the public media automatically become subject to this relatively impersonal process of judgment on behalf of collective ideals.

This definition of photography may appear counterintuitive. Photography can be intrusive, and photographers have been known to be arrogant; where is the humility of small things? Visual images are not texts, so why look for a language? Do the countless images of violent demonstrations and natural disasters, or those flesh-and-blood mannequins populating advertising images, represent ordinary life? And what is public about the millions of images taken and shared every day on private devices in private circles of association? Well, media are distinct from those who use them, and so photographers, poets, and anyone else can be arrogant or humble, intrusive or reclusive, and yet communicate much more than their personal traits. Likewise, all media have to be described in terms of other media if they are to be understood adequately, as when writing has a "voice" and music is "colorful." And although the photographic archive is overflowing with extraordinary events, those images depend on continuities with everyday experience that also is cataloged extensively and that, once we learn to look at it, may not be so ordinary after all. And whatever their origin or destination, photographs always are viewed within a public context, which is evident from how people hide or share them, find them to be sentimental or scandalous, and otherwise weave together public norms and private experience in a medium instantly accessible to strangers.

These observations point toward a sense of paradox: we find that photography's media plasticity, rhetorical power, and global sweep are due to its relatively humble capabilities. At issue here is a misunderstood or underappreciated feature of popular media arts. Note how photography is faulted for its lack of skill relative to painting, just as popular music is faulted for its lack of skill relative to poetry, as is pulp fiction versus literature, television versus theater, and so forth. One can easily demonstrate, for example, that the rock lyric is insipid in print even though the song remains deeply moving to those who love it, including those who have high degrees of cultural literacy. Those who try to counter by pointing to hidden levels of mastery are still swimming against the current. A great rock lyric falls far short of a Shakespearean sonnet, and most photography does not approach the deep encounter of the best work in the art museum. But that is to miss the point. The lyric is not the song, which is a much richer cultural experience, and the photograph is not the image in the frame on the wall but part of an encompassing virtual experience that permeates modern consciousness. More to the point, sometimes the small form is capable of doing heavy lifting emotionally and politically *because* it is small. This paradox was captured by Lou Reed when he remarked that "you can do serious writing in a rock song if you can somehow do it without losing the beat. The things I've written about wouldn't be considered a big deal if they appeared in a book or movie."[32] Although it is not a big deal to discuss war in a scholarly book, if the same idea is embodied in a photograph, with the emotional encounter that is the medium's equivalent of having a beat, something larger happens. The photograph is a small, accessible artifact, yet photojournalism uses that artistic form to speak of the most serious events in the world. Each image is dispensable, and none may live for the ages, but like a good song they can linger in memory, evoke deep stirrings of connection, and challenge habits of indifference and disregard. Skill is still involved, of course, but what remains to be understood is how the intelligence of a public art exceeds the relative simplicity of its artistic medium.

Our previous work includes considerable discussion of photography's middlebrow status and public function that need not be repeated here. It is important, however, to reaffirm that photography is not only a medium of representation but also one that operates performatively. It not only records something but displays it to a spectator for dedicated, artistically enhanced observation and response. Moreover, by foregrounding the distinctively social qualities of human behavior, it reveals how events themselves are self-contained social performances while adding the viewer along with other potential spectators to the audience. So it is that photography can both record ordinary life and yet present it for thoughtful reflection, and do so in a "language" that has a capacity for eloquence precisely because it is at once largely unspoken and immediately accessible. Photography is not the only art having these capabilities—film, its cognate technology, is one obvious example—but it remains the public art most entangled with both ordinary life and the news media, and thus the one that regularly connects individual experience with the expectations of citizenship.[33]

We define "spectatorship" as a civic capability, one similar to literacy in its contribution to the public sphere.[34] Like literacy, it is a pervasive dimension of any modern society. As Jacques Rancière has summarized, "Being a spectator is not some passive condition that we should transform into activity. It is our normal situation. We also learn and teach, act and know, as spectators who all the time link what we see to what we have seen and said, done and dreamed."[35] Spectatorship is not a series of behavioral reactions; it is an extended social relationship that works more like a process of attunement or affective alignment than a logic of direct influence. Thus photography offers a way of being in the world with others.

This capability is defined further by Ariella Azoulay's distinction between ordinary, technical, and civic modes of seeing: defined by neither the natural attitude of everyday perception nor the technical discernment of expert observation, the civic spectator is one who sees through a frame of ongoing discussion about public affairs, who assumes that other spectators also are seeing and discussing the same or similar images, and who forms opinions and enters into political relationships by doing so.[36] Obviously the space between ordinary and expert vision also will be filled with many other ways of seeing: advertising, entertainment, fashion, work, and many other social practices saturate vision, and do so through modes of performance that direct audience response. Public discourse and political relationships cannot be wholly separated from those influences, and that is why photojournalism can become so important for public culture: it simultaneously activates civic spectatorship and includes other social contexts. Nor are they subsumed under a single optic; they are part of the radical plurality of the public image.

From Addison's *Spectator* to contemporary norms of transparency, the modern public sphere continues to be defined as a type of spectatorship.[37] Criticisms of degraded publics typically involve images of inappropriate spectatorship, such as the mob at the gladiatorial games of imperial Rome, frenzied fans at sporting events or rock music concerts, anomic individuals watching TV or playing video games, and everyone involved in the "media circus" of the American presidential election. Publics vary in how they see the world and those around them, and a habitual way of seeing may or may not be conducive to good judgment. Not surprisingly, governments, advertisers, entertainers, and many others are continually encouraging one way of seeing the world or another as it brings them some advantage. The media institutions of film, television, and advertising have developed enormous cultural power as a result—a power that at times serves the public interest but that most of the time pushes the audience in very different directions. Fortunately, the visual medium best suited for seeing as a public is the one that is the most widely available, inexpensive, and otherwise democratic.

Seeing in Public

Human beings live in a world that is simultaneously real and virtual, material and symbolic, sensate and mediated. Nor are these dimensions of human experience easily separated: we really do see the weather map and plan accordingly; our clothes and other material objects articulate a collective relationship to the world; we are startled by unexpected noises and frightened while watching formulaic movies. The media saturation of modern societies intensifies this complexity and creates both pathologies of and possibilities for community. One of the distinctive features of modern life is that photography has become an important medium for collective association. Instead of living only in a clan, village, neighborhood, or other local setting, many of us become habituated to seeing and being seen in a global city.

The photograph in figure 1 took up almost a full half-page above the fold for a story in the Weekend Arts section of the *New York Times*.[38] The caption said, "The New Museum of Contemporary Art: From the sidewalk, onlookers inspect the lobby and facade of this seven-story structure on the Lower East Side, which opens tomorrow."

So it is a photograph of people looking. That is not exactly news, and why are we being shown the onlookers and not the building that they find so interesting? The photograph itself would not seem to be the reason, as it is hardly a study in dramatic intensity. The viewer's gaze is directed every which way, whether cued by the many different sight lines of the onlookers or by the way the view expands unevenly but consistently outward across the rear of the frame. The division of the horizontal axis by the posts into uneven thirds further breaks up the scene. The image becomes a triptych, but one that doesn't tell an obvious story and that has only accidental coherence.

It is a remarkable picture, nonetheless, one that could hang on a wall of the museum. The photographer has captured what usually is

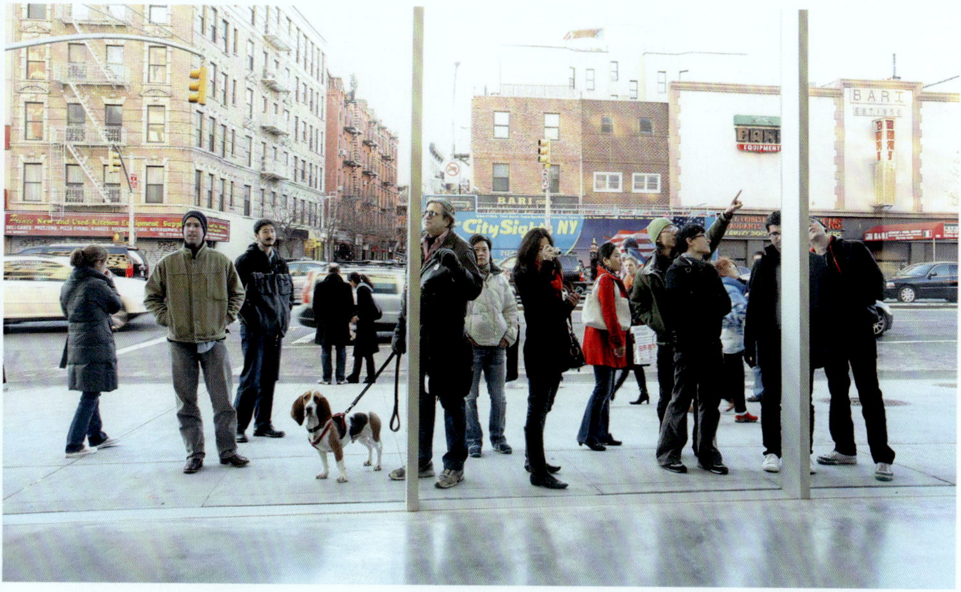

Figure 1. © Suzanne DeChillo / The New York Times / Redux.

only a blur in the background of our consciousness but now can be seen in pristine clarity. And what is seen? Society. Modern, urban, liberal-democratic society.[39] Not all of it, of course: those we see are predominantly young and generally from relatively privileged demographics with plenty of social capital in their wallets. But that's easy to see. The street scene is defined not by those attributes so much as by habits of civic interaction that are much more broadly distributed in the developed world today. Look, for example, at the spacing between the individuals and the several groupings of people. The proxemic ratios there are not universal, but they are typical of civic interaction on many city streets and other public places around the globe. The "culture" of modern art may be the pretext for the photo, but it is capturing the performative habits of a public culture that flows around and through the museum and other modern institutions.

This photograph exposes an important dimension of the complex social experience on display. Public life depends on visual norms, habits, and practices. The discourse on photography can misrecognize these forms as long as it depends on assumptions that visual media are largely instruments of power by which elites create spectacles to manipulate the masses. If public culture is something different from manufactured consent, the difference might lie in how it includes mediated experiences of seeing one another. The photograph above provides one example of what one might look for if taking seriously the idea that modern civil society depends on seeing and being seen.

Let's catalog the many ways that sight is marked in this photograph—how it exemplifies what Mitchell has labeled "showing seeing."[40] The caption features an art museum—an institution devoted to public viewing of visual artworks. The people in the photograph are identified as "onlookers"—defined by the act of looking. They may also be citizens, or New Yorkers, or connoisseurs of the arts, but all that is folded into "onlookers." And looking on is a specific type of seeing: one is not within the scene being observed, not part of the action. They are spectators, but are not degraded by that condition. In fact, they are "inspecting" the building; although not inspectors, they are engaged in an inherently visual act that includes an assessment, in this case an aesthetic judgment. That is what the architect assumes, and so we are seeing the other side of architecture: not the building but the culture within which it makes more or less sense. The building will be judged according to how well it meets the visual challenge carried by the story caption, "New Look for the New Museum."

And that is merely the caption. In the image itself we see people defined by looking, which clearly goes in many different directions probably reflecting different points of view.[41] Even the dog is looking. More specific attentiveness also is evident: someone pointing to direct others' view, the woman pointing her camera, the couple in the background who have to watch for traffic. The city is a place to look, from streets to signage to buildings. It also is a place to look at people: those in the picture are posed by the still image as if for inspection. The red coat in the right middle fixes that dimension of the scene. The fashion statement signals a culture of display, while the informal pants, coats, shoes, headgear, bags, and postures throughout the scene suggest a general level of comfort within that culture. Like the woman in red, albeit to varying degrees, everyone has agreed to be seen by others.

This shared visual experience is given a reflective touch by the large windows (a transparent barrier) and the reflections off the polished floor. We see, but always through things (even the air can distort) or with things (such as this photograph). One reason people go to art museums is to become more intelligent about how they use their eyes, and the photograph is doing some of this work for those of us who, like the onlookers in the photo, are not yet inside.

The final touch is provided by the sign in the center rear of the composition: "City Sights NY." This cheap sign for what may be a low-grade tourist operation is perfect here. On the one hand, it is the art museum's opposite: a commercial, artistically worthless advertisement for prepackaged "sightseeing" by those lacking the cultivated tastes that confer social distinction.[42] No wonder it is getting exactly zero attention from those interested in the museum. On the other hand, it is just the other side of the same street: the city is a place for seeing, and people go there for that reason. The cheap commercial signage tells us why the museum is there, for both are all about "City Sights NY." And that is a story about not only New York City but also anywhere people are to mingle together in modern civil society.

It is only part of that story, however. A full appreciation of public culture requires that one become comfortable with the idea that much of the time we are mingling with images. Images, whether statues in antiquity or photographs today, are an essential means for creating a public world.

In figure 2, one man walks down a street along life-size photos of six other people in an advertisement. The photo is mildly comic: they could be fellow citizens, were they real; he could fit right into the ad, were he an image. They have been carefully posed to model what the retailer wants people to wear; seemingly by accident and without needing to buy a thing, he is wearing clothes that qualify as suitably stylish. The caption embellished the point: "Real style on display as a man walked past an ad for clothes in Pristina, Kosovo."[43] He is real while the photographs are not real; likewise, his style is real while theirs is imaginary.

The caption also provides an example of how words are unreliable. The sentence could mean either that the man displays real style in contrast to the visual fiction behind him, or that the ad displays

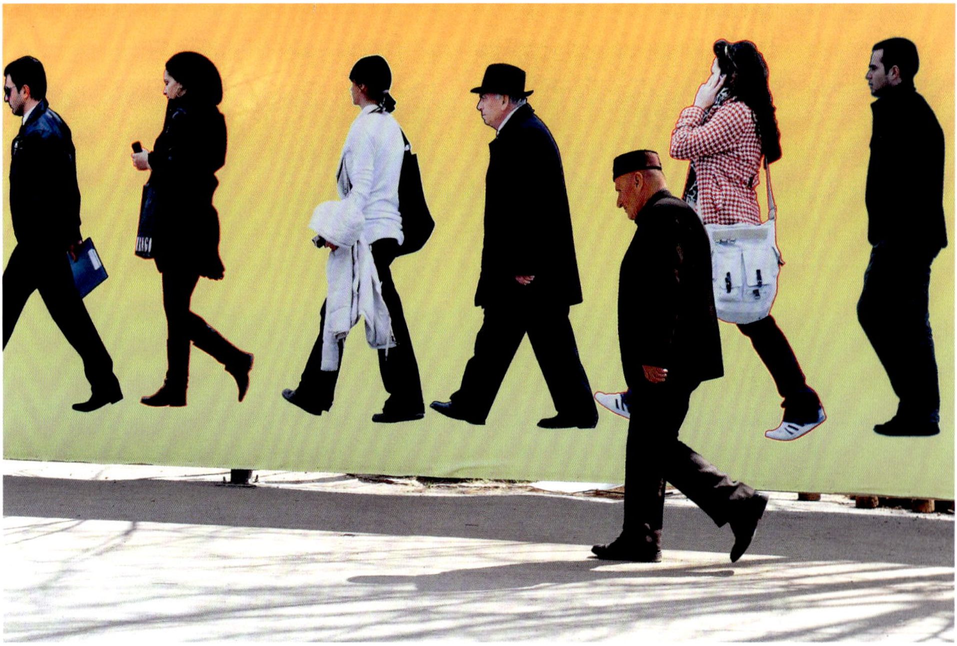

Figure 2. © Armend Nimani / AFP / Getty Images.

real style while the man walking in front of the ad is but the lesser approximation of that style. The second interpretation is less likely, because it isn't supported by the typical contrast between image and reality or by the real man being placed in the foreground of the photograph. The ambiguity, however, runs deeper than a case of sloppy sentence construction.

The basic dilemma here is that the man—whom you see—isn't real, either. Real style or real human being, the question is the same. The photograph has created a sense of its own reality through an internal contrast between a transparent image and another that is obviously a copy of something else. We know that the real models are no longer in the advertisement, yet we assume that the man on the street is really there. The photograph is a near perfect example of what Roland Barthes labeled the reality effect: "that unavowed verisimilitude which forms the aesthetic of all the standard works of modernity."[44] In a nutshell, realism is fabricated, signified, suggested rather than being a direct reproduction of reality. What is equally important, however, is that images are no less useful or the virtual world less important for relying on rhetorical artistry.

Both academic and public discussions of politics and photojournalism are rife with anxiety about the danger of images displacing reality.[45] Writers such as Daniel Boorstin and Neil Postman—among many others—have issued dire warnings across the decades about the moral and political decline that is sure to occur as visual media create a world of pseudo-events and manufactured experiences.[46] What they fail to understand is that collective life depends on illusions as much as it does on more material realities. The photograph of a man walking past images of people walking reveals the role that photojournalism plays in creating the civic strangers populating the imaginary space necessary for citizenship.[47] The man in the photo is in the same relationship to the viewer as the six figures in the ad are to him. He is one of the imaginary citizens placed beside us by the media. Instead of seeing images as copies of real people, why not, once in a while, see ourselves as people who live among images?

The contrast between image and reality is used, almost as a talisman, to ward off awareness of how modern civil society depends on seeing, copying, and imagination. But the visual illusion that creates a reality effect is more than mere deception. It can be a necessary fiction for collective life—and perhaps especially so amid the strong emphasis on individualism that defines liberal societies. Instead of cast adrift as a single person surrounded by empty space, anyone also can be walking down the street amid imaginary citizens. They aren't "real," but their presence allows us to feel both connected and individuated, distinctly positioned and part of larger patterns of aesthetic, moral, and political recognition. Likewise, although everyone sees oneself as a unique person, "real style" can be located more in the collective imagination than in the individual statement, while the reality effect of individual subjectivity is precipitated out of the social world of images.[48] Although merely an aesthetic backdrop to actual interaction, these public images constitute the civic space in which interaction will be more or less threatening or rewarding, pleasing or discouraging, difficult or helpful. That virtual presence also can create social pressure, distribute social goods unfairly, place unreasonable demands, and induce alienation and disengagement, so social critique still is essential. But the image itself is not the problem.

Developing the Public Image

The chapters that follow develop several themes intended to advance important features of photojournalism as a public art. Chapter 2 addresses some of the concerns that dog image analysis, not least as these are amplified by the comprehensive technological and social changes known as digitization and globalization. More than sensitivity to the contemporary environment is needed, however, as the public image reflects an anxiety about communication media that was expressed in Greek antiquity. As the photograph came to assume this burden of representation, it was sure to be faulted for being both inadequate and dangerous. Similar issues then emerged regarding its interpretation, and so it is easy for claims about the meaning of a photograph to appear both subjective and domineering. There is no escape from this predicament, but neither is it debilitating. We suggest how engaged spectatorship can benefit from the radical plurality of the image, especially as the globalized new media environment makes a virtue of decontextualization.

Chapter 3 takes up the central predicament in understanding photography, which is that the recorded image is both realistic and artistic. We argue that twentieth-century critique advanced an unduly reductive and pessimistic conception of both realism and the imagination, and that one result has been a retreat to an implicit doctrine of literalism that inhibits civic spectatorship. What is needed instead is a reinvigorated realism that requires a stronger conception of the photographic imagination, which is a way of seeing beyond ordinary observation or conventional belief. We provide several examples of how photojournalism frequently achieves that standard. Such images guide spectators to extend the scope of what they see, and do so through use of both distance and empathy along with many other artistic techniques, including even the idealization associated with commercial photography. Through the complex intertwining of what was and what might be, the public image becomes capable of invoking photography's democratic vision.

Chapter 4 takes up photography's entanglement with modernity, modernization, and the aesthetic and political ideals of cultural modernism. Instead of defining photography as an all-too-typical example of modern technology colonizing the lifeworld, we consider how the relationship is deeper and more ambivalent. We suggest that modernity is in fact the distinctive content of photography and that the medium therefore is capable of profound reflections of modern life. Whereas photography theory has focused on photography's relationship with the past, we consider how the medium reflects modernity's characteristic orientation toward the present as an implicit future. Thus photographs can capture both utopian dreams and processes of dispersion, enact both allegorical and prophetic attitudes, and feature characteristic habits such as waiting for progress to prevent catastrophe. One result is that some images offer an archaeology of the present, which invites consideration of contemporary civilization as if it were in ruins.

Photography's cultural scope is matched by its attention to the details of social interaction, and so chapter 5 considers how the photograph operates as a characteristic medium for social thought. Rather than begin with either class stratification or conflict, we consider how photography is aligned with society as such, that is, with society as a relatively autonomous dimension of modern life. Photography is acutely attuned to social performance and social relationships—including those that it creates through spectatorship. Representative photographs articulate this performative optic and how it reframes ritual events, tracks social mobility, and provides an aesthetic awareness of social texture and social structure. This aesthetic can double as a basis for thinking about political and economic relationships during a time when it is becoming easier and more profitable to make labor invisible. When left with the asymmetry of the individual within a social structure, photography can feature both the unique moment and processes of repetition.

Social experience can be harsh, and the recourse to violence is the worst of it. Humans kill for much more, and less, than food or territory, and war continues to thrive within the modern era. Chapter 6 takes up photography's intimate relationship with warfare. We push back against claims that images of violence provoke either perverse pleasures or moral anesthesia. Following writers such as Linfield and Azoulay, we focus instead on how photographers are providing an anthropology of contemporary violence. As images capture the changing nature of war, the spectator is confronted with untethered violence, regime-made disasters, and refeudalization, as well as processes for normalizing war within otherwise civil societies. We suggest that photography is documenting more about violence than its most horrific traces—particularly how a war culture is becoming increasingly entrenched in everyday life across the globe. To face this danger, what is needed is not skepticism about the medium but rather a more explicit ethic of spectatorship.

Photography cannot be resolutely serious, however, as it remains ridiculously ubiquitous. It is everywhere, from the image on the cereal box to the lunchtime digital news scan to the selfie uploaded in the evening. In our final chapter we consider this supersaturation of the image world to be a sign of cultural vitality, albeit not without its problems. These are not the problems of scarcity, however, which have dominated cultural criticism since the allegory of the cave. Instead of a few images capable of enchantment for want of better light, we offer the idea that abundance is an important feature of both the image world and any other world we might want to inhabit. We also note how often doctrines of scarcity lend themselves to antidemocratic attitudes in aesthetics and politics alike. So it is that the vast, ever-growing photographic archive might provide a schooling in democratic habits of mind and feeling—if we give some attention to how to see on behalf of an abundant life for all.

Each of these chapters could be developed at far greater length, and we are open to criticism on that basis at virtually every turn. All that we ask of the reader is that before any image or idea is rejected, you consider carefully what might go in its place. Dismissal is easy, but the point of our brief for the public image is to encourage discussion. As we have said before, healthy democracies are those in which citizens are accustomed to arguing thoughtfully about how they are influenced.[49] Such conversations certainly should include reminders about how each of us has only a limited view of the whole, as well as skepticism about the reliability or intended effects of any image, but the art of democracy needs more than this conventional wariness.

The Spectator in the Mirror

Democratic public cultures depend on citizens who enjoy being spectators. Public arts have to appeal to that audience, but they also will make communication itself an object of reflection. One reason we believe that photojournalism is a public art is that it periodically discloses the image world itself to reveal how spectators are part of the show.

Fashion isn't timeless, but the photographer's artifice has captured something essential about photography in figure 3. Perhaps the over-the-top aesthetics of the fashion show gave the photographer more artistic license than usual: by creating an effect of extreme overexposure at the focal point of the image, the audience is brought out of the darkness while the model is turned into a creature of light. Which, of course, she always was.

But which is stranger: to see an all-white silhouette or to see the act of spectatorship offered to view? One answer is that both are strange, with the emphasis depending on where you want to go philosophically. When one focuses on the model, images of haunting come to mind, and one might recall how images of ghosts, fairies, spirit worlds, and other premonitions of life beyond death were a prominent part of the early history of photography.[50] Ultimately, although not completely, realism trumped those phantasmagoric projects, but photography has remained a medium in several senses of the word ever since. As the bare outline of the model suggests, the camera is capturing only traces of what is there, with the rest to be supplied by the imagination. Likewise, one can imagine how photographic images are already within the camera waiting to be released, and also floating unseen through the air waiting to be captured. Haunting, we might imagine, is omnidirectional.

But is there one ghost or many? As the members of the audience are brought out of the shadows, we are reminded how they also haunt the camera—always there, unseen and often unbidden, waiting for the image to appear. Without the audience, there is no need for the image, so in one sense they always have to be there, unseen, as the potential force that allows the camera to flash.

They, more than the model, appear like those viewing the photo. They double our viewing, as we do theirs. The experience of seeing

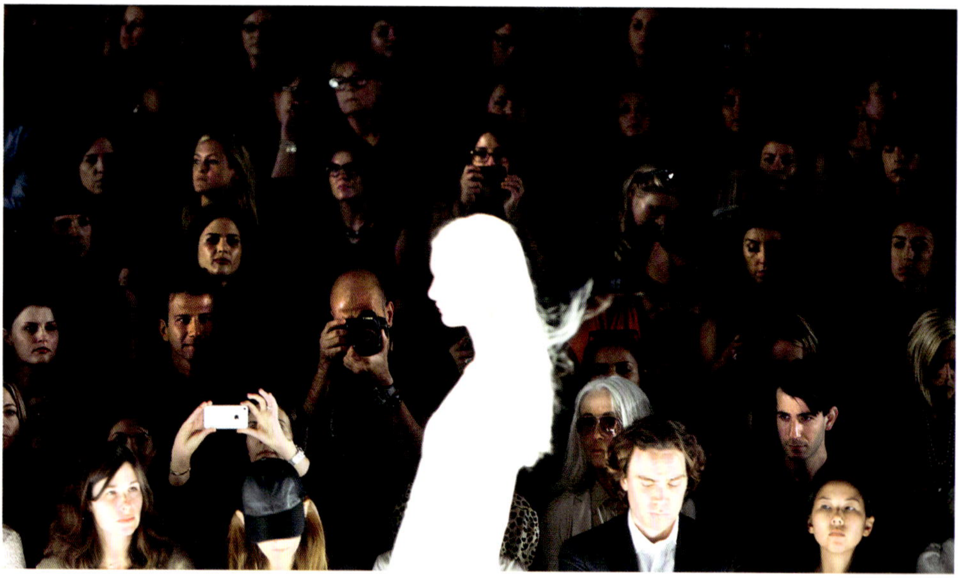

Figure 3. © Reuters / Andrew Burton.

them seeing may be a bit troubling, somewhat like seeing oneself unexpectedly in a mirror. But instead of a single face, here we see many different modes of response, for (as with the spectators outside the museum) the image is "showing seeing."[51] The gazes in the audience are by turns appraising, calculating, desiring, distracted, bored, and more. Some are taking photographs, thus also doubling the act of taking this photo. The full measure of audience subjectivity cannot be taken here (if anywhere), but we at least can see that they are not trapped in what David Levin has rightly labeled the "terrible double bind" of the conventional paradigm: "The subject is invariably positioned either in the role of a dominating observer or in the role of an observable object, submissive before the gaze of power."[52] Photography is a study in plurality, extended further by its own reproduction, and ultimately about itself when it can show what it means to see and be seen. And to see what often goes unseen, even during Fashion Week.

And yet Sontag may get the last word after all. The spectral photo places us back within a cave where spectators look up at a dumb show of images. Runway models, like the clothes they wear, are created for display. The audience gazes on fashions that will flicker momentarily and then disappear, leaving only the necessity of another show, another ritual activity dedicated to reproducing a world of appearances. Plato makes it quite clear that happiness is not to be found in that world, a world in which images are used to keep people content with ignorance, superstition, and bondage.[53] The model is a creature of light, but her beauty will keep others chained in the dark.

Nor is it enough to reply that model and spectators are there voluntarily. Fashion is among the most social of phenomena: it is a study in minor variation on behalf of conformity and in superficial choice on behalf of compulsion, all the while maintaining hierarchies of wealth and privilege. These features are also there to be seen in the photo. The spectators can look one way or another, but they have to look. The model will be wearing a unique outfit, but we see instead how she also is abstracted into mannequin impersonality.

But compared to what? One complication with using the allegory of the cave is that Plato was *not* advocating release from visual enchantment into direct perception in everyday life. Instead, he was comparing "the region revealed through sight [outside the cave] to the habitation of the prison, and the light of the fire in it to the power of the sun." To Plato, the real world of human experience is actually illusion, and liberation comes from seeing the true forms of reason and goodness as they exist in another realm beyond ordinary perception. Likewise, we are to understand that anyone who had obtained this enlightenment would no longer be willing to occupy themselves with mere human affairs, as they would once again be trapped in a world of "the shadows of justice" and other mistaken conceptions. Nor should we omit that Plato frankly identifies his allegory as an image or that his higher reality is one of ideal forms, that is, things to be seen having decidedly aesthetic properties, and that one can see them not literally but through an act of imagination.[54]

In sum, a recurring critique of images on behalf of another reality cannot avoid its own complications, not least an incapacity or unwillingness to grapple with the messy, always somewhat deluded world of human affairs. In place of that critique, we offer another approach to the image world. By focusing on photography and especially on photojournalism, we pay attention to the most ubiquitous and important visual art for modern liberal-democratic public culture. Whatever their limitations, these images provide remarkable resources for thinking about what it means to see and be seen and about how we might live well in a world connected by lines of sight.

CHAPTER TWO

FOR INTERPRETATION

The fundamental scandal of the public image is that it is not limited to communicating specific information to a specific audience about a specific event. Instead, the image has more value, wider circulation, and much more to say. Unfortunately, those messages often are overlooked, and not for want of sophisticated methods of analysis.[1] The problem is larger that that: an attitude that sets responsible use of the image against interpretation.[2] In the name of documentary proof, photographic meaning is locked up in old anxieties about representation, mistaken assumptions about persuasion, and a doctrine of contextualization that denies the radical plurality of photographic meaning.

The encounter with an image is never determined only by direct reference to the event depicted or the immediate circumstances of reception. Context does matter, but it consists of layers of assumptions, permissions, and prohibitions. Some of these are provided by the conventional discourse on photography. For example, professional standards suggest that the public image should be defined only in respect to its immediate point of origin, that public meaning should be limited to determinations of authenticity and accuracy while all other responses are merely subjective, and that failure to adhere to these protocols will lead to dangerous distortions.[3] As we shall argue in this chapter and the next, the situation is neither that simple nor that dangerous. To see the image anew, one has to admit to what viewers are doing all the time: decontextualizing and recontextualizing in order to engage with different dimensions of the image, different perspectives on what it shows, and different conceptions of its audience.[4] Engaged spectatorship includes more than the baseline interest in reliable perception that we bring to all viewing; it also requires practice in selecting and reframing images within settings that are both personal and public, shared and subject to debate.

The anxiety about grounding meaning in a stable context of direct reference has been both amplified and complicated by photography's remediation into a globalized new media environment. As Fred Ritchin has suggested, these comprehensive changes are "bending the frame" of documentary photography, often to beneficial effect.[5] Stated otherwise, photographers and spectators today are conducting what might be thought of as a worldwide crowd-sourced conceptual art experiment that mashes up diverse practices of documentary witnessing and citizenship. The results expose not so much the limits of photography as, rather, the limitations of prior conceptions of photography. Often what seems new was always available, and sometimes even in use, but thought to be something else. To understand the cultural work that has been under way through a succession of technological innovations, it is necessary to reconsider how photographs are bound not by fidelity to the moment but by assumptions about representation and influence that run from old media to new.

The Burden of Representation

One of the more revealing discussions of new media comes from antiquity. The new technology of writing had become linked with the public art of rhetoric in the democratic city-states of the Greek world, creating the new media genre (and seeming oxymoron) of speech writing. The philosopher Plato was not pleased, as he rightly sensed the transformative capabilities at hand. In the dialogue *Phaedrus*, his interlocutor Socrates lays out the problem. Writing will provide "not true wisdom . . . but only its semblance," and although readers will "seem to know much," for the most part "they will know nothing." And why might this happen? "There's a strange thing about writing, which makes it truly analogous to painting. The painter's products stand before us as if they are alive, but if you question them, they maintain a most majestic silence." Worse, they quickly get away from their original context: "once a thing is put in writing, the composition, whatever it may be, drifts all over the place, getting into the hands not only of those who understand it, but equally of those who have no business with it." In sum, writing produces only "a kind of image," something lacking the meaning that could be supplied only by those in the original speaking situation. Worse yet, the unseen gap between knowledge and delusion becomes magnified through the new medium's easy dissemination to other audiences.[6]

The irony that this critique of writing was placed in a written text was not lost on Plato, but it has eluded many of those still under his spell. Although writing came to be seen as the guarantor of meaning, successive innovations in communication technologies would be born under the same shadow of illegitimacy: they created illusions that displaced reality, fomented misunderstanding and lack of accountability through dissemination, and alternatively empowered and enthralled those audiences who had the impertinence not to know their place. Were a technology to combine the mute vitality of a painting with the industrialized power of mass dissemination, surely it should come with a warning label.

And so it has, as when we are told that photography provides only "knowledge at bargain prices—a semblance of knowledge, a semblance of wisdom."[7] By virtue of this warning and others, photography has been tagged with "the burden of representation."[8] As we use the term, this burden refers, first, to the extent to which communication media are held responsible for social ills and, second, to the extent to which one medium is held responsible for problems that in fact are found in all media. In the first sense, one can observe how the media are singled out as leading causes of juvenile violence, voter apathy, a rush to war, or any other complex problem. Similarly, one can see how any new medium is saddled with the same list of dire consequences: medical, educational, juridical, and moral authorities have averred that photography or radio or television or the Internet is essentially degenerative as it impairs memory, analytical ability, social capability, moral sense, and political engagement. The logic is that of blaming the messenger: the communication technology is singled out as a powerful cause of problems the society presumably would not have otherwise. Any new medium provokes a new staging of the drama, as it provides both a new scapegoat coincident with many other changes and a chance for the older media institutions to pass the burden on to the new competitor.

Photography has not escaped this role, one that has been renewed by digitization. Is politics superficial and craven? That must be because pols are playing to the camera. Are people becoming too self-centered? That must be because they are taking selfies with their cell phone cameras. New media, old discourse. Sontag's *On Photography* remains emblematic for this reason, as it provides an exhaustive litany of ill effects that follow from not having the properties of older media such as painting and, most notably, writing. What is most telling about these comparisons is how they let the prior media off the hook. For example:

> The industrialization of photography permitted its rapid absorption into rational—that is, bureaucratic—ways of running society. . . . Photographs were enrolled in the service of important institutions of control, notably the family and the police, as symbolic objects and as pieces of information. Thus, in the bureaucratic cataloguing of the world, many important documents are not valid unless they have, affixed to them, a photograph-token of the citizen's face.[9]

You may not have thought of the family as a bureaucratic organization, but Sontag paints with a broad brush. And, of course, the family is an organization of social control, and bureaucracies do use photographs (and perhaps the more demeaning "photograph-tokens").[10] That said, the passage is a stunning work of substitution. To begin, *writing* is the media technology that was essential for the emergence and spread of bureaucratic organization, both in antiquity and in the modern era.[11] Second, the ratio of texts to images in bureaucratic organizations is overwhelming, and photographs are even prohibited in many cases. Third, even with digitization, images still present significant difficulties for archival organization, while "data mining" of texts and anything else happening at a keyboard is advancing by leaps and bounds. Perhaps most tellingly, note how Sontag's alignment of photography with bureaucratic processes depends on terms derived from writing: photographs were "enrolled" in institutions of control, involved in "cataloguing" the world, and affixed to "many important documents." Bureaucratic practices remain modes of inscription even as they are being attributed to photography. The burden has been shifted, however: through a substitution that has little historical merit or contemporary relevance, social control now works through images.[12] As photography assumes the burden of representation for a large-scale, complex social practice that defines modernity for both good and ill, it becomes freighted with anxieties regarding impersonal organization and political surveillance. At the same time, writing, Sontag's medium of representation, presumably escapes any sense of shared accountability.

This discourse about photography continues to spool uncritically throughout media commentary. As it does so, it carries with it a corresponding model of persuasion, one that becomes most evident in discussions of photojournalism. The most characteristic rendition in the twentieth century was the conception of "hypodermic effects," which became a cottage industry in media studies.[13] Neatly combining the ancient idea that persuasion is a drug with modern medical technology, the term implies that modern media are capable of effects that are targeted, unidirectional, and powerful.[14]

With or without the term, this idea has informed a lot of media commentary, and it acquires additional purchase with photojournalism. Photographs are supposed to persuade with the causal force of reality itself, and any failure to do so then motivates increased ethical scrutiny of the medium. If tasked with recording human misery, then press photography also should be capable of motivating the appropriate moral response and political action. When that doesn't happen, there is a need to know why the better reaction did not occur. This failure and subsequent scrutiny are most likely to occur when the stakes are highest, that is, with atrocity photographs.

This model of persuasion can be summarized in three steps: the horrific image should create a direct encounter, which produces a moral shock, which produces a decisive effect.[15] The model seems intuitive because each of the three experiences does occur, and not only with photographs but with language and other media as well. We all have felt the intense connection that can arise in face-to-face arguments or when engaged with a work of art; we all have been stopped in our tracks by a personal revelation or documentary photograph; we all have seen a statement of fact or a graph change the entire tone of a meeting, or watched a speaker turn an audience on a dime. Persuasion such as this does happen, and it does happen with photographs. But it is exceedingly rare.

To see how rare this is, reflect on the rest of your experience—say, arguing at home, on the job, or anywhere else. And consider how strange the world would be if the decisive effect happened all the time; and consider by contrast the enormous amounts of energy and redundancy that are needed to get any kind of agreement on political issues. "It takes time to turn a battleship," "Rome wasn't built in a day," and similar adages are much closer to the actual conditions of consensus. Or, recalling that the burden of representation is not distributed equally, consider how the lack of direct audience response to an atrocity also holds for vast amounts of written reportage, first-person testimonies, government and NGO reports, editorial commentary, public art installations, poster campaigns, documentary video or films, television coverage, and Internet postings.

Nor is this merely because human beings can be stupid and lazy. We are separate individuals, living with other individuals who often have different needs, beliefs, values, and goals, in the midst of institutions that have enormous inertia. The result is that for each of the three ideal results to occur, a great deal has to be in place. When we do observe those dramatic transformations, much is already in place—so much, in fact, that we can assume that the image or text or speaker alone is doing the work. With atrocity photos, the case is even more complicated, as the paradigmatic images continue to be the images from the Holocaust, which came out only after the need for action had passed. So it was—and is—that many could experience the moral shock in almost pure form, without having to face questions of commitment and constraint. Images do persuade, but the range of effects is much wider and less immediately obvious than is typically assumed.

None of this assessment argues against moral and political engagement or for a status quo of doing nothing. It does suggest that the political imagination is being held hostage to a myth of how public action should occur. The model of direct encounter, moral shock, and decisive effect is that myth: it is relevant some of the time but taken to be relevant all of the time, which allows other elements of the social structure to escape accountability. Instead of worrying about either the image or the spectator, perhaps we might ask instead just what and who else should have to answer for modernity's continued entanglement with horror.

Of course, modern media are powerful determinants of modern

life—that is, they are not merely messengers—and serious investigation and discussion of their influence is continually necessary. It is unfortunate, however, that visual media are singled out in a world where both images and text have been increasing exponentially. Photography continues to be subjected to an intense interrogation of its cognitive, moral, and political effects, while the ways the same problems haunt every medium, including, most notably, the printed text, are ignored or at least downplayed.[16] Can photographs be faked? Of course, and texts can lie. Do photographs require a sense of context to be interpreted correctly? Of course, and so does every form of textual representation, as e-mail misunderstandings can make all too clear. Can photographs be used to advance vicious stereotypes? Of course, just like *The Protocols of the Elders of Zion* and many other screeds.

There is a difference, however, that supposedly makes all the difference: photographs are assumed to be accurate recordings of what really existed, while words are known to be crafted, mediated, intentional constructions rather than indexical reproductions. The claim is true enough, to be sure, but isn't the truth more complicated in each direction? On the one hand, photography has been a familiar part of everyday life and culture for 150 years, and warnings about its limitations have been voiced frequently from the beginning. On the other hand, people are constantly, incessantly taken in by words, and their many subsequent experiences of disappointment or betrayal don't seem to make a dent in the general level of stupefying gullibility. Political manipulation, to take one good example, can thrive (as it often has) without ever needing a photograph. Indeed, photographs can achieve moments of rhetorical power on behalf of justice or other ideals because they, better than words, are able to expose the distance between speech and reality, abstractions and experience, ideology and the common good. Yet public and professional commentary cannot say enough about the dangers of digital image manipulation, even as a significant portion of verbal reportage begins as press releases and columnists spread fraudulent claims supporting partisan memes.

Instead of assuming that images have the status of reality, we might ask who believes that people are the size of their photographs, or that magazine covers or their cousin's wedding photos haven't been altered, or that the starving child isn't being used to elicit a donation? As John Edwin Mason noted while commenting on the cell phone's acceleration of vernacular photography (and contra public anxieties about the deluge of amateur images): "There is no evidence—none—that people think that photos of sunsets and photos of body parts are equally important. Quite the contrary, people wielding camera phones—people like you and me—have demonstrated time and again that they understand the difference between amusing their friends and recording something of significance."[17] Modern societies are defined by their communication technologies but also by the media literacies that have become pervasive. Some viewers will be naive, of course, but the more common experience is that the natural attitude toward photography is a dense, rich, and flexible set of habits that includes, as a matter of course, variable levels of trust and skepticism regarding mediation. This thick repertoire comes to be forgotten, however, when visual media are saddled with anxieties about technological dependency.

The reason for privileging print media is well documented (of course): printing and the verbal arts, genres, and institutions that developed across the modern era were central to the rise of the bourgeois public sphere.[18] Public culture emerged out of the essay, the novel, and the newspaper, and also the advice book, journal, and pamphlet. That is only part of the story, however, for it also emerged out of the theater, Wild West shows, parades, posters, graffiti, and many other performative and visual arts. In short, the modern liberal-democratic public sphere depends on both verbal and visual media, and public thought needs both good writing and good photography as well as successful remediation of both practices into the digital environment. The public also could benefit from a discourse on photography that allows them to explore not only the negative but also the positive features of the image world that they hold in common.

This is where the road splits. You can take one pill and go through the looking glass into the image world, the virtual reality of public culture. Or you can take the other pill and continue to believe that your consciousness is firmly anchored in reality, however much it might also be looking at screens and images. That reality might be the pleasures and pains of bodily experience, or the routine activities and demands of everyday life, or the hard ground of the laws of nature, but it is there and forever capable of correcting delusion. By committing yourself to reality you will unquestionably (but perhaps ironically) be on the side of the angels: standing for truth and against fantasy, deceit, and manipulation. And you will assume that each time you have exposed an image for what it is, something important will have been said.

And you won't be entirely wrong. What you will not have, however, are precisely those values that were promised: objectivity, certainty, moral truth. You will continually expose one kind of mediation while pretending that others do not exist. You will confuse the claim that reality exists independently of consciousness (which it does) with the claim that understanding can be independent of mediation (it cannot). Which is why this is a decision and not a matter of being in or out of step with reality. Reality is there no matter what, so the key question is what you want to see.

And if you take the other pill? Welcome to the Matrix, Oz, Wonderland—and your laptop. In this world, nothing is innocent and everything might be tinged with magic. Politics is important but also crazy: much closer to a circus than we want to admit. Society is an ongoing play, but one that is lived onstage, backstage, and in the audience all at once. Modern societies are gleaming marvels of technology, but they also are playing a dangerous game with nature as if they were drunken gamblers on a roll at Vegas. Which is why the stakes are high even when we are living within a virtual world. Illusion is there no matter what, so the key question is what to make of it.

By being so dramatic, we obviously are pitching the choice toward one type of spectatorship rather than the other. The choice remains nonetheless. As Errol Morris has argued, believing is seeing: the interpretive frame that you bring to the photograph will shape its meaning.[19] Photographs can be seen as artistically accomplished depictions of social reality encouraging public thought, and they also can be seen as typified perceptions encouraging mythologies of political participation that serve those projecting the shadows on the wall.

Few would claim that any modern society is free of such vices, so the issue is not proving or denying their existence. What might matter is acknowledging that this crisis in perception is lodged within society itself: that is, modernity's highly mediated, complex, large-scale societies create processes that are used to both liberate and control, educate and enthrall, enrich and impoverish. Keeping the focus where it has been will have all-too-familiar results: some media will get off too easily, while photography will continue to be faulted for problems that no medium can avoid. Predictable alarms will continue to sound, but it will be difficult to appreciate how photography is one of the engines of the modern world and an important resource for public identity, thought, and action. Stock questions—is it excessive? is it limiting? does it excite or distract or numb?—will lead to the same answers. And not much will change. By asking different questions, however, a stronger conception of photographic meaning might lead to a more engaged understanding of a world that is both virtual and real, dangerous and abundant.

Image and Interpretation

In a digital world, the image appears to be a vanishing object. In a global world, interpretation appears to be a parochial act. But what is about to vanish reappears, and what seems to be merely local turns out to be the site of globalization. More prosaically, we hope to encourage an interpretive encounter with the public image during a time when technological and social changes are redefining the basic conditions of democratic spectatorship. Because of those changes, our approach might seem out of date while paradoxically being faulted in respect to criteria that are out of date. Thus, to realize the artistic and civic potential of democratic spectatorship, we first need to clarify basic concerns about the object and method of our approach.

One might ask how the image can be disappearing amid the incredible deluge of images in contemporary life. And that is part of the answer: given the changes in image reproduction and circulation, the photographic image itself is losing a sense of autonomy, integrity, and influence. (The same fears have been applied to the individual in a mass society.) In place of the silver gelatin print framed in a museum, there are the billions of digital files being shared across billions of devices. In place of the indexicality and authenticity of the documentary record, there is Photoshop and all that it represents. In place of a relatively small number of skilled practitioners and elite institutions producing and distributing press photos, now there are an endless number of inputs and outputs within an enormous system of dynamic networks large and small. In place of the conception of a mass public, now there is a fragmented media environment while everywhere people also are involved in vernacular production and circulation of media content. For these reasons and more, theorists rightly are rethinking photographic practices in terms of human-machine interaction, swarms of circulation, and other concepts that might capture how digital technologies are actually being used and how they are changing social behavior.[20] What isn't needed, it seems, is curatorial attention to the individual image.

Interpretation faces a similar challenge from globalization. A global world is a decentered world. The biggest city is in Japan; the biggest airport is in the United States; the biggest film industry is in India; the biggest banks are everywhere. English is the international language—the majority of English speakers speak it as a second language—but bilingualism and multiculturalism are the new normal. In this context, any definition of the public image may be much too ethnocentric—may be, for example, obviously centered on mainstream media in the United States without comparative study of other nations or regions, or of subaltern or diasporic communities of reception, or of the social, political, and commercial networks that now brachiate through all cultures, much less the decentering and divergences within a global system where alternate modernities are developing beyond the normative, aesthetic, and political conventions of the United States and Europe. Why speak of a democratic art when so many people live without democracy? Why celebrate communication when deep gaps in awareness and recognition persist both within and across cultures? What can spectatorship be if it is not encultured, embodied, and situated in respect to actual conditions of production and reception? Isn't any more general statement an example of imperial overreach? For these reasons and more, scholarship rightly is exploring the many ways in which meaning is created and shared in specific settings. This ethnographic approach assumes that the meaning of any photograph is radically dependent on the circumstances of its production and reception and that much of what might be said there won't translate easily or won't apply elsewhere. What isn't needed, it seems, is an extended exposition from any one standpoint, much less one centered on US media.

We are not in a position to criticize advocates of change tout court, but there is a reason many of the anxieties about communication media are perennial concerns. For all the noise and scatter, the individual image remains at the center of individual experience. No one looks at the deluge of images, while the small material practices of everyday life contain many techniques for centering, featuring, revering, or enjoying individual images—and as one way to anchor experience and identity within the media maelstrom. Many images are whisked away with the flip of a finger, but another always comes to the fore. Indeed, this process of selection now is an important feature of image consumption: decisions that once were largely limited to or constrained by media institutions are now part of daily life. The media institutions have responded by providing ever more images for personal use independent of the traditional news function. Most important, the encounter with the individual image reveals much of what is in play in our media experience. That is where decisions will be made, and where influence will occur. It is not the only place, as everything from background processing to the encounters with texts and other media also are important, but the encounter with the image is a crucial intersection of self and society. The image, like the individual, cannot vanish, because it is a place for regeneration.

The creative encounter with the image happens through interpretation. Much of the time that process is tacit, and often it is banal. You see again what you have seen before. You file the new image into the old category, not paying attention to the fit. Some of the time, however, the image becomes a place for challenging or enhancing one's experience of the world. Whether eliciting revulsion or awe, or revealing the familiar as strange, or fragmenting what had been whole, or joining what had been separate—whatever the encounter, the image is at that point prompting important reconsideration of how one lives with others. That reconsideration involves reprocessing the image in terms of a scheme of interpretation; it is cultural work, and there is no technological or geographic change that ever will replace it. They inflect it, but never to overcome basic problems of translation between showing and telling, or co-orienting self and other, or using common codes to communicate specific experiences.

The public image is interpretive in an additional sense as well. It is used to do some of the heavy lifting in modern civil society: that is, helping to create a virtual world shared by strangers regarding the general welfare. This work typically is identified with the institutions of the press. Because of the drastic changes occurring within journalism due to digitization and globalization, some have wanted to double down on professional norms of objectivity and neutrality.[21] Likewise, scholars and pundits decry the decontextualization that is an increasingly obvious feature of image circulation and appropriation across all media. Digital images floating in the global media sphere quickly become untethered from knowledge of their original context, exactly as Sontag and others had warned. Taking images out of context is said to be the first sin of interpretation, and now it is a habitual experience of ordinary media consumption.

This is one point where a paradigm shift is necessary. In order to cultivate a rich encounter with the public image, it is necessary to affirm both that photography continues to do important cultural work and that decontextualization is an important feature of that work. Digital technologies and global media make evident what was always the case, not least how imagery works through some of the fundamental conditions of all communication. The image was always an ephemeral precipitate of larger social processes and yet a vital resource for public thought. There is no universal language of photography, but interpretation is never entirely local, and it is an important basis for communicating with others about what might be held in common.

Consider the continuity with language in this regard. Words necessarily are meaningful beyond literal reference, to which they still can be tied precisely in specific cases for specific purposes. Descriptions of events regularly move across genres, media, topics, and audiences, always involving shifts in meaning, and can be both remarkably consistent and put to widely different and still valid uses. The richness of a public text can be extensive, even if never fully evident at any one time. Nor is this interpretive range limited to texts: people use all symbolic materials to make sense of the world and communicate with one another, and for this to work the distinction between virtual and real is both obliterated and re-created moment by moment. You read something as true until you question it, and you see an image as true until you question it, and in each case both processes are occurring continually. What you do *not* do, except in very limited and instrumental conditions, is withhold understanding of the text or image until you know the specific circumstances of its original referential statement.

To grasp this claim about image content, consider the following comparisons: a photograph is like a poem; like a quotation; like a painting; like an old photo; like a stock photo; like you. Poems certainly can be explicated in terms of the events they recount and the circumstances of their making, but those elaborations are not needed for the initial encounter or loving recitation, and they are provided only when they might illuminate other, more compelling features and more wide-ranging audience interests. To take one example, appreciation of Ezra Pound's "In a Station of the Metro" need not depend on knowledge of the specific day or station, though a scholar might productively make the determination to better tease out the poem's relationship to the imagist movement that influenced its creation and reception at the time. The poem circulates nonetheless, for its richness allows the reader to apply it to recurrent features of modern experience.

The same holds for quotations: they circulate widely, and as they do so they regularly become detached from their original circumstances.[22] As Gary Saul Morson has demonstrated, many popular quotations acquire different wording, varied author attributions, completely erroneous references, and fabricated histories—and these features are signs of the richness and usefulness of these small texts.[23] The value of the quotation doesn't turn on whether Churchill's witticism was to Lady X or Lady Y or whether the droll insight was by Twain or Wilde or Alice Longworth Roosevelt, even as the specific attribution is there (unwittingly) to enhance use for a specific speaker or audience. What does matter is that the text is a formally accomplished distillation of social intelligence and that it circulates and is appropriated when writers create other, longer texts that also are doing the work of sustaining a culture.

The same holds for other media as well. Paintings, which rightly merit the extensive attention that they receive from curators and art historians, nonetheless receive that attention only because of a radical decontextualization. As André Malraux observed: "A Romanesque crucifix was not regarded by its contemporaries as a work of sculpture; nor Cimabue's *Madonna* as a picture. Even Phidias' *Pallas Athene* was not, primarily, a statue." These later valuations came through the emergence of the modern idea of art, particularly as it was institutionalized through the museum. "They [museums] . . . have imposed on the spectator a wholly new attitude toward the work of art. They have tended to estrange the works they bring together from the original functions."[24] Malraux's brief for a "museum without walls" is curiously similar to claims made subsequently about the photographic archive and new media today: wide dissemination and democratic accessibility put the artifacts into a new, relatively abstract space, one in which their status as images comes to the foreground.[25] The difference then is in valuation: whether to see the loss of an original meaning or an emergent pluralism; a reproduction of prior social authority or a prompting of more comparative, creative, and interrogative capabilities. Even the critique of the image world requires that one see images as (decontextualized) images—an alignment of artifact, archive, and spectator that depends on the virtual reality it faults. The viewing public generally follows suit: the preferred typification might be limiting ("Great Art") or personally enlightening ("that family is like my family"), but it has to involve more than circumstantial knowledge.

And so it goes. Old photos reveal a feature of all photos: the local knowledge either is missing—"is that Auntie May?"—or is unable to account for the attraction—"yes, and look at how barren it is." Stock photos provide a similar demonstration: we sift through them daily without hesitation, moving among people and locales that were somewhere sometime but now are simply part of the background of a continually recurring present. Just as we are part of the background for a continually recurrent present: not ours, but for those around us. Nor is this a matter of distinguishing between greater and lesser intimacy, although that is part of it. The disturbing truth about communication is that most of the time we are not dealing in intimate knowledge of the world, or even of each other, or even of ourselves, but rather somehow getting to better and worse approximations of those relationships through symbolic materials that are typified, impersonal, recurrent tokens of meaning.[26] What saves us from comprehensive superficiality is that we also have the capacity to artistically and interpretively enhance our texts and images, to load them with experience and with connections to other people, places, events, ideas, values, desires, and dreams. And these "additions" are part of the process of developing the public image.

But one might reply, Isn't the news image by definition created for the specific task of relaying information about specific events? The short answer is yes, of course. The more comprehensive answer is yes, and due to both necessity and historical accident it has come to do much more as well. In this regard, new media practices are once again revealing a feature of all media. The news was never only about the news and always a cultural practice serving many social needs while creating a public context that is one of the distinguishing features of modernity.[27] All readers were reading selectively, and all were making sense of larger conditions based on exceedingly limited examples, and the news photograph was always getting away from its institutions to circulate and be "repurposed" elsewhere; as that happened the media were creating virtual communities in which people could imagine themselves as members of cities, nations, or a common humanity.[28]

Of course such practices involve dangers: for example, radical decontextualization can contribute to superficiality, ignorance, enthrallment, and emotional responses that are too vague or too cheap to be reliable. But context is only one part of any media experience, which also depends on processes of generalization and identification that rightly override literal specificity, and moderate decontextualization is essential for creative thinking, moral reflection, and other attributes of good communication. Although each communication practice settles on norms of referential attribution, in each case there remain alternate modalities that also are necessary for understanding. So it is that accuracy can vary across everyday conversation, press reportage, and scientific demonstration, while these interpretive communities also rely on jokes and editorial commentary and high-quality visual displays. Thus public culture includes both ordinary reportage and a plethora of images that are relatively freestanding, awaiting recontextualization by the spectator. Their value is determined not by how they illustrate the news but, rather, by how they provide an ongoing, dynamic, and complex engagement with the world.

This book includes our interpretations of a few photographs as examples of how a revised discourse on photography might help any spectator appreciate the complexity and value of the public image.[29] And interpretation starts with our selection of each image: selection itself is an important act of spectatorship. In that small curatorial moment, one is resisting the instantaneous amnesia that necessarily accompanies the conditions of modern media production. Even those photographs that could be acutely revelatory often are experienced as ephemeral flickers in a vast light show of continuous signage on countless screens. This constant stream of visual information requires protective viewing habits to guard against cognitive overload and emotional exhaustion. So it is, in Howard Becker's memorable words, that "laymen learn to read photographs the way they do headlines."[30] And to forget them just as quickly.

This amnesia is facilitated by the standard schemes of categorization that are evident in the news media. The image is dispensable because it is one example of a familiar category such as news, sports, or fashion. This conventional organization can suppress the artistic or critical value of many images. A curatorial selection, by contrast, can collect images because of how they exemplify artistic achievement or any other feature of cultural engagement. That selection may be based on nothing more explicit than the "wow factor," as when you are stopped in your tracks by the beauty or visual distinctiveness of an image. Or it can develop beyond that first encounter to communicate something important about the historical conditions confronting the viewer. These photographs are not necessarily "the best" in terms of technical accomplishment and certainly not the most inventive or unique, nor do they have to capture the decisive moments of great events or even be especially newsworthy. They can, however, ask that you take a second look.

The photographs in this book have been selected as examples of this larger, more explicitly cultural project. We remained centered on photojournalism, even as that term is becoming more diffuse; on photographs that appeared in mainstream media, even as those media are being pulled into or displaced by diverse networks of circulation; and on contemporary images, even though digital archives are making past images more accessible. Our selections are drawn from the daily stream of photographs accompanying news stories or in online digital slide shows that are provided by news institutions and periodicals as well as news or photography services in the United States and, to a lesser extent, elsewhere (*New York Times*, *Washington Post*, *Guardian*, *Boston Globe / Big Picture*, *Atlantic Monthly / In Focus*, *Time/Lightbox*, *National Geographic*, Reuters, etc.). Some of the images we have selected were prominently displayed as news photos—front page above the fold in print editions—while others come from the slide shows that pull in images from diverse sources and have become a new media genre. These "photos of the day" are a representative sample of the transitional period in which we are working: they have obvious continuities with and differences from older genres such as the photo-essay or spot news photo; they include both hard and soft news images (an increasingly outmoded distinction); and they can include breaking news but often are shown days or weeks after the news event. These photographs come with basic captions but usually with no other narrative or reportage, and they float in a relatively contextless media space that might be thought of as an art gallery without the status of art.[31]

Whatever the platform or genre, the news media today provide a remarkable stream of images that reveal both the ordinary conventions and the extraordinary artistry to be found across the photographic archive. These images also exhibit the blurred categories (professional/amateur, reportage/entertainment, news/advocacy, politics/fashion, documentary photography / commercial photography, news media / social media) that are coming to define the new media environment without confirming either the dire warnings or the utopian pronouncements that have filled opinion pages and not a few academic journals. Most important, however, is that they are provided at all. Like so many other images across a wide range of media and platforms, they are presented for viewing by whoever might pass by: the readers, viewers, onlookers, sightseers, and other strangers who constitute the public sphere. They are a mode of civic performance, a call for an ongoing spectatorship that is dedicated to a shared world but not limited to matters of governmentality.

Our interpretations are offered in the same spirit. They are not statements about the inherent meaning of the photographs; they are examples of an engaged encounter with the image. They also can be dismissed as idiosyncratic, ethnocentric, and insufficiently attentive to context—and they may be so. We have tried to do better than that, but in any case what is most important from our perspective is to free the interpretation of public images from the all-too-limiting assumptions of the conventional discourse on photography. Whatever else may be affecting interpretation, it is always shaped by a discourse about the medium, art, genre, or audience. The conventional discourse of the last century has been shaping understanding for too long. The time has come to consider what can be learned about the public image—and the public world—if interpretation is not fettered by old assumptions and anxieties.

Out of Many, Many

Our approach pushes back against claims about the inherent (universal) incapacity of the image and against making a fetish of literal reference and uniquely situated responses. We grant that images can alienate viewers from their immediate lifeworld, but we also insist that images are rightly valued precisely because of how they communicate across situated contexts of reception. (All media are situated and transitive, particular and abstract, encultured and coded for strangers.) We believe that rigorous explication will account for how images are marked by local, national, and transnational practices and are open to divergent interpretations directed by different cultural habits, but we also believe that the encounter with the image has to begin and end as a statement from one's own standpoint. (*Every* claim that is made about any artifact is grounded in a particular standpoint. There is no universal standpoint, and all analysis has to work upward through one's cultural experience, regardless of how ethnocentric or cosmopolitan that might be.) Most important, we value the public image precisely because it is so well suited to promoting public discussion—that is, discussion oriented toward comparing viewpoints to share experiences and forge agreements. Thus we talk about the media we are familiar with, in the context that we cannot escape, as one example of how spectators might better understand their media experience.

Our interpretations take the images as we find them already relatively decontextualized: news images that are bearers of culture more than any specific news story, framed for dedicated viewing as if in a museum, but thoroughly ephemeral, sure to drop out of circulation as others like them take their place. In other words, they are very much like most of the images that you see every day. The paradox in our approach is that we find these ephemera to be remarkable works of public art. To bring out the aesthetic and political richness of these images, we frame them in ways that have been denigrated in the conventional critical discourse. We focus on formal composition, we appreciate beauty, we rely on emotions, and we accept the obligations that come from being placed in a social relationship with those in the photograph. To draw out the potential meaning of an image, we identify how it offers or rewards connections with specific issues, themes, concerns, or challenges in public life as we understand it. We can be wrong about any and all of this, but not merely because we take the image out of some sovereign context.

We believe that the photographic meaning is radically plural: it cannot be contained by any one interpretation. We are hardly alone in this, but it can be difficult to accept the full force of the idea. Susan Buck-Morss provides the direct statement that is needed:

> The complaint that images are taken out of context (cultural context, artistic intention, previous contexts of any sort) is not valid. To struggle to bind them again to their source is not only impossible (as it actually produces a new meaning); it is to miss what is powerful about them, their capacity to generate meaning, and not merely to transmit it. . . .
>
> Meaning will not stick to the image. It will depend on its deployment, not its source. Hermeneutics shifts its orientation away from historical or cultural or authorial/artistic intent, and toward the image event, the constantly moving perception.[32]

This condition is a logical consequence of what may be the central idea in the twentieth-century discourse on photography: the idea set out by Roland Barthes that the photograph is "a message without a code" and thus a communicative act involving a new relationship between denotation and connotation.[33] Curiously, the idea has become more relevant precisely as digital technologies have made it obsolete. Barthes's claim was based on the assumption that a photograph could show what was before the viewfinder without having to first transform the event into a system of signs. The analog image was an indexical trace of the event, the result of a causal chain of photons bouncing from object to film. Instead of signs throwing off multiple meanings that have to be formally consistent, the photographic message was a conjunction of a direct analogue and whatever coding was brought to it by the viewer. For example, the conjunction of photograph and caption could be an example of all photographic meaning: image and text that can be each apprehended alone have been joined, but only contingently as there is nothing in the image that mandates those words as opposed to others. The conjunction of a direct copy and additional coding guaranteed that any photograph contained a "plenitude" of meaning precisely because what it showed could not be directly or fully articulated.[34] Showing is not telling. At the same time, showing is not sufficient to communicate and permit viewers to understand all that is shown, and so interpretation is inevitable. Any interpretation of a photograph has to bridge that gap between the silent analogue and its possible articulations. More to the point, the photograph exists to prompt that crossing.

But what happens when the image is no longer an analogue of reality? Photographs today begin as data that then are coded by algorithms for display.[35] In place of direct reproduction, there are norms of representation and processes of verification. To comprehend the change involved, consider how intelligent machines would have no need for much of the internal processing that goes into making a photograph; their cameras could input data directly into computations of distance, mass, viscosity, or any other variable for the task at hand. Faces, social distance, Albertian perspective, and other features now coded into the image could be dispensable. They are supplied for us not because they are there in the world but because we want to see them. Indeed, as Brian Massumi has argued more generally, "digital technologies have a connection to the potential and the virtual *only through the analog*."[36] The comparison also reveals how current coding reflects long continuities (not certainties) in human perception. Digital cameras are programmed to conform both to features of ordinary vision and to conventions of analog photography, and for good reason: so that they will be purchased for everyday use around the globe. Despite all the commentary about digital manipulation, the most unassailable observation is that for most people the transition from analog to digital cameras was seamless.[37] The corresponding shift from stand-alone cameras to billions of smartphones will have enhanced this continuity of experience: the image's relation to reality is ratified by the camera's becoming even more closely woven into everyday life.[38] Whatever the reason, billions of people traded one technology for the other without any awareness of the difference in image production or any adjustment in their use of the medium except to use it more often, in more situations, and more creatively.

Digital photography thus confirms both the importance of the reality principle to the medium and the necessity of interpretation if the medium is to exist at all. (Machines have cameras, but they need not have photography.) Even though coding now goes all the way down, the distinction between analog and code is re-created through the act of processing the image. In fact, direct perception is a fiction, as seeing is highly discontinuous and cognitive processing is indispensable to the production of a mental image: our brains run algorithms that put the most expensive digital camera in the same class as the pencil. In like manner, optical memory can be influenced by many factors, but it does not substitute words for parts of the image. Whether in ordinary perception or in memory or as a material artifact, the image is not directly continuous with the discursive coding that might be supplied. Stated otherwise, there are codes and there are codes. To translate the optical data into a linguistic code might be possible, but it would not be a photograph.

The photograph's relative autonomy from language creates a paradoxical outcome: it presents reality as it can be seen, but without means for restatement. One can circulate the image, but to understand and share its meaning, something has to be said. By reaffirming ordinary perception, the digital image also affirms the necessity of interpretation. This might be thought of as the "postprocessing" that accompanies any image, whatever its origin. That may be exactly why context matters: it is part of the computation needed for us to see more than the raw data. Contexts need to be fixed to allow specific things to be seen, and they need to be changed so that other things can be seen. The fundamental problem defining photography need not be the question of representation—how it does or does not involve accurate copies of the real—but rather how its use involves varied forms of contextualization and decontextualization.

Just as the analog image changed the relationship between denotation and connotation, the digital image has changed the relationship between image and interpretation. Amid the general continuity of conventions, there is no doubt that digital technology "changes everything" and that digital cameras now produce more than photographs. As we become habituated to photographs, visual networks, and data arrays, to smart phones, cars, and clothes, and to "simulative, heuristic, and layered" images, neither ordinary experience nor public consciousness can be anchored in a single conception of representation or authenticity.[39] The image is now thoroughly and unavoidably interpretive, and thus it has to be developed and stabilized through use. As Melanie Bühler summarizes:

> Whereas the relation between reality and representation was a key concern of classical photography, now, as photography has become digital, the focus has shifted from this single relation to a multiplicity of relations that extend from a photograph. Value is no longer primarily derived from the special relation between the object in front of the lens and the way it is depicted in the photograph. . . . The question of the original is no longer relevant.[40]

New media lend themselves to overstatement, but the observation is rich nonetheless. Instead of undercutting the validity of the photograph, digital technologies have provided platforms through which the inherent plenitude of photographic meaning can be developed and shared, often to critical effect. Fred Ritchin has pointed out how this "linked, dynamic, node-like photography," at once literal and metaphoric, could "open and amplify the image, allowing it a more vibrant, dialectical role on a multimedia platform" in which photographers create images to activate discussion, and both distributors and spectators can add links and alter contexts to create "a collaborative, multi-vocal interrogation of both external and internal realities in which the initial exposure is only a minimalist starting point."[41] As W. J. T. Mitchell has stated, "It is not 'adherence to the referent' that is endangered by digital imaging then, so much as the adherence to a controlling intention in the production of the photographs."[42] Mitchell's examples include the Abu Ghraib photographs, which were explicitly digitized but rightly granted indexical power, and which started as "trophies of sadistic domination" but became "revelations of a structural, social, and political reality that would have remained, but for this existence, at the level of rumor and verbal report."[43] As David Campbell observes, the range of interpretations an image evokes through global circulation "shows how photographs are polysemic and polyvalent—as part of their condition, they are inescapably open to multiple readings."[44] The new medium has enhanced what always was a feature of the old. Each image is both distinct and one of many; a single moment and part of multiple patterns; a specific intention and something defined by others; a mute perception and a figural performance awaiting restatement.

It is this deep pluralism that makes the photograph an important object for civic spectatorship. The public value comes from the distinct combination of a plenitude of meaning with the continuity provided by shared perception. The photograph is a distinctive and useful interpretive object not because different viewers can each see what they want but rather because whatever is seen is open to other views of the same things. This utility is realized fully only in discussion about what the image reveals. You might see environmental degradation where your father-in-law sees economic growth, but for either claim to be meaningful, the viewer has to articulate a connection between what is shown and what is said, between what is visible and larger patterns never seen comprehensively. You might see an image of a professional athlete signing autographs at a National Guard camp, and we might see an image of the normalization of war, and the choice is not between right and wrong interpretations (although mistakes can be made at each level) but about whether one is willing to stay within or move beyond the conventional wisdom that is already a part of, but not wholly determinative of, the photograph's meaning. As Wendy Kozol has argued, this *ambivalence* is a crucial feature of spectatorship, reflecting how the image is both caught within hierarchies of difference and able to resist them, and thus an unavoidable condition for ethical witnessing.[45]

Photography's radical pluralism is evident in an image (fig. 4) of mirror reflections at a shopping center in downtown Tokyo. Photography becomes reflexive when it focuses on its own or other optical

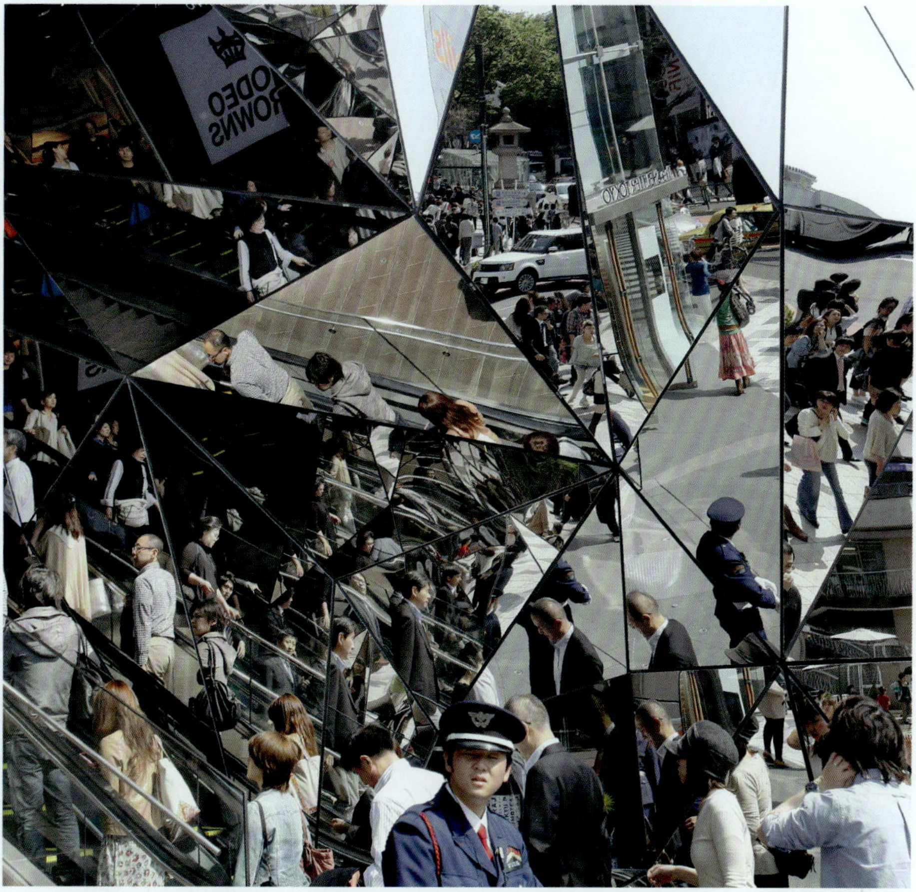

Figure 4. © AP Photo / Koji Sasahara.

technologies or reflective surfaces; by "showing seeing," the image features some of the conditions of seeing and being seen in public.[46] The reflections in figure 4 provide a fragmented panorama of people coming and going. Because the glass is cut in a variety of geometric forms that were then welded together at odd angles, the panels resemble fun-house mirrors in crazy-quilt arrangements. Individuals are reflected accurately enough to be recognizable yet also are slightly distorted: we see double images, transected images, oblique angles, and unusual perspectives. Each shard of glass is accurate enough, but the jumble of those fragments leaves us with a scene that is chaotic if not altogether incoherent. Those in the scene are so accustomed to being viewable that they can walk by the mirrors without giving them any notice, and yet many of them are mirrored in ways that are closer to surveillance optics than face-to-face interaction. State surveillance is hardly out of the question, as the police are evident both outside and inside the mirrored space. That double image neatly reproduces the reality effect: because the cop in the foreground is in front of the mirrors, we see him and therefore the photograph itself as real. It also constructs the mirrored space as emblematic of the public sphere: a space of representation and spectatorship separate from the state yet also now including state institutions. The police look rather small and clueless, however, and this is very much a portrait of civil society, especially because the mirrors are in a shopping mall.

Perhaps the strongest contrast is between the many signs of social organization evident in the clothing and behavior of the pedestrians and the chaotic, almost incoherent assemblage of images. A seemingly ordered world becomes distorted in representation: duplicated, fragmented, duplicated again, broken up and reassembled differently, and never in a stable configuration precisely because the process is occurring constantly and mechanically. The conventional paradigm would seem to be validated: the public image is at once fragmented and overwhelming. What should be in the background has taken over the frame; what should be a technological supplement to the real world has become an image world that distorts as it absorbs everything into its madly refracted hall of mirrors.

Photography does provide only fragments that become part of a massive jumble of images that includes varied and never wholly coherent perspectives. The photograph says as much, but it also places that condition within a reflective space—one where the dominant attitude need not be anxiety. The images are continuous with yet also obviously broken out of the natural attitude, conventional wisdom, habitual orientation, and characteristic blindness of ordinary vision. Each one of them, on inspection, can reveal something from an ordinary street scene that might otherwise be overlooked. Together they foreground and defamiliarize social and cultural assumptions that are everywhere visible and yet rarely observed: characteristic features of modern society and urban design. Because of the jumble of perspectives, we can see more of the street scene than would be available from any one angle without the mirrors. Perhaps the collage suggests that the real jumble is present *before* conventional awareness—as if the photograph were showing us something like a raw file of the street scene before it is processed into preset patterns of civic order and consumer consumption.

The image captures a deep tension between fragmentation and coherence within photographic spectatorship, as well as the idea that each public image is at once a fragment of an incoherent whole and a collage of many different perspectives. We see a plethora of possible angles on a single scene, while the internal transections draw attention to how smaller vignettes can be broken up further for observation—say, for observation of the many intersections of social conformity and individuation defining the public space. Most important, perhaps, the messiness of the image might signify that for all the similarity of this city to other high modern cities in the most economically advanced nations, the transnational civic culture on display is a construction having no sure logic—and no basis for believing it is the destination of the more explicitly jumbled public cultures and alternate modernities emerging in Nairobi, Mumbai, São Paulo, and elsewhere.[47]

The camera reflects the mirrors that reflect the camera: one image, many images; one place, many places; one viewpoint, many viewpoints. The image obviously is limited by the circumstances of its making: it is but a fragment, reflecting an affluent world, and so forth. Those features are not hidden, however, but reflected in the image. The photograph is one fragment showing a few of the many facets of the public image in its inherent multiplicity, plurality, openness, and resistance to any one totalizing regime of intelligibility.

So it is that we have selected and interpreted a few dozen photographs in order to provide one model of how to cultivate a mode of civic spectatorship. We hope that our use of the images might motivate viewers to build their own archives and bring other images into their conversations and other creative activity. The images are there every day, asking for a response. We have to ignore most of them, but the supply, at least for now, seems endless. Instead of authoritative gatekeeping, this book points to an embarrassment of riches.

Instead of definitive claims about the meaning of the image, we offer a process of attunement to a public world that can be familiar and strange, conventional and revelatory, disastrous and beautiful all at once. Interpretations undertaken to engage with this dimension of the news image often assume too much for many readers. We hope, however, that some of the time they can suggest how much remains to be seen.

CHAPTER THREE

REALISM AND IMAGINATION

Photography is defined as a medium by its relationship to reality and as an art by its relationship to the imagination. These distinctions have shaped the discourse of photography from its inception, and each successive reformulation of the discourse involves a new understanding of how reality and the imagination might be entangled together in the still image.

Perhaps the most succinct formulation was provided by film theorist Siegfried Kracauer, who was trying to identify how "each medium has a specific nature which invites certain kinds of communications while obstructing others."[1] Kracauer defined photography as being shaped by two generative principles: "there is on the one side a tendency toward realism culminating in records of nature, and on the other a formative tendency aiming at artistic creations."[2] As he also noted, this tension generated the aesthetic problems for the medium. He could have added that it offers one explanation for the conventional division between documentary photography and fine art photography, as each side emphasized one media capability or the other while trying to avoid compromises that could undermine either ethical integrity or artistic innovation.

We might call this model the photographic matrix. As a matter of necessity, every photograph consists of both a referential and an imaginative orientation. Any photograph is both more or less a record of what happened and more or less an artistically enhanced experience; both more or less empirical and more or less interpretive; both more or less accurate and more or less suggestive. A photograph of a dog is not a photograph of a cat, and whether one sees a beloved companion or future show dog depends on extension into a larger context, one that already may be coded into the artistic composition of the image. Of course in many photographs the imaginative element may be minimal, say, limited to the most basic technical enhancements such as framing and tonality. Likewise, in other photographs the referential element may be spare—a small candle burning in the darkness—yet have strong emotional and symbolic resonance.

These two principles do not have equal status, however. As Kracauer correctly observed, the media specificity of photography comes from the primacy of the realist principle. Although "a minimum requirement," it is almost absolute: photographs are expected to show something that was in front of the lens prior to the creation of the image.[3] That said, Kracauer recognized that the imaginative and realist principles don't have to conflict: indeed, the formative tendency "may help substantiate and fulfill" the realist tendency.[4] What might seem like a minor caveat is in fact a radical insight: *realism has to be the first principle of photographic meaning, but it cannot be achieved completely without imaginative presentation and response.* The camera records the surface of the world like no other instrument, but the truth of what is shown can be *realized* only through an act of imagination. Stated otherwise, the photograph is inherently not reducible to a single principle of representation and instead is a "heterogeneous object" where different sources of meaning intersect, and the intersections are lodged in the formal design and explored through interpretation.[5] How such intersections occur can be described as the relationship between image and text, image and context, image and optic, denotation and connotation, studium and punctum, and so forth. These are "hermeneutical circles" defining interpretation, similar to those active in other media.[6] They are *not* evidence that the image is inherently meaningless by itself, or that its claim to show the world accurately is fraudulent, or that image consumption becomes pitched toward aesthetic pleasures that will corrupt judgment.

Failure to appreciate photography's dual nature as record and artifact has led to a serious disconnect between theory and practice. As Patrick Maynard has summarized, "Both among theoreticians and in the popular mind . . . industrial technologies (quaintly associated with our 'needs')" were defined in contrast to the fine arts, with "imagination as the very antithesis" of industrial production.[7]

Instead of the imagination considered as "a crucial practical skill" and photography as a technology for amplifying imaginative powers, the separation of mechanical reproduction from aesthetic experience became conventional wisdom.[8] More recently Jae Emerling has concluded, "The contemporary impasse of photography is, in large part, a result of this rejection of aesthetics, something which one finds throughout its discursive history."[9] This separation and a corresponding skepticism regarding mass culture have long been the dominant attitudes in academic, professional, and public commentary. One result has been puzzlement or embarrassment regarding the continuous stream of images having both representational validity and imaginative power, not to mention popular appreciation. Another result has been widespread acceptance of a tame conception of photographic realism—what we will label "literalism"—and with that, a weakening of the political imagination.

We want to be very clear that we are *not* insisting on a single definition of either realism or reality. The habitus of photography contains varied conceptions, criteria, and standards of photographic reference.[10] Those differences reflect everything from pragmatic variations in use (a family album is not a court of law), to philosophical debates about representation, to fine art experiments with the conventions of visual perception, to professional and public controversies about Photoshopping the news. Fortunately, engaged spectatorship does not require a comprehensive theory or professional doctrine, but it can benefit from making specific aesthetic and political commitments against a background of multiple perspectives.

We believe that the camera's capacity to directly and inexpensively produce reliable pictures of the world remains an essential technology for democratic societies, but the full benefit will be realized only through imaginative interpretation of the public image. Such spectatorship attempts to develop the full richness of the image and the archive, in order to place the viewer in an engaged relationship with the real world and those who live there. To do that, each generation will have to work through the fundamental tension between trace and artifact, reality and imagination. Unfortunately, the current legacy provides a weak sense of both dimensions of the photographic statement.

From Realism to Literalism

The invention of photography in the nineteenth century was a profound and yet curiously pleasing shock to modern habits of representation. In retrospect the effect seems to have been one of receiving a large and unexpected inheritance. By so perfectly and easily capturing the observable world, this obviously modern technology offered a new, more immediate, unbiased, and comprehensive relationship to reality itself. In fact, the removal of human mediation was thought to be the supreme achievement of the technology, an idea captured by Henry Fox Talbot's label, "the pencil of nature."[11] Louis Daguerre had already gone one better, claiming that the daguerreotype was "not an instrument to be used to draw nature, but a chemical and physical process which gives her the ability to reproduce herself."[12] Reality now could communicate directly, without need of or distortion by human artistry. A French journal summed up the matter succinctly: "We can hardly accuse the *sun* of having an imagination."[13]

Photography's exclusion from the fine arts followed directly from this statement of the obvious: photography was not an art, could not become an art, and any attempt to do so could only corrupt both art and photography. Charles Baudelaire got closest to the problem with his disdainful account of how the new medium was changing the public and, with that, artists who would pander to the sensationalism of the real. Thus "progress" was decline—"by progress I mean the progressive domination of matter"—as photography drove the artist to paint "not what he dreams, but what he sees." Because the camera was aligned with both the material force of matter and "the great industrial madness of our times," it was driving out the imagination, leaving a void sure to be filled only by banality, mediocrity, and sentimentality.[14] What actually was happening, of course, was that the definition of art was changing radically due to the pressure of photography's mimetic power and widespread circulation, and by being freed from the imitation of nature, modern painters unleashed one of the most significant bursts of creativity in the history of art. Even so, Baudelaire was prescient in recognizing that photography was distinguished not merely by a close fit with nature but also by its industrial production, and that a major effect was the change in public spectatorship.[15]

Despite the strong separation of reality and imagination in these early debates, other voices were developing a more nuanced view of the technology, one that recognized artistic potential beyond veridical representation. Oliver Wendell Holmes was an avid promoter of photography and also one of its most insightful commentators. His account of the medium includes a phenomenology of seeing in which "the mind feels its way into the very depths of the picture" to sense an "inexhaustible" complexity where "there will be as many beauties lurking, unobserved, as there are flowers that blush unseen in forests and meadows"; perhaps most important, he broached the idea that "form is henceforth divorced from matter" and thereby something that can be reproduced, shared, studied, and enjoyed easily.[16] As these and other quasi-artistic experiences were being explored in practice, the trafficking between photography and the imagination became a busy streetcorner where eccentrics, charlatans, artists, and journalists worked side by side. Victorians indulged an appetite for photographs of fairies and other traces of a spirit world, pictorialists and surrealists redefined the camera as an instrument for artistic experimentation, and photographers such as Alfred Stieglitz, Edward Weston, and Henri Cartier-Bresson developed the idea of photographic artistry as an important, though carefully circumscribed, marker of professional value.[17]

While the debates about photography continued to focus on whether photography merited the status of a fine art, the scope of visual media was expanding greatly. Lighter cameras, faster film stock, industrialized printing, the cinema, the expansion of advertising, social reform documentary photography, explicitly politicized artworks and culture wars, the rise of the Frankfurt School—the list is a long one. These and other developments could not be handled adequately by policing entrance to the museum. In a near-perfect example of a paradigm shift, Walter Benjamin declared that "*commentators had earlier expended much fruitless ingenuity on the question of whether photography was an art—without asking the more fundamental question of whether the invention of photography had not transformed the entire character of art.*"[18] Photography was no longer a newcomer in the salon but instead a force shaping the modern world. Equally important, questions of aesthetics were aligned with the noxious politics of Europe in the 1930s. In Benjamin's most famous statement,

"*Such is the aestheticizing of politics, as practiced by fascism. Communism replies by politicizing art.*"[19] Art was giving way to the mass media, and photography was one of the media to be manipulated in order to control the new mass society. Benjamin and the Frankfurt School writers devoted a lot of thought to this new problematic, as did Soviet photographers with their development of photomontage and photocollage, as did László Moholy-Nagy at the Bauhaus and elsewhere, and—to be sure—critical thinking has been immeasurably improved by their work.[20] But perhaps because of their alignment on the Left, as well as the exhaustion produced by the war, this discourse was largely ignored until it was rediscovered and promulgated by Susan Sontag, John Berger, and other theorists in the 1970s and 1980s.[21] Until then, and sans any critical challenge while riding the wave of the postwar economic boom, photography was acquiring all the benefits and characteristics of institutionalization.

By the middle of the twentieth century, photography had achieved a complacent stasis in respect to both reality and the imagination. It was solidly institutionalized as a modern recording technology that served science, industry, advertising, art, and most notably the press, but always in a subordinate role. As part of the professional segmentation that accompanied this ubiquitous use, fine art photography also was recognized as a minor form of the fine arts. More generally, aesthetic appreciation was accepted as a common feature of ordinary consumption, just as artistic skill was recognized as one feature of good photography. *Life* magazine and *National Geographic* epitomized this cultural consensus: the photographs were taken by highly skilled photographers for an audience that wanted to be both informed and entertained but not troubled or changed. In sum, the photographic image was securely ensconced as the instrument of accurate observation, and some photographs were valued for how well they enhanced the viewing experience. Along the way, with few exceptions, the discourse on photography had gone largely dormant: beyond the technical manuals, there wasn't much sense that the medium might exemplify important problems in modern culture.[22] Perhaps for that reason, both realism and the imagination had been tamed.[23] Reality was there to be seen through ever more advanced technologies such as cameras in space, undersea, and inside the body, with little concern about selective perception or political bias.

Imagination was largely confined to technical artistry or, at the cutting edge, the selection of subjects (as in the work of Robert Frank, Bruce Davidson, Garry Winogrand, Lee Friedlander, and Diane Arbus), or to avant-garde experimentation in fine art photography that had no significant effect on the larger viewing public. Photography had become part of a standard world whose only horizon was one of continued progress. Although described by some as a golden age of photojournalism, the time had come for someone to upend the table.

Enter Susan Sontag, who convinced her readers that photography was both characteristically modern and deeply problematic: "the quintessential art of affluent, wasteful, restless societies—an indispensable tool of the new mass culture."[24] Equally important, she changed the relationship of photography to both reality and the imagination. The key restatement is this:

> Photographs are, of course, artifacts. But their appeal is that they also seem, in a world littered with photographic relics, to have the status of found objects—unpremeditated slices of the world. Thus, they trade simultaneously on the prestige of art and the magic of the real. They are clouds of fantasy and pellets of information.[25]

Sontag has defined photography along Kracauer's two axes: the photograph is simultaneously artifact and fact, fantasy and information, an imaginary world and a small piece of the actual world. So far, so good.[26] That colorful vacation photo, that astronaut on the moon, demonstrators shouting across a police line, a starving woman holding a starving child—each depicts a tiny slice of what was there then, and also activates visions of leisured happiness, technological progress, political action, or ethical community. This framework doubles as a highly concise critical method: for any photograph, one can ask how its fragmentary record of the event or process is too selective, and how it appeals to the spectator's desires as these have been shaped by larger practices of cultural domination.

The problem is in the specific inflection given to each of the two generative principles of photographic art. Sontag's formulation is radically reductive, and doubly so: both representation and imagination are recast in their least adequate forms.[27] The photograph's relationship to reality is reduced to mere information, and in the most demeaning sense that can be attributed to that term. "Pellets" denotes the product of an industrial process, one that produces endless numbers of small identical objects. The photograph is seen through Baudelaire's eyes: fused with the most alien aspect of reality, its sheer materiality, devoid of consciousness, and with the most impersonal and powerful form of modern society, its relentless industrialization.

The damage done to the imagination is at least as bad. Information is legitimate and legible in a modern society, but fantasy is a cheap thrill at best. As before, however, Sontag does have one leg to stand on: If photography replaced imagination with fantasy, that could be considered an example of cultural decline (compare even today the relative status of "literature" and "fantasy literature"). And some photography certainly will indulge fantasy, particularly if one looks to advertising, travel photography, and other commercial practices.[28] That said, the easy path of fanciful artistry is a constant temptation in any area of creative work, and no small number of bad poems, novels, films, and buildings are evidence of that. Sontag's distinctive emphasis is to redefine a negative tendency in any imaginative process as an essential condition of photography. Photography cannot be imaginative, yet it is an artifact; therefore it must be phantasmagoric. Which, not surprisingly, would seem to explain why it would be so appealing to the mass culture audience.

This model became the foundation of late twentieth-century discourse on photography. Note, for example, the double denigration in John Tagg's assessment of the FSA photography project: "We cannot be innocent of the values which inhere in the 'realism' of these photographs. . . . We may live the space of the picture, its 'reality,' its ideological field. But as the picture draws us in, we are drawn into its orbit, into the gravitational field of its 'realism.' . . . We seem to experience a loss of our own reality . . . we are invited to dream in the ideological space of the photograph." He concludes by quoting Freud: "'When the work of interpretation has been completed, we perceive that a dream is a fulfillment of a wish.'"[29] The supposedly realistic image is a fabrication that takes the spectator away from reality and substitutes a dream world. Photography misleads because of both how it shows the world and how it invites imaginative response to what is shown.

From this platform and through the application of semiotics, rhetoric, psychoanalysis, and other critical technologies, the two principles of realism and imagination were each subjected to withering attack.[30] On the one hand, photography did not provide adequate representation of the real world. Instead of being a transparent window on the real, the photograph was an artifact, a designed object that shaped perception according to technological or ideological imperatives. Instead of being directly apprehended, it was essentially meaningless until provided with contextual information. Instead of recording exactly what happened, it provided only the thinnest sliver of any event, a tiny fragment of time with no sure indication of what happened before or afterward. Instead of being the objective result of a mechanical process, the photograph was the product of desires and conventions that affected every element of its existence and use. Instead of providing veridical evidence of actual events, the images of the world were being used to make social hierarchies appear natural. In Martin Jay's succinct summary, "By the late twentieth century the realist paradigm was practically obliterated."[31]

On the other hand, photography also was faulted for being incapable of artistic extension into the more creative and critical modes of perception. Instead of being oriented toward the imagination, photography was doubly banal: a cheap, disposable object documenting the most ordinary circumstances, people, and events of everyday life. Instead of being used to think critically, it was taken by the public to be merely descriptive, informative, factual. Instead of elevating thought, it was a relentless mixer and leveler that fueled popular culture while making amateurism into a virtue. Instead of channeling the emotions to break through convention or complacency and motivate action, it substituted faux experiences of empathy and other bourgeois sentiments. Instead of enhancing perception, it "aestheticized" reality, prettifying the ordinary and converting horror into perverse fascination. Instead of providing a bracing encounter with the unknown, it encouraged voyeurism, tourism, and other irresponsible habits that converted people into images for consumption. By 1990 Fredric Jameson could pronounce the sweeping verdict on modern visual experience: "The visible is *essentially* pornographic: which is to say that it has its end in rapt, mindless fascination."[32]

Most people don't talk like this, but the critical discourse has seeped into public consciousness.[33] And this is not a mysterious process. The discourse became the lingua franca of higher education and other cultural institutions, and the criticisms were identifying real problems: it becomes widely evident in a media-intensive society that representation is both unstable and powerful, and this combination is a pervasive source of anxiety. People want to be grounded in reality, not reality effects, and they want to control their lives, not be controlled. Nor is renunciation a viable option: it is difficult to be employed or be a parent or enjoy one's leisure time without using modern media. Caught squarely in this dilemma, journalism has developed a means for coping with photography's uneasy combination of reality and imagination. In place of a strong sense of either photographic realism or photographic artistry, the default mode now is a commitment to literalism.

According to this model of visual meaning, the photograph is taken to be a veridical record of reality, but only if it is presented and interpreted in strict accord with neutral determinations of fact. The photograph is literally true, or disqualified if found to be altered, but that is all. No other kind of speech acts are recognized: photographs state what is, but they do not explain, predict, judge, confront, suggest, plead, or otherwise call for a response. Photographs do all of those things, however, so exceptions have to be taken into account. First, some photographs are acknowledged to work on a higher plane: iconic photos are the leading example.[34] These moments of eloquence are admittedly exceptions, however; ordinary images are supposed to be seen and not heard. Second, all the aesthetic, emotional, symbolic, moral, or other resonances are limited to private, subjective experience: these are thought to be merely individual reactions and not as reliable as ordinary perception. Even those photos that shock the viewer activate only subjective reactions; they provide no moral knowledge that might be shared.

This hermeneutic, which dominates professional journalism and public discussion, is appealing in part because it intuitively responds to the critical deconstruction of both the referential and the artistic dimensions of the image.[35] Is reality constructed? Well, then, we will insist on the most basic model: the who, what, where, when of each single event. Can artistry divert or enthrall? Well, then, we will relegate such reactions to private experience: they will not have the status of public acknowledgment. So it is that the press promises unaltered images, photographers or editors provide relatively neutral captions, commentators state that their opinions are their own and not those of their organization, and public discussion includes continual fretting about digital manipulation. Admittedly this helps one avoid both flights of fantasy and errors of fact. (Make no mistake, these are important concerns for both the press and the public.) Literalism also is legible, as anyone can identify some fantasies and various facts, whereas the intermediate realm of beliefs and values is harder to pin down, much less lead to agreement. Unfortunately, the easier path leaves spectators ill equipped for critical discussion or democratic solidarity.

From Literalism to Realism

Whatever the cultural domain, literalism is not far from fundamentalism. One sticks to the letter of the text or the law or scripture in order to stay close to the essential elements of a doctrine. In the case of photography, the doctrine is the modernist commitment to objectivity on behalf of rational deliberation. If the image is found to be too artistic, emotional, or suggestive, these are biases that pitch it away from its referential function and toward fantasy and political manipulation. The knowledge that perfect objectivity may be impossible is not a deterrent but instead cause for increased vigilance. For example, the popularity of digital cameras and amateur photomanipulation has only heightened anxieties about the reliability of the image, rather than becoming evidence that the question of literal accuracy might be merely a preliminary basis for understanding the photographic encounter.

Photographic literalism has received additional promotion through Errol Morris's *Believing Is Seeing*, which followed from his essays in the *New York Times* on visual truth and deception.[36] The book provides an engaging set of detective stories, what Morris refers to as the "mysteries of photography" in the subtitle of his book. As others have noted, Morris is a careful (and appropriately obsessive) Sherlock Holmes as he interrogates the facts of the matters before him: Can we determine where and when a photograph was taken? What is the order of photographs in a sequence of images? Is the placement of objects in a scene empirically verifiable? As these and similar questions are answered, it becomes clear that the mysteries of photography are altogether secondary to Morris's primary concern, which, as Kathryn Schulz has observed, is epistemology.[37] The goal is knowledge, at the cost of bracketing from consideration everything that cannot be demonstrated conclusively in respect to the specific circumstances of image and event.

This shift from photography to epistemology is exemplified by the first half of Morris's title: *Believing Is Seeing*. His phrasing reverses the terms of the cultural aphorism "Seeing is believing." This is not just a stylistic affectation. The more common phrase calls attention to the nature of seeing as the source of belief. As Aristotle remarked in his *Metaphysics*, "For not only with a view to action, but even when we are not going to do anything, we prefer seeing (one might say) to everything else. The reason is that this, most of all the senses, makes us know and brings to light many differences between things."[38] To "see" is more than just to "look at" or to "gaze upon"; to see the world is to be in it and to be of it; it is to discover, compare, categorize, and otherwise understand the world actively. This sense of active discernment is captured metaphorically by the phrase "I see what you mean." By reversing the terms, Morris prioritizes "belief" as the active agent that controls seeing, and in the process he reduces the latter term to a condition of passivity.

This is not just a chicken-and-egg question. To privilege belief in this way underscores a narrow definition of truth and what counts to establish truth. For example, Morris attends to two famous Roger Fenton photographs from the Crimean War. In one photograph the road is covered with cannonballs. In the other photograph the cannonballs are on the side of the road. And the mystery is, What accounts for the movement of the cannonballs from one location to the next? And which of the photographs was shot first? The first question is never fully answered, although Morris does ultimately provide an answer to the second. But what, really, does it tell us about the truth of the matter? Or more to the point, the truth that it uncovers seems ultimately trivial in relation to the horrific conditions of the war and the suffering that it caused—a truth that doesn't change, no matter where these cannonballs actually landed.[39]

This is another way of saying that one very quickly gets to the limits of literalism. The epistemological questions can never be answered in full, and they displace other substantive questions. The literalist asks whether the photo is accurate but not what other statements it might be making. Although the displacement of all social, cultural, moral, and political questions is hardly Morris's intention, one can see exactly that use of literalism in ordinary commentary. From elite forums to online comment threads, people regularly insist either that a disturbing or challenging photograph can support only the most minimal account of the event, or that since it is not perfectly reliable it should not support any judgment. As Jörg Colberg points out, "These mechanisms are now essentially being used to discredit stories. It doesn't even matter any longer whether the allegation that a photo was staged is true or not. What does matter is that the allegation points to an increasingly widely spread worry about the medium, and the story becomes discredited automatically."[40] Whether due to political legerdemain or the simple desire to be free of ambiguity and conflict, an insistence on literal accuracy alone can sever the most vital connections between the photograph and the world.

What we have, then, are two different paths for the interpretation of photographs. From the first perspective, any photograph might provide a limited but accurate representation of the objective world: the tree really was there whether you thought so or not, as were the power lines that nobody had noticed when the picture was taken. And "OMG, did I really look like that?" Here interpretation is focused on considering how the fragmentary image could be a valid representation of an event. Was it altered? How much did things change before or after the ¹⁄₅₀₀th of a second in which the photograph was taken? What really happened? We might label this perspective the referential model. It relies upon indexicality, and it constitutes the ground floor of visual literacy.

From another perspective, photography is a medium of social interaction: photographs depict people in relationship with one another, they are used to make sense of the social world, and they create and inflect relationships among those who use them. "OMG, did I really look like that?" is a question not only about what happened but also about social acceptance. And about politics: in Ariella Azoulay's terms, each photograph creates a "civil contract" among all parties to the photographic event and thus joins viewer and viewed as virtual citizens.[41] We might label this model the relational model. Not surprisingly, it opens the door to a much wider range of questions about what an image might mean, in what contexts, for what reasons, and to whom. More to the point of this chapter, the shift from literalism to realism is also a shift to an imagined community, that is, to a relational understanding of the photographic event and of everything depicted in the photo.[42] That imaginative extension of the image is at once aesthetic and ethical and therefore often intuitive. Thus a more robust conception of photographic realism moves upward and outward from the specific image: it follows the artistry of the photograph to trace extrinsic patterns and ethical obligations, including those created by the act of viewing the image.

This is not to deny the importance of detailed observation and media reliability for evidentiary purposes, whether in a court of law or in the court of public opinion. There are times when the stakes are very high and all can turn on the veracity of the literal image. It should also be noted, however, that almost all photography is accurate enough for the purposes to which it is put. From tourism to scientific research, the cameras and images in use have been selected because they are sufficiently reliable for the task at hand. The problem is that literalism elevates an occasional concern into a preoccupation. Of course context matters, and so the photograph used in a scientific report operates with a different standard from the cover of a fashion magazine, but in general, when discussions of photography are restricted primarily to questions of whether the image was Photoshopped, it is rather like limiting literary criticism to an exclusive focus on plagiarism. In each case one might conclude that we are hearing about an interesting problem but still well short of taking the measure of the art.

Literalism includes a general suspicion of both aesthetics and rhetoric—and for good reason, as they invariably dismantle the assumptions necessary for believing in the inerrancy or objectivity or neutrality of literal statements. They also contrast with literalism's own implicit aesthetic norms, which typically involve some minimalism, iconoclasm, or other aversion to excess in representation and response. From this perspective, fantasies are by definition excessive, and when they occur it can only be because audience response is no longer adequately tied to text or reality. Thus when realism is reduced to questions of referential accuracy about "pellets of information," imagination has to follow a corresponding redefinition as "clouds of fantasy" providing willful, superficial enchantment.

This redefinition neatly reproduces Samuel Taylor Coleridge's distinction between imagination and fancy.[43] Imagination is the vital ability of the mind to see its way into new perceptions, new creations, new syntheses; it is the human ability to create ideas, images, and relationships that had never existed before, and to do so in a way that brings us closer to the real nature of things. Fancy, by contrast, is merely the mind at play with things it already knows: it is the mechanism by which we assemble and reassemble memories without regard for reality in order to pander to our desires.

To bend these ideas in the direction of photography, we might think of imagination as a way of extraordinary seeing—that is, how one sees beyond the horizon of ordinary observation or conventional belief. Astronomy, for example, began as an incredible act of imagination: by looking at a pale disk and points of light in the sky, people came to understand that the earth is a planet, and by looking at telescopic photographs and other electromagnetic traces, we have learned that the universe consists of billions of galaxies that will never be visible to the naked eye. Likewise, photography has been a remarkable exercise in imagination, for by showing distant people, places, and events it has brought spectators around the globe to realize that they are part of a common humanity living in myriad different cultures that no one will actually see together.[44] In both cases, moreover, the mode of extraordinary seeing brings the viewer closer to reality, and to a larger reality, not further away from it.

These examples also demonstrate that works of the imagination will not be accessible to everyone and that they can be misused. But we knew that. The important contrast for the moment is with fancy as a mode of all too ordinary seeing. The sad truth is that when people are being fanciful, they also are all too predictable. Fancy is party hats and balloons and drinks on the sly at the office; imagination is the single mysterious flower waiting for you at your desk.

Photography can provide works of the imagination, but they risk being merely fanciful confections. It can bring viewers to see anew or to enjoy a habitual blindness. Sontag was half right: fancy is a risk whenever the imagination is in play. But what she missed is this: the imagination is necessary for reality to be apprehended at all. If only fantasy is possible, then a better way of seeing reality is no more accessible than it was by means of those pellets of information, facts incapable of carrying with them the ideas and emotions needed for thought and action.

Stated otherwise, a photograph is always both image and optic: a picture of some part of reality and a way of seeing that reality more extensively; a recording of specific facts and an act of imagining a world. And just as we can say that the photo shows more than one thing, or that it can mean different things to different people, so can it contain multiple optics. Thus in looking at the iconic photograph of a man standing before a row of tanks near Tiananmen Square, one might see Cold War geopolitics, democratic revolution, liberal individualism, global citizenship, and other perspectives as well, including the Chinese government's focus on the restraint of the tank driver, as well as high-modernist aesthetic simplification that reinforces "seeing like a state."[45] Most important, each perspective is simultaneously grounded in the particular event being depicted and extended beyond that moment to other actual or potential events that are part of some larger pattern. The optic has to have some purchase in the event that the viewer can recognize or it won't be activated at all, and it has to imply additional extension if the event is to have any significance.

The extrapolation from the single moment may be why so much emphasis has been placed on both semiotic composition and discursive contextualization. The formal composition and iconography of an image provide springboards for inference: central placement implies importance, a farm denotes a rural setting and connotes tradition, looking up can be aspirational or intimidating, and so forth. Likewise, captioning and other texts direct elaboration of the scene: those facing each other are antagonists, the rain helps one side more than the other, a third party predicts a stalemate. So it is that believing is seeing, for the beliefs brought to bear on the image also are resources for imaginative consideration of various possible meanings. Form and context are both crucial to photographic meaning, but not because they are safely ensconced wholly inside and outside of the image. Each is a modality for imaginative extension of what is shown so that it can be more adequately intelligible and useful. Form extends beyond the image, while context has to be grounded in the image if it is to work imaginatively rather than be merely fanciful.

We should note that this is precisely the point where the critique of photographic representation should apply. The semiotic extension of the image does involve a sleight of hand: any pattern of meaning is attached to more basic properties of perception and thus can acquire a sense of inevitability that obstructs any relevant sense of individual choice or collective action.[46] That said, the critique cannot retract to a literal degree zero of visual representation, as that would make photographs either unrecognizable or completely useless.

There are three levels of inference that should be noted in this regard, as they provide a basic structure for imaginative extension. The first level is the ordinary experience of regularity in the natural world. A photograph shows a man pitching over a cliff and the viewer concludes that the man is falling; one literally sees a man in the air and then adds gravitational force, continuation of motion, and other suppositions to complete the picture. Action can be seen at all only because we can extrapolate causally beyond the single moment. Likewise, one concludes that the man is falling, not flying. One might have a fanciful conjecture about flight, but the photographic imagination works with, not against, nature. Thus any visual experience, whether photographic or otherwise, begins with basic considerations of physical continuity and causality that cannot be literally evident in the still photo (if anywhere). Most portraits show only portions of the whole body, but no one assumes that they are seeing actual dismemberment. The imaginative supplement is labeled "closure," and Scott McCloud's discussion of graphic art perfectly captures those properties that often are faulted in photography: in both media, the framed images "*fracture* both *time* and *space*, offering a *jagged, staccato rhythm of unconnected moments*. But closure allows us to *connect* these moments and *mentally construct* a *continuous, unified reality*."[47]

The photograph is inherently imaginative in a second sense as well. For any record of human behavior to make sense, it requires inferring others people's intentions and thus other ways of looking at the scene. This exercise in higher-order intentionality—that is, imagining what other minds are thinking—is fundamental to human communication.[48] (Turn taking requires it, for example.) The basic intelligibility of a scene as well as any ethical response depends on some degree of intentionality—at the very least, why the photograph was taken[49]—and generally involves complex patterns of social interaction that can be evident on the surface of things. One sees that the man is wearing a swimsuit and gracefully arcing toward the water, and thus sees a dive instead of an accident. Or, as there is more slippage when dealing with social conventions than with physical laws, one might imagine an unusually polished suicide or a terrible accident in the making on the undersea rocks below. To "see" at all, however, one has to complete the picture by providing missing information about the internal states of the actors, which requires an act of closure in the social realm equivalent to closure regarding physical continuities. Just as one can assume that the person in the photograph has a lower body that is not present in the image, so one can assume that the smile denotes approval, and that it could be genuine or feigned, and that the action could be appropriate or ironic, and so forth. Seeing is believing, but belief has to work through the imagination, which draws on our ability to extrapolate intentions and other mental and emotional states from others' behavior.

This imaginative capability works through psychological processes, but it also becomes elaborated into the complex patterns of interaction and implication known as societies and cultures. Communication media are the essential means for doing so, and so they inevitably are caught up in articulations of presence and absence, self and other, and other paradoxes of the human condition. Most notably for our purposes, modern media are the infrastructure for the public culture that provides distinctive conditions for modern political legitimacy. Thus the third extension of the photographic imagination occurs as it fills out what Hannah Arendt has called the "space of appearance" that is the warp and woof of public life.[50] That space consists of the places, media, and discourses in which people create a shared world that becomes the basis for collective organization and action.[51] This is a world where "innumerable perspectives" intersect, and a world that has to be re-created continuously out of that condition of radical plurality through interactions with others as they are seen by others. As Roger Silverstone summarizes, that re-creation is defined by "the visibility of the other, of the stranger as well as the neighbor, the capacity for dialogue and the manifestation of discord, the presence of alternative views and the struggle for an audience."[52] It also is a continuing act of imagination, one in which we see images as reality and strangers as fellow citizens, while continually adjusting our conceptions of what other people are thinking, feeling, and doing.[53] As Arendt and many others following her lead have argued, this virtual world is one that depends on disclosure and response, a willingness to be seen and an engaged spectatorship that is, as Barbie Zelizer has argued, at once contingent, imaginative, and emotional.[54] And the linchpin in this motive constellation is imagination, through which the reality of a shared world is created out of the elaboration of fragmented appearances.[55] When an image activates this public optic, the spectator is being called into a higher-order intentionality that can see sameness and difference, plurality and solidarity, which become the assumptions of a shared world.

If the reality of that world is to be experienced through photography, the medium has to be capable of activating and guiding the interpretive resources that allow generalization beyond the literal setting and behavior. Realism requires imaginative presentation and response, which then become pathways to deeper modes of engagement. This would have been part of what Holmes was after when he spoke of feeling one's way into the depth of the picture. The photograph's relative immobility allows time for such consideration, and that time is used for an imaginative shuttling between self and other. This also is a crucial point of intersection of Kracauer's referential and formal principles: the aesthetic dimension of the image is most important when it activates empathic connection with strangers.[56] Whereas literal reference can be all too narrow and familiar, photography can bring the spectator to see beyond what he or she already knows and to encounter what has not yet been labeled.

Realism Today

A strong conception of realism need not be defined by nostalgia for previous examples such as the social reform photography of Jacob Riis and Lewis Hine in the early twentieth century, or the FSA photographs documenting the Great Depression, or the gritty urban photography and courageous photojournalism of the 1960s (and beyond), or any other historically specific achievement, although these and many other models can be provided. Nostalgia is unnecessary, because powerful photographic encounters with the world are constantly available. The present moment is particularly rich in this regard, as digital technologies have accelerated the blurring of distinctions between documentary and art photography, reportage and advocacy, and professional and amateur practices.[57] These are not regrettable deviations from a prior model of professional practice but rather means for reconsidering and strengthening photography's relationship to the world. As W. J. T. Mitchell has argued, contrary to the technological determinism that ignores how media are shaped by social practices, "digitization has produced a general 'optimization' of photographic culture, one in which better and better simulations of the best effects of realism and informational richness in traditional photography have become possible."[58] A robust realism need not be threatened by digitization, which has prompted exactly the artistic experimentation that is creating a more engaged encounter with reality.[59] Or, one might say, with what really matters.

Realism in this sense is a commitment to achieving the greatest public benefit from photography's ability to provide a veridical representation of the external world. The opposing tendency, at least initially, is idealization—a process easily but mistakenly confused with artistic inflection. Obviously a great deal of commercial photography is idealized, ranging from the selection of subjects to the artistry of the image to the manner of circulation, all of which is composed to project desired conditions as if they were already available through purchase of the product. By contrast, realist photography strives to document the material conditions, social relations, and actual experiences of ordinary life as they are shaped by economic and political practices. As we argue in chapter 4, this commitment is part of photography's special relationship with modernity. The legitimacy of the modern age depends on the quality of everyday life for ordinary people, and photographic realism provides one measure of how well any society is meeting that standard.

This commitment involves several assumptions regarding photography's subject, purpose, and audience. First, the camera is capable of documenting how the material conditions of everyday life reveal social, economic, and political relationships. Spacious or crowded, rich or poor, free or restricted, these and other structures of distribution are there to be recorded in detail. These larger patterns are evident only as traces and textures—for example, an old car or new coat, worn heels or good teeth—and often are found to be complexly articulated: for example, plenty of children to play with in the slums, isolation in the private jet as a hidden cost of affluence. In any case, the material surface is a record of causal processes and of how the people in the frame are coping with the circumstances and contradictions defining their common world.

Second, realism offers photography as a democratic mode of communication, one that is about ordinary people and for the common good. Through the social relationship created by the viewing of the photograph, the image offers a connection with the lives of others that might not be expected otherwise. When the image focuses on the everyday lifeworld, that relationship is simultaneously grounded in common experience and identified in terms of actual distributions of power. As John Roberts notes, "Realism, essentially, is a fallibilistic account of a transitive, stratified and differentiated world; it is not a window on a homogenous and present or phenomenal reality."[60] Thus it provides "practical knowledge" for negotiating the contradictions of social organization while calling for (rather than presuming) democratic community.[61] Consequently, the photograph also is an intervention into that world, an attempt to praise or blame, maintain or change what is shown; reality is represented as part of a rhetorical act. As Roberts summarizes the early revolutionary theory: "The 'everyday' was where the world was to be remade," and photography was to be an important part of that work.[62] Every image of the contradictions defining ordinary life is also an image of what could be changed for the better.

The final element of realist photography is the presumption of a high level of critical and collective spectatorship. Viewers are assumed to be entering into an ethical and political relationship with those in the photograph. This is not the sentimentalism decried in the conventional discourse on photography, much less "voyeurism" or "tourism," but rather an on-the-ground humanism that presumes common rights in a shared world and critical engagement in a public sphere. Roberts summarizes this orientation as "a recognition of the deep historical connection between representation and the possibility of a public, not just a professional, culture for art."[63] Realist photography shows what is and says that those conditions are in fact objective, not subjective; as they are, not as they are claimed to be; and part of a common world, not separate domains of interest. Thus the realist photograph presents itself as an emotional encounter leading to collective identification: the image takes the spectator inside another world, asks how it is also the viewer's own world, and offers solidarity on those terms.

To make a long story short, "realism" is one marker of how photography provides essential resources for public thought, which of necessity has to be attuned to both facts and values, and to the relationship between conventional beliefs and particular experiences, and to how well state and society are serving the general welfare. For this reason, it should not be surprising that each of the elements of photographic realism depends on artistic, imaginative development: the depiction of how ordinary people are affected by and coping with material conditions; the connection between actual experience and possible changes to achieve a better society; the viewer's identification with people and places that could be ignored. These elements of representation and response are not provided by the camera alone. Instead, photographers and everyone else working with the image have to be able to draw out its revelatory and rhetorical powers.

Photography's relationship to reality has to be more than either factual or fraudulent. After all, ordinary perception provides an endless supply of facts: this wall is here, that plant is there, the mailbox is empty. Ordinary perception is continuous, while photography, despite its wide proliferation, has a more uneven flow that requires imaginative stitching together of the images in various overlays of optics, archives, and cultures. Photography is not simply a mechanism for capturing the world as it is, but rather a capacious public art that participates with all other media in making reality meaningful. And to follow this path is to recognize that the simple presence of an object in a scene—a cannonball on a road—is less significant than the visions being evoked by the small world of the photograph. In addition, as images are circulated throughout a public culture, they can lead to important truths about what it means to see and to be seen as citizens—a result more important than whether objectivity has been sanctified or fantasy avoided one more time.

The imagination is not an innocent place, of course, but one traversed by vectors of power and colonized by societies and their institutions. Thus critical awareness has to be brought to bear, both when imagination is stunted or co-opted by the powers that be, which happens all too often, and when mere fantasy can mislead those who have few resources to waste. Imagination is a political resource—including fantasies of power by both the strong and the weak, but much more as well—and it needs to be used well.[64] One of the functions of journalism is to create the imaginative space of the public sphere—a space in which citizens have the freedom to consider alternatives to the status quo. Another is to report reliably on what is actually happening so that planning and other acts of political imagination can be grounded in reality. Professional journalism has described itself as if a carefully managed literalism is sufficient to serve the public interest. It is not sufficient, and fortunately journalism's actual practice exceeds its disciplinary norms, in part through the photographs published every day. What still is needed, however, is a stronger understanding of photojournalism as a public art—that is, an understanding that returns from literalism to a more complex and nuanced mode of spectatorship.

Seeing What Cannot Be Seen

Realism is powerfully identified with specific documentary conventions and dramatic periods in the history of photography, which today can seem to be limitations on both artistry and uptake. But realism is not limited to black-and-white photography, portraits of the poor, or any other of its signature instantiations. Today it also includes brilliant color, aerial photographs, conceptual artworks, and more. Conventions have evolved not only due to technological changes but also to confront important questions about what can and cannot be shown and how the public viewer should react. To suggest how spectators are being invited to contend with these issues, we can look at how realism includes images that challenge seemingly fixed borders—for example, between the visible and the invisible, and between humans and other species.

Even when documenting suffering, the traditional realist image was laudatory because it conferred visibility on what otherwise was ignored. By displacing the human figure, contemporary realism can achieve the same objective. The baseline condition in each case is that visibility can be an important property that represents status, legitimacy, rights, privileges, and powers.[65] To consider how that is so, think of the men and women who still are trapped in the closet, or the street people who are treated as if they don't exist, or the elderly who have to endure others' talking about them as if they were not in the room. Consider also what it can mean for an ethnic group when one of their own achieves celebrity, or when they can see themselves without caricature in entertainment and advertisements, or when strangers nod pleasantly as they pass by. Not everyone needs such recognition: those who are very rich prize not being seen by the masses, but they already have what they need otherwise and are assured recognition and deference within their own circles of entitlement. For most of us in a modern society, however, a baseline sense of value comes from being visible—more specifically, from the experience of being seen without social stigma or stereotype and as if we belong in the picture.

The problem of Native American invisibility continues to be part of the prolonged catastrophe that otherwise is known as their history in the modern era. This invisibility is not for want of paintings and photographs; in fact, they are part of the problem. Even today, there are few images of Native Americans that are not of a feathered warrior, or alcoholism and poverty, or a casino. Photographers return to the reservations and urban ghettos, but no matter how hard they try, it seems that the mix of persistent social problems and ritual trappings will defeat any attempt to see. Stereotypes are rechanneled inadvertently through conventions of "poverty porn" that lead at best to pity, and through romantic conceptions of native spirituality that can excuse material deprivation.[66] Were these documentary habits overcome, there still would remain that irrevocable barrier between the present and all that was lost when oral cultures suffered conquest and displacement.[67] What is seems forever sundered from what was, so much so that the traces of the past can offer neither solace nor a basis for reconstruction. Because of their geographic isolation and how that compounds dysfunction while reducing assimilation, the native peoples of the Great Plains may be in for the worst of it.

Figure 5 is from the Pine Ridge reservation in South Dakota. The photographer is trying to break through the wall of invisibility that prevents any understanding of both the failures of the reservation

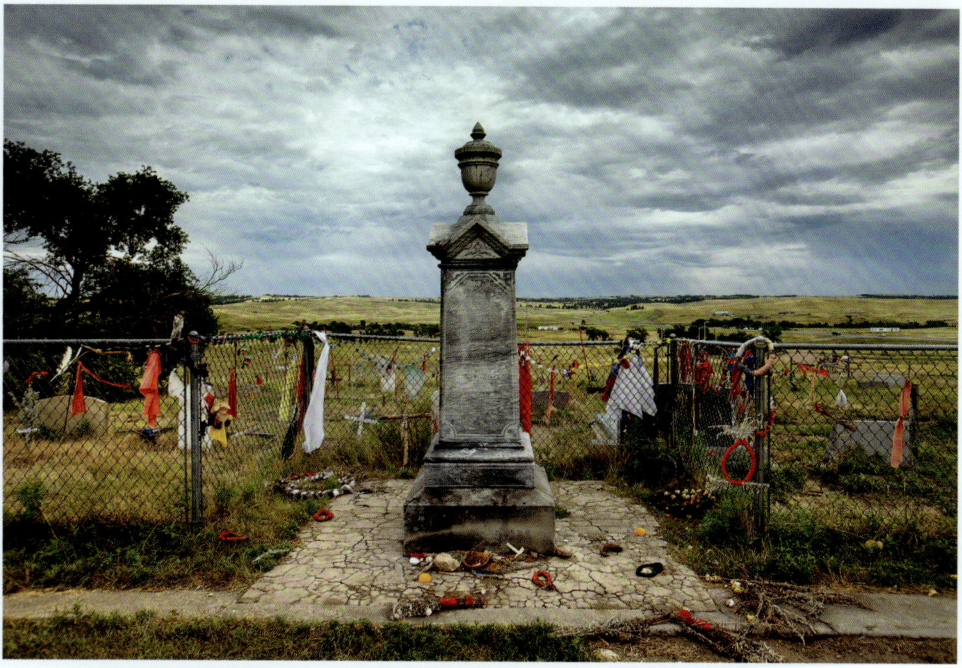

Figure 5. © Aaron Huey.

system and how, for all that, people are finding ways to care for one another, preserve their shattered culture, and perhaps even one day receive justice.[68] Even so, the news is not good, as might seem evident from this photograph. Although both monument and photograph provide a memorial—that is, a site oriented toward the past—the image also projects a damaged future. It accomplishes this by featuring the persistence of the past, including the relative lack of visibility that has defined Native American history. No one is in the picture, and the West can continue to be imagined as a largely empty landscape awaiting development.[69] Once again Native American culture appears almost immaterial, ephemeral, a collection of feathers, scraps of fabric, and other ornamental flotsam that will be carried away by the prevailing winds.

But that's only part of the tableau, for European culture doesn't come off any better. That monument was never an award winner and has gained nothing with the passage of time, but above all it was out of place from the start. What would simply be overlooked (invisible) in today's urban park—or in almost any public square throughout Europe—here looks distinctly anachronistic; worse, it can stand for all that did not follow, the promises of compensation and a common future that never came to pass.

Instead of a city or the prairie, we have the fence, and with that the political fact of forced enclosure. That fence is too banal to really qualify as a symbol, but it will have to do: like the reservation system itself, it is a cheap but effective barrier. To see more than that, you have to look more intensively, peering through it to see crosses and gravestones and, if you look very closely, a few houses scattered across the plain. The spectator then has both additional information and a greater awareness of how little is known. A community must be there, but one marked by death and solitude. And catastrophe: the caption tells us that this is a "mass grave at the site of the 1890 Wounded Knee Massacre."

So it is that another roadside memorial tells a story, but it is not the whole story. The memorial tableau depicts two cultures that reflect contrasting optics.[70] Instead of seeing only scraps of material on the fence, those within the Wounded Knee community can see signs of continuous attention and respect. The dead have not been forgotten but rather are being honored by a community that is present, active, and ethical despite all that it has suffered in that place. Likewise, the neoclassical monument still marks the hybridity of the Native American memorial, but instead of incongruity one can see a history of cultural interaction—one that changed the visual vocabularies of both Native American and Euro-American cultures. Instead of keeping a people interned in the past, the photograph suggests that history continues to be both forgotten and reinscribed in the present. By focusing on signs rather than people, the photograph aligns a history of warfare, defeat, and occupation, the problems of invisibility and representation, and the challenge of finding a way forward through interpretation and reinterpretation.

That challenge is not merely one of widening one's perspective to neutralize earlier misconceptions. There is one more thing that goes beyond both restrictive convention and activist commitment: that impossible sky. At once beautiful and foreboding, it suggests a natural history of the civilizations that have passed below, each sure to disappear like yesterday's wind into the vastness of time, and yet also a sign of something higher, stronger, more enduring than any human thing.

Thus the photo invites consideration of the relationship between myth and reality: the memorial, a sad remnant of two cultures that tragically collided, and its backdrop of sublime natural beauty with all the spiritual power and promise that still holds. To live under that sky is still to be impossibly rich, unless of course you are impossibly poor, sick, abandoned, and traumatized. If the spectator concludes that spiritual richness compensates for material poverty, then the photo has been read back into those conventions that perpetuate injustice and indifference. But the sky is heavy with storm clouds, and goes from there to exceed representation itself. It reminds us that no monument can compensate for material want, and that poverty is an indictment of those who rule on a planet that is vast and abundant. Under that sky, the landscapes of reality and the imagination merge to become not one story but rather an invitation to a shared future.

There are a few white settlers still living under that sky, and some of them can still see it, but for most of us on all sides, that experience has been lost to either disaster or affluence.[71] It is odd that the sky could become invisible, but that, too, is part of the history signified by the photograph. What may be hardest to imagine in a world made by photography is that anything could be omnipresent and not seen, but that is the condition that haunts both photography and modernity. Hence the drive to record anything that is approaching extinction—as was done with the painting and photographing of the "American Indian." What is needed instead, however, is the ability to understand how photographs are warning us of catastrophes still in the making.

Photography is deeply implicated in modernity's encounter with its own destructiveness. It bore profound witness to the Holocaust and continues to document genocides and other atrocities. Some argue that it has nonetheless made promises that cannot be kept. Sontag's meditation on photography and suffering concludes with the emphatic declaration that "we don't get it. We truly can't imagine what it was like. We can't imagine how dreadful, how terrifying war is, and how normal it becomes. Can't understand, can't imagine."[72] For once, the limit condition of representation is comprehensive: no medium can communicate the trauma that is known only through direct experience. What is a psychological fact may also be moral wisdom, but it offers only a negative solidarity, an almost sacred acknowledgment of radical difference. One cannot share the victims' suffering, and so all that is left is to honor them by keeping one's distance and refusing any pretense of a common life. If photographic "realism" suggests otherwise, it is a lie and an insult to those in pain. In the imagined community created by the photo, there still remains a terrible divide between the spectator and the victim. Honesty, it seems, is the best that one can do in that situation, while compassion is imaginative excess, a delusion reinforced by the faux intimacy of the photograph.

Surely those are genuine risks of any attempt to communicate about or respond to horror. Yet the same critique also has taught us to be suspicious of discourses that make social divisions appear natural, put disturbing experiences beyond the pale, and deny possibilities for egalitarian community. In any case, photography continues to bear witness to modern destructiveness, and even to extend the promise of solidarity with victims across supposedly natural barriers to moral consideration.

Few could look at the widely circulated photograph shown in figure 6 without being utterly, viscerally affected. The image is doubly disturbing, for although the impending gag reflex might make one turn away, it is nevertheless hard to stop staring. This would seem to be photography at its worst, creating a perverse fascination with the grotesque, a gaze that borders on disgust, fixating on what is aesthetically and morally hideous. Worse yet, perhaps, it does so while suggesting that we can imagine what it is like, that we can cross the barrier between victim and spectator, even when the divide could not be more obvious: how can we claim to understand another species? And isn't the more pressing task that of understanding the oil spill, something that requires backing out of the photo to obtain a wider view, a sufficient context for deliberation about the complex political and technological factors that encompass both the problem and its solution?

Yes, but . . . Let's not be too quick to cast off emotional entanglement with other species, or the role that particularity should play in moral and political assessment, or the ideological pressures evident in the detailed circumstances of ordinary life for those at the

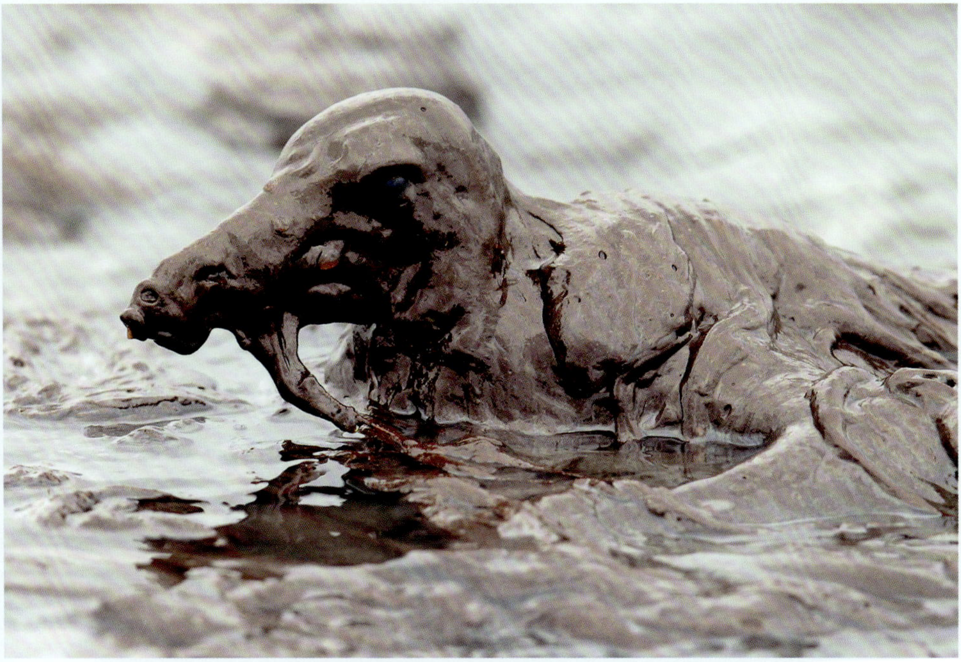

Figure 6. © AP Photo / Charlie Riedel.

bottom of the social order. These elements of a robust realism articulate through the complex emotional response evoked by this photograph, and they are the reason that the image can activate public awareness of the catastrophic potential of modern oil production. Photos such as figure 6 "speak" to the twenty-first century's unfolding environmental disaster precisely because of how they work as photos.[73] The tight close-up shot may seem to lack context, but here decontextualization functions as a means for critical reflection—and for a recontextualization in terms of a morality that extends beyond merely human costs. Although a study in thick particularity, the image clearly is about more than one bird.

Curiously, it also incorporates many of the conventions of portrait photography: focus slightly off-center and with the subject filling the frame at a three-quarters angle so as to put itself on display. Perhaps that is why it invites anthropomorphic projection by the viewer. There is something of a regal quality to the bird's pose: sure to die but still holding its head upright; reduced to nakedness by the slime yet striving to endure; on view for all to see and yet refusing to succumb to the humiliation of being immobilized by filth. It is not a stretch to say that the bird exudes a sense of dignity that resonates with the better part of the human spirit. Thus the photo may have stronger moral force than typical glosses on human loss in the Gulf: "The workers are free to work elsewhere. The economy would collapse without the oil industry. The technologies to prevent and repair spills are continually improving." When neither nature nor society apparently merits compassion, a dying animal may nonetheless activate our moral sense.

This identification, or interspecies connection, may be helped by our not being able to see the creature directly. Only the eye, looking as if the animal is in shock, is visible through the mud. We see the organ for seeing, one that can mirror, prompt, or guide our viewing. But most of all we see the thick crude oil, and the bird trapped in the muck as if in the petroleum seepage of an ancient tar pit. Through that allusion the photograph stuns, because it shows how a modern technological disaster has so fouled the earth that it has re-created a prehistoric calamity. The bird is here in the present and yet in a time out of time, both making a direct call on our compassion and scrambling past, present, and future. The poor beast is a living fossil, one that could become the trace of an extinct civilization.

This dislocation in time is easier to sense precisely because there is nothing in the photograph that directs our attention to the immediate cause of the bird's plight. The caption locates the bird on a beach in Louisiana's East Grand Terre Island, and so we might be inclined to point our fingers at British Petroleum or perhaps the oil industry more generally. But the photograph itself fails to provide any direct evidence to support that conclusion. If any blame is identified in the photograph, it must come from elsewhere, and like any portrait this one urges us to look inward, to see ourselves lurking in the image somewhere. When we do that, we have to recognize that although BP is culpable for the catastrophe in the Gulf of Mexico, the responsibility for this bird's quandary is not BP's alone.[74] Everyone who depends on the use of petroleum and oil by-products is complicit in the system of production. As a society we need to view the effects of our use of oil in the context of a larger moral universe.

What we see in the photograph, then, is an image of ourselves. The negative affect we experience in viewing the photo can include implicit recognition of modern society's waste, impurity, and carelessness. This emotional reaction can do something too rarely achieved in public discussion of energy and environmental policies: fuse individual and collective responsibility. The muck that looks like liquefied shit is the waste product of a civilization, and there is no way to pretend that it doesn't exist or that all aren't caught in a wide spill of obligation. The trapped bird signifies a skein of social relations, it locates both harm and change in the everyday world, and it creates an empathic bond that is essential for democratic communication. Although initially shocking, our first recoiling back from the image leads to a reverse movement back into the image; like Holmes feeling his way into the very depths of the picture, the imagination struggles through the tar to comprehend not only the bird's catastrophe but also how it is the moral center of a much wider indictment.

Ideal and Real, Reconsidered

One might expect a robust realism to have an antagonistic relationship with idealization. Isn't all the work being expended to see through any pretension that things are better than they are, to confront society with what actually is despite what it may claim to be? Perhaps, but it would be more helpful to consider how the real culprits are vapidity, denial, and similar accomplices to exploitation—vices that can be found in every medium. More important still, one might recognize that realism and idealization have important intersections and resonances, and particularly so in respect to the political imagination. Although they are not the same thing, each rises above literalism, and each may have something to offer, something that can become evident when we compare specific images.

One of the standard criticisms of photography is that it produces an idealized conception of reality. Framing, depth of field, and many other techniques are used to feature what is attractive and ignore everything else. As Sontag summarizes, "Often something looks, or is felt to look, 'better' in a photograph. Indeed, it is one of the functions of photography to improve the normal appearance of things. . . . Beautifying is one classic operation of the camera, and it tends to bleach out a moral response to what is shown."[75] The implication seems clear: to allow moral response, idealization must be checked. Ordinary habits of moral indifference would seem to fit the formula. Much of the time we see single events, not the surrounding confusion or complexity; clean surfaces, not inner turbulence; smiles, not heartache. Of course photojournalism and art photography alike strive to escape these conventions, whether to document what is going wrong in the world or to explore extraordinary modes of perception. But for every one of those images, there are thousands from commercial photography, advertising, public relations, travel and snapshot photography, pornography, soft news—in fact, just about everything else, including those great pictures of distant galaxies from NASA. And did we mention sunsets?

If we had a dollar for every photograph like figure 7 . . . Yet they continue to appear, and not only on Flickr and Facebook but on desktops, greeting cards, corporate reports, news sites, and just about everywhere else. The more conventional they become, the easier it is to disdain them: "Photographs create the beautiful and—over generations of picture-taking—use it up. Certain glories of nature, for example, have been all but abandoned to the indefatigable attentions of amateur camera buffs. The image-surfeited are likely to find sunsets corny; they now look, alas, too much like photographs."[76] One could go further and point out that the stock image provides an idealized portrait of nature, and one that, like the dog waiting for the stick to be thrown, has been thoroughly domesticated. Except that you can't domesticate the sea and the sky, so we have only a delusion of control and reciprocal beneficence.

The photo also assumes that the woman (and dog) can easily escape any bad turn in the weather and that she can take the leisurely stroll because she doesn't have to depend on finding something to eat along the shore. Her leisure and ours in enjoying the image depend on a prior, taken-for-granted surplus; without it, the photo could be only a weather report or a guide for foraging. Any thought that somewhere, somehow, sustainable food, shelter, and other protections might be at risk is put to rest by the vision of natural harmony. Human, animal, and inanimate nature share a common beauty—what more do you need to know?

That is one account, and it may help with understanding why so many similar photographs are taken, although it doesn't leave much

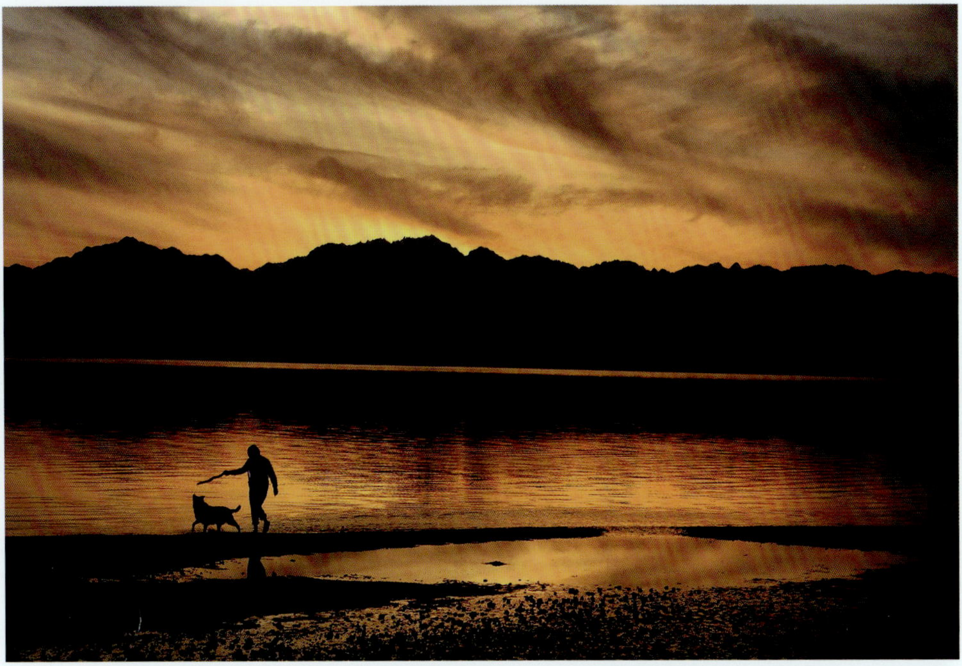

Figure 7. © Larry Steagall / Kitsap Sun, Bremerton, Wash. Used by permission.

for those who find beauty or solace or other kinds of resonance in the image. In chapter 7 we will suggest how landscapes and other seemingly superficial images and conventional emotions can provide important resources for living together—for example, by inviting us to a more abundant life than we might think possible. That said, Sontag is correct to the extent that it can be all too easy to forget just how idealized many images are. But not all of them.

The original caption of figure 8 said, "A crow eats it's [sic] prey sitting on the roof of the Chancellery in Berlin on May 6, 2014." That's a model caption—who, what, where, when—which doesn't begin to capture our emotional response to what is being shown. There may still be a small measure of buffering, as at least in this instance the prey may not be alive while being eaten, but many spectators probably would conclude that they are close enough, thank you.

The photograph may be unusual (if you don't watch the nature shows on television) because of its close depiction of predation, yet it records an event that occurs just about anywhere just about any-

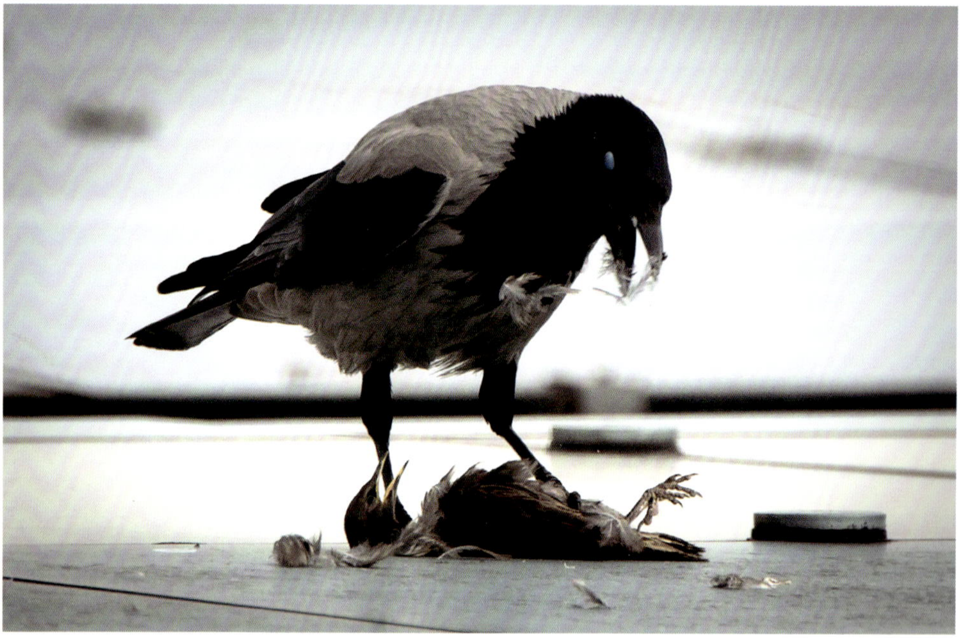

Figure 8. © Odd Andersen / AFP / Getty Images.

time. Some birds are carnivores who will eat other birds, and they do so again and again around the globe every day. Even with the reference to a government building, the event is hardly news in the typical sense of the term, yet the photograph was presented in a slide show on a major news site. Something is being shown, but what? The answer comes from seeing the image not in respect to the rooftop in Berlin but in respect to the photograph of the sunset. Each presents a very different vision of nature, and in figure 8 survival is front and center. The photograph depicts a world where the options are kill and be killed, and while there may be pleasure, there is no room for remorse. Thus it presents a different view of photography as well.

By focusing without flinching on a single meal by a single bird, the photographer has exposed the pervasive idealization that saturates so much of our mediated experience of the natural world. It would be a small step from there to conclude that the second image is superior to the first: showing us reality as it is and not as we wish it would be; reminding us that we, too, are animals who kill to eat, and not pretending that we treat all animals like pets; showing that nature is wholly indifferent to whether any animal lives or dies, and not assuming that we fit seamlessly into a natural order of transcendent beauty.

It would be easy to stop there. We believe, however, that doing so would be mistaken. A vigorous realism has to go beyond the claim that life is harsh, and idealization might indeed be one way that we rise above that condition, however precariously. Consider, for example, how this photograph is very different from the image of the bird in figure 6. The animals in figure 8 are not suffering from human action, nor does their relationship suggest a similar fate for us. Consider also what it would be like if the second photo were the norm and we saw thousands of images like it every day. (One could say we do but don't know it because they involve humans preying on other humans. Let's leave that for chapter 6.) Imagine that photography's consistent message was that nature is cruel, that life is only a struggle to survive at others' expense, that fairness and every other social value have nothing to do with it, and that there was nothing to be seen that suggested any other way of being in the world. Of course that message *is* being promulgated from one end of the political spectrum, but fortunately they do not have photography on their side. The consequences probably would be gruesome.

Note also that figure 8, though brutal, is artistic. The close framing, hard surfaces, soft background, gray-blue tonality, symmetrically inverted yet vastly unequal bodies, precisely detailed features, and single impersonal blue eye of the crow all cohere to create an intensified experience of something that seems to be autonomous, complete, and sovereign without any need for human awareness or intervention. The powerful sense of nature's struggle for survival is a reality effect of these artistic techniques, which in turn provide an optic for seeing nature without sentimentality. Thus even a direct depiction of predation, and one that calls the bluff of most photography, is no less an aesthetic achievement, and one that is completed through imaginative extension to all of nature. Without the imagination there is no "nature," and without the imagination there is little reason to show the photograph of two small birds on a rooftop in Berlin to the rest of the world.[77] Even so, it is a limiting case. Realism is cramped, not confirmed, by a vision of amoral survival.

The difference between the photographs of the crow on the roof and the seabird in the sludge exemplifies the crucial distinction between realism and fatalism. Both require imagination, but to different ends. The difference is that the image of the crow presents a world that is fundamentally determined to be as it is, while the image of the seabird presents a world that can be changed for the better. In figure 8's image of predation, all change is superficial—this bird or that one, but always the laws of nature. Entire species may adapt, evolve, or become extinct, but always within the same structure. In figure 6, however, there is an invitation to human agency. This bird or that one, but the oil need not always be there.

This is exactly what Azoulay has labeled the "political imagination": "the ability to imagine a political state of being that deviates significantly from the prevailing state of affairs."[78] The transition from monarchal subject to national citizen was a momentous example and expansion of the political imagination, as is the ongoing development of the concept of human rights. The political imagination need not be progressive on European terms, as the contemporary vision of reborn caliphates attests, nor need it depend on photography. Photography nevertheless provides the most widely available medium, and one that may be more progressive than not. Azoulay argues for a further development that grounds a "civil imagination" in photography: a virtual space in which the egalitarian basis of visibility doubles as a potential relationship among all who are ruled, regardless of whether they are deemed to be citizens by a nation-state.[79] That imagination already has brought modern societies to accept a practice of shared visibility and norms of institutional transparency and civility among strangers; ideally, the "ontology of photography" can continue to provide imaginative extension of that way of being in the world to encompass a wider conception of citizenship that is postnational, extrajuridical, and the more ethically and politically significant for that.[80]

Given the deep relationship between freedom and plurality, a civil imagination is never fixed as a state of nature. Indeed, these performative spaces have to be continually re-created through "interpretive effort, the assimilation of facts and work of the imagination, because nothing is given in advance in the photograph."[81] "Nothing is given" in the sense that the spectator's participation in the civic space of the photograph has to be taken up and engaged, not mandated.

"Interpretive effort" is required because the image does not simply record the real or indulge fancy. Facts and imagination have to be fused because these are the two principles of photographic meaning. Azoulay's project provides one model of how this interpretive labor can serve the public interest, and the doctrine and history of photographic realism provide others as well. But these are a few among many photographic practices and genres, many of which overlap and provide distinctive contributions to the task of envisioning a better world.[82]

So it is that idealization may not be so bad after all. Not all of it, and not without deliberation, criticism, and other reminders of how it can be misleading, but compared to a severe insistence on the struggle for survival, visions of a beautiful, peaceful world might be worth having. Better yet, perhaps they could be inspirations to create such a world in reality. That world is already in the making, of course, across a vast and constantly growing photographic archive. So it is that idealization and realism cohere, whether to hold up conceptions of a world without violence and want, or to insist that such a world is both not present and still possible. In every case, they also project that world through photography's distinct combination of reality and imagination, particularity and abstraction, single events and complex social relationships.

Real Vision

Images such as those included in this book are offered as temporary stand-ins for what is a potential capability in any photograph. The importance of recognizing this richer conception of the image was captured by William Carlos Williams:

> It is difficult
> to get the news from poems
> yet men die miserably every day
> for lack
> of what is found there.[83]

One might say that there is precious little poetry in the news media, but we maintain that there is quite a bit there, present but unrecognized. The poems in this case are the photographs that are available every day, waiting only for the spectator to see them as public images rather than pellets of information. By learning to read this richer sense of the news, one might acquire ways of knowing, feeling, imagining, and associating with others that could be used to change a civilization's habits of human sacrifice.

This insight connects directly with what Wallace Stevens has called "the pressure of reality," by which he meant "the pressure of an external event or events on the consciousness to the exclusion of any power of contemplation."[84] This was not a plea for a reclusive life but rather an account of a modern tendency toward stupidity and violence, and of how art must respond to that reality. The photographs in the news certainly are part of the pressure of reality, but they also can push back to suggest other possible futures beyond the relentless continuation of the same. As a public art, photojournalism might be working, however fitfully, to disrupt and reshape the powers that maintain an iron cage of inevitability and sacrifice. To the extent that those powers rely on reproducing the world as it is, it can be enough for the art to present a reality suffused with both fact and imagination, reality and aspiration. In other words, "a reality adequate to the profound necessities of life today or for that matter any day."[85]

This richer sense of realism is not merely disruptive. It is also a capacious affirmation of a deeply ethical way of seeing, one in which images and the imagination are understood to be not diversions or enthrallments but essential for realizing collective ideals. In the vision of a biblical prophet, an active imagination would be the sign that a community is in right relationship with heaven and earth: "I will pour out my spirit on all flesh; your sons and your daughters shall prophesy, your old men shall dream dreams, and your young men shall see visions."[86]

So we return, ironically, to Baudelaire, who was objecting not to this rich sense of a common life but to the "pressure" that society exerted as everyone became convinced that they were seeing reality itself. So he proclaimed defiantly, "*It is a happiness to dream.*"[87] And so it is, especially when one can *see* how the dream might already be part of reality. Realism requires imagination to be more than mere information, but the imagination needs realism as well, which is why photography is so well suited to be a public art. One of the responsibilities of photography is to strengthen the imagination, and especially the civil imagination that can envision actually achieving a better life for all—one so real that it could be photographed. This is no small task. As Stevens knew, imagination "has the strength of reality or none at all."[88]

CHAPTER FOUR

THIS MODERN ART

The photograph was a technological innovation encountered amid vast changes in society and culture wrought by industrialization; thus it was from its inception experienced as "a decidedly *modern* device, a sign and prophecy of changing times."[1] This representative aura did not diminish as modern life became saturated with images: successive developments from the hand-held camera to color photography to digitization have been both symbols of progress and lightning rods for anxiety about change. Where early commentators lauded its likely value to the sciences while debating whether it would help or harm the arts, today the scope of its influence is summed up in the book title *Photography Changes Everything*.[2] In the supposedly innocent act of objectively recording the world, photography has changed the way people in modern societies see—and thus how they think, feel, relate to one another, and otherwise share a common world, that is, a culture.

The common world of photography is the world as it is observed and imagined within a modern society. That culture is, by definition, ambivalent in respect to questions of value, for modernization has always been experienced as both creative and destructive, marked by both gain and loss, "winners" and "losers," as these are inevitable outcomes of continuous and often radical change. Famine disappears, but so does tradition. Prosperity increases, but so does loneliness. One can "see the world"—and watch jobs migrate to other countries. So it is that photography bears responsibility for another burden, the weight of modernization pressing down on society to remold ordinary life in its own image. Both effect and cause of modernization, agency of both enlightenment and alienation, instrument of both civilizational progress and the deadening uniformity of a machine age, photography is in the curious position of being an inexpensive medium having very high stakes.

This also is the point at which the emerging discourse on photography has both the greatest continuity with and a distinctive break from the older paradigm. The great achievement of Susan Sontag's generation was to lift discussion of photography above middlebrow complacency, holding the medium accountable for its complicity with modern ways of seeing, modern social relations, and modern regimes of domination. What was equally important, however, was that the emphasis was on the *negative* consequences. Any positive benefits went unmentioned, while the task of critique logically focused attention on what had gone wrong. And apparently a lot had gone wrong:

> Needing to have reality confirmed and experience enhanced by photographs is an aesthetic consumerism to which everyone is now addicted. Industrial societies turn their citizens into image-junkies; it is the most irresistible form of mental pollution. . . . Ultimately, having an experience becomes identical with taking a photograph of it, and participating in a public event comes more and more to be equivalent to looking at it in photographed form.[3]

Industrial production, mass consumption, psychological dysfunction, political deterioration: such is life in the image world, and it is not a pretty picture. It also is a characteristic lament of modern life. The critique is itself trapped—"ultimately"—in one side of a modern dialectic: chronicling the dangers of a communication technology without exploring how it is for the same reason suited to serious reflection on its cultural location. Modern technology both empowers and weakens, it both liberates and creates new forms of dependency, it is both progressive and catastrophic, and its potential for either good or evil can be adequately discerned only by keeping each side of these contradictory tendencies in play.

We believe that photojournalism is documenting the fundamental characteristics, contradictions, and possible futures of modern civilization. As a public art, it has to work within specific constraints on what can be shown, but it does so with respect to the basic questions and values defining the public sphere. What the archive never does, however, is present anything systematically or articulately. Photographs are indeed mute fragments, and the archive is an enormous jumble of images depicting endless details of everyday life across the globe. Whatever you see, you see only in part, and there always are other images reflecting other ways of living and other viewpoints. Even so, all photographs are artifacts, and some achieve high levels of artistic truth: that is, they frame and focus our attention to see with intelligence and empathy the deep patterns and problems that define human relationships. Such images are available every day, replaced by others continuously, and encountered haphazardly, but they are there.

This is where the spectator has to step up. If there is to be systematic reflection, themes identified and developed, and judgments made, it will not be done by the images themselves. Images have to be selected, placed alongside others, and otherwise used as a way of thinking about a complex common world. But they also have to be interpreted: not to discern the pragmatic intention of the photographer, or even the intentions of those in the photo, but interpreted as artifacts that are capable of revealing collective choices we would rather avoid. This chapter provides one example of that spectatorship: we react to and think through a set of images that we find to be especially prescient, revelatory, or otherwise suggestive of distinctively modern predicaments.

There is one sense, however, in which our spectatorship is fundamentally *not* modern: the photographs themselves, and their selection and interpretation, prove nothing. We are not providing a scientific demonstration of what is or has to be, we are neither meeting nor challenging specific epistemological criteria, and we certainly are not saying that specific photographs mean exactly or only what we find there. Ironically, modernist habits of analysis are not the best means for unlocking photography's relationship with modernity. Instead we rely on subjective aesthetic and emotional responses and draw on the antique mentalities of allegory and prophecy to express our understanding of the photographic statement. This is not to evade scrutiny but rather to open up the image and the public conversation. We think photojournalists are doing what artists do: creating artworks that resonate with larger cultural patterns, reward dedicated seeing, and prompt insight into a common world. The images are not dispositive, however, and there should be no doubt that our example is but one of many needed for public discussion. The one really serious mistake would be to avoid that discussion for want of better evidence. Photography's entanglement with the modern project is not trivial. Whether modernity advances or collapses or changes into something else entirely, it will not be because we could not see it coming.

Seeing Modernity

No media art should get a pass, and photography has problems aplenty. Yet the conventional litany of complaints misses the artistic core—and challenge—of the medium. What is most important about photography is not that it requires machine-age and now computer-age technologies, or that its products can be reproduced cheaply (and now ever more cheaply) and widely (and now ever more widely). Though the medium is shaped by these attributes, the single most important characteristic of photography is that *its distinctive content is modernity itself.*

To work our way into this idea, let's begin with the obvious caveats. All of modern culture is, in the most basic sense, about its own time and distinctive conditions. Any art form, no matter how ancient its lineage, can be and probably has been used to represent and reflect on modernity. As cultural forms—high and low, refined or quotidian—are used for any purpose in the present, they will inevitably reflect the conditions of their time. Some of the most profound works of painting, music, literature, drama, and other arts are so because of how they explore modern life. Those works of any period that are deemed classics merit that status because of how well they continue to speak to the present. And no wonder, as "we have never been modern"; lacking the distinction it craves, modernity has no great need for a unique means of self-reflection.[4]

That said, both fine and popular arts are understood to have varied relationships with modern society. No one would look to tempura painting to channel the spirit of the age, although some contemporary painters work with tempura. Photography, by contrast, has from the beginning been explicitly aligned with modernity's salient features, including scientific knowledge, technological innovation, industrialized production, and democratic extension. As it became incorporated into journalism, modernity's distinctive form of public information exchange, it also became aligned with the idea of the public sphere and the ideal of civilizational progress. Everywhere it was used to chronicle everyday life and to record the ways the lives of ordinary people were being improved or degraded by modernization, which then became a major test of the legitimacy of the modern age.

These alignments are grounded in a set of temporal relationships that lie within every photograph. The fundamental fact of photographic reproduction is that one cannot take a photograph of anything except as it is in the present. Literature, painting, and other arts can go where they will—far back into the past or far into the future—but every photograph is locked into the depiction of the present. The decisive question then emerges: Why is the photograph taken? Why record what is already present? The answer is that the photograph is taken for use in a future defined by change. The photographic *énoncé* includes the assumption that something in the photographic event has changed or is changing or will change. Every photograph records what is so that one might see it relative to what came before and what came after. Most often the focus is on recording what is before it changes for better or worse, or (if it is assumed to be fixed) on cataloging how it will fare relative to other changes occurring around it—often, how it will become a marker of obsolescence or loss. Thus the camera records the present before it is altered or replaced or displaced or lost or degraded or destroyed, and perhaps to show how that happened. The photograph itself mimes this temporal pathos: taken in the present, it instantly falls into the past, only to be redeemed when seen at some point in the future. Whatever its durability, the photograph is defined by its relationship to a vanishing present and an emergent future. Photography is thus geared to modernity's sense of linear time and continuous change.

Photography's conception of an evanescent present is mirrored by its relationship to its own history. A literary or plastic artwork is defined by its relationship to the history of that art; even the concept of the avant-garde depends on a strong sense of the past for its meaning and significance. Photography's history, by contrast, is a very weak force, while the photograph can never escape questions about its relevance. More conventionally, most arts are valued as their work can become "timeless," a transcendent status reflecting the artist's mastery of technique to fully realize a mode of perception or express an essential truth. Photography is considered to be timeless only in the rarest of exceptions, and not without dissent. Instead it is caught in the dilemma of recording a present that is continually disappearing. The fact that all of vernacular life has been recorded confirms the scope of modernity's relentless transformation.

This relationship to modernity may be an accident of birth or quirk in development that bonded the medium to the self-awareness of its historical epoch. It nonetheless has become a feature of the medium, a contingent capability, neither self-sufficient nor likely to last but available for those who want to use it: photography is the archive of vernacular life, displayed to allow reflection on how everyone is being affected by the ongoing changes that define modern societies.

To get inside this orientation, we might draw on Erwin Panofsky's distinction between subject matter and content. Panofsky first distinguishes between all forms of communication and those that aspire to being works of art. All communication involves focusing on "the idea of the work, namely, on the meaning to be transmitted, or on the function to be fulfilled." In the work of art, however, "the interest in the idea is balanced, and may even be eclipsed, by an interest in form."[5] After noting the futility of distinguishing exactly between pragmatic and artistic intentions, Panofsky then proclaims: "One thing, however, is certain: the more the proportion of emphasis on 'idea' and 'form' approaches a state of equilibrium, the more eloquently will the work reveal what is called 'content.' Content, as opposed to subject matter, may be described in the words of Peirce as that which a work betrays but does not parade. It is the basic attitude of a nation, a period, a class, a religious or philosophical persuasion."[6]

Thus the subject matter of a painting is whatever the artist uses as figural material: Christ on the cross, an old man, haystacks, a Campbell's soup can. Although the distinction makes sense immediately in painting—Monet's paintings surely are not prized because collectors want to look at haystacks—it might seem misplaced in the context of photography. When one is taking a picture, isn't the subject matter the point? Yes and no. The representational principle is paramount, so the "idea" must be evident in the specific features framed by the viewfinder. Yet what Panofsky calls artistic "eloquence" also is possible: the image, by virtue of its combination of form and subject matter, is able to point toward a more basic orientation in collective life.[7] The photograph records its subject, but it also can reveal something more: the technological, economic, social, political, or cultural tendencies of modernity.

Photography thus is a representative practice of modern life to a greater extent than Sontag and other critics imagined. It not only carries all the defining features and troubling effects of modernization and democratization but also casts all of modern life into a reflective space. Photography doesn't merely record modern society; it provides a performative reenactment of how that society gets through the day and how it is shaped by viewpoints ranging from a stolen glance to satellite images of cities aglow at night. And it asks whether modernity is moving into a future of continued progress or impending catastrophe.

Seeing Modernism

Photographs of industrialization and urbanization have long had an important place in the modern archive. Photography documented factories and slums, cataloging the productivity and the social costs generated by large-scale concentrations of technological and economic power. The cover of the first issue of *Life* magazine is illustrative, for it featured Fort Peck Dam, which was being built by the Public Works Administration (fig. 9).[8]

The photograph of massive concrete art deco towers looming above lilliputian figures on the ground articulated a strong affinity between the design arts, the machine age, and photography, with a good dose of national pride on behalf of progress, the New Deal, and the American Century thrown in. The photo essay inside featured the everyday life of the workers and how the construction project was both improving and disrupting life in rural Montana.[9] These and thousands of other images depicted modernization as a continuously unfolding process, at once creative and worrisome but certainly inevitable.

The stylistic continuity between dam and photograph may have provided one source of assurance.[10] Modernization subjected human

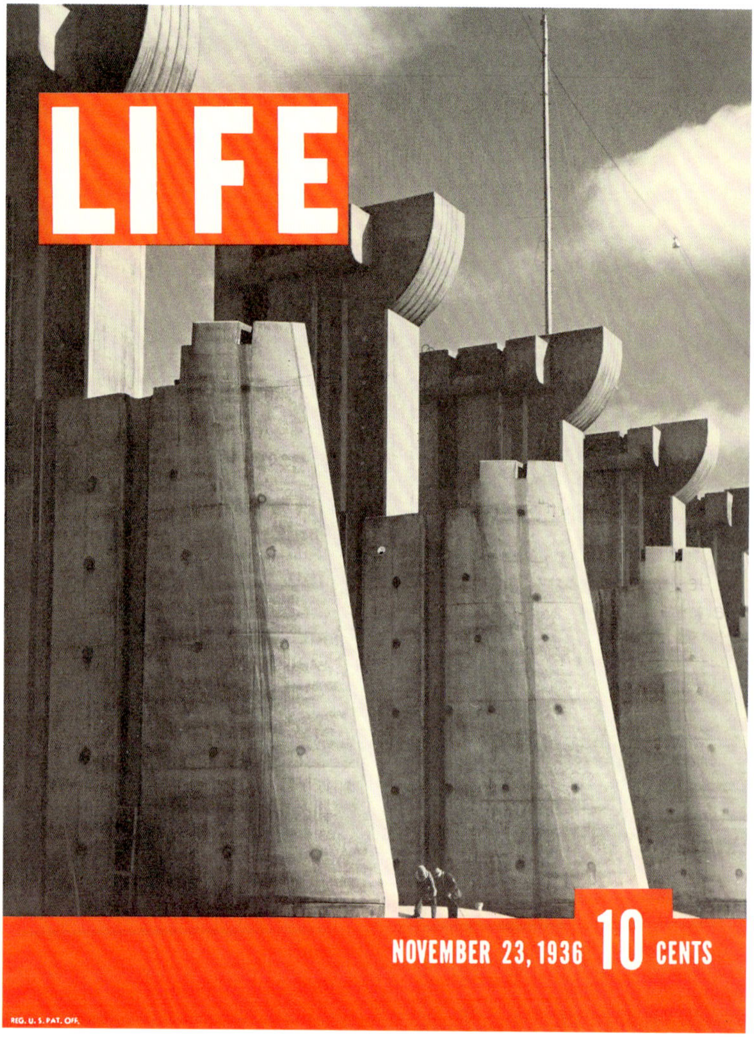

Figure 9. © Margaret Bourke-White / The LIFE Picture Collection / Getty Images.

beings to technological, economic, and governmental processes of enormous scale, but photography could offer a point of view needed for civic spectatorship. Note how the distance between the people in the photo and the towers high overhead is matched by the distance between the dam and the spectator. Although still unable to see the full magnitude of the project and all that it represents—a magnitude marked by the explicit cropping of the structure—its extension of tower after tower, dam after dam, is monitored through the technological reproduction of the camera. As an individual observer, anyone is in the position of the tiny figures in the picture, dwarfed by the structures of modern engineering. As spectators, however, all can avail themselves of the photograph's own manipulations of distance and scale.

Such photography had critical capability, as a long line of reform movements have demonstrated.[11] That said, much of it was tilted more toward appreciation than critique by virtue of the fact that modernity seemed endlessly progressive. The only serious limit condition was the threat of nuclear annihilation. That possibility was largely neutralized by a Cold War optic that either kept the threat contained within a closed circuit of technocratic control or imagined it as a single blow: the stroke of midnight in the Doomsday Clock that, should it come, would end time itself.[12] Short of that, modern civilization stretched forward endlessly; the only question was when the less-developed areas of the globe would catch up to the West. As Catherine Lutz and Jane Collins said about the temporal logic of *National Geographic*, "Their present is our past," and thus our present is their future.[13] Modern time was on continuous display in the photographic archive.[14]

The archive is changing, however. One of the significant developments of contemporary photojournalism—and culture more generally—is that modernism is becoming a period style.[15] As it had been modernity's most representative cultural style, this is a change of some importance. Modernism always defined itself against a premodern past and toward a future of its own continuously inventive expression. What twenty-first-century photography suggests, however, is both a disturbing simultaneity and a different type of succession.

Figure 10's portrait of a wildly colored exotic ritual performance captures a jarring exception within a supposedly advanced society. Our present is now a garish imitation of some primitive rite of symbolic mortification. Modernity's deep investment in colonization had from the start included a fascination with "primitive" cultures, which then became a source of both energy and innovation, especially as modern art and fashion appropriated premodern iconographies to channel energies thought to be suppressed by the structures

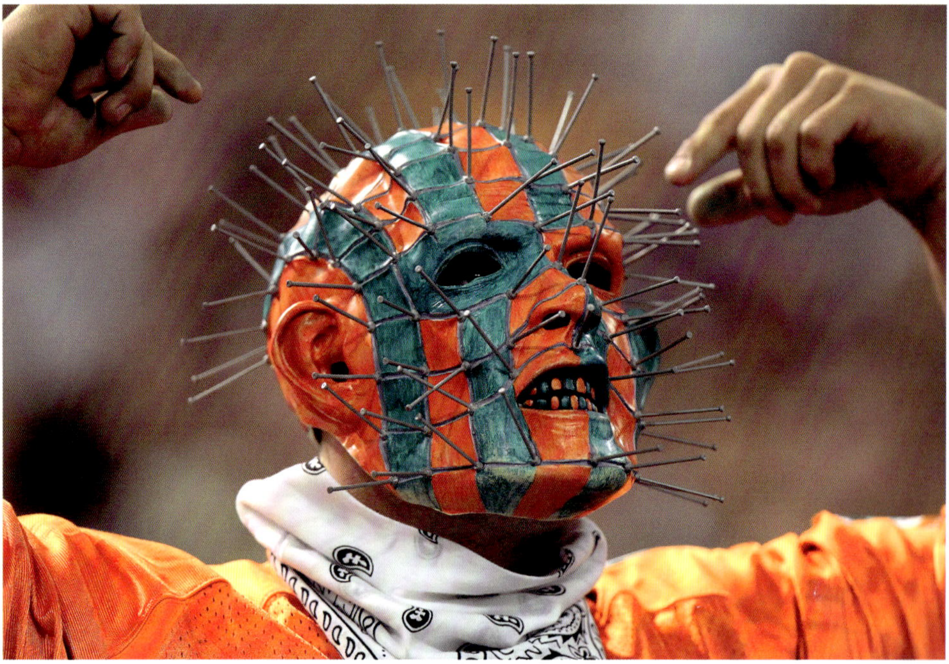

Figure 10. © Allen Eyestone / Palm Beach Post / ZUMA Press.

of modern life. The image of a football fan in figure 10 reprises that sense of primitive forces resurgent within a modern world. At once artful, machined, and hideous, he appears like Frankenstein's monster within the high-tech spectacle of mediatized entertainment. Those nails are a product of the machine age, as is the plastic material used to form the mask, which removes the individual's face and personal identity from public view, while he is painted, draped, and otherwise transformed externally and internally for ritualized combat. That combat has to be imagined between individual warriors, as there is no point in one man trying to frighten a platoon or a plane. The attempt to terrify is more intimate still, for he bares his teeth as if to rip your throat out. The fact that they are painted the same colors as the mask adds to the threat, for it says that he has been made into a single being for a single purpose. Man and mask have become one thing.

If you have any doubt of his now inhuman will to power, look at the nails. He has cannily challenged his adversary by mortifying himself first: what can be done to terrify him when he has already mutilated his own image? But who is he, anyway, now that he has fused his identity completely with his team, his tribe? Although merely a very modern Miami Dolphins fan enjoying the carnival culture of a live football game, he is channeling the artistry, psychology, and mythic resonance associated with primitive societies. The fan performs his identification with his team by creating a monstrous double of the player on the field, revealing the passions being sublimated through the game.

The primitive is a back-formation of modernism, with modernity then defined as the necessary condition for protection against any resurgence in the political sphere of those forces being sublimated through cultural expression. One shouldn't be surprised to find that expression to be so obviously demotic—or so well executed. Yet the photo does surprise because it captures the combination of popular culture, psychological immersion, and performative art so well, and thus it can prompt us to think about how much energy is being expended to supplement or escape (temporarily) the dominant designs of modern life.

Designs such as figure 11, for example. Although wearing wrinkled corduroy slacks, this museum visitor is neatly turned out for public viewing; you might call it uptown casual, and you can find it any day of the week in the museums and similar venues for art and culture. The basic black jacket, corresponding gray slacks, and gray-white hair with just a hint of muted color in the scarf for accent, along with the sheer geometric surfaces devoid of ornamentation—these are standard features of modern design (and, since men started wearing black in the nineteenth century, of modernity itself).[16] If you aren't sure, just look at the painting, where the design principles have been perfected, although not without irony, which also came into its own in the modern era. Centuries of enlightenment, experimentation, and artistic freedom have led to—what? An artwork that is a completely flat, blank, black surface, absorbing all light.

Like figure 10, the image is striking because of the homology that ties person to thing. Just as colors joined mask, teeth, and tribe, now color joins spectator, painting, and modern design. And where the first image was carnivalesque, this one is gently humorous. What is there to see in that black void? Will intent peering discover anything

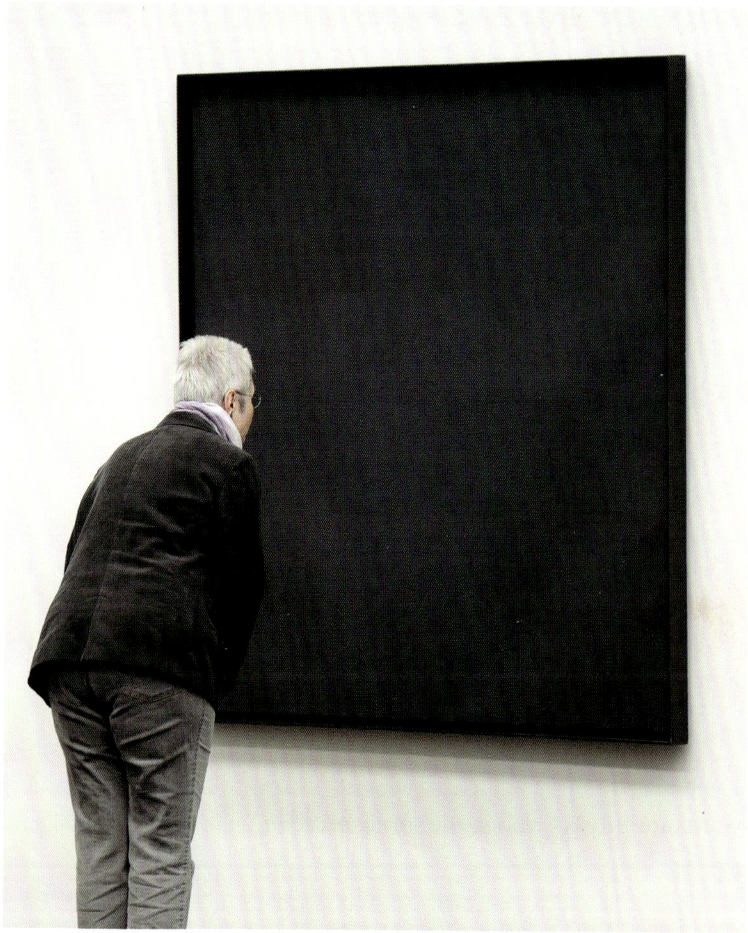

Figure 11. © Julian Stratenschulte / DPA / LANDOV.

in black but black? Isn't it amusing that person and artwork seemed to be doubles—that a blank surface mirrors an actual person?

It takes only one more step for the joke to turn into something else: perhaps the painting does mirror the person, who may be largely a void after all, and also not much more accessible to the rest of us who can only see the individual from behind, as it were, and as a social type. And is art imitating life, or is life being made over according to an aesthetic that is abstract, impersonal, dehumanizing—an expression not of the individual person but of mechanization? Does the photograph bear witness to Nietzsche's admonition that "when

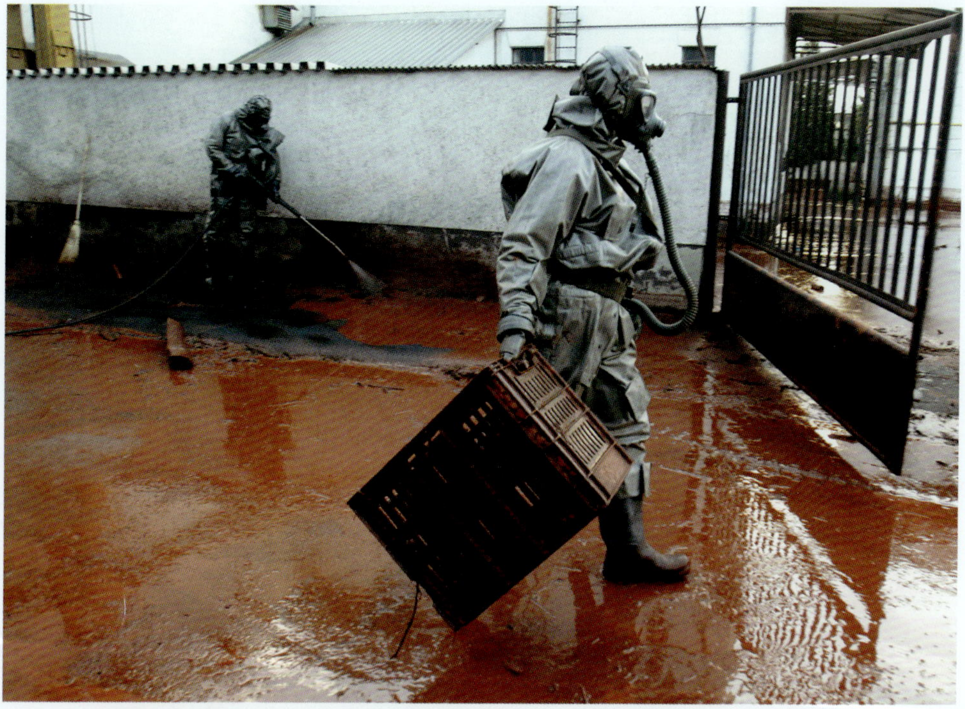

Figure 12. © Reuters / Bernadett Szabo.

you stare into an abyss, the abyss also stares into you"?[17] Perhaps this photograph is a study not only in modern design but also in a distinctively modern form of terror.

But not the worst terror. In figure 12 we have a third thing: simultaneously primitive and modern, machined and animal-like, alarmingly Orwellian yet an actually existing scene from the present. The workers in their hazmat suits are cleaning up a toxic-sludge spill that inundated a village in Devecser, Hungary. The uniforms are awful, grotesque. They are not intended to scare anyone, yet there is something terrifying about them, partly because the workers seem so completely habituated to them—as though this were just another day on the job.

And that's one more thing all three images have in common: each is a photograph recording a relatively unusual event rather than a typical day's activity, and yet each of them suggests that something both terrifying and deeply continuous is in fact present. Blood lust is always there; the question is, how is it sublimated? The abyss is always there, along with the grinding uniformity of modernization; the question is, how to live well anyway? The disasters that result from industrialization, environmental exploitation, and the continual assault on the commons are becoming woven into the fabric of everyday life in far too many places; the question remains: who is going to clean up the mess?

Figure 12 represents a significant shift from modernism to postmodernism. Modern civilization continues, but now into a future that is increasingly likely to be horrific. Modern and primitive have become fused into a new creature that is both mechanical and organic, at work yet isolated from the environment and those in it. Worse yet, primitivism is no longer contained within the context of leisure and the ritualized space, time, and activity of the sporting event. At the same time, the emotional structure of the image has shifted. In the first two photos, any emotional content was in the image itself: expressiveness was on display in the one and ascetic concentration in the other. Note also that both figure 10 and figure 11 are images of spectatorship and that they articulate the two opposing poles in the modernist conception of modern cultural experience: mass culture versus fine art; overemotional lower-class enthrallment in a mass spectacle versus ascetic higher-class edification in an arts institution. In figure 12 the spectator is not visible and yet is being hailed more affectively. Nothing beyond functional behavior is visible, while the emotional charge is transferred to the spectator. It is similar to the *Life* cover, except that we now are much closer to the action, and our response is likely to be more visceral than when buffered by distance.

Perhaps you enjoy seeing swinish cyborgs treating toxic waste as just another day's work, or more likely you sense that something already is seriously wrong if so much has been invested in coping with industrial-strength poisons. In either case you are seeing modernity as already containing the wrong future, and the emotional weight of the photo is placed *on* you rather than *before* you. Those in the photograph cannot do the seeing: their vision is obviously obstructed by their masks and the instrumental gaze required by their work. The same applies to the spectators in the other photos: neither immersion in mass cult entertainment nor isolated reflection on art devoid of political content can be a model for a robust public art.

Photographs such as these get close to the central challenge of photography, to lead spectators to look thoughtfully at the distinctive tendencies defining modern society. As modernity transitions into its next phase, as modern becomes postmodern, and as human becomes posthuman, the art will face its greatest challenges—and perhaps its demise, that is, its passage into another epoch where it becomes merely another technology like air conditioning. But that day is not yet here. In the meantime, we can ask how photography brings us to see a world defined by changes that are amazing, dangerous, and relentless. As we shall suggest, that vision is realistic, imaginative, and especially evocative when it can frame modernity within the antique modalities of allegory and prophecy.

Dream and Dispersion

Instead of the institutional time out of time and the specific forms of emotional management provided by the sporting event or the art museum, a postmodern optic carries a sense of forward movement that is not necessarily a form of assurance. This shift in temporality and emotional valence allows one to see modernity as it is caught between a utopian dream and its own processes of dispersion, and as ambivalent about its prospects.[18] For modernity was always a golden dream—an act of imagination, a vision of the future.

Taken on the morning of the fiftieth anniversary of the city of Brasília, figure 13 evokes both a vision of the future and its melancholic shadow. The epitome of high-modernist urban design, Brasília has become a monument to both the utopian dream and social poverty of modernism.[19] With its economy of line and the sharp complementarity of light and dark surfaces, the photograph exposes at once the precision, the promise, and the danger of a society organized around modern technologies. Building and sky, technology and nature, radiant energy and functional discipline exist in a pure space of perfect harmony, while the human interest is reduced to a lone silhouette of an individual shuffling offstage to no longer mar the abstraction that will dominate like the full glare of the sun. The

Figure 13. © epa / Fernando Bizerra Jr.

golden dream, it seems, will persist even if no one is there to experience it. The golden hue may be not a sign of transcendental ascension but rather the sunset of a civilization. It is small consolation to imagine that at least we, too, might be remembered for our beautiful sense of design.

The image (and there are others like it) captures modernity's promise and pathos. Even so, it might seem too close to being a work of modernist art and thus to be primarily about itself.[20] Better to have something a bit more familiar and yet still able to feature a relationship between form and function—and art and society—in modern life.

Figure 14's woman striding through a gallery in London seems obviously stylish. High heels, short skirt, long sleek hair, ramrod posture, stiletto figure, all in basic black—one can go right down the fashion magazine checklist. Less is more, however, and her lean minimalism and striking pose suggest that she is not merely stylish but as much a work of art as the two paintings on either side of her, as

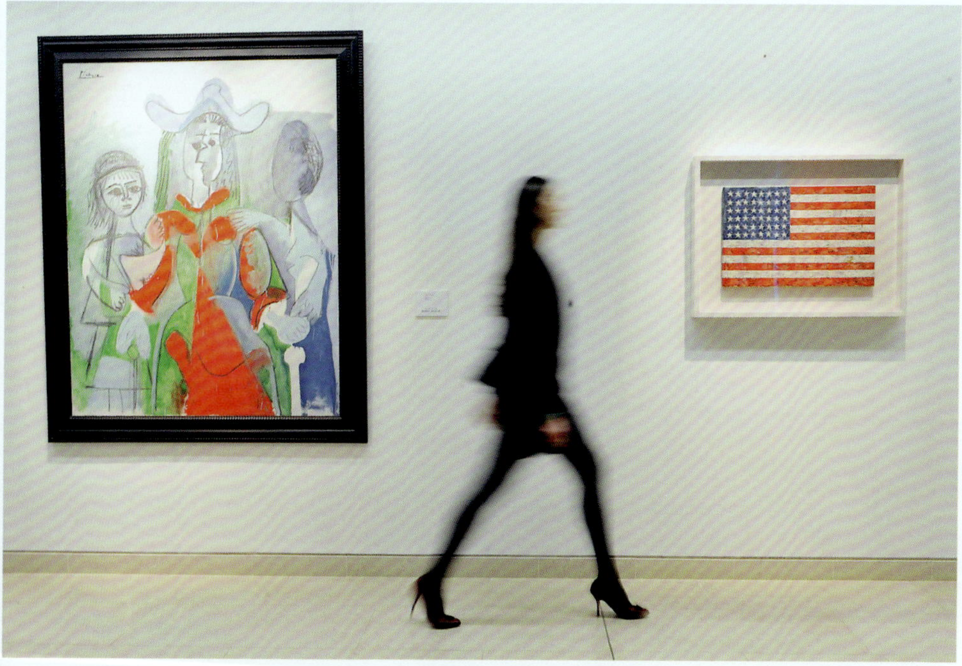

Figure 14. © PA Archive / Press Association Images / Tim Ireland.

if she were the middle panel of a triptych. But for the blurred edges that indicate motion, she could be a sculpture by Alberto Giacometti.

And not just any sculpture, but the *L'Homme qui marche I* that sold at a Sotheby's auction in 2010 for £65,001,250.[21] That fact may account for the existence of the photo, as the publicity about the sale may have activated the Giacometti neuron in at least one photographer's brain, and the photo was taken at Christie's, a competitor of Sotheby's. Even so, the woman had to be there for the photograph to be taken at all. One artist may have been paying homage to another, but at least in part because the artistic influence was so pervasive that life was already following art.

No one gets up in the morning to put on their Giacometti outfit, but many do spend a lot of money and effort to appear stylish, and the hundreds of Giacometti stick figures that populate museums, books, posters, and other media of the art world have played a role in defining the aesthetic norms of contemporary cosmopolitan society.[22] That modernist norms can be traced across art, fashion, and

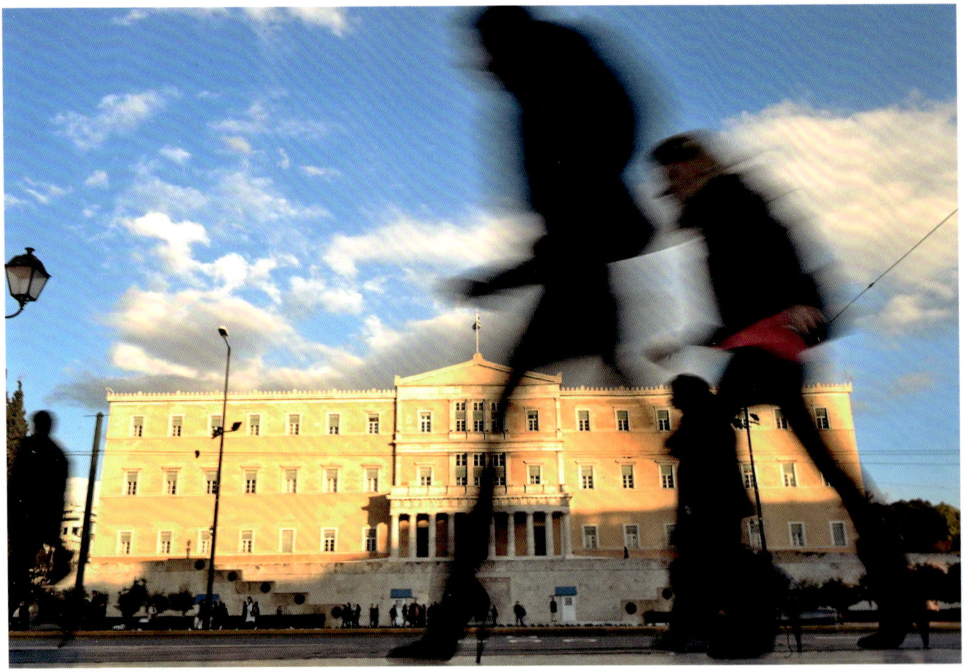

Figure 15. © Louisa Gouliamaki / AFP / Getty Images.

photography as well as interior design, architecture, and other arts is hardly surprising, as a universal economy of representation was the point, but perhaps something more than homology is at stake.

Perhaps a second photographer had been cued to Giacometti's gaze. Figure 15 is not merely a study in influence, however, but evidence that Giacometti may have seen something then that is becoming ever more evident now in modernity's continued development.

People are transformed into shadows, women are styled into nothingness, mass is consumed by motion, life crafted for the gaze reverts to the vanishing point, all that is solid melts into air . . . Each of these ideas is a start, but just that, at understanding what is being revealed. And perhaps it is worth noting that the photo was taken before the Greek Parliament building in 2010, during a week when the Greek financial meltdown was threatening the European Union economy. As would happen again a few years later, billions of dollars hung in the balance, and ordinary people suffered because the European political process had been hijacked by financial interests.

Greece itself was not innocent, as it had a shadow economy and a government that avoided transparency, not unlike the representative figures for state and society in the photograph. Despite the blue sky of a Europe at peace, the shadows are lengthening, and those in the picture seem to be striding back into the past—a past that the world would do well to avoid. The public square is largely empty, so political action seems to be vanishing as well in democratic Athens. Both fashion and tradition are evident as the speed of consumption is set against a backdrop of political rigidity, yet it's clear that both success and failure will be found offstage. In place of a vital space for political action, we are left with shadows, emptiness, and stony impersonality. Instead of creativity where it is needed most—in the public sphere—we find anxious movement that, for all its stylishness, is still an evacuation. And Greece's repeated crises are only local versions of the overextensions and crashes that occur elsewhere as well. So it is when modern financial systems operate with a radical autonomy and disregard for common sense that may be keys to artistic innovation but little else.

By capturing modernist art and fashion against backdrops of top-tier consumption and governmental paralysis, these photographs prompt one to ask how much that is caught within modern processes of change will simply vanish. More to the point, they suggest that disappearance will not be limited to supposedly premodern holdovers such as primitive peoples, folk cultures, religion, and violence. Those already modern are also caught up in a vortex of change that can spin everything into something else and then into nothingness.

This photographic chronicle of dispersion isn't limited to artsy shots of stylish modernistas; it also extends to those lower down the economic scale. Like dispersion itself, they often are hidden under the euphemisms used to describe economic destruction. Descriptions of the recession that began in 2008 featured terms of contraction: "cutting back," "downsizing," "retrenchment," "shrinkage," and so forth. Companies were reducing inventories as people were eating in instead of going out because bubbles, markets, and sectors had collapsed. With the Dow at a fraction of its former value and the global economy cooling like a dying star, it seemed that drawing inward was a universal law of hard times. Unless, that is, you looked at figure 16.

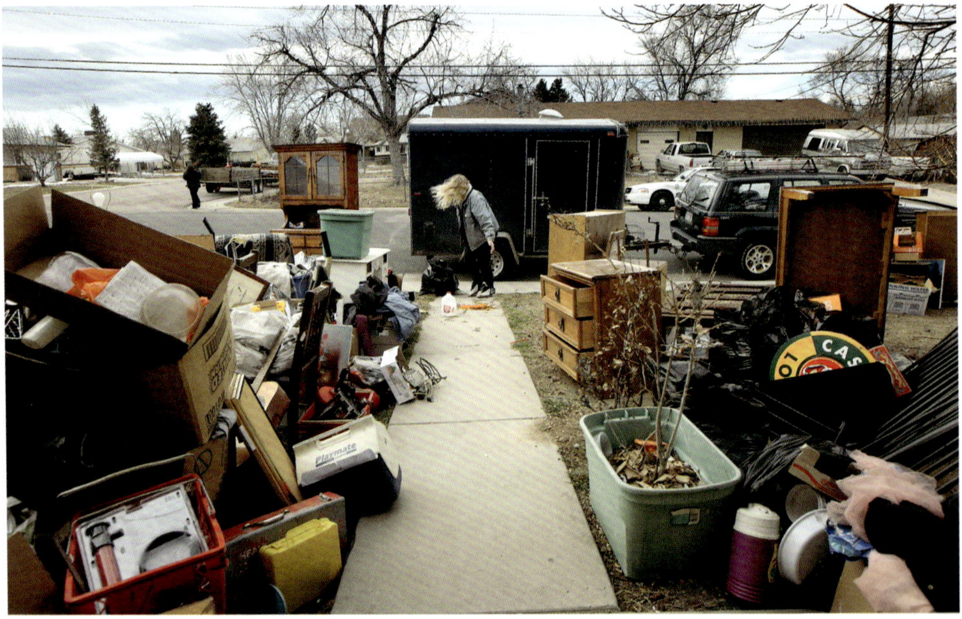

Figure 16. © John Moore / Edit / Getty Images.

A woman is standing among her possessions after having been evicted. She had been renting the house from an owner who took the rent but stopped paying the mortgage, which led to eviction by the bank and the local sheriff's office. She is seen at the back of the photograph, at the end of the bare concrete sidewalk leading to the street, on the line to the vanishing point. The wind blows her hair across her face, adding insult to injury. She stands as if at a loss. Like the splattered mess on the sidewalk beside her, some things that have been broken can't be put back together. What to do? How can she gather this all up and put it somewhere safe, much less back where it belongs? How can she hold on to anything of value?

The garbage bag in front of her makes the question seem particularly futile: she could put something in it, except that it is already full and likely to tear when she tries to carry it, if she can carry it far at all. No wonder that she looks as if she is having an exasperated conversation with the bag. Who else can she talk to? The rest of her stuff is strewn along the sidewalk and out into the street. It is in no discernible order save the haphazard mess made by the eviction crew. Drawers are pulled open, a table is overturned, the cabinet stands empty and precarious at the curb, boxes are piled helter-skelter, a plant dies in the winter air. It would look much the same if it had been done by vandals, but then she would know whom to blame. In any case, she is not likely to see the people who got her into this mess.

This is a scene of personal desolation. It also is a sign of collective danger. The economic implosion does not lead only to the frugality and togetherness celebrated in nostalgic memories of bygone days. Economic disasters also release terrible centrifugal forces: winds of dispersion that tear lives apart and scatter people across places that will never be called home. Paul Krugman put it well when he spoke of "the Great Unraveling."[23] The significance of the photo is that it captures that process. One does not see poverty; there *is* relative poverty, but one also sees possessions that reflect the relative affluence of modern societies: wood cabinetry for each room, plastic coolers for picnics and vacations, all in a suburb with two-car garages. The focus is on dispersion rather than insufficient accumulation; this is what can happen even when we've made it out of poverty.

There also is a corresponding change in the way of seeing. The photo avoids the bright close-ups that would be used to sell any of the products now forlornly lining the sidewalk, and the darker close-ups used to expose hidden recesses of urban slums, and the sunny panoramas of suburban real estate ads, and the action shots taken from inside a dramatic event. Instead the photo shows how distance has infiltrated all of the spaces in this suburban setting, a constant presence that keeps people removed from one another, from their settings, even from their own possessions. Rather than any promise of improvement, rising prosperity, or growth, the muted colors suggest depression and decay, and the best the woman can do is to turn her back to the wind and hold on, all her energy focused on a doomed attempt at stasis.

Thus the optic within the photo shows the economic disaster by means of a visual recession. Recession may require not only cutting back on luxuries but also cutting back on the visual extravagance of dramatic action shots, decisive moments, and iconic images. The photojournalist's task then includes documenting dispersion, retraction, erosion, and sad quietude. This approach may bring us to dwell on the dull surfaces of ordinary life. That banality is a resource, however, not something to be overlooked.[24]

Equally important, the banal clutter of the photo cues its allegorical significance. The woman becomes a small vernacular counterpart to the angel of history in Walter Benjamin's meditation on the Klee painting *Angelus Novus*: "Where a chain of events appears before *us*, *he* sees one single catastrophe, which keeps piling wreckage upon wreckage and hurls it at his feet. . . . This storm drives him irresistibly into the future, to which his back is turned, while the pile of debris before him grows toward the sky. What we call progress is *this* storm."[25] Benjamin is shifting from one sense of time to another. We want to see a linear, rational sequence of events, something that could make sense as a forward movement occasionally delayed or deflected. The angel sees something more revelatory, a single catastrophic event repeated endlessly, a replication that makes a mockery of the illusion of progress. The angel "would like to stay, awaken the dead, and make whole what has been smashed," but the storm of progress is blowing, so much that the angel can no longer resist its force. The woman, too, would like to stay, awaken those who are dead to the injustice of her plight, and make her life whole again. But that is not an option for her. The question remains whether it is for the viewer of the photograph.

The angel also stood for Benjamin futilely trying to sound the alarm. We can consider how the alarm still may be sounded, albeit by the mute medium of photography. Photographs such as figure 16 reveal a process of collapse and dispersion, one that is sure to continue in societies, such as this woman's, that refuse to provide adequate regulatory barriers against forces that are becoming ever more turbulent in the economic equivalent of global climate change. The image also provides an optic, a way of seeing that records but also questions modernity's characteristic sense of time, its sense of historical progress, and whether it values anything more than profit.

Seeing is also valuing, and valuing is seeing. The image of an eviction doubles as one of a lone individual unfairly put out in the cold to be buffeted by the winds of a harsh neoliberal economy. Even without a full articulation of the allegory, the distance between viewer and subject is an important part of the image content. How far apart are individuals in this common world of the image? How much is the individual person valued, and by whom? Is she to be left to the help of any family or friends who might be available to help her move, or are there larger responsibilities that might involve the viewer or other people or the state?

These questions acquire more or less significance as they are coupled with one sense or another of modernity's forward movement. As long as we see a chain of events moving toward a bright horizon, the golden dream justifies leaving some things, and people, behind. A more tragic view recognizes that history can flow backward, that disaster can return endlessly.

The Archaeology of the Present

Modernity is always about time: the continuous, linear flow of time from past to future, and the inevitability of change in the present, and an endless vista of a better world to come.[26] Modern societies have placed clocks on buildings and in factories and classrooms, and in pockets and then on wrists and by every bed, and then in every car, computer, and cellphone, now often calibrated to GMT at atomic accuracy. Modernity officially acknowledges no time other than ordinary time, an endless progression forward without any possibility for magical interludes, eternal returns, apocalyptic ruptures, or other supernatural distortions.[27] Of course all that is suppressed seeps back up, and there remain ritual events to provide small interludes in the prevailing discipline—New Year's and Super Bowl parties, carnivals and other seasonal festivals, religious holidays with their liturgical calendars—but they are mere epiphenomena, superficial distractions that no longer channel deep tensions in the social order. Ritual has been reduced to just another spectacle in a culture of images, as if the society were being examined by archaeologists from a later time.

Figure 17 is a double image. On the one hand, it is an image of modern technology and governance on display. Civilization can be hewn out of rock, common goods such as transportation facilities can be gleaming monuments to efficiency, everyone can benefit from this investment in shared infrastructure for enjoying liberty and prosperity, and this can be done not only well but beautifully.

On the other hand, it is also an image of the fate that awaits every

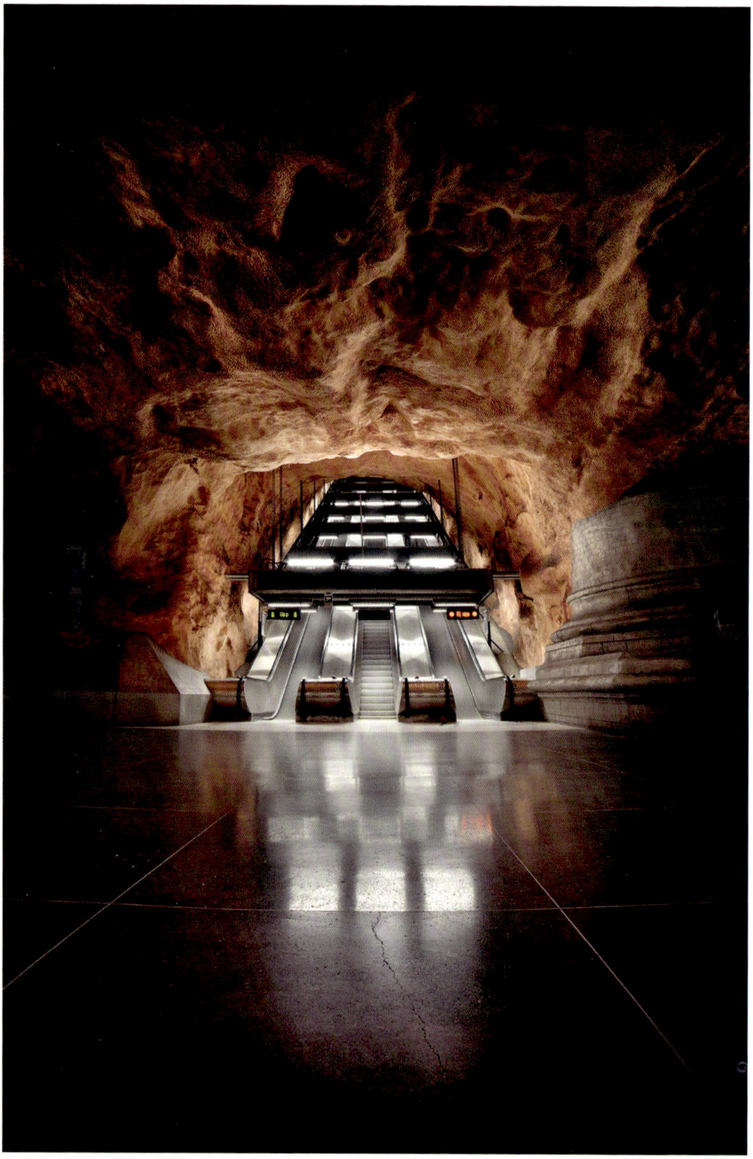

Figure 17. © Valentijn Tempels.

government, every state, and many a species, including perhaps our own. Those ancient civilizations that now lie buried were once vibrant, sometimes *most* vibrant just before they were overcome by a moving desert, invading horde, ecological crash, or other catastrophe. We already have self-made ruins such as missile silos, defunct nuclear reactors, and highways to nowhere, but that is the least of what could follow. Better perhaps to imagine how something both practical and beautiful could become an empty, abandoned fragment of a lost civilization. (And note how the reflection of the metal on the floor—another doubling—suggests dissolution.) Although this machined space was wrested out of the earth by skill, labor, and organization, the rock will outlast anything not renewed, the silence will reign far longer than society, and just maybe the inadvertent monument will receive the accidental tribute of someone wondering how a people so advanced could have disappeared.

Call it an archaeology of the present: the images that can remind us of how close we might be to becoming ruins. This archaeology is not merely about the present as if it were the past; instead, the optic reveals how potential demise is already coded into the present, already one possible future extending from the present. Barbie Zelizer has suggested that photography's subjunctive voice becomes evident in the about-to-die photo; what remains to be seen is how there are many more such photos than had been recognized.[28] These images provide a vast, continuously unfolding gallery of an ever-closer relationship between goods and junk, advancement and abandonment, prosperity and catastrophe. They show how modern society is changing not simply to advance and render present goods obsolete but rather to produce its own unmaking. They suggest how the unmaking of a world can appear at the time to be only temporarily disruptive, and how the accumulation of goods can become so much wreckage.

As Benjamin, Sontag, and others declared, by reproducing the past as millions of individual images, each but a nugget of time (a "pellet of information") separated from the others without regard for narrative continuity, photography like modernity itself shattered tradition. For the same reason, however, photography became a pervasive technology of memory, a democratic compensation for what was being stripped out of the lifeworld. Kodak made snapshot photography a cult of nostalgia (that distinctively modern emotion): children are photographed to capture a vanishing childhood, and eventually everything else is photographed because that, too, is vanishing in a world pitched toward change, innovation, and novelty.[29] Roland Barthes made the photo an aide-memoire, creating an almost tactile experience of a past that can be known only in fragments.[30] Yet there was no place for such sentimentality in the critical discourse of photography. Instead the photographic production of the past became another form of social control and political domination, and with that a battleground.

What is missing from both commemoration and critique, however, is a deeper appreciation of what photographic time offers for thinking about collective life in the contemporary moment. The past is always an artifact and always maintained through repetition, whether of stories, speeches, place-names, or photographs.[31] Photography offers specific resources and creates distinctive problems in that regard, but it should not be evaluated primarily in respect to its effect for good or ill on collective memory. Instead we suggest that photographic time provides distinctive capacities for thinking about the relationship of the present to the future. Photography is part of modernity's continuous unfolding and is uniquely positioned to document and reflect on how that happens. Taken time after time, photographs school people in seeing the present as if it were already passing away and in seeing the future as if it were already emerging in the present.

Even when enlightenment may no longer mean what it used to. The image in figure 18 is not easily legible and therefore asks that you look more carefully. That request, coupled with the odd juxtaposition of decorative window and washing machine, suggests that we are looking at an image in a virtual museum. The window is a source of light, and the machine the thing illuminated, yet each is both functional and aesthetic (the one colorful, the other streamlined). This dark interior contains no light of its own, as if it were a cave. The weak shaft of light seems to have to bend to get there, as if refracted along canyon walls before entering this animal's den. The animal seems to be human, although his shadow looks ratlike, and that feral insinuation might be closer to the truth of his circumstances.

The caption says, "A Free Syrian Army fighter carries his weapon

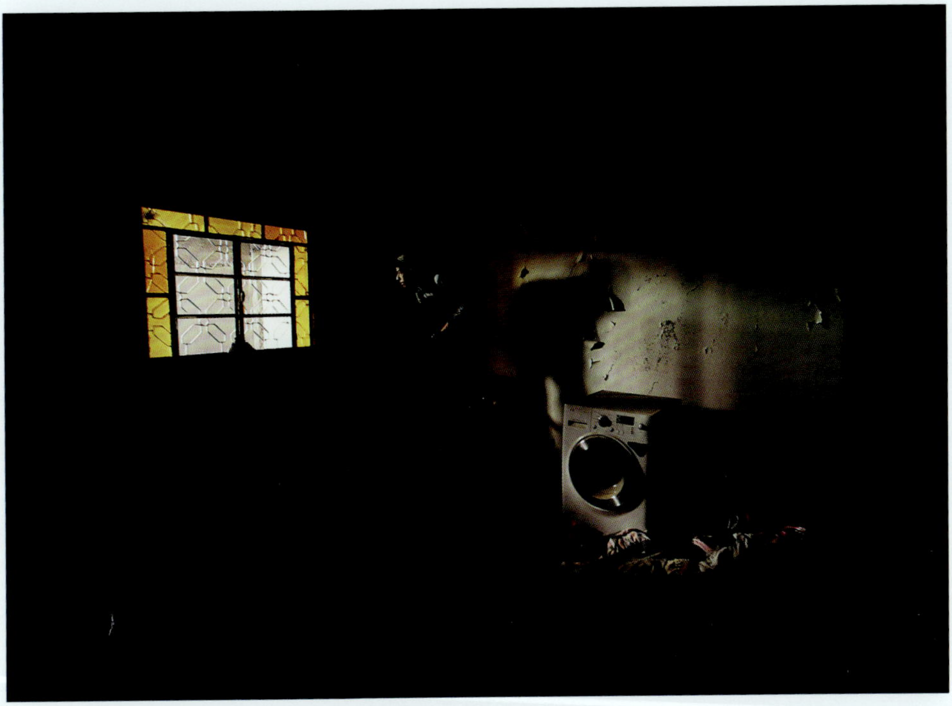

Figure 18. © Reuters / Khalil Ashawi.

as he takes position inside a house in Deir al-Zor." One could almost say "*what had been* a house." The place seems to be returning to darkness, to an inchoate void that soon will absorb everything there. Imagine how much has been lost already. Walls that will have echoed with conversation and laughter now are pockmarked from neglect and destruction. What had been a piece of furniture now is the soldier's perch. What appears to be clothing and other domestic goods are piled on the floor, thrown perhaps because they couldn't be taken to a refugee camp, or so they wouldn't be in the way of the fighting. Whatever the story, it is one of lives being undone.

And so we get to the washing machine and the window. Each is remarkably salient, each has a presence as if it were something uncanny, each is both where it is supposed to be and yet dramatically out of place. In other words, each now has the properties of a work of art. The machine stands there like a surrealist object, a machine of domesticity framed as a thing in itself, or perhaps as a historical curio—say, a Soviet capsule intended to send a monkey into space. Such options are far-fetched, but compare them with the impossibility of the washer still being what it was: a banal part of ordinary life.

And that window! Was it ever banal? Perhaps there are many like it, and on close inspection it looks like a machined knockoff of merely decorative designs. But still, it is at once beautiful and so vulnerable. You cannot believe that any soldier on any side in this street fight is going to hesitate to shoot through it the second he sees a target. And such a shame, as the stained glass and abstract pattern resonate across art history, sacred and secular, from Gothic cathedrals to Islamic calligraphy to modern design. Of course it was just a nice window in someone's house, admired occasionally and ignored much of the time, but that's how a good society works. When ordinary life is well above the level of living in a cave, that is, because ordinary things are continuous with so many fundamental achievements in art, science, government, and the other modes of civilization.

If a tank fires, the entire room will be obliterated. At that point, all that will remain of the remarkable objects in the room will be the photograph. Thus the image provides an archaeology of the present, revealing how close a society can be to becoming a lost civilization. As this realization sinks in, it becomes evident that the photograph is showing how one can move from enlightenment into darkness and from the time of progress into a time when human beings, like rats, survive by following their predatory instincts through the ruins.

Messages in Ruins

Where photographers once labored to capture the massive scale and awesome productivity of industrialization, their descendants have returned to memorialize the abandoned Rust Belt factories and the communities that were traumatized by the economic tsunami of neoliberal globalization. Detroit in particular has been singled out, and for good reason: the devastation was astonishing, reducing what had been the fourth largest American city to a wasteland, and the photographs are eerily beautiful. The disconnect involved in admiring the remnants of a human tragedy was not lost on those living there, some of whom complained about being misused for "disaster porn."[32] That term comes straight out of the critical discourse of photography, which, incidentally, was created during the period when the American auto industry and much of the industrial Midwest was sliding into a precipitous decline. So it is that a "decontextualized aesthetics of ruin" exemplifies what might have gone wrong visually.[33] By abstracting those living there out of the picture and not respecting how they were coping with hardship and trying to improve the city, the images could convert human experience and political struggle into a merely aesthetic object, an item for pleasurable consumption safely distant from either want or obligation.

That critique will catch some of the viewing experience, but it also misses what may be most important for engaging with the powerful forces and amoral elites driving the global economy. It could be that there is a thriving market for photographs of ruins because those images, more than others, provide resources for thinking about modernity in the present historical moment. More to the point, they provide the archaeological optic and prophetic voice that allows reconsideration of the relationship between present and future, capitalism and the common good, progress and catastrophe.

The room in figure 19 is a wreck, yet still completely familiar—and that may be the key to the photograph's troubling reverberations. Everything there could have been used again; allowing for the stylistic upgrades, you can see the same setting every time you go to the dentist. Thoroughly mundane and yet constantly new, the dental office might be the ideal example of how modern technology and design are at once so taken for granted and continuously beneficial. So why would it be abandoned? The scene suggests a science-fiction narrative, as if those working there had succumbed to an epidemic or been vaporized or simply walked out one day, entranced by strange music in their heads, to board waiting slave ships. Although obviously far-fetched, these suggestions hint at the imaginative potential of the image. There is something horribly wrong when a civilization appears to have been abandoned.

The traces of modern civilization do not age well. There is little irony in the fact that modern structures make shoddy ruins—compared to stone, they break apart and deteriorate far too quickly—but it does make deterioration all that more telling. The peeled paint undoes the color coordination that gave the room and the equipment a uniform veneer suggesting smooth efficiency. Lacking that

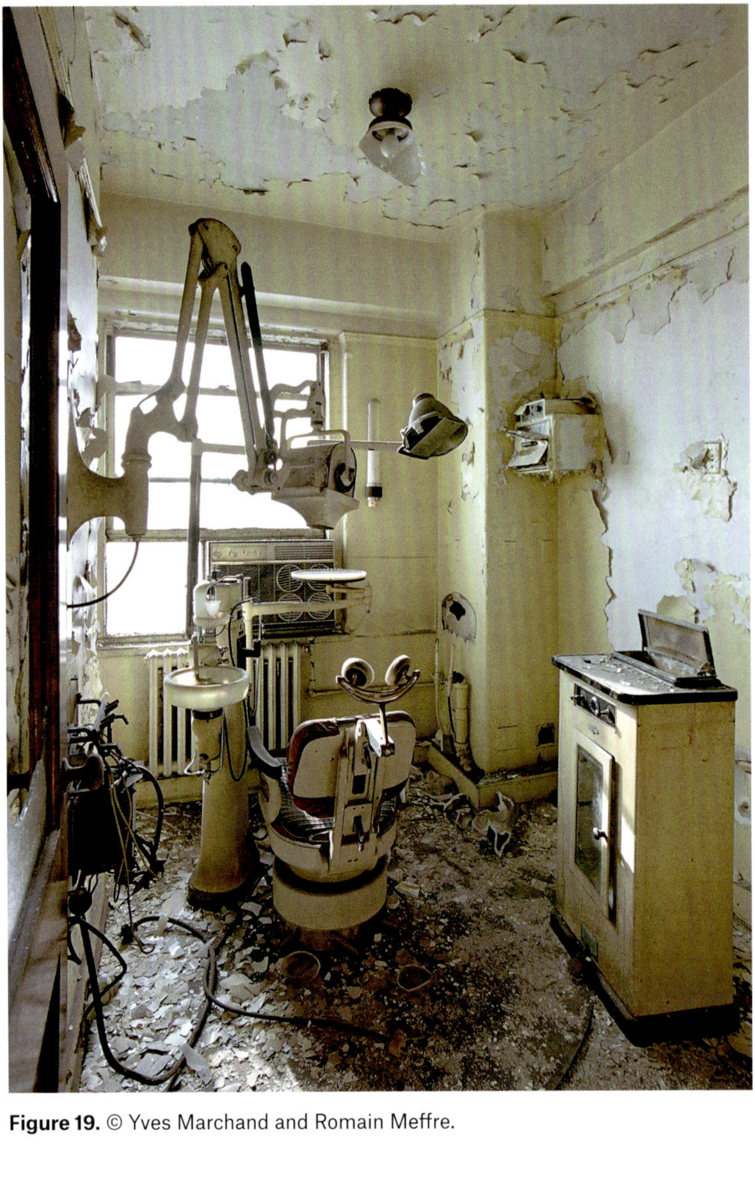

Figure 19. © Yves Marchand and Romain Meffre.

soothing assurance, now the equipment acquires a somewhat macabre cast. The cyborg chair and robotic arm for the x-ray and lighting look vaguely threatening, as if used for human experimentation, while cables snake across the floor and along the wall as if connected to some sinister machine that both supplied and extracted energy. And where once the floor would have been spotless, it is covered with the debris of broken lamps and windows; what once was illuminated now is shrouded in the half-light of melancholy.

Melancholy is the natural attitude of allegory, just as the ruin is its central motif.[34] The photo of the ruin of a dentist's office perfectly activates these figural resources for thinking about the historical process. A dentist's office is not monumental; it began with no signs of grandeur, which makes its demise all the more poignant. Unlike monumental structures—and monumental history—it never was built with an eye to outlasting its age. It has been ill-used when that happens, although not by the dentist or the photographer. What should have been another example of an improved present evolving into a better future instead is a sign of an economic disaster large enough to suggest that the future will be a place of ruins.

Benjamin remarked that "allegories are, in the realm of thoughts, what ruins are in the realm of things."[35] The ruin is a fragment, a trace, a sign of time's corrosiveness, a thing reduced to being an accidental sign, a call to memory, and more as well. Note that each of those descriptions apply—and have been applied—to photographs. More to the point, photography often has been framed in melancholic terms, in a supposed compact with nostalgia, loss, or death. John Roberts claims that this "elegiac and mournful" attitude suggests that photography "is at its most perspicacious and relevant when it *foregrounds* its mordant and memorial role," which is done by emphasizing aesthetics rather than documentary truth and contemplation rather than interruption of political hegemony.[36] Roberts is both insightful and sharply critical regarding anyone who "identifies the political allegorically with the ruin and the remnant."[37] We must acknowledge the central point, for Roberts himself is on the edge of allegory: a photograph's depiction of ruin could be a metaphor for the demise not of a social order but rather of the cultural form of documentary photography, and that substitution could deflect political awareness from its appropriate target. That caveat aside, the allegorical potential was present in photography from the beginning, and photography need not be trapped in binary conceptions of present versus past, truth versus art, and contemplation versus action. The constraints on any public art in today's media environment can be refashioned artistically and discursively to become critical tools. Most important, many of the contemporary photographs of ruins disrupt the myth of progress to expose systemic dangers that are, by definition, hard to visualize.

Allegory, ruin, and photograph are all resources for thought: not only something to think about but also something to think with and through to understand the passage of time. When ruins appear in the photographic record, they need not be allegorical—say, when ancient backdrops are used to mark modernity's supersession. Allegory and ruins have a backward resonance, however, for they each are a trace or a retelling of what has happened before, and so they acquire an ability to confound and trouble overly optimistic conceptions of modernity. Likewise, some photographs intensify one's sense of ruin—or impending ruin—and with that they open the door to allegorical meditation. When the ruins involve modern buildings in Beirut, Chernobyl, or Detroit, or suburban housing tracts reverting to prairie, or surplus equipment abandoned in the desert, modernity is being shown through a different lens.[38] Through this allegorical mentality, as well as straightforward documentary reportage, contemporary photojournalism provides a continuing revelation of the public world. That world is no longer history on the march, however, but rather a chronicle of progress upended.

The unraveling of modernism involves the emergence of catastrophe as a major concept for understanding the historical process.[39] A tsunami's death toll in Japan will continue for years due to the meltdown of three nuclear reactors; floods, wildfires, and tornadoes are creating vast swaths of destruction in the United States, while a major city has been largely abandoned; hundreds of thousands of women have been raped amid millions of civilian deaths in the Congo; sixty million people have been herded into camps and otherwise displaced by war; seven trillion dollars in wealth was destroyed in a few months by a few firms; bustling airports provide the infrastructure for global pandemics. These and similar stories are accumulating and acquiring a new significance. Instead of marking where nature has not yet been controlled, they expose the hidden costs of contemporary regimes of control.

A catastrophe is a sudden and widespread disaster that threatens the core sustainability or legitimacy of a social system. Epidemics, oil spills, financial crashes, earthquakes, and other disasters reveal how seemingly secure structures were actually fragile. Such events expose the moment when control collapses, fatality is exposed, and everyone is reduced simply to watching as destruction becomes so extensive as to inspire awe. At that moment it may become possible for humanity to "experience its own annihilation as a supreme aesthetic pleasure," which would be the final insult to any conception of human grandeur.[40] Yet there is another sense of catastrophe as well, captured in Benjamin's insight into how an unjust system can persist: "Definitions of basic historical concepts: Catastrophe—to have missed the opportunity. Critical moment—the status quo threatens to be preserved."[41] Thus the financial meltdown was one catastrophe, and the continuation of the same system without significant reform is another. This wider sense of the concept carries with it a wider optic—that is, a way of seeing how the future disaster is already nascent in the response to the present one.

The Prophetic Image

There is another premodern mode of public speech that also can challenge belief in modernity's ascent into a better future. Prophecy declares that a future calamity will follow from a way of living in the present.[42] The claim is both predictive and normative: the assumption is that all action is consequential and that moral failure will lead to destruction of the community. What is needed, then, is to identify the moral fault and awaken the collectivity to the danger of not reforming their behavior. It is only nominally predictive, however, because the focus is on what is already happening. The fault is already occurring, and the possibility of change is already present as well. It is necessary to see these potential patterns as they are already present, albeit occluded by corresponding habits of distraction and denial. Prophets articulate an archaeology of the present: they confront their audience with a view from the future, looking back on their society as if it had been reduced to desolation.

Prophecy as a form of speech may depend on optical projections, on vivid depictions of unjust opulence and vivid imaginings of harsh punishments. Photography usually does not speak in a prophetic voice, but it does at times serve a prophetic function in public culture. More to the point, there are photographs that appear unbidden to confront the public with its complacency and to call for a more ethical way of life. To understand how spectators might respond in kind, we can turn briefly to the model for prophetic criticism provided by Michael Walzer.[43] Most notably, prophetic speech is (1) *particularistic*, that is, set out in terms of a society's own mores, experiences, and values rather than a universal rule; (2) *public*, that is, drawing on common materials and addressed to a wide audience deliberating outside of institutional settings, rather than an esoteric discourse for institutional decision makers; (3) *poetic*, that is, lending eloquent expression to discourses and values already available in the society; and (4) *dedicated to solidarity and fairness*.

Note how each of these conditions is part of the habitus of news photography: such images are inherently particularistic and depend on easy legibility and aesthetic familiarity; they are addressed to a large audience for public judgment; they are artistically enhanced depictions of a common life; and the last criterion of solidarity and fairness is met by photography's being grounded in vernacular life and extended across civic spectatorship to form egalitarian sympathies. Of course this critical potential is just that: a conceivable or hypothetical activation of the image among many other possible uses. That is where the critic steps in: the task is to show how images are exposing possible futures. Benjamin located this potential deep within spectatorship:

> No matter how artful the photographer, no matter how carefully posed his subject, the beholder feels an irresistible compulsion to search such a picture for the tiny spark of contingency, the here and now, with which reality has, so to speak, seared through the image-character of the photograph, to find the inconspicuous place where, within the suchness [*Sosein*] of that long-past minute, the future nests still today—and so eloquently that we, looking back, may rediscover it.[44]

The eloquence of the small language of the image is found in its ability to connect past, present, and future. The fascination of the spectator is redeemed in that moment: "compulsion" represents not irrational desire but rather the need to be connected to a sense of how reality is unfolding over time. The most consequential sense of this revelation is when one needs to connect past failings with disastrous future consequences, as they each are found nested in the present. That image calls the audience to engage emotionally and deliberatively with each other, in order to choose—while they still can—the better vision of a common life.

In March 2011 the Fukushima Prefecture in Japan was hit with earthquakes and a tsunami. Press coverage included photographs of the devastation, rescue efforts, and victims living and dead, including those wounded by grief, sometimes watching helplessly or walking aimlessly through a world turned upside down. Many of these reports were just what journalism should be: highly informative and emotionally engaging accounts of a distant event having global significance. That significance was heightened by the fact that the damage included a partial meltdown at the Fukushima Daiichi nuclear reactor. Reactions to the events included humane concern about others' loss of life and property, economic assessments of the costs of the disaster that would have to be borne by those outside the contaminated zone, anxiety among millions of people worldwide who live near or depend on nuclear power plants, and warnings about how the tsunami that triggered the meltdown might be a harbinger of more dangers to come due to accelerating climate change. All these are captured in figure 20, which says much more as well.

The caption describes their interaction as "An official in protective gear talks to a woman who is from the evacuation area."[45] The description is puzzling, as the woman clearly is speaking to the official as well. The difference reveals more than gender bias, although that should be pointed out. We are to believe that the official is instructing the woman, guiding and helping her for her safety and that of others. Shouldn't communication during a disaster be from the official to the citizen, and from those who are equipped with modern technology to those who are wrapped in blankets? Well, yes and no, because effective response to a disaster depends on two-way commu-

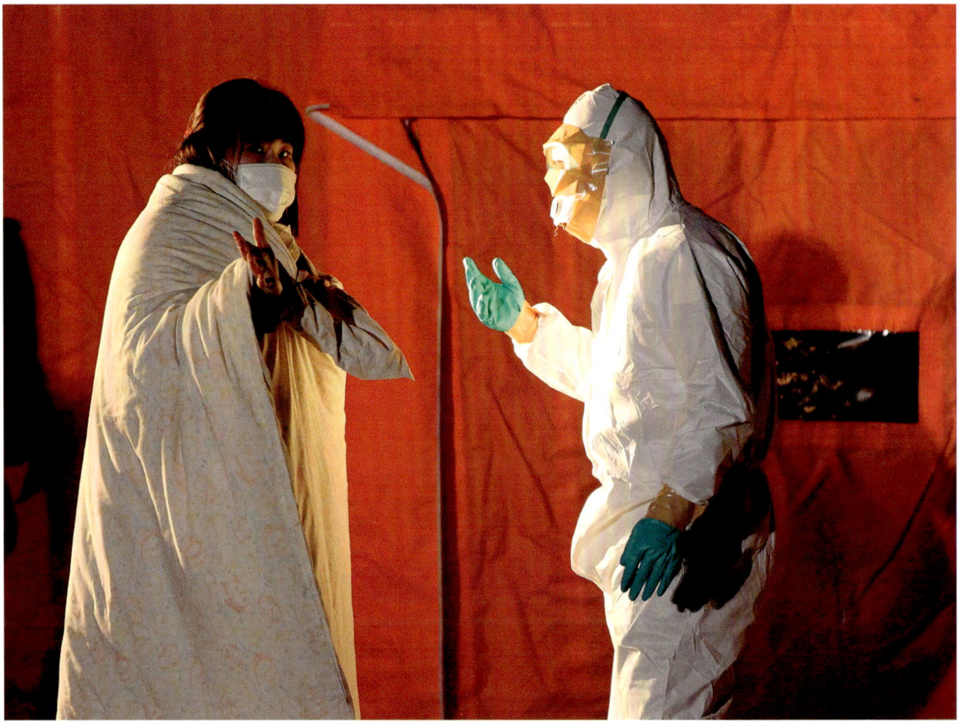

Figure 20. © Reuters / Kim Kyung-Hoon.

nication: those who are deployed need information from those who have direct experience of what is happening on the ground.[46] Given the sensory deprivation involved with that hazmat suit, she probably *can* help.

But we digress. One reason this photograph is remarkable is that it seems to be a still from a science fiction movie.[47] More precisely, by considering it as a movie still we can begin to discern its imaginative capacity to reveal something about modern civilization. There she stands, one of the new nomads, continuous with primitive peoples from tens of thousands of years ago and yet newly vulnerable. Her blanket and mask were machine made, but she seems to be illuminated by firelight, and her gesture suggests that she knows the terrain and even how to negotiate with the alien questioning her. But we know that she is in danger; it is as if the red tent behind them is blaring a continuous state of emergency.

As well it should, for what kind of world includes the figure on the right? Its clothing is not something that was grabbed while scrambling for safety. The suit and gloves were designed, tested, manufactured, ordered, and worn in training because they are part of the normal operation of managing the nuclear reactor. That is to say, because responding to nuclear catastrophe is part of the normal operation of this society.[48] And the scenario does not change if some reactors are shut down or oil reserves expanded: nuclear power epitomizes the promise and the dangers of a capital- and technology-intensive civilization. And when protective clothing once imagined for outer space is required to survive on Earth, modernization comes to be defined more by its backwash than by any dream of escape.

The earthquake had to come, and the reactor, despite the many precautions taken, was likely to crack and release radiation, and both happened because of natural and social processes that were under way, day after day, well before the bad news arrived. Thus we might consider how the photograph reveals not only that a dystopian future could happen but also that we already are getting used to it. By assuming a prophetic voice, the image not only warns the public of dangers to come but also confronts society's characteristic habits of denial. In observing how specific disasters are contained and compensated, one can overlook how the response is already part of the breakdown and can lead to a larger catastrophe—say, becoming a society divided into separate castes joined only by emergency measures, with fairness and solidarity long past. The prophetic image shows how potential futures already are discernible in the particularity of social practices, albeit waiting on what capacity for choice still remains to be used or ignored. Because that capacity is encased in denial, the images, like the prophets of old, have to be repetitive. If these warnings are ignored, it will become all too easy to look back and see how they already were traces of a future awaiting our arrival.

Waiting for the Apocalypse

There are other images of rupture and regression revealed by dramatic events, but the most insightful photographs may be those that capture more ordinary experiences, particularly those moments when time is passing habitually. Images of people moving through the day, rising early or working late, speeding along the expressway or stopped in traffic, hurrying across the street or waiting for the light to change—these and similar modulations in everyday life provide a choreography for staging what it means to define oneself in respect to a forward moving present. By depicting how people are continually moving through time, but never smoothly or without consequences, one can begin to discern how much contingency and risk are built into even the smallest patterns of interaction in a complex society, and how much the future can turn on habits of observation and of blindness in the here and now.

Of course the fire makes the picture in figure 21, but the silhouettes have the most to say. Which is interesting, as they are necessarily enigmatic. The caption tells us that this is a photograph of firefighters in a back-burning operation in New South Wales, but by being depicted as silhouettes they become only partially legible abstractions. Because abstractions need not have any one locale, the scene could be in California or Greece or any other place that has been aflame. The dark forms may have the traces of Australian clothing and deportment, but there is no need to make too much of it. For any given purpose, some details don't really matter.

So what does matter? That's a double question here. First, what matters in the composition? The answer seems to be the stark contrast between the holocaust in the background and the calm, silent, reflective poses of the people in the foreground. Keeping their distance from one another, staring in different directions, hands in pockets, each seems to be lost in thought, while all of them seem to be standing as if waiting for a bus or train, strangers on a street or commuter platform, nothing out of the ordinary, just another day in the life. They stand as many stand while enduring the obligatory routines of traveling through impersonal public spaces, safe but not familiar with the strangers around them, biding time until they can get to their destination, each on a private journey made possible by but still separate from what they have in common. Even when what they have in common is territory on fire on a planet that is getting hotter every year.

This gets us to the second sense of what matters: what is the photo's content? The answer to this question takes us both closer to those in the picture and farthest from the actual circumstances of

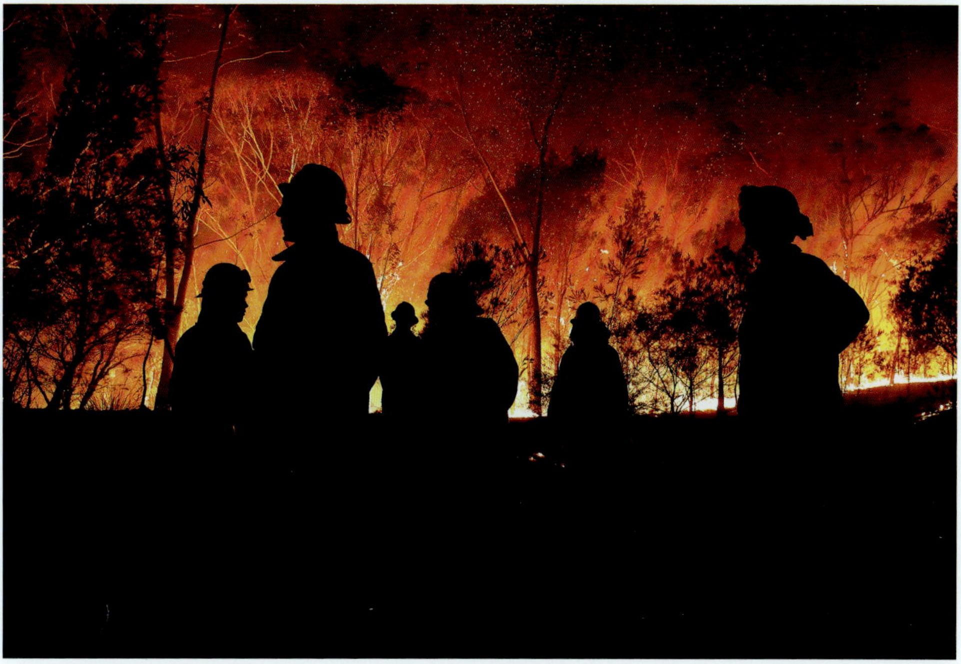

Figure 21. © Brad Hunter / Newspix / Getty Images.

the moment. More detailed knowledge of the scene probably would verify that they are a close-knit, well-trained work crew, that the fire (which they set) is under control, and that they are relatively safe at the moment due to their skill, knowledge of the terrain, available escape routes, and similar precautions. Our take on the image moves away from all of that, to get closer to what is being shown.

What matters is that people can get used to anything, that Western culture will follow its commitment to controlling nature to the gates of hell, and that denial of global warming comes as easily as waiting at the bus stop because it comports so well with maintaining the routines that are among the few anchors we have in an era of rapid change. So we can wait for the cosmic bus to come and take us away to some better place, or we can turn and look around and see each other.

What matters in the world today is that people stop pretending that there isn't a fire raging in the background. The photo shows us just how close we can get while still in denial. "Just a back burn; we've got this one under control; move along now, these aren't the causes you want." In sum, what the image shows is how modernity has habituated citizens to waiting it out whenever "it" involves controlling nature. The photograph is an image of waiting, and of waiting too patiently. One waits in that manner when confident that the passage of time is in one's favor. Although initiative, boldness, investment, and other elements of change are celebrated when products and markets are being developed, a different set of motives seems to come into play when the unintended consequences of modern development are being addressed. If history is progressive, then patience is a virtue. If.

Waiting is not characteristically modern, but now it may be symptomatic of a felt incapacity to influence the future. Expecting to be saved by the forces that threaten you and settling for abandonment in a dangerous world would be much the same: a mode of resignation. Time simply has to pass, whatever the outcome. Thus progress and fatality might not be as far apart as one would think. Perhaps progress is just fate with a happy face, as if smiling for the camera.

CHAPTER FIVE

SEEING SOCIETY

"To see life; to see the world; to eyewitness great events; to watch the faces of the poor and the gestures of the proud; to see strange things—"[1] So began Henry Luce's mission statement for *Life* magazine. The publication now has only a zombie afterlife of commemorative issues that appear alongside celebrity magazines in the checkout aisle. Luce's statement seems only to invite parody or, more likely, scathing dismissal, as it is suffused with evangelical confidence while easily reproducing conventional hierarchies and masking his often reactionary politics. The son of Presbyterian missionaries had found a much more effective way to colonize the world. This attitude may have been what Susan Sontag had in mind when she claimed that "to photograph is to appropriate the thing photographed," which creates "a chronic voyeuristic relation to the world which levels the meaning of all events." Nor was the effect on the spectator a good one: in "an even more image-choked world," photographs are "inexhaustible invitations to deduction, speculation, and fantasy."[2]

The "image-choked world" now includes stacks of *Life* magazines piled up at flea markets, while expanding far beyond a few weeklies and the television in the living room. Those "specialized tourists known as journalists" are still at it, moreover, and the ever greater proliferation of photographs would seem to invite near total mystification of actual social relations.[3] One might wonder, however, if the gap between authenticity and alienation is so comprehensive, and we might consider instead what this conception of photography is missing.

What is notable about Luce's statement is that it charts a movement into smaller spaces and more nuanced attentiveness. "To see life; to see the world; to eyewitness great events; to watch the faces of the poor and the gestures of the proud; to see strange things." From life wherever it might be (remember, he believed in life after death), to this world, to specific events, to the surface of things and signs of character, to what puzzles, confounds, or is not initially familiar. One shouldn't make too much of Luce's capacious prose, which is characterized by promotional zeal more than syntactical discipline, but there is a hint here of something important. Just as Sontag identified a fundamental danger of photography's expansion, Luce suggests something equally important. Photography can become a way of participating in the world that we already inhabit.

To photograph anything is to put the viewer in a social relationship with what is being shown: this lizard, that desert, those people. The camera's ability, along with the "*compulsion*" to photograph anything and everything one sees, embodies this inclusive and expansive sociality.[4] The photograph is a virtual transaction among those showing, those being seen, those looking, and those who might look. The photographic archive is a vast social space in which these relationships become interchangeable. Thus the fear of living in an "image world" actually points toward an important feature of photography: it is a technology for seeing society from the inside. The images on the wall of the cave are not mere shadows but reflections of the social relationships around the fire. By looking at a photograph, we can observe the relationships recorded there and also as they extend along lines of sight, involve fluctuating sensations of proximity or distance, and confirm or disrupt our sense of place. Further, one need not see only a society, this one or that one, but society as it is the distinctive habitus of modern civilization. For the same reason, photography also can become one basis for self-reflection, and the images themselves can become a medium for social thought.[5]

But what is society? As the only social animal with a camera, human beings have a unique opportunity when answering this question. The complex patterns of interaction within families, neighborhoods, workplaces, markets, networks, and many other forms of association necessarily involve visual cues, from eye contact to the window office. Social relations are modes of coordination that require recognizing each other's behavior as more or less intentional, more or less appropriate, more or less appealing or threatening or useful. Social relations thus become evident on the surface of things, and social influence depends on being affected by what one has experienced—say, by looking at a photograph.

Any social relation begins with the definition of being inside or outside a group: "we're a team," "this is a family matter," "that's their business," "he's not one of us." As relationships proliferate, overlap, and become organized, society emerges as the envelope within which all such definitions are brought to view and thus capable of being judged. Modern societies are particularly complex and dynamic: large-scale, high-tech, and committed to innovation, growth, and other forms of change, they produce astonishing alterations in status, rights, opportunities, protections, capabilities, and prosperity, all of which in turn can disrupt traditional customs and beliefs. Perhaps most significantly, modern societies are societies of strangers: the representative place is a city, not the village.[6]

In the modern world, then, one lives not only in a particular place with its own mores and local knowledge but also within society, which is *the realm where everything intersects*. It is the symbolic space, behavioral field, built environment, and virtual reality encompassing human coexistence. There is indeed a "social fabric": the tapestry through which every thread of human experience runs. That fabric acquires patterns known as art, business, entertainment, fashion, law, politics, science, sports, travel, war, and more, but without the common weave each eventually would fray into meaninglessness.

The camera is uniquely capable of depicting social meaning because it will capture everything that is visible in the viewfinder.[7] The photograph is a society in miniature—a place where everything intersects, all visible discriminations and patterns mixed together, whether finely coordinated or jarringly obvious. Class, race, gender, sexual orientation, age, occupation, affectation, health, stress, comfort, wariness—to the extent that these and many other elements of identity and responsiveness can be seen, they will be recorded. Thus photography is a medium of modern social thought not because it is mechanical but because it shows how in any moment, myriad relationships are already intertwined.[8]

Once one is inside the world being shown, the terms of spectatorship become revalued as well. Luce unabashedly says that his magazine will allow one to "see and to take pleasure in seeing; to see and be amazed; to see and be instructed." It is the iconoclasts who are modernity's ascetics, while the missionary's kid celebrates taking pleasure and assumes that amazement and instruction go together. (If one thinks of an amusement park, the critics may have a point, but it also is true that "philosophy begins in wonder.")[9] Likewise, spectatorship involves particular modes of attentiveness. Pleasure and amazement are important: if nothing else, they motivate exploration, but they also suspend ordinary habits of pragmatic observation and assessment—that is, the familiar terms of conventional judgment. Spectatorship focuses on the surface of things, on trying to "see the world" by being grounded in particularity rather than abstraction, and observing and pondering the distinctively social media of faces and gestures. Having an experience may be displaced by taking a photograph of it, but one also could come to see the taken-for-granted world as wider, more varied, and more marvelous than one had thought. By following familiar lines of sight—the significant event demanding attention, the face being presented, or the gesture giving away the game—one might come to see the familiar as strange. Society is constantly enveloping the spectator, but as it is placed on stage, it can be seen as it might appear from the outside, alien and yet uncannily close to what had seemed unique, authentic, or natural.

Because the photographic image provides a performative framing of whatever is shown, it always places its subject on stage and so always turns the viewer into a spectator. Nonetheless, some settings are better than others. At least one of the figures in the photograph from the Crystal Bridges Museum of American Art (fig. 22) is a sculpture, but how many of the others are not?

Jim Dine's *Walking to Boras* occupies the center of the display space.[10] The pedestal and the four short poles for the ropes to prevent contact assure us that it is an objet d'art, just in case we had any doubt about a seven-foot boy in lederhosen. But what about the two figures on the left? They are so perfectly caught in time, and so gracefully posed in a moment of dynamic equilibrium, and so absolutely isolated in visual space that they seem at once almost together and yet completely separate, and both specific individuals and social types . . . The composition seems too good to have happened naturally, while it could be a key to a larger composite grouping. We look for the statue contrasted with the people around

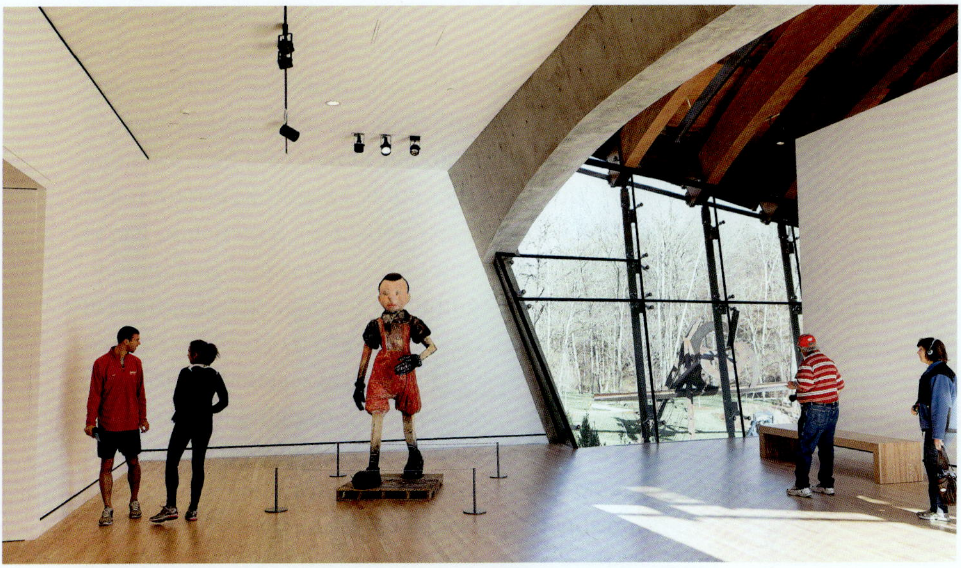

Figure 22. © Steve Hebert / The New York Times / Redux.

it, only to discover that the photographer has tricked us into seeing people as statues.

Perhaps in the next millisecond the couple leaned in toward one another to confer or confide or otherwise get closer together, or perhaps a brief word or glance was enough to break the pause and they vectored off along the path each was on, going in opposite directions. Or perhaps they are still there, perfectly posed in a moment of aesthetic perfection, but of course inert. But if they have moved on, what about the two figures on the right?

They certainly could qualify as statues, as their all-too-ordinary clothes and postures echo the sculptures of George Segal. And it would be a good joke, as well as a moment for genuine reflection, for a museum in the Ozarks to feature its most local visitors as works of art. And what if everyone in the room was a statue rather than a person passing through the aesthetic space? Would the space become less welcoming or more stimulating? More an occasion for reflection on art and life, or a disturbing walk through an uncanny valley of simulation?

Questions such as these are prompted by the photographer's superb ability to re-create the deep experience of the aesthetic encounter as it is available in any well-designed art museum. Stated more simply, a good museum, like the art it holds, brings the spectator not only to see the artworks as they are but also to see everything else aesthetically. There need not be one definition or purpose for this kind of perception. However it works, the result can be to see more of what is there to be seen, and with more clarity, insight, objectivity, empathy, humor, desire, and respect. We can see how others are at once alien and human, typified and unique, needy and mindful, beautiful and doomed, achingly desirable and hopelessly out of reach, inhabitants of alternate worlds and caught in our shared catastrophe, exposed by appearances and forever unknown.

A good museum does that. Photographs can do the same. Photographic space can work like museum space: tuning the senses to see the artistry in ordinary life.[11] It has an additional function as well. Because the museum is an archive of society's past, it provides a replica of the society as it was. One enters the museum space as a way of entering into a more considered relationship with the society itself. Photography does the same. In the image above, the museum space is featured, both by emphasizing the volume of the room and through contrast with the natural environment seen outside the window. (Fittingly, another artwork occupies the liminal space between the window and the tree line.) The museum stands in for society as it is a constructed space, one separate from the natural world, and one within which our lives can be seen in concert with others. This seeing is then modeled by the photographer's depth of field. Through a pulling back, outside the space of ordinary interaction with other people and direct observation of objects such as artworks, a more distant, estranged, objective mode of observation is created. The figures are not quite silhouettes because they still remain vividly present in the particularities of age and clothing. They are as separated from each other as the statue is from everyone around it, and yet they are connected by the many small signs of contemporary consumption. They each will be attending to pragmatic interests—what do you want to do next? where is the restroom?—but the spectator is being shown something else: how, by stopping the action, one can see the social setting within which everything is more or less familiar or strange, meaningful or enigmatic, predictable or up for grabs.

To do that, photography features events as performative settings for thinking about social relationships. This line of thought should include attention to how consciousness can be hijacked by those in power, but it also should consider how photography provides additional resources for thinking about social behavior. What is needed is a more active viewer, one who can collect, compare, and delve into images in order "to see life" as it is lived with others. That process of reflection can be activated by any image that combines aesthetic perception with concerns about social organization, and it can be advanced through exhibitions designed to encourage further observation and discussion. We offer one of many possible exhibitions. This chapter highlights features of social experience that are highly conventional and perhaps overlooked for that; the task is to consider how photography works within conventions of social thought (what might be called middlebrow social theory) that can become rich modes of spectatorship. By selecting photographic displays of ritual, social mobility, the texture of everyday life, and social structure, we identify a few of the elements of social experience as it is there to be seen.

Ritual Photography

Any ritual supposedly is a premodern social practice, albeit one that may have persisted into the modern era. Ritual events such as coming-of-age ceremonies, weddings, holidays, birthdays, retirement receptions, and the like remain small duties and temporary disruptions in the stream of work and other responsibilities, but they are not seen as having comprehensive significance. Likewise, the standard technique for marking any group as (relatively) premodern is to feature its ritual activities, decor, and costumes. Whether traditional cultures in the developing world or subcultures lodged within modern societies, the not-yet-wholly-modern is indexed according to its ritual display. These are at once excessive—colorful, expressive, costly beyond standard norms of functionality and efficiency—and yet highly constrained: channeled within the same time periods and theatrical routines, and fated to cyclical repetition rather than change and growth.

Photography has been thoroughly complicit with this conventional wisdom. All of the developing world and every marginalized group within the West probably has been portrayed in this way: presented as more colorful than productive, while living in a place or manner somehow anterior in time to the modern world.[12] Along with this ideological distortion is the fact that, of all the media that one might use to capture the experience of being caught up in a moment of collective expression, photography probably is the worst choice one could make. Instead of all the noise and sounds and physical sensations of being pulled along by a crowd, intoxicated with sensual overload, freely yelling and laughing gleefully, we get . . . an image. Mute, two-dimensional, static, and lacking taste, smell, sound, or touch: there is not much to get excited about. The fact that it is the medium of choice suggests that the sensory deprivation might actually be reassuring and that visual engagement is preferred because it can be merely pleasing rather than disruptive. This *tourism* (yes, we'll grant it's a real temptation here) is all the more limiting now that ethnic displays, and especially those by indigenous peoples, often are thoroughly self-aware performances for hire that show little of their culture's actual hybridity. Thus a thoroughly tamed sense of ritual assurance can be provided regularly to supplement the dominant sense of modern development—and so it is that the public is treated to images of Chinese New Year, Carnival, and so on around the globe and around the calendar.[13]

Such celebrations are photographic attractors, and for obvious reasons: brightly colored costumes, outlandish floats, dazzling light shows, and other displays of over-the-top theatricality in ordinary settings provide a ritualized departure from the humdrum routines of ordinary time, as well as plenty of eye candy. Which makes it all the more plausible that the alignment of photography and ritual practices would seem to offer a poor basis for thinking about any society, much less a modern society. Or it might help if it could show how seemingly dynamic and productive practices actually are ritualized, and how displays of modernization are exercises in enchantment, but that doesn't go very far. The focus on ritual is itself outdated, so why go there to understand modernity?

The stunning photograph in figure 23 is a powerful example of how the camera can do more than capture the color and excitement of another culture. Photography still goes there, of course, but some find a way to see through and yet think with the conventional reportage.

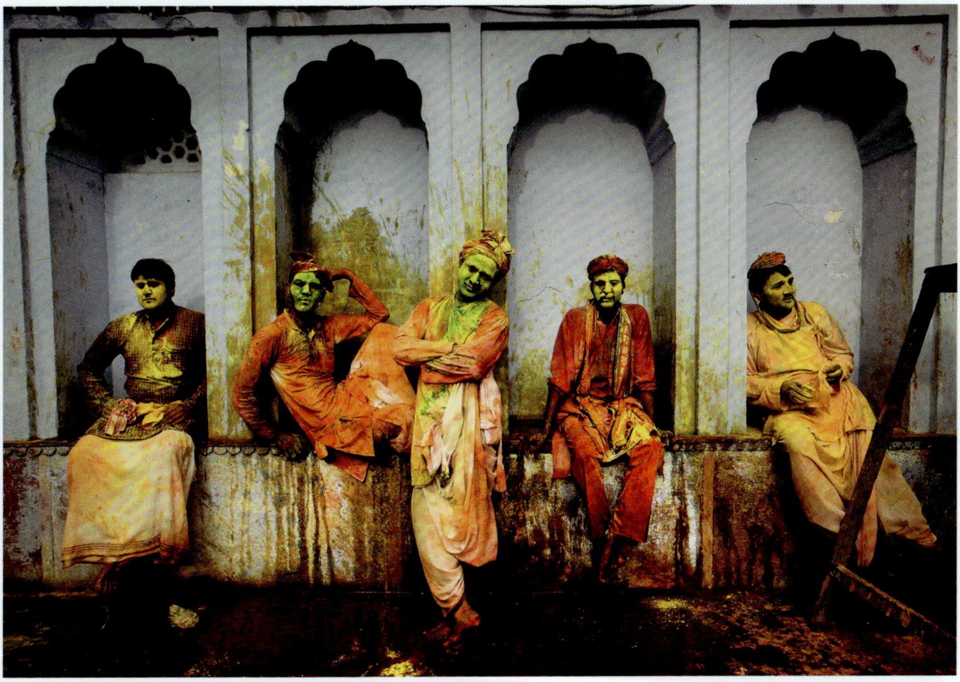

Figure 23. © AP Photo / Manish Swarup.

The image is from Holi, a festival of color: individuals festoon themselves with paint while great crowds of people are drenched in dyed powders of every hue. Colored water bombs explode as people sing, dance, and surge through the streets. There also are vernacular theatricals replaying mythic stories, which is why, in the photo here, "Indian villagers from Nandgaon wait for the arrival of villagers from Barsana to play Lathmar Holi at the Nandagram temple famous for Lord Krishna and his brother Balram, in Nandgaon, India."[14] Many viewers will not know the story, but the photograph provides other paths into the festival. The five actors appear as if they were in a painting, and perhaps they acquire additional status and individuality for that. The four arched spaces could have been taken from a Renaissance altar, now updated to feature Hindu saints. Or they could be statues on a cathedral, giving us apostles, angels, and perhaps a defiant gargoyle on the inner left. Krisha has no need of a cathedral, of course, but some of his viewers might need a little help in appreciating what is right in front of their eyes.

These aesthetic hints don't compromise the photograph's fidelity to the festival, but even so this photo is quite unconventional. Many festival images feature thick washes of color, the energy and excitement of people in motion, and displays of massed exhilaration. By contrast, here we see the riot of color framed and subdued by the blue-gray building, static poses instead of movement, individuals instead of a crowd, and attitudes ranging from bored to indifferent. Instead of being in the middle of the action, they and we are waiting for something to happen. And while that isn't happening, we can sense that what is yet to come already is on its way to being over: the red/orange/yellow/green stains look more messy than festive, and it is easy to imagine how the clothes will be washed, the walls hosed down, and the bodies scrubbed to return everyone and everything to ordinary time and business as usual after the ritual celebration.

That hint of the ordinary world is one clue to what the photograph has to say about social consciousness. Consider how figure 23 provides a more institutional sense of theatricality and, with that, a basis for serious reflection on the relationship between drama and life. The guys in the picture are not merely villagers out of role but are behaving like experienced troupers long accustomed to waiting backstage. And they are backstage, which provides a reverse shot on the explicit theatricality of the festival while channeling the dramaturgical social theory developed by Erving Goffman and others.[15] Because the convention derived from colonial-era photography is to see individuals as types, an image today can bring us to see types as individuals and then to typify individual features as distinctively human attitudes that can be inhabited by actor and spectator alike.

Thus individuality becomes something to be found within social relationships, not against them, and in place of either fixed roles or unique personalities, photography highlights successive moments in continuous patterns of social interaction—on stage, off stage; acting, reacting; imitating, adapting; performing, pondering; and so on. Like other arts, photography typifies and also personalizes; it objectifies and also exposes objectification. Rather than to create a world of either types or individuals, it explores how that tension is fundamental to social experience, particularly in distinctively modern societies. Equally important, it transfers that tension to the spectator: making the manner in which one sees the other a choice, and one produced through the social pressure of seeing in common. And while viewers are still spectators, that virtual experience is modulated further by the photographer's being able to move through and around the event.

The slide shows on Holi and the other festivals contain quite a few backstage shots. The photographers are doing what they have to do to file the story to compete in a marketplace of attention, but they are doing more than that as well. Precisely because the photo in figure 23 is so static and composed, it gives us some insight into the carnival's celebration of excess, playacting, and role reversals. On the one hand, human beings are always on stage, always acting, always in character even when no one is supposed to be looking. And if waiting is part of the frenzy, then likewise the madness that is supposed to be released during the festival is always with us, no matter how mundane ordinary life may seem. On the other hand and at the same time, we retain an ability to step back, be still, carefully look at one another, and marvel at the strange, beautiful fallen angels before us, just as they look back at us. Indeed, all the distractions of color and action might be there in part to avoid seeing how much can be seen in ritual repose.

The opportunity for reflection that is gained here is not radical, not erudite, and not state-of-the-art social science. Notice that we have avoided a discussion of the academic domains of visual sociology and visual anthropology (both are subdisciplines with their own journals and book series). Whatever the individual scholar's commitment to praxis or public engagement, these are expert, not public, gazes, similar to the expertise that geographers or radiologists bring to their visual practices. There may be a relationship between the sociology and photojournalism of any period—it seems a strong feature of midcentury photography and especially the exploration of subcultures at that time—but we are not prepared to track that here. The critical discourse of photography absorbed the normative commitments of cultural studies during the past few decades, and progressive inquiry will continue along those lines: the critique of the male gaze may be old news, but the production of whiteness is not yet adequately theorized.[16] Scholarship remains an important tributary to public culture, but it is not itself a way of public seeing.

At the same time, photography's observation of social performance is not a wholly unreflective exercise in objectification. The claim of objectification may be the bedrock on which all critiques of domination through representation stand. It has been applied without qualification in photography, as when Sontag declared that "photographs objectify: they turn an event or a person into something that can be possessed."[17] No ifs, ands, or buts, while the process of symbolic substitution is immediately transformed into its most suspect use: possession, ownership of the person, as if slavery were the objective. One also might note that there is no equally familiar term for the equivalent act of converting an event or person into words: *nominalization* isn't used, and *abstraction* has less impact since it can apply to other media as well. Yet if we look for objectification where it would be likely to occur, as in an AP photograph of ritual performance in the Global South, we can see that it is only one option among many.

More to the point, the public gaze developed by photography has to avoid objectification if it is to do everything else that needs to be done to maintain public culture. Pluralism, a nonthreatening relationship with strangers, a sense of egalitarian reciprocity, and other social habits are nurtured by photography precisely because it does more than objectify. Consider how the photograph, instead of setting people at a distance from one's personal space in order to transform them into objects, makes distance part of the scene to be observed while also putting the viewer into a social relationship with those being viewed. Distance—social distance—is an important part of social interaction, a feature of modern societies having both positive and negative effects, and something modulated within civic spectatorship to encourage varied forms of response. It is not prima facie evidence of social estrangement, but it is a constitutive feature of modern social experience and something that can be bridged (or at least made more tolerable) by media technologies. Look again at the photograph from the Crystal Bridges museum (fig. 22): distance is made visible, it isolates the individuals for observation, and it is what is being crossed or maintained through their interactions and the viewer's response. Curiously, then, objectification and the theoretical gaze are joined at the hip, for both are attempts to *use* distance, whether to order and manipulate or to analyze and change the world. These are available positions along the wide spectrum of spectatorship, but they are not the same as the public optic that has developed out of photography's exploration of the pathos of living among strangers.

So look one more time. Notice that those in the Holi photograph (fig. 23) not only are being looked at but also are looking: at others outside the frame, inwardly, and at us. As we study them, they study us, each mirroring the other. Modern individuals are always looking at one another, aware that they are being seen, and posed accordingly—even when just killing time. By putting the spectator in a social relationship with those in the picture, the photograph emphasizes that seeing and acting are reciprocal forms of social behavior. What then is needed is to show how they are also constantly in flux, not fixed by ritual practices but moved by the dynamic forces that define every modern society.

Social Mobility

Museums and rituals remain spaces of confinement, and modern society is nothing if not dynamic and capacious. It expands across the globe and forward through time. Both geographic and temporal changes are captured in figure 24.

Six young people stand before a dazzling backdrop of the city of Shanghai aglow in the night. Of course they also are *in* the city, which is showcased by its corporate skyscrapers. But a river separates the six individuals from the concentration of wealth, which is set above them a bit like heaven. Because the image is divided high and low by the distant shoreline, the visual grammar makes the high-end architecture an ideal that is set over the reality below. Because their heads just break the line, they may be tending toward the bright lights, as is suggested also by the middle-class consumer consumption evident in their clothing and accessories. Indeed, one implication is that they are destined to become the next generation of adults living within Chinese capitalism.

One might ask, then, How are they doing? The photo suggests several answers. One is that they are doing fine, because they obviously are sharing in the prosperity that they will one day claim as their own. The city was built up while they were being prepared to thrive

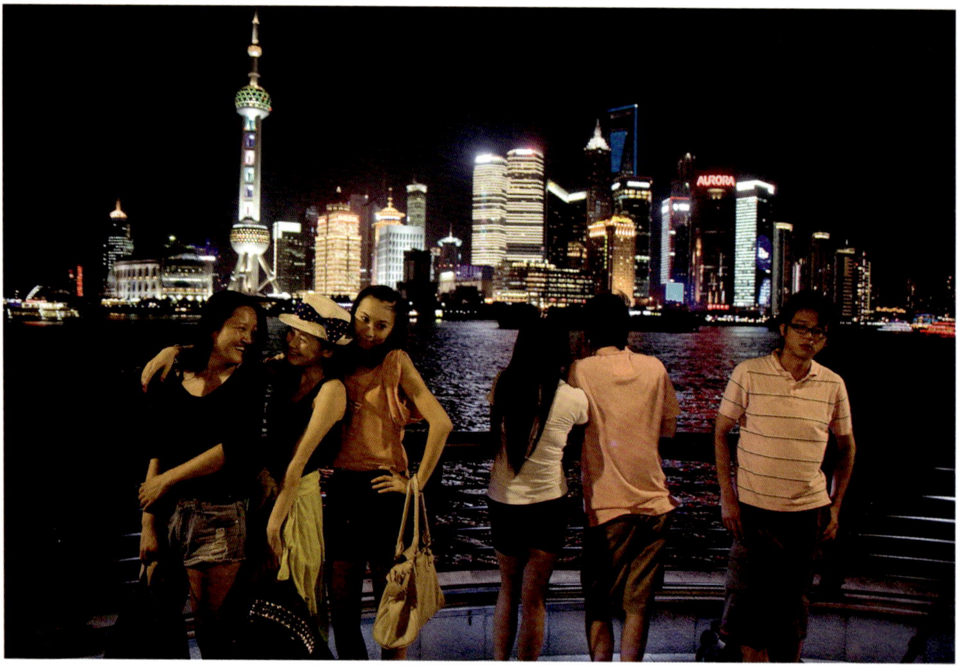

Figure 24. © Bruno Barbey / Magnum Photos.

there, so life is good. Indeed one might think that China can skip the anxieties about modernization damaging the young who then damage society. One might recall the midcentury public discourse about the social and moral effects of modern development: Bruce Davidson's photo documentary of a street gang, the Jets and Sharks in *West Side Story*, "juvenile delinquents" in newspapers and magazines, and earnest discussions about "teenagers." Now that gangs are murderous million-dollar cartels, the allegory is less appealing, but youth retains considerable metaphoric value, not to mention market share.[18] In this case they are passing into early adulthood, so the sense of change is amplified, and no one is going to cross the street to avoid this group.

Even so, one implication is that China has developed well enough that its children can experience the distinctively modern definition of adolescence, which is considerably elongated for extended education and uniquely susceptible to developing a youth culture dominated by popular entertainment and merchandising. That may be both good news and bad news, but it implies a universality for modern societies that can hide other differences—say, the likelihood that everyone in the picture is an only child who has intimate knowledge of loneliness.

Another implication might be that China is now in the adolescent phase of modern capitalist development: growing by leaps and bounds, and look at how much carbon that city eats! Within such a framework, virtually anything can be excused as "growing pains," as long as the kid doesn't pick up a gun or kill someone with the car or get pregnant; no military expansion, then, and please be careful about emissions, but otherwise we'll wait it out. Such a view is exceedingly condescending, of course, but it is sure to have plenty of adherents, perhaps for that very reason.

The photo does better than that, however. There is another dimension to the image, one suggested by its dark tonality and the separation of the people from the cityscape. These qualities push universality further to suggest that China's youth are destined for other uniquely modern experiences as well, including the social fragmentation and anomie that are side effects of modern development. Furthermore, we have to pay attention to the photo's almost painful depiction of typified social behavior. As the eyes move from left to right, we see three girls hugging, a girl and a boy close together, and a lone boy. Thus in the center the teen dream of romantic coupling, and on each side (girls on the left, boys on the right) the gender segregation in which many young people spend much of their time. It is more than a matter of time, however, as the boy on the right seems quite alone and at least pensive or even sad. If you look closely, you'll see that the girl on the right side of the threesome also is a bit outside of that grouping gesturally and emotionally. The intense social awareness of youth inevitably is accompanied by separation, self-consciousness, and sadness. Despite their evident prosperity and bright future, life still could be tough.

So it is that the photo provides an allegory after all, and one that is not just about China. One of the major questions of the twenty-first century is how to live well in a world dominated by modern capitalism. As China demonstrates, the shopping mall is one answer to that question, and it shouldn't be dismissed out of hand. But it is not enough, nor are GDP, the level of foreign investment, and other macroeconomic variables the full measure of success. More to the point, the photograph provides two views of society, which reflect two dimensions of social determination. Society is the gleaming superstructure of modern technologies and economic development, and it is also the smaller circles of association that people form to make the impersonal megalith habitable. These small worlds are part voluntary, part obligatory, part accidental. They are the places where expressions and gestures matter, where character counts, where feelings get hurt. And even if the social drives are as powerful as the dynamo that is Shanghai, the actual groupings are very fragile. But then there may be more to the photo yet: the young people stand in contrast to the towering buildings, but each side of the river also can be seen as a mirror image of the other. They will acquire the powers of the city, unless the city's future proves to be as unpredictable and fragile as their own.

As modernization spreads, the idea of society becomes more encompassing. The less awareness there is of an outside, the more upward mobility matters. This is usually thought of as economic mobility for both individuals and peoples, but corresponding social and cultural changes are both inevitable and visible. Corresponding anxieties emerge as well: wealth unsettles things, especially if it is acquired too fast or displayed too garishly. Children and especially young people become symbols of both the promise and the risks of modernization. In that light, what may be most important about the photo above is that it is somewhat enigmatic. Modernity without predictability is not a reassuring condition.

Social Texture

Instead of seeing a photograph as supplemental information about what could be superficial or irrelevant features of an event, we suggest that a photographic image provides a different and much richer mode of reportage, one that features social context in order to describe the event as it really is—that is, as it already is shaped by the many influences that constitute a modern society. Moreover, the photograph does so not by identifying structural causes—there writing is the better medium—but by showing the surface of things.

Thus the *texture* of the scene becomes important, for that is where social influence is evident.

By texture we mean the manner in which social context is evident on the surface of an event and how that modulation is one dimension of the overdetermined, performative, and dynamic quality of social experience.[19] Just as surfaces are rough or smooth, so are surfaces rich or poor, relaxed or tense, bureaucratic or sentimental, and each of these designs reflects habitual practices. In the same way, surfaces in any scene are more or less coordinated or uncoordinated, resonant or dissonant, uniform or dissimilar. Surfaces thus display social relations and emotional valences, and one can consider how they are "talking" to one another, this wall to that chair to the person sitting in it to the person standing before him, hat in hand. Such communication is possible because the human world is organized according to conventions of social behavior: as viewers recognize the conventions in otherwise fragmentary scenes, they can instantly supply the social meaning that is not being voiced directly. (Of course misunderstanding always is possible and is more likely as the audience is less familiar with the culture, but that is true of all communication.) These conventions are maintained and extended through repetition, including repeated display through photography.

Photography, then, provides a continuing case study in the texturing of social reality: although the material surface of the photograph itself is uniformly smooth, texturing extends from its print tonality to all the elements of visual composition to all the surfaces presented together in the single frame. Indeed the contrast between smooth surface and continuous texture in the image itself highlights the social content, and not as a surface and depth exchange but as a series of surfaces with their transcriptions traced across them and awaiting activation by the viewer. The image is a richly textured social object.

Figure 25, a photo of Egyptians uploading video from Tahrir Square, is both a portrait of political action and a study in youth culture. They could get beaten, imprisoned, and tortured for what they are doing—and they are completely at home in the hip casualness of student fashion, sporting laptops, cameras, and other electronic gear, and blending hacker intensity with the easy jive of sharing cigarettes. We particularly like how the color of the hard drive matches

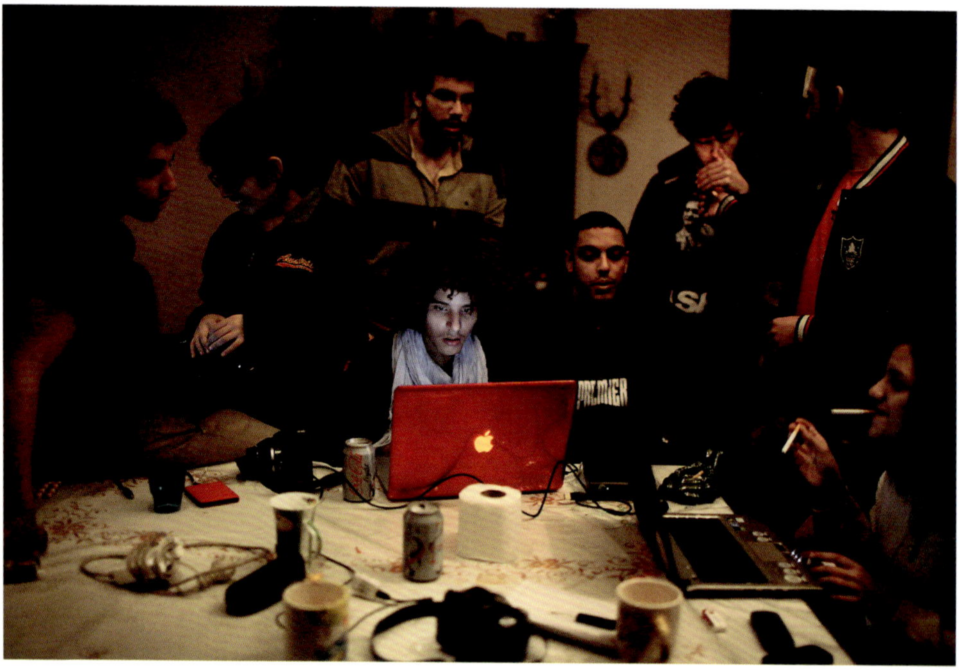

Figure 25. © Ed Ou / The New York Times / Redux.

the laptop, which also gets picked up on the Coke cans and the decorative pattern on the tablecloth; these horizontal connections might not matter for many purposes, but they are present. At the same time nothing is too neatly coordinated, for that would nullify the wonderful informality and messiness that most characterizes the tableau. They don't have to wait for an election: this already is a portrait of democratic life.

Of course the image also plays on sentimental memories, for those who have them, of student days—the ashtray and toilet paper are near-perfect touches—and these revolutionaries also are middle class (or better), Westernized, and otherwise liberal-democratic elites in the making. They do not look like those demonstrators who were poorer or who embodied more traditional customs and Islamist commitments, and less privileged viewers might be quick to notice and resent those who do not have to go to work as soon as they are able. No one should conclude that they are or ought to be the face of the revolution or that democracy cannot include wearing jellabiyas or that every viewer should warm to the glow of the Macbook Pro laptop.

Equally important, taking "superficial" features of political action seriously does not mean that one should disregard other sources of power. Many regimes still rule the old-fashioned way: by brutally beating, torturing, killing, and otherwise terrorizing people. More comprehensively, as Martin Jay summarizes: "The egalitarianism produced by the camera can be interpreted in positive or negative terms, depending on one's attitude toward the society it depicted. For those who stress the still class-riven structure of that society, photographic democratization is only ideological."[20] This is no small point, but it should not be overstated either. The risk of ideological capture attends any representation of community. Democracies may depend on symbols more than other regimes and thus may be more susceptible to mystification, but they do not have the option of doing without the risk.[21] The creation of a democratic polity out of a more authoritarian establishment may have to address obvious deficits in democratic imagery, not to mention the need for support from other democracies. We assume that the political intention of the photograph is to encourage identification with the protesters. That said, one must beware of being beguiled by mere surfaces and allowing appearance to become a substitute for a more durable reality. What is equally important, however, is to realize how much social knowledge is available on the surface. The study of texture is about observation, with questions of judgment and action to follow. The photograph shows what is in place on the surface of a society, and that often can be a reliable indicator of both horizontal networks and deep structure. It also, as above, can show what needs to be in place, and from that one can discuss what else would have to change for the scene to occur not once or twice but reliably and sustainably.

The camera's capacity to record texture is closely tied to its egalitarian potential. That valence has several dimensions: equality is performed through the representation of everyday life, as all can be subject to the same conditions of erosion or granted the dignity of portraiture; it is reinforced through its broad horizontal production and distribution, and so "the people" can have their own image; it shows equality as it can be seen in actual practice and as it can be denied by customs that continue to demean and deny fellow human beings. Photography's egalitarianism is not a universal solvent of social discrimination, but if they are placed in an egalitarian frame, the textures of other social orders then become all the more available for judgment. And while visions of equality may be merely ideological, sometimes the character of another regime can become all too obvious.

Figure 26 displays the interior of a nondescript building somewhere in Damascus. The *New York Times* caption had little to do with the photo as such: "The escalation in Syria, where Mr. Assad has vowed to end a 10-month-old uprising that he has characterized as the work of foreign-backed terrorists, came within a few miles of the epicenter of his power in the capital on Sunday."[22] So what is the photo doing? We don't see a recognizable building or evidence of warfare or anything specific to the day-to-day struggle being reported in the text. The photograph is there to communicate something, however, and perhaps something about the nature of the Assad regime as it can be seen at "the epicenter of his power."

Institutional buildings often have a dual texture: on the one hand, they can be dull, unadorned, vaguely depressing places given over to sheer functionality; on the other hand, they can include suggestions of grandeur or at least stature, as with ornate porticos or gleaming atria. Each design is part of the look: one can see efficient and egalitarian application of the rule of law and the authority and collective resources needed to make that happen. The building in figure 26 has it down: marble floor and wainscoting and elegant crown molding frame the scene, which contains drywall, standard-issue metal frames, and no-smoking signs. The message might be "admire and obey," even without the large picture of Assad, which adds another layer to the room's political statement. The portrait of Our Leader is the stock image of authoritarian regimes, accompanied by the elimination of most other images and their implications of pluralism. This photo captures that and more, including a sense of social impoverishment, as if the energy is being leached out of everything. Even Assad's portrait is fading into ghostliness. Perhaps he's on his way out, but this photo says that the authoritarian regime has already reduced its society to a kind of lifelessness. Those flags could be in a mausoleum, whether one run by the state or one used for the state's interment. Small signs of deterioration, from the cracks

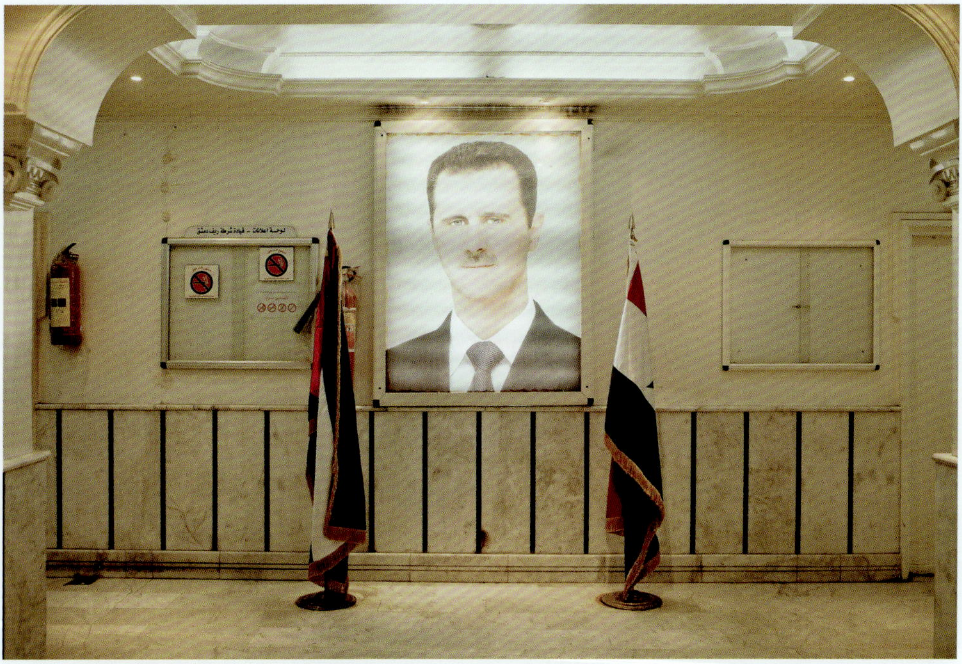

Figure 26. © Tómas Munita / The New York Times / Redux.

in the crown molding and the walls to the stains at the edges of the portrait and around the bases of the flag stands, suggest that this is an empty, negative space. Decayed surfaces, listless symbols, and a fire extinguisher: welcome to the Syrian government.

Egypt is doing better than Syria, but we are not interested in obvious or simplistic contrasts. One comparison does apply, however: it is telling that the government, and particularly the military, is not visible in the photo from Egypt. The Egyptian military is a multibillion-dollar economic cartel, the recipient of an additional two billion each year from the US government, and the single most central, powerful, stable, and self-interested party in Egyptian politics. Subsequent events proved that they would continue to control the country ruthlessly and with no thought of easing their financial stranglehold on the economy. Figure 25 can be faulted for not capturing any of that, or worse, for pretending it didn't exist. But some photographs, like the revolution itself, are about hope. It would be unrealistic to portray a political uprising otherwise. What matters is how it was done. The signs of high-tech communication and mass-market consumption offer a liberal politics that is more dream than reality, but along the way they also remind us that politics and society are profoundly intertwined. And one is not left with only a liberal politics that defers collective action to a future of individualized consumption. The photographs of military wealth and corruption are waiting to be taken—the officers' upscale colonization of Cairo cannot be hidden—and next time around the democratic movement might consider what was missing from the picture.

Photography offers a robust realignment of social and political thought precisely by showing how politics is textured: that is, how the social context and consequences of political action are evident on the surface of things. By paying attention to the social surface, we can understand how both individual experience and collective action might be shaped by many different factors coming together in a particular place and time. And we can see how different political practices can make the world more richly interwoven and vibrant, or more relentlessly ordered and depressing.

The focus on texture also raises the importance of social objects. Alongside photography's capacity for capturing facial expressions, bodily gestures, and the dignity and grace of the human person, it also can bring out the communicative potential of objects. More to the point, some features of our social nature are revealed more clearly when we are not in the picture. The human figure reveals but it also distracts, not least as personal features invoke personalized reactions. To see society as such; to see how social behavior is systemic and habitual; to see the category system that undergirds social performance; to see how these things are literally set in stone and also in steel, plastic, wood, and glass; to see how the individual is constantly surrounded and prompted and guided by social cues in the built environment; to see how that environment is painted, carpeted, decorated, furnished, and otherwise suffused with meaning; to see how the individual must live amid networks of association that are deeply embedded, historied, and largely unconscious; to see how the familiar could appear strange, alien, or hostile precisely because it is human artifice—to see all these things, one needs to be able to see *things*.[23]

A portrait of inert things can show how every moment is an intensified convergence of social energies that are constantly in circulation and often no respecter of persons. When the camera focuses on the social thing, it extends photography as a medium for social consciousness. Along with the tensions between inclusion and exclusion, association and isolation, and similar dynamics of relational life, photography also highlights how any scene has more than one potential outcome. Although justly celebrated for documenting what is actually there, photography is an art because it also can suggest how social behavior can flow one way or another. The decor of a room, the width of a street, the tilt of a telephone pole, a frayed hem, and many other surface features of the human environment suggest not only actual conditions but prior tendencies and pending choices. The camera records how seemingly fixed conditions are powerful but temporary consolidations of social forces, and how people might conform, adapt, cope, resist, succumb, overcome, or otherwise respond to the inheritance of the moment. Equally important, this deep negotiation of social pressure includes those viewing the photograph. The image puts a scene with all its potential energy before us, thereby creating a double encounter: we feel the tensions defining the moment, and we are asked to imagine, judge, enjoy, suffer, and perhaps even act along with those who are caught in that social space.

Even when no one is there. The abandoned house in figure 27 has acquired a paradoxical richness of texture. Were it well-maintained and occupied, many probably would pass by without noticing. Another bungalow with a nice porch, at once too small and too open for contemporary housing developments, an example of a cramped yet comfortable past, it would have its niche but nothing more. And now the realtor's gaze can see only an eyesore, a dirty wound in the visual body of the neighborhood.

The photograph reveals much more, however. The decay of the house is all the more evocative because of the lushness of the grass and the plants rising up before it. And not only grass but a rich panoply of species, all vibrantly thriving from the homeowner's neglect. The bushes and trees towering in front of the porch seem almost like alien conquerors, taking or now guarding their prize. As the building rots, it is taken back into a vegetative state, slowly being converted into mold, then soil, and eventually new growth, wholly without human influence.

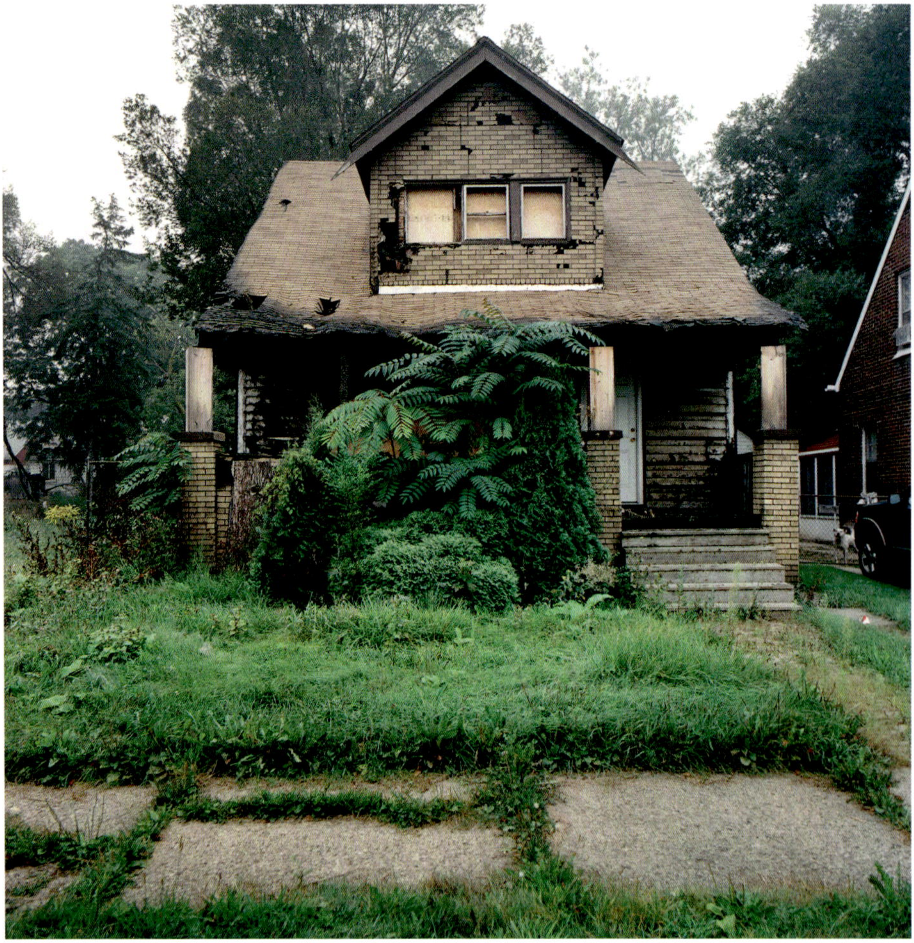

Figure 27. © Kevin Bauman.

But not quite yet. The house is posed as if for a portrait, and it retains a residual dignity as it wastes away. The strong thrust of the dormer seems almost defiant despite visible decay and bordered windows, as do the pillars still standing after the overhang has rotted away. This once was a place that mattered. And mattered to those who once lived within, an entire world of experiences that now is shuttered from view, locked up like so many secrets in a vault no one will even bother to open. And so the photograph becomes an image of foreclosure—of literally shutting out, closing early, stopping. We see layers of blockage: the expanse of fissured sidewalk, overgrown lawn, dense foliage, pillared and shadowed porch, closed door, and boarded windows—every part of the image says you might go forward but should not. Likewise, the viewer's gaze, which is pulled toward the vanishing point in the middle of the picture, is abruptly interrupted by the plants and then the boards. The image might be described as adding insult to injury, as it stops any attempt to discover anything beneath the sad surface of decrepitude.

But is this only the texture of decline or something more complicated? The lushness of the natural world is not only reclaiming human engineering but confronting it. How could there have been such a failure of substance amid such bounty? Yes, the built environment is being eroded continually by nature, but it also is part of nature and has access to those energies and materials. Corporate practices and governmental policies (or the lack of them) are far more corrosive than wind and rain. The conjunction of house and lawn may hint at the kind of social thought that is required to connect the particular case to systemic processes. The visible surface is produced most immediately by natural forces, but they are an index of how social pressures are brought to bear on the material conditions of daily life. The house was an economic achievement that is reverting to nature, but nature is only the proximate cause. The incredible detail in the decline of the sidewalk, front walk, steps, and the house itself testifies to how it was an intricately available place for social experience, and also a repository of enormous amounts of potential energy that can be channeled or dissipated according to the decisions of both specific individuals and large institutions.

This texturing of human, natural, individual, and corporate factors is given additional emphasis by the second house in the photograph. As if bleeding in from another image—and another neighborhood—the scene on the right edge both underscores and further complicates the portrait. The second house is well maintained, as is evident from the clean, well-painted lines of the white eave and window frames. Nature is still evident, but now as a domesticated animal, the dog looking curiously at the photographer. There still are signs of enclosure, but now as a fence and window shades, which signify private property and privacy. The vehicle adds mobility as well, and its complementarity with the inhabited house is emphasized by the neat white line along its side. The air conditioner in the upper window may be a step down aesthetically, but the owner does well enough to sleep comfortably. We're back to the baseline condition of ordinary life for many people: making do, getting by, and not being noticed for the wrong things. Against the unintended majesty of a ruin, the texture of everyday life can seem very mundane. It can be an achievement nonetheless, and perhaps one best seen with a sideways glance.

Spectatorship can be enriched by banality, blockage, and emptiness.[24] The encounter with surfaces ranges from awe to delight to interest, to indifference, boredom, and frustration, to disgust or worse. Once artistically directed, every part of the spectrum can be a resource for thinking about and relating to others. The denial of access to the house as it was lived in is a moment of hesitation, frustration, and reflection. The gaze that cannot go forward is refracted back, and in place of having sufficient knowledge we enter into a mood. That emotional response can become atmospheric and thus limn other surfaces as well. That lateral extension—going across surfaces "horizontally," as it were, instead of a "vertical" movement to a transcendental or foundational reality—can lead the viewer to a wider sense of scene, one that can include both the focal object and a marginal supplement, the central subject and others as well. It also can lead to a more direct engagement with broader economic and political conditions that are evident only through their surface effects. In the terms of critical theory, the photograph's fascination with the surface can direct the spectator to think about the material relations between persons by featuring the social relations between things.[25]

Social Structure

Photography's ability to depict the texture of human interactions is one of its most important properties. It also is a property that has been almost wholly overlooked or incorrectly appreciated in the critical discourse on photography. That said, by focusing only on texture, one would miss other elements of social intelligence; more important, one would not face the problem that does confront any visual medium, which is how to depict phenomena that are abstract. Equally important, immersion in particularity can foster blindness regarding what critical discourse rightly features: how power and domination are exercised through impersonal structures of control and compliance.

Many of the central terms in modern social organization refer to quasi-metaphysical entities: "society," "the state," "the market," "the public," and "human rights" have real properties and yet also are abstractions. These things are not things but ideas, models, relationships, processes, habits, or norms. They also are virtual realities that are maintained via circulation through a society's channels of communication. Whatever their presence, whether articulated by a judicial proceeding or by a video game, they never exist in only one place. One might go so far as to say they are products of the more abstract medium of language, but in any case the question arises: can photography adequately represent the relatively abstract dimensions of collective organization? The answer is yes, but indirectly. Abstraction captures realities that operate at a scale exceeding literal observation, but these realities do not exist in a separate plane of existence; they still have to work materially, and that can be seen. Virtual realities can be visible on the surface of things: because they absolutely depend on mediation, they can be brought into view within a medium capable of creating mirror effects.

These capabilities were brought to the fore when the press faced the difficult task of capturing a drastic crash in the global economy. Trillions of dollars were destroyed through fiscal mismanagement by a small number of firms, but the actual changes consisted of ledgers not balancing, stocks dropping in value, orders not being placed, taxes not being collected, and other largely invisible changes. Grievous material consequences would chain out for many years, but often in relatively small-scale events that could be dismissed as normal vicissitudes in any case: small businesses closing, people out of work, families having to live on less. And, in fact, public discourse generally is impoverished regarding economic policy, where ideology reigns supreme.

Even so, the right photograph can highlight just how much is at stake in the definition of economic realities, showing how the economy, no less than politics, is always experienced within a social context.

Figure 28 is the image of a reflection, which neatly duplicates

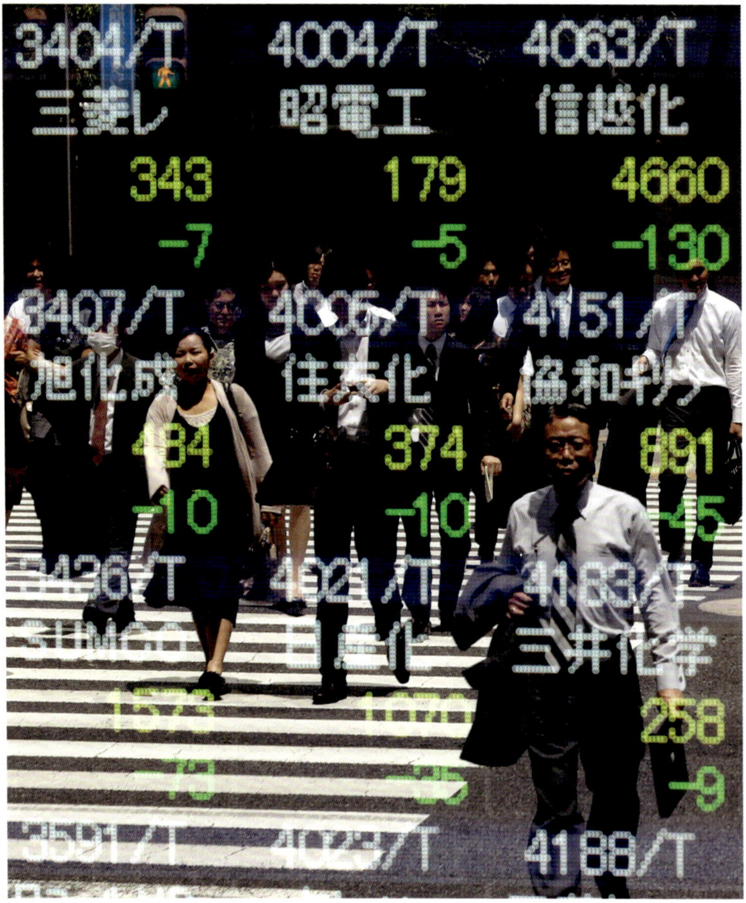

Figure 28. © Reuters / Kim Kyung-Hoon.

what any camera has to do to record the economy. "Pedestrians are reflected in a stock index board outside of a brokerage," while the superimposition works in reverse, as the people on the street appear to us through a scrim of data that seems to be the reflection. The textures are revealing: the numbers are obviously ephemeral, having the flickering half-life of a digital projection of rapidly changing figures, and instrumental, having the rough fonts and meager colors of workplace informatics. Likewise, the pedestrians are almost dreamlike, as if in an alternative reality, but one with the anonymity and functionality of an urban crosswalk. Behind that is only blackness, the back wall of this black box theater. One might wonder: which is more real, the data or the crowd? The question exposes and contests neoliberal fantasies now regnant in many elite institutions.

On the one hand, the photo seems to say that labor and stock prices are indivisible parts of the same economic whole. For there to be profits, there have to be workers; for there to be workers, there have to be profits. Labor and capital are seamlessly integrated into a single system. In that system, the relatively abstract, fluid investments are backed by the labor they fund and organize, which in turn prospers from that investment to acquire the many benefits of modern life such as good clothing, shelter, health care, transportation, and communications. That's the dream, and one that has been realized in significant areas of global economic development.

On the other hand, the photo could also reveal how labor and finance are not coordinated and how the electronic data flows of the stock market obscure, displace, and literally write over the body of labor. Now labor and capital can become alienated from one another, so much so that the work, lives, and interests of most people can recede behind a screen of financial activity that moves upward while they become increasingly secondary, ghostly, unreal. Those shown are not the blue-collar workers whose jobs are being automated or shipped away; the latter are already invisible, with only the next to go being shown. The people massed to cross the street are still somewhat discernible but relatively inchoate, emerging into visibility only as they enter the visual field of the numbers, spreadsheets, and abstractions that have become not merely representations of productive work but their own reality. The photograph has captured the essential substitution in the creation of the commodity fetish: the process that "transforms every product of labour into a social hieroglyphic."[26] We see both the phantasm and its effect, which is to make labor disappear from public consciousness. Of course many other photographs (particularly in advertising) promote comprehensive commodity fetishism, but by placing both the abstract symbols of market exchange and embodied labor (and consumption) in the same reflective space, equally present and equally ghostly, this photograph becomes an object for social thought.

The "real economy" of jobs and the virtual economy of finance are equally real, but they are not held to the same standards. Amid the neoliberalism governing economic globalization, labor too often has been rendered invisible. In its place is a phantasmal world of derivatives, debt-to-GDP ratios, stock-market indexes, and even unemployment statistics, and a refashioning of everyday life through bar codes and online shopping supported by globalized and increasingly automated production. Many people are still doing the work, of course, but the work and the people doing it are disappearing from public consciousness. As capital superimposes its image on labor, society acquires the form of a palimpsest, with the older values and social contract covered over by abstractions. Although the large-scale processes elude visibility, photography can nonetheless provide glimpses of the logics of superimposition and of how visibility is structured.

The transformation of labor may exceed any medium, but the question for both photography and society is whether it will be seen, recognized, and rewarded. Figure 29 depicts workers and a visitor at a German Oktoberfest. Needless to say, the photo is a bit different from the promotional images of cheery waitresses serving tall steins to happy customers. Whereas those stock photos mask actual working conditions, this photograph of people temporarily not working exposes what had been hidden. Now the workers are backstage, caught in an unguarded moment that might not be subject to company surveillance and proprietary control. The waitresses are on break, catching a smoke, making a phone call, and perhaps texting a message. These last details are informative: although still a part of the global data sphere depicted in the previous photo, the ratio of bodies to electronic display has been reversed. This is a place of physical work. Unlike the smiling faces and effortless activity seen in ads, these working people can be bored, tired, and having to manage the rest of their lives around the edges of their work, which is tightly scheduled and often includes having to deal with people, like the guy on the left, who are not exactly at their best.

The tableau may be grimmer still. Look again at the spaces between the four figures, as those channels of separation also are what is being shown. Another contrast emerges, along with those between working and taking a break from work and between being on stage and back stage. The folk costumes imply a folk community, a rich fabric of close association over long periods of time, with palpable

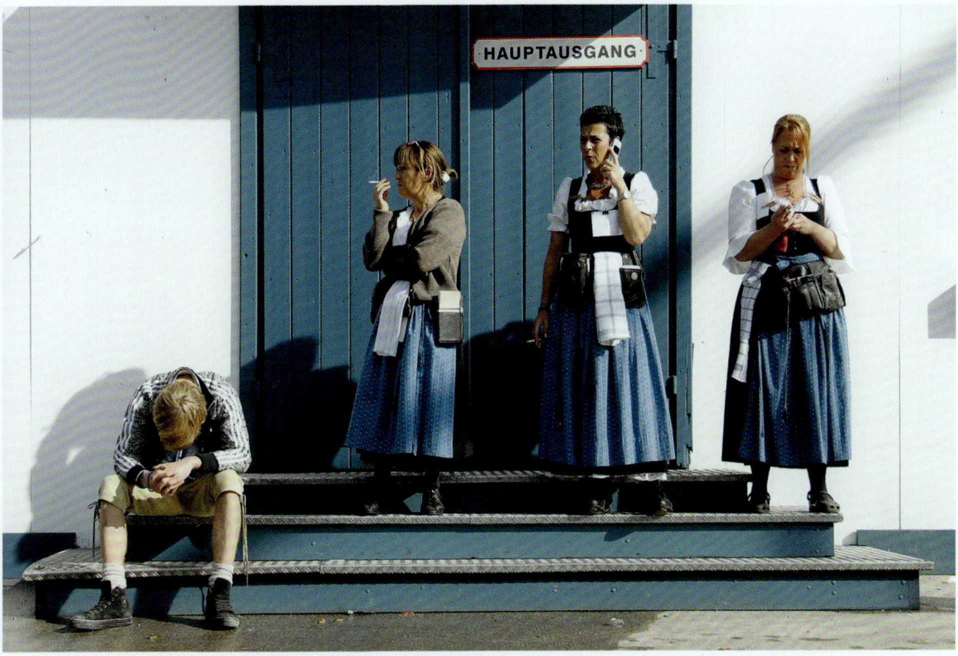

Figure 29. © AP Photo / Matthias Schrader.

bonds of kinship and familiarity and a stable foundation of shared beliefs. These assumptions are in part nostalgic, of course—a by-product of the modern society that replaced the folk cultures it now preserves for commercial purposes. The photograph captures this transformation: the four figures are individuals starkly separated from each other. Whether they are communicating via modern technologies with those not present, or present but having nothing to say to one another, the social space is defined by its distances. The common culture of their traditional clothing is an act for paying customers; at the end of the shift, the costumes will be taken off and replaced by blue jeans and other accessories of contemporary fashion. The dresses match the color of the steps and door, suggesting the deep homology of a traditional society, but the women stand on prefabricated gray industrial material. The photograph is a sociological study: *Gemeinschaft* and *Gesellschaft*, community and society, two ideal types as they actually are evident in ordinary experience, as the one way of life continues to transform the other.

Figures 28 and 29 could each be faulted for substituting an image for a complex economic reality, but isn't the better insight that they are showing other, much more powerful processes of substitution? Actual workers are being transformed into the flickering data of market behavior, and traditional cultures are being made into images of themselves for commercial appropriation. Photography has played a role in each of these changes, but so have many other technologies. Photography, however, is suited to becoming emblematic of the transformations wrought by modernization, and for that reason it also can provide a capacity for critical reflection.

The crux of the transformations wrought by modernization is the relationship between the individual and the social order. Individual autonomy, freedom, and rights are in fact extended, but only through systems of organization, from markets to rule of law, that are necessarily impersonal. The results in any specific case can be mixed. For example, note again how distance is part of what is being shown: the distance between workers on break contrasts with the nostalgic sense of community coded into their costumes. Isolation clearly is part of the modern experience of social structure, especially when that structure distributes goods according to class and other markers of relative inclusion or exclusion. The people in figure 29 are set apart as individuals and free to live their lives for better or worse on those terms, yet they also are very small and completely dispensable pieces in vast economic and technological networks.

That relationship might well be the subject of figure 30. The photograph features a world-class athlete at a warm-up event for the 2008 Summer Olympics. The diver is entrained with her background—black and white or black and gray, each is a study in geometric form. Oddly, she is placed off to the side, as if the building were the subject of interest and she were merely an ornament hanging there to complete the architect's design. The immensity of the horizontal space may imply an equally deep vertical drop, but the effect is not one of action or risk but rather of order, of individual and structure in perfect equipoise.

The idealization is advanced by how the photo features its ability to stop time. A dive that is a whirl of motion has been stopped, but for an instant, which allows one to see the high degree of expertise, discipline, and training required by modern sport on the global

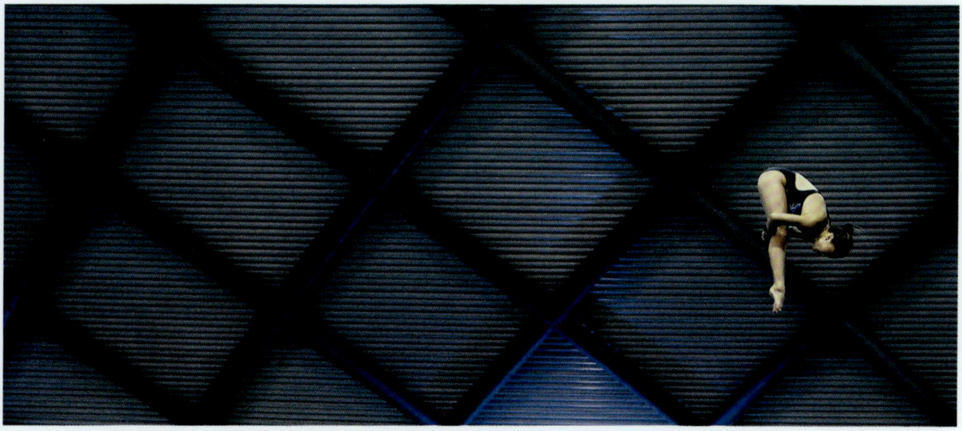

Figure 30. © Leon Neal / AFP / Getty Images.

stage. The curl of the toes, the right angle of the head from the upper torso—these along with every other part of her body exhibit extreme control, a perfect coordination of individual will and natural forces to achieve astonishing levels of athletic performance. Nonetheless, one cannot help knowing that she is plummeting toward the water. She is suspended for a brief moment of glory and then disappears. The individual athlete will drop from sight, but another will appear in her place, and another, and always as successive iterations of the same. The dives may differ, but the fall and much else is constant. The individual flies through the air, but the structure of repetition remains. It is modern society's answer to ritual.

CHAPTER SIX

WATCHING WAR

Imagine an image world full of nothing but smiling faces, pleasant occasions, and lovely vistas. Not even advertising is that uniform, but it is close enough that the rest can be visualized. The result would be ghastly: false, alienating, and yet pressuring the viewer to quash other emotions and conform all expression to the Happyville norm. Desire would be warped into sunny banality and fetishistic consumption, while conscience would atrophy.

Now imagine the opposite: an image world full of nothing but destruction, beatings, rape, torture, murder, and all the suffering of the victims and those around them. Photojournalism isn't nearly that explicit or comprehensive, but it is close enough that the rest can be brought to mind, especially because of the boost provided by television and film. The result would be horrific: fraught with confounding experiences of terror, revulsion, fascination, anger, sorrow, and depression, while provoking dangerous reactions ranging from self-loathing to cold, brutalizing indifference.

Photography has been faulted for taking society in both directions. On the one hand, it falsely "beautifies" the world, cosmetically remaking everything into a good picture or granting every mundane thing its day in the sun; doing so can enable denial of moral ugliness, while it plays to a society defined too much by consumerism and other distractions from political awareness.[1] Worse yet, when violence is shown, it is said to be "aestheticized": the transformation of real violence into visual artifact advances the political aesthetic of fascism while promoting voyeuristic objectification of the victims and pornographic enjoyment of their suffering.[2]

On the other hand, photography also has been faulted for the unsettling realism and pervasiveness of documentary reportage about war and other forms of physical violence.[3] Despite considerable respect for norms of decorum in image selection, and despite warnings at online news sites that allow viewers to skip potentially disturbing images, editors regularly are criticized for publishing photographs that some readers believe are too gory.[4] And instead of aesthetic buffering, persistent exposure to images of violence is believed to harm one's moral sense: photography can induce either compassion fatigue or a sense of helplessness, both of which inhibit political action to reduce the suffering of others.[5]

Offsetting critiques should not imply that photography is innocent. The new medium soon became complexly entangled with war, while lynch mobs, rapists, and drug lords have discovered that it can be a useful technology for humiliating and blackmailing their victims.[6] More "civilized" institutions are not excused, either. "After several decades of analyzing the structure of Jeremy Bentham's Panopticon, Hollywood's male gaze, the imperial colonialist gaze, and the racist gaze, we are now accustomed to accepting the idea that looking is often a mode of violence, an act embedded in regimes of power."[7] This complicity is highlighted by a critical phenomenology that finds the photograph to be inherently violent, as when the camera is said to shoot, cut, capture, rape, or kill.[8] More prosaically, studies of propaganda describe how photography is used to mobilize for war and other forms of state aggression.[9] Although such government control is supposed to be countered by the press serving as a watchdog on behalf of the public interest, the reality can be quite different. Government "embedding" requirements to control photographic access to the war zone are thought to be a significant restriction on what can be shown, while some regimes skip the niceties and censor, bludgeon, imprison, rape, or kill journalists who refuse to comply with the party line. In any contest between vision and violence, violence seems to have the upper hand.

Such concerns have had some influence on professional practice. As Liam Kennedy has demonstrated, some of the most influential conflict photographers of the last several decades have been laboring to develop more ethically sophisticated repertoires for representing violence.[10] For the most part, however, professional and public discussion has focused on relatively pragmatic questions about intervention, appropriateness, and censorship. Thus photographers are faulted for not dropping the camera to stop the perpetrators or help the victims, and the press is faulted for publishing images of graphic violence or death, and the state and any cooperating institutions are faulted for limiting access or censoring images. It can become easy for professionals to assume that they will be damned no matter what they do, while being resourceful enough to keep on doing it, and so the cycle continues.

As we have noted before, the general effect of these conversations is that public and academic commentators can conclude that photography is morally dead on arrival: already too fettered to expose the full trauma of human suffering, too compromised to bear documentary witness to evil, too ineffectual to speak truth to power, too enervating to provoke public action, and for these reasons and more, too complicit with the violence it would expose.[11] And as we have also noted, until recently the only widely circulated reconsideration has been the condescending claim that although it cannot provide moral knowledge, the photograph of extreme violence can shock viewers out of their presumed complacency into a rudimentary awareness of harm. Fortunately, neither photography nor human beings are that simple.

As Susie Linfield has argued eloquently, the photographic encounter with violence reflects the unnerving complexity of the human condition. Representations of violence are both riveting and incapable of full disclosure, emblems of horror and calls to conscience, inherently perverse and a deep form of solidarity. Against this understanding of the medium, Linfield has no patience with conventional critics: "They want the worst things on earth—the most agonizing, unjust things on earth—to be represented in ways that are not incomplete, imperfect, or discomfiting. Is there an unproblematic way to show the degradation of a person? Is there an untroubling way to portray the death of a nation? Is there an inoffensive way to document unforgivable violence? Is there a right way to look at any of this?"[12]

There is not, yet questions nag the portrayal of violence; given Linfield's insight, they would have to. Ariella Azoulay expresses a similar frustration, while giving more definition to the idealization that underlies the standard critique of photography. This "phantasmagoric model" is one where

> the much sought-after object of vision is a sort of pure object that makes it possible to see war with utter clarity. It is an ideal object of vision, which is why all the available images are either more or less than what is supposed to be offered.
>
> The other side of this passion for a pure object of vision, which no existing image can equal, is the passion for a pure spectator who will encounter the image, be appalled by what is revealed, and successfully change the world through her active response to it. Such a hope inevitably results in disappointment.[13]

In fact, images are "partial, obscured, fissured, and questionable," while viewers are constrained by many factors and forces. Sometimes the best to hope for is that one can "steady one's gaze," look at what is revealed, and speak on behalf of what is shown.[14] The photographic encounter with violence cannot do without critical and collective ideals, but it has to begin with humility.

That does not mean that either the old suspicions or more recent counterarguments provide a sufficient basis for thinking with the images of the wars burning like gas flares around the planet. (We will not succeed fully, either.) It is not enough, moreover, to credit photography for its capacity to provoke ethical reflection (as Sontag came to do in her later work), or to provide an emotional connection to the reality of individual suffering (as Linfield emphasizes), or to invoke a social contract grounded in spectatorship (as Azoulay does). These are important elements of the photographic encounter, but the image of violence is doing much more as well.

We believe that photography is an important medium for understanding and confronting violence, particularly the violence of war. There are indeed obvious limits on the medium's ethical capability, but its absence only benefits the perpetrators. Equally important, photographic evidence often can cut through verbal rationalizations that are much more powerful means for damping moral response. Even so, such relatively "extrinsic" effects still do not do justice to the depth of the photographic image or the breadth of the archive. Indeed the entire question of effects is somewhat misplaced.

Consider how much lies between what we might call the psychological and global boundaries of photography's capacity for influence. On the one hand, seeing does not convert directly to action. If it did, we would be very primitive life forms or automata: wholly reactive, incapable of thinking or making decisions about our perceptual inputs. Instead we have the good fortune to be able to mediate perception, which has led to the development of prosthetic extensions of the brain's capacity for imaging. Were photographic effects more reliable, we wouldn't have been able to develop photography in the first place. On the other hand, there is reason to believe that photography has been essential to the development and widespread acceptance of modern conceptions of humanity and human rights, and one factor in the relative reduction in violence in the modern era.[15] As Steven Pinker and others have demonstrated, primitive societies' rates of death by conflict were staggering in modern terms—roughly 15 percent of the population—and the carnage included torture, the slaughter of women and children, and genocide as relatively common practices.[16] The fact that such practices have been reduced, and that where they persist they have to be hidden, is due in part to the role of photography in human rights advocacy.[17] Thus the synapse between any photograph and behavioral response is always unreliable, and yet global adoption of the medium has improved the moral context for observing all human behavior.

The use of photography to understand and manage violence can reflect what it means to live between these end points. When one then considers the incredible force of war and the inertia that it acquires, the idea that one could simply see carnage and throw oneself against the war machine appears absurd. As James Nachtwey has stated, "The greatest statesmen, philosophers, humanitarians . . . have not been able to put an end to war. Why place that demand on photography?"[18] And yet, as Linfield reminds us, even though images document that we arrive too late, that justice will never be met, and that the suffering of the victims will never be redeemed, the same archive also testifies to the dignity of the victims, the scandal of abandonment, and the possibility of change.[19] We believe that it provides not only cause for hope but also some of the tools that are needed to convert the slaughter pens of the present into a more habitable world. To that end, one might consider how the photographic archive provides a daunting but illuminating anthropology of contemporary violence.

The first step in this program of study is to acknowledge the scope and variety of the image world that we do inhabit. Admittedly, it is a world of smiley faces and Shock and Awe, and of canned emotions painting over habitual indifference, and the worst effects reflect ever-present tendencies toward either delusion or brutalization, which are two kinds of tyranny. Let us consider, however, what else is being shown. The images of war also include American generals looking completely at home in an imperial palace; bagged bodies being lifted into the industrial maw of an armored transport vehicle; a boy stricken with fear as soldiers ransack his home during a raid; a severely wounded soldier and his wife mired in depression and bitterness; a father collapsing in grief . . .

These and many other images every day have filled out an image world that reflects a real world of suffering, hubris, folly, perseverance, and much more. Although constrained by many factors, these images are not merely propaganda, entertainment, or a substitute for documentary witnessing. Instead of driving us toward extreme states of media dependency, they provoke engagement with a world of power and pain that otherwise could be easily ignored. They remind us that for many living in the world today, the media are the least of their problems. They challenge the spectator not simply to act but to think about actions already taken and their implications for a shared future. Most important, they show how war and related forms of violence today are not exceptional events in relatively isolated fields of battle, but rather a continuous disruption of ordinary life that millions of people have to adapt to, pay for, and endure without end.

The critical discourse on photography appears increasingly outmoded in this world. That should not be surprising, as it reflected historically specific developments in both political violence and media technologies. Despite many geopolitical and technological changes, however, the limitations are not what one might think: fascism does remain a serious threat, the decreased likelihood of Great Power conflict hasn't made a dent in military budgets, and many photojournalists are killed every year in the line of duty. Instead, as with any paradigm shift, old questions are not settled so much as redefined while being partially displaced by different problems and methods.

Instead of fretting about photography's moral and rhetorical limitations, we offer a conception of the art as it can be an anthropology of violence. Obviously the metaphor doesn't escape the old critique, as the histories of both anthropology and photography include ethnic profiling on behalf of imperial conquest.[20] The goal is not moral purity, however, but to appreciate what has been accomplished subsequently—in this case, to understand how photojournalism is recording the relationship between everyday life and larger forces of domination, disruption, and change. Likewise, the habit of focusing on small, subordinate societies fits well with the distribution of violence today. Precisely because major-power conflict is largely neutralized, the margins of the global system become the most representative sectors. Video clips from the aircraft carrier and flyovers at the football game depict the awesome power of the imperial state, but there are other stories, one of which might become the future, that are being acted out in the seams of the geopolitical system. Moreover, were an order of violence to emerge that was not defined by the state's monopoly on violence and the institutional practices of international relations, then it would be likely to become visible at the margins: in failed states and quasi-states, occupied territories and zones of anarchy. Photography is already there, documenting the texture of destruction that is unfurling around the globe.[21]

If a new discourse of photography is to emerge, it must be able to follow how photography has taken the lead among the public arts in documenting the changes in modern violence that seem to elude conflict resolution and the restoration of something like peace. That is an unending task, but we will suggest that photography has been cataloging important changes in the nature of war, including untethered violence, regime-made disasters, refeudalization, and normalization. Such claims are admittedly provisional, not least because they identify symptoms rather than causes. The tendencies being identified are there to be seen, however, and they can motivate important commitments regarding spectatorship.

This perspective inherits a sense of visual history. For photography, as for much else, World War II continues to be thought of as "the good war," one whose pictorial archive seems aligned with ethical imperatives and sanctions.[22] If that archive culminates in Holocaust photographs, the story is complete. As it happens, however, the archive also included photographs from Hiroshima and Nagasaki, and so the first hints of ethical ambiguity emerged.[23] Subsequent wars became a story of ethical unraveling: Korea was a lesson in hubris, anticolonial wars of liberation led to decades of dictatorship, Vietnam proved to be one of a series of neocolonial fiascos, successive wars in Israel have produced the world's largest ghetto, and the second US invasion of Iraq demonstrated how US leaders refused to learn the lesson of their own imperial legacy. Nonetheless, a set of twentieth-century assumptions about modern warfare remain pervasive articles of belief: war is politics by other means, military forces fight primarily against each other rather than civilians, war is becoming less prevalent amid progressive globalization, and billions of people are now experiencing peace as a stable condition of modern life. Each of these assumptions underwrites important features of modern society, from civilian control of the military to increased integration of the global economy, and they should not be taken lightly. That said, each idea is increasingly subject to exceptions. As the exceptions multiply, it becomes possible that war is changing in a manner that appears progressive but nevertheless is quite dangerous, and we might already be able to see the features of an emerging order of twenty-first-century violence. There is no morality play to be had here: the Army is not evil, and Art is not redemptive. What can be said, however, is that photography is documenting how each of the stabilizing features of the familiar world is crumbling.

Untethered Violence

In place of the idea that war is politics by other means, Linfield has argued eloquently that violence "has become less tethered to its political aims." Drawing on the emotionally exhausting encounter with photographs of mutilated children from Sierra Leone, adding to that all we know about the brutality and scale of destruction in the African wars, and contrasting it to identification with the fighters of the Spanish Civil War, World War II, and the wars of colonial liberation, Linfield confronts the profound disintegration of a previous structure of feeling, moral response, and political action.

The breakdown is comprehensive. First, war itself has become disengaged from ideology. This is not merely the loss of a rationale: in place of being motivated, directed, and constrained by political objectives, the conflicts become wars of disintegration. "Such conflicts are expressions not of imperial expansion, national liberation, socialist revolution, or even fascist counterrevolution, but are more akin to auto-exterminations."[24] Linfield recognizes that these wars do have causes, but she emphasizes that conventional analysis in terms of political objectives cannot explain, for example, the horrific escalation from "the battle over the Congo's coltan reserves to the carving up of young girls' vaginas."[25]

A second breakdown follows: faced with endless, senseless violence, the viewer is cut off from identification with agents of change. There are no political leaders, idealistic volunteers, or even martyrs for the cause. "Internationalists drew their spirit and their energy not only from a protective concern for helpless victims but from a positive identification with fighters for just causes. In the post–cold war conflicts, this sort of connection—this sort of fraternity—is more and more difficult to find. Indeed, it may be a luxury we can no longer afford."[26] The loss is both moral and political. Without ethical direction and political purpose, one's affective response to the image of victimization is pitched headlong into mere emotionalism and worse—the emotion of pity, and then, as one confronts one's helplessness, of self-pity. Conscientious encounter with the actual war becomes displaced by one's painful encounter with the image, and so most people will simply turn away. There is little else one can do, as the loss of political reason also means that there are no reliable channels for political action. Comparing the maimed child in Sierra Leone with the victims of the Spanish Civil War, Linfield notes that viewers then "had a pretty good idea of what was to be done," as the conflict existed within a realm of "traditional political aims and understandings."[27] As violence becomes disconnected from any mechanism for conflict resolution, the rest of the world becomes incapable of knowing how to respond. It would seem, then, that continued exposure to images of senseless brutality would only extend moral and political paralysis.

Linfield's argument requires some caveats. One problem is that of legibility and ethnocentricism. An apparent absence of purpose may be merely an absence of some *familiar* purposes and perhaps a romantic ideal lodged within the European state system. Motives that are not legible to a particular viewer are still motives. A more ethnographic immersion in the wars would have to confront the appalling violence against civilians but might find that it was not merely violence for its own sake. Assessment is further complicated by the fact that the images cannot help evoking deeply rooted racial ideologies: Africa is still dark, it seems, and it may be too easy to assume that raw emotions prevail there. Linfield acknowledges these and other complications, but the result could be another reason for some viewers to conclude that political action would be hopeless. A third concern is that the argument, despite its attempt to identify a transformation under way in this specific historical moment, cannot help but reinscribe historical amnesia. The Crusades, the sack of any city (say the sack of Rome in 1527), and many other episodes provide plenty of evidence of how violence can become untethered from an ideological superstructure. Thus the point might be better put if we considered how violence was becoming untethered once again and attended to how the causes involved more than an absence of political aims. And of course plenty of international violence, including highly visible examples of both terrorism and conventional military operations, continues to be driven by ideology and institutions.[28] Finally, one has to say that for those who are being destroyed, it really doesn't matter whether violence is rationalized or not. Nazi extermination camps remain the model of tethered violence, and one would never define that slaughter as reasonable or constrained. Even so, Linfield demonstrates how the study of photography can provide a profound examination of the nature of violence in the early twenty-first century.

It also is important to stress that untethered violence represents a shift in the conditions of visibility. Compared to major military offensives, carpet bombing, and prolonged battles that can be given place-names, now horrific violence occurs at the relatively small scale of plundering a village or kidnapping children. Likewise, much of it occurs well away from major media coverage. Racism could be involved, but there are many more obstacles as well, including the economic and political status of a region and lack of an obvious reason to cover events that seem to have no purpose, no basis for response, and no remedy. And although amputated limbs have horrific visual salience, it is difficult to depict the horrors of gang rape, sexual mutilation, sexual slavery, and forced conscription of child soldiers.

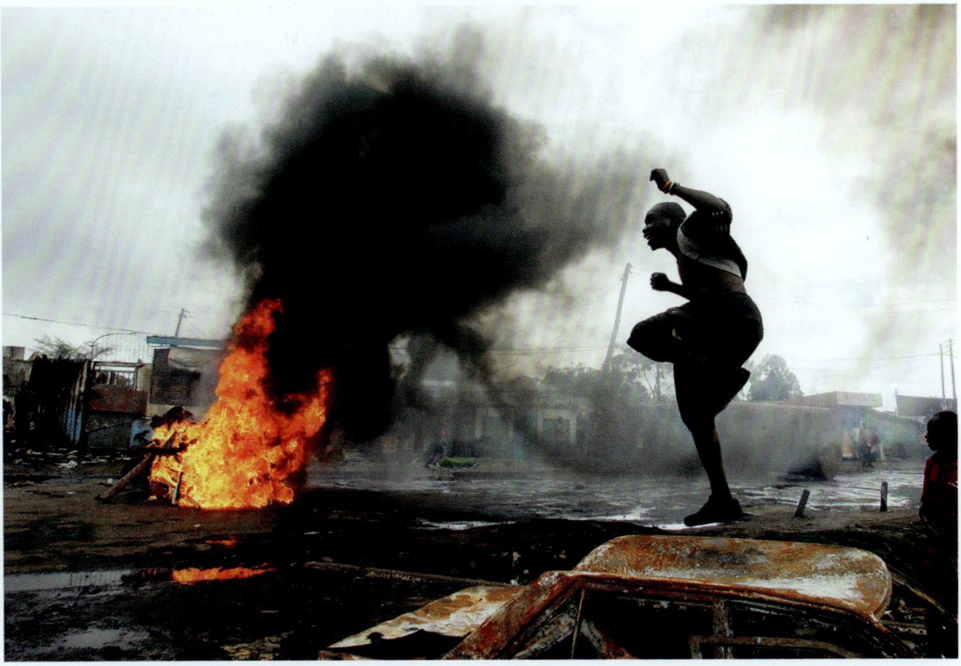

Figure 31. © Simon Maina / AFP / Getty Images.

Even if the attacks could be photographed, the trauma can be either too graphic or largely invisible and in any case a long way from the conventions of military journalism. So it is that photographers have had to become more artistically inventive to record how violence is spreading and changing. Figure 31 is illustrative in this regard.

A man dances on the roof of a ruined car before a bonfire in a slum. Wreckage of one sort or another extends in every direction as fire and the thick black smoke of burning tires billows upward. There are no weapons or uniforms or war dead, or any sign of warfare or the state, and yet the photo from Kenya's civil crisis of 2007–8 is unmistakably a portrait of violence. But what kind of violence? The photo tells us little about the crisis, and certainly not who the man is, which side he is on, how this slum matters in the conflict or its resolution, or what issues are at stake. Perhaps it could be placed with images from around the globe of civic protest turned violent; typically these are photographs of demonstrators battling with police or rival mobs. Those images look much the same, however, as if there were one long-running political spectacle in the theater of the Arab / African / Asian / Latin American / North American / European street. The images are legible, and the violence depicted generally relates to clearly defined antagonisms. By contrast, here we see only destruction and dancing combined, and the photograph itself seems untethered.

That may be why this image is at once familiar and scandalous. Instead of the stock characters of dissenting citizens and bullying cops, or mob frenzy and state terror, or soldiers and guerrilla fighters, or any other political scenario, we see a man exulting in the sheer ecstasy of destruction. An obscene truth is being revealed: what is violence and burning and horror to some is for others an experience of raw freedom that can be perversely but powerfully known only through violent revenge and ruin. The sound track could be the Ode to Joy—as heard in *A Clockwork Orange*.

One might ask whether this photograph exemplifies an analytical mistake: Is the untethering argument an artifact of decontextualization? Would putting image and event back into the original context reveal how violence is tethered? The short answer is yes, but that answer also can mislead. It is true that the civil strife in Kenya was legible according to standard political and ethnic ascriptions, and that legibility is evident in or consistent with the caption for the photograph. Opposition leaders had called for political rallies to protest a rigged election; if the situation descended into anarchy, mob rule, and horrific violence, local knowledge was a short step away for anyone following the news, and the initial motives were still part of the mix.[29] At the same time, the language of "elections," "rallies," "opposition leaders," "ethnic groups," and "civil war" misses important features of how violence can spin out of control. Likewise, the corresponding supposition that violence must be tethered contains questionable assumptions about both human nature and the spasms of destructiveness disrupting large areas of the world. In addition, the evidence compiled by Linfield and others includes many photographs that are part of highly detailed documentary accounts. The basic problem, however, is that the reasonable question about political legibility can also carry a forensic perspective that will never be able to recognize what hides behind the mask of rationalization. If one grants that violence can lead to more violence beyond reason, then the door is open to considering also that decontextualization can aid recognition of untethering as it actually occurs.

Thus the photograph is valuable because it captures how violence can become disconnected from political legibility. Stated otherwise, to see what the photograph can add to an anthropology of violence, we need to look at the image without seeing it solely through the original caption, which refers to events in a single place and time. Its occasional reproduction suggests that its value lies not in reproducing specific features of the Kenyan situation but rather in capturing fundamental anxieties about twenty-first-century warfare.[30] In its most decontextualized incarnation, it reveals a truth fueling explosions of carnage around the globe: that anarchy and uncontrolled violence can involve not only terrible victimization but also full-throated pleasure. And one can easily imagine how anarchy and hatred could spread from there to create a chain reaction that would unleash horror across an entire region. By capturing a moment that seems primarily, if perversely, aesthetic rather than political in any conventional sense, the photographer has captured something vital and terrible about the way that war can break loose from political restraints. Yet the photograph also is subject to concerns raised earlier: violence seems inescapably racialized, and one should recognize that even slums have a structure and that the seeming lack of political reason here would say more about the audience than the image. In fact, the option of a more legible response may be coded into the image via the other figure, barely visible in the right margin of the photo. That same figure also underscores the photograph's ability to signify more than one dimension of the scene, and also perhaps the likelihood of valorizing more restrained forms of spectatorship. Whatever the interpretive focus, the image compels more than balanced deliberation: it challenges the viewer to recognize that war can mutate far beyond reasons of state, and that as violence spreads humanity can end up dancing in hell.

The Regime-Made Disaster

War is not one thing, however, and Linfield's model is not the only way to bear witness. Ariella Azoulay has identified the regime-made disaster as one of the distinctive forms of war in our time. The term describes the condition of a population that is deprived of resources and otherwise injured to the point where it is just above becoming a humanitarian disaster, and then kept there. Azoulay argues that Israeli governing techniques keep the Palestinians in the Occupied Territories and Gaza in this condition indefinitely.[31] Were the subject population actually dying in the streets from starvation, that would be evidence of criminal misrule by the occupying authorities. If they were conscripted for forced labor, that would be another obvious violation of international law. However, if the population is able to eat but has to devote inordinate time and energy to get to work while continually being subjected to shortages of power and of other resources necessary for economic and civic development, then there is little basis for international military intervention.

This system of military partitioning and administration includes its own conditions of visibility. The regime-made disaster produces a continuous stream of suffering but not massed or spectacular suffering. Untethered violence metastasizes in areas far removed from intensive Western media coverage but often can be immediately condemned by media exposure; by contrast, the regime-made disaster usually operates below the threshold of demonstrable violence and produces effects that can be mistaken for the ordinary vicissitudes of a hard life. Hence the paradox: on one hand, it occurs within the full glare of media coverage; on the other hand, it is hard to confront a process of continuous but distributed deprivations. A farmer has to go through a checkpoint to get to his fields, or a pregnant woman to get to a hospital, and the checkpoint can involve lengthy, uncomfortable, frustrating, frightening delays, and might be closed unexpectedly at any time, and *is* closed time and again when someone desperately needs it to be open. But what does one show: a line of people waiting (they don't look like they are starving)? a guard standing by an empty road (that has been closed for hours)? When violence is distributed through a system of state practices and often reduced to the "petty sovereign" making decisions at a checkpoint, the result is a comprehensive assault on civil society, but in a manner that is visually banal.[32]

So it is that the regime-made disaster depends on the very mechanisms that should alleviate it. These include humanitarian aid and Western media coverage. Consider each case. Because the situation is obviously distressed but not to an extent that justifies military intervention, it invites humanitarian responses. The subject territory becomes dotted with aid agencies, which help people live on the verge of catastrophe but also inadvertently define the situation as humanitarian (like a famine) rather than political (like a civil war). Were they to withdraw, the result would be an unmitigated disaster, leading to international condemnation and more costly administration by the occupying power. But they do not withdraw, and thus they help to stabilize what should be seen as an unacceptable use of state power. The same holds for media coverage: because the media are drawn to the few violent exchanges that do occur, their presence constrains overt violence, which motivates further refinement of the less overt mechanisms for domination, which can continue to be hidden in plain sight for want of a spectacular quality. Any flare-up leads to images of physical destruction and funereal rituals, whereas there remains little reason to photograph a freeway running through the Territories even though Palestinians are prohibited from using it and have to use a winding dirt road instead. Photography, a vital medium for the humanitarian project, becomes, if not quite an instrument of domination, neutralized on behalf of abusive state power.

That is not Azoulay's conclusion, however: instead she argues that photography provides essential means for exposing the regime-made disaster and developing an alternative conception of citizenship. The regime is exposed when visual literacy is developed as a civic skill: specifically, the ability to see how a photograph documents both regimes of domination and an inescapable plurality of experience. Thus one should learn to read the traces left by past violence and distributed violence and to recognize other perspectives, especially what is seen by those for whom the status quo is a catastrophe. This visual literacy carries with it a civic relationship: the civil contract of photography, which declares that photographic subjects and spectators are oriented toward each other in a condition of equality independent of any governing authority or attribution of civic status. That attitude has particular relevance to conflict zones, occupied territories, and borderlands, and photography becomes a cultural resource for overturning an insidious form of warfare.

Warfare, for example, where there need not be soldiers, or guns, or courage. The photo in figure 32 appeared on page A8 of the morn-

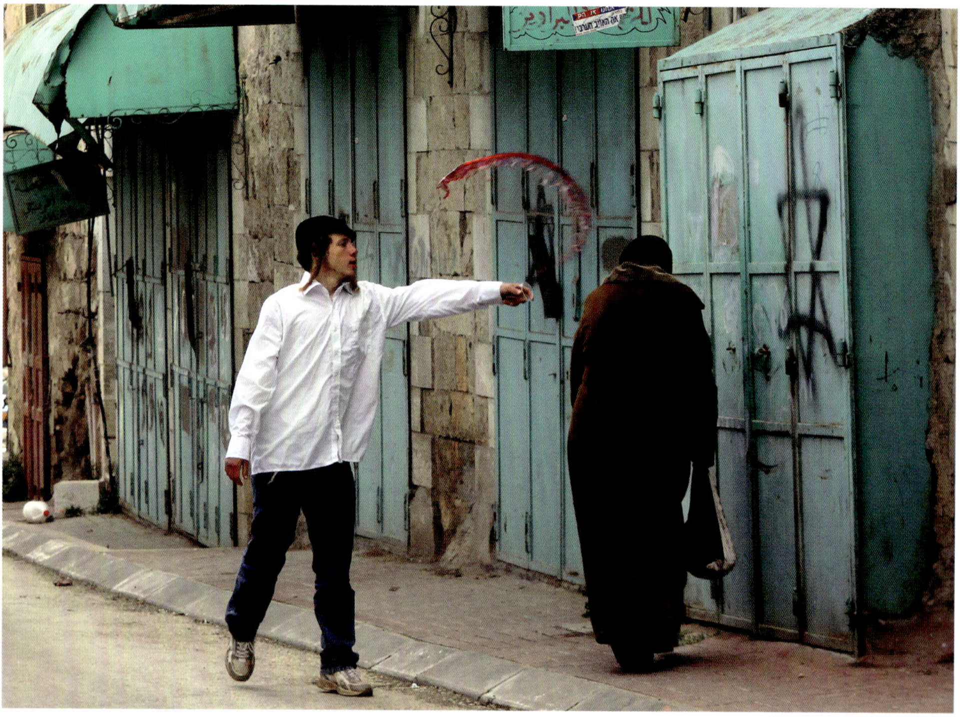

Figure 32. © Rina Castelnuovo / The New York Times / Redux.

ing edition of the *New York Times* with this caption: "Tinderbox in Hebron, a Jewish settler threw wine at a Palestinian woman. The city is a center of tensions between settlers and Palestinians."[33] The complete set of images, which included a photo on page 1 of an Israeli child being bathed and three other photos on page 8 labeled "Veneration," "Remembrance," and "Preparation," clearly favored the Israeli settlers. Even so, the photo of the settler throwing wine undercuts the myth of taming the frontier in the Holy Land.

But why does it shock? He is not hitting her, and surely spraying her with wine is less of a crime than, say, razing a house with a military bulldozer. Or blowing up a bus with a suicide bomber. Since there is violence enough on both sides, why make so much of a minor incident of teenage insolence? One reason to do so is that the photograph reveals what is rarely shown: the small acts of personal viciousness and humiliation that make up the practice of domination in an occupied land. The argument of the more and the less also applies: if a boy can do this, imagine what adults can do, and if a civilian acts so imperiously, imagine what soldiers at checkpoints will do. Even more important, it is clear that both the boy's aggression and the woman's self-protective reaction are often-practiced, habitual responses. Were he taunting an older woman for the first time, he would be likely to look much more ragged, uncoordinated, and either furtive or overly demonstrative. Instead he could be a figure out of Whitman: throwing his weight around without breaking stride, a figure of youthful grace on the city street. Likewise, she isn't being caught by surprise. Her head is already turned, her body hunched against the impending blow. She's been through this before, and she's learned that direct confrontation is not an option. This may be her neighborhood, but it's his street.

The photograph's power also derives from its capacity for analogy. Look at the woman's coat and hat and at the Star of David scrawled on the storefront; she could be in a German ghetto, and all it takes is a change of costume to see him as a German soldier. Or they could be an African American woman and a young white teenager in the Jim Crow South. Whatever the comparison, it stems from recognizing that a regime of violence can become deeply embedded in the habits and personalities of those in the space of domination, and that it is at once evident on the surface of things and yet seemingly banal, highly constrained, and not even overtly political.

Part of the artistry of this photograph, which rightly won a World Press Photo award, is that the underlying structure of power has been exposed through an incidental but visually salient moment. The stream of blood-red wine arcing through the air snaps like a whip from the young tough to the older woman. The green metal facades provide just enough color to accentuate the overall shabbiness of the neighborhood: a place kept on the verge of catastrophe by the continual run of shortages, blackouts, curfews, lockouts, and embargos. Even the temporality of the image is significant, as the obviously ephemeral action will leave only a trace of its violence: the stain on her clothing, requiring the choice of whether to bear the cost of removing it or the humiliation of continuing to wear it. The regime-made disaster benefits from specific conditions of visibility, but even so it is there to be seen.

That said, power is not likely to grow out of the lens of a camera. Azoulay has demonstrated how photography exposes a distinctive and powerful mode of violence in our time, but her argument is not without problems. One qualification pertains not to Azoulay herself but to the likely use of her work, which is to assume that the regime-made disaster is a recent innovation. One could say that Ireland was a regime-made disaster for centuries, and one that didn't depend on unintended effects in media coverage. A more pointed objection is that in the Palestinian case, and perhaps others as well, the subject population and the allied state actors bear some responsibility for the nature and longevity of the disaster. A third concern is that intentionality can appear both essential for judgment and difficult to identify. The system of social partitioning, military administration, destruction of infrastructure, embargoing of trade, and the like may reflect an original intention to divide and conquer, but it also seems to develop much more impersonally, and it then can operate without ordinary people having extraordinary motivations. That is, the system can produce dysfunctional polities on both sides, but at the end of the day there seems to be no one to blame.

The visual record is compromised as well. One problem is that the archive is by necessity made up of fragments and traces. Regime dominance influences media coverage, and there have been few visually salient incidents to record anyway. Second, the hermeneutic can appear circular: to see the traces of prior partitions or deprivations, or to see the plurality necessary for an alternative "potential history," one has to already assume that damage has been done and that responsibility lies primarily on one side.[34] Third, when civic literacy becomes yoked to a forensic attitude, as often happens, one can be held hostage to technical standards that, given the rest of the situation, are not likely to provide a basis for pressing charges. This case becomes even more difficult if one is confronting the origin myth of the state, as Azoulay is doing in her work as a political dissenter.[35] Regardless of the stakes, the final difficulty is that the civil contract of photography will seem idealistic—that is, too much at odds with the realities of state power and the fact that human rights still depend on protections provided by state citizenship.

Yet this is precisely where photography's capacity for moral witness comes to the fore. The photograph's call on the spectator is not a juridical obligation but a mode of recognition and empathy grounded in everyday experience. The political situation in the West Bank is complicated, snarled, difficult to untangle, but it is not beyond understanding how power affects character and how anger is internalized.[36] Apportioning blame across a half-century of war is not easy, while verbal constructions of moral equivalence remain the easy default, but one can see how power is not symmetrical and how it involves random physical and psychological assaults on the weak. No image should trump all other considerations, but what the image can do is communicate the social knowledge that is necessary for adequate moral judgment and legitimate political action. By framing a performance of domination in a vernacular setting, the photograph features the regime's scope geographically, behaviorally, and psychologically; it presents that exercise of power in the terms of a familiar moral context (would you want your child doing this, or this done to your mother?); and it makes that context one basis for participation in the public debate.

This mode of recognition and empathic participation is particularly important for the challenge of confronting the regime-made disaster. Recall how this mode of control is able to deflect criticism because the violence only rarely attains the visibility of a battle—and then seemingly in response to a provocation rather than as a continuous operation of logistical interdiction. All that one has are banal settings and ordinary frustrations: Waiting at a checkpoint can look like waiting in traffic, so what's the big deal? Refugee camps can have streetlights and hospitals, so how can that be so bad? This relative advantage in avoiding moral scrutiny has its own weak spot, however: the degradation of everyday life can be evident in very small things, which the small language of photography can communicate effectively. One can see and connect in a way that will never match the grand strategies of great powers, but it can make the spectator another factor in their equations.

There is another point to consider as well. If patterns of degradation evident in the camps are spreading elsewhere—say, in the spectator's own society—it cannot hurt to have seen them before, and now perhaps to be able to see them for what they are: not accidental irregularities in the economy or political process but another deliberate disaster that is the result of, and for the benefit of, those who could prevent it.

Refeudalization

Modernity is supposed to move forward, not backward. In politics any reference to regression, devolution, or primitivism is negative: brutality will be called "medieval," "savage," "beastly," even if it involves torture and killing conducted by modern states with modern technologies. And much of the time the production of violence itself is moving forward, becoming ever more professionalized, efficient, and constrained. Time is a funny thing, however. Even as violence is becoming less of a concern in many affluent nations, it is morphing, metastasizing, spreading throughout areas of the world that had been relatively civil. These eruptions can be explained as, for example, the continuing disruption and realignments occasioned by the midcentury collapse of colonialism, or as a result of the wide-open global arms market and the oil and drug money that fuels it. These and many other factors will be present, but one should not be too quick to explain too thoroughly. There is need as well to look for any signs that some change is not yet being recognized for what it is or could become. If the apparent anomalies prove to be trivial or easily explained, then not much time has been lost. What photography might do, however, is provide evidence of changes that just don't compute.

One sign of an unexpected future might be evident in how warfare is producing a steady accumulation of ruins. Beirut, Sarajevo, Grozny, Baghdad, Aleppo—when it comes to the utter destruction of cities, no one even makes the pretense of saying "never again." What is equally important is how the ruins persist: Instead of a Marshall Plan for reconstruction, the world is becoming littered with trashed buildings, broken roads, burned-out tanks, and other examples of an infrastructure of abandonment, while people cope as best they can. Neither occasions for renewal nor remnants of a classical civilization, these ruins might be signs that some already are living amid the shadows of an impending dark age. Instead of being temporary, these swaths of destruction seem to be harbingers of even more gun running, militia violence, and other patterns of dysfunction. Where once people lived in vibrant communities, now they live in Rubble World, a development with exciting growth prospects in the twenty-first century. The future may involve a particularly perverse form of creative destruction: one in which the new city is being created by the same machines that are destroying the old one.

This geographic change is coincident with other changes in political action and in the way that power is exercised and exposed through display. One of the characteristics of contemporary politics is that street demonstrations are becoming an increasingly important part of the political process.[37] The political action that then becomes most salient is the riot. Riots happen more often than you might think around the globe. When they happen in London, Vancouver, or other upscale locales, the shocked response is always the same: how could that happen *here*? The combination of a European locale and the seeming lack of reason have led some to label such violence a "peasants' revolt."[38] The modern world is not supposed to contain peasants, and thus irrational behavior by the urban masses can be dismissed as a throwback to more primitive impulses. This dismissal may be prophetic, however, or at least point to aesthetic changes that may be signs of deeper transformations in social organization.

For example, instead of inspiring images of democratic solidarity, some of the images coming out of Cairo, Athens, Kiev, and many other cities are becoming surreal—as in figure 33. He is so distinctive that you can even see another photographer in the picture trying to get the shot. The bizarre gas mask is hardly standard issue, and its white rubber both contrasts with his dark clothing and matches the white smoke pouring out of the tear gas canister. The smoke streams back along his path as he runs forward, for this is definitely an action shot: a revolutionary in action. The photograph captures key features of a popular revolt defined more by its opposition to a corrupt establishment than by a shared vision of what the new polity should be. Yet even the sense of opposition is scrambled by that alien, almost unintelligible mask. He doesn't fit any available category, so what are we seeing?

Although surely human, he looks grotesquely simian, as if political demonstrations were a form of devolution. Worse yet, this falling backward is also a cyborg projection into a future in which organic and mechanical natures have been horribly fused. The close-fitting headpiece reveals a human skull in all its distinctiveness and fragility, yet the mechanical mask destroys any hope of wholly human

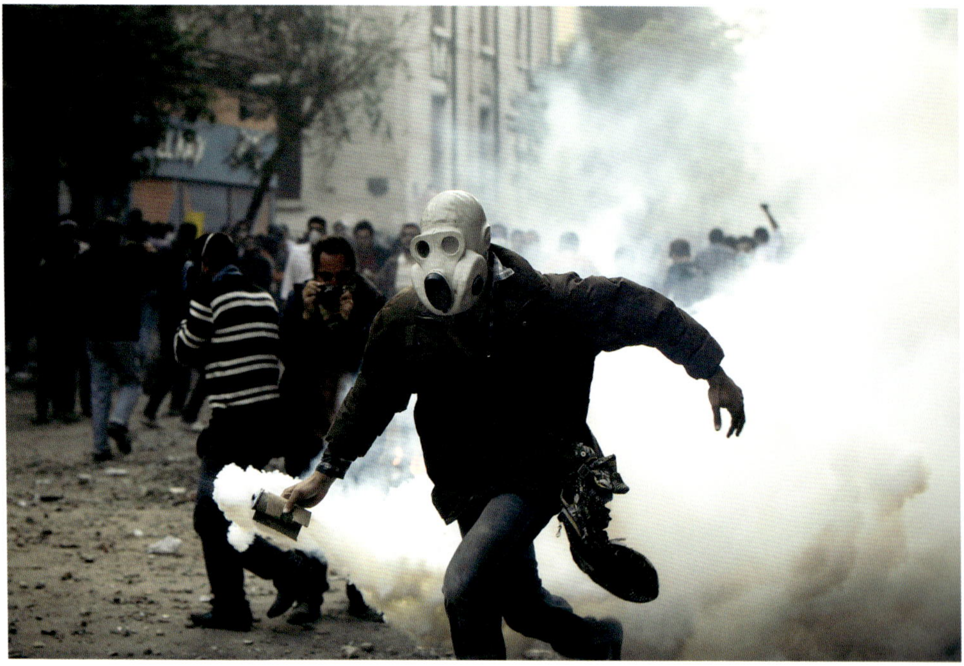

Figure 33. © AP Photo / Tara Todras-Whitehill.

sympathies. The bare hands make the dark clothing seem like a pelt, while the loping limbs suggest a life alternating between predation and flight. The bag hanging below his waist looks like another limb and thus another example of organic life distorted, whether by bad science or by the pressures of a harsh environment. Five-limbed with a machined face, he provides little basis for identification. Nonetheless, he might be a transitional figure.

To take a page from science fiction, technological progress can proceed with and contribute to regression along every other dimension of human experience: social organization, economics, politics, culture, you name it. Thus rather than merely supporting or undercutting the demonstrations, photographs such as figure 33 might be working more prophetically to identify how a harmful future is emerging in the present. Along the way, they also are showing how ordinary people are already coping symptomatically with deprivations and more explicit forms of systemic violence, adapting to those harsh conditions at the very moment that they are fighting against them. This is one place where imaginative projection and realist encounter intersect: the provisional, ragged bricolage of everyday life in the war zone requires stitching together fragments of a history still in the making.

Susan Sontag argued that photography was essentially, "natively" surreal—and that was not a compliment. Its "takeover of the modern sensibility" created a "reality in the second degree" that was "more dramatic than the one perceived by natural vision," ruled by accident rather than intention, drawn to exotica, extremes of wealth or poverty, and the city's "dark seamy corners" rather than its "official realities," and creating "abrupt changes in the social level and ethical importance of subject matter" rather than respecting hierarchies. Sontag was nothing if not bold, for she was claiming that a medium defined as inherently realistic was in fact surreal. Nor did she pull her punches normatively: surrealism was a "bourgeois disaffection," the medium of middle-class fantasy life and a technology of acquisitiveness.[39]

It is true that photography, like surrealism, has "always courted accidents, welcomed the uninvited, flattered disorderly presences."[40] (Apparently an art should know whom not to invite to the dinner party.) And one can imagine the generals and other elites seeing the masked figure on the street in Cairo in much the same way: this is photography theatricalizing politics and pretending that those pushing up from below are fascinating, when in fact the stability of the society depends on a firm hand maintaining social order. There is another perspective to be taken, however, which is that the admittedly surreal spectacle may be closer to reality than the more standard photographs of more orderly confrontations.[41] Not closer to the reality of the political conflict, which is indeed defined primarily by conventional political ideals, organizations, and maneuvers. Instead some of the images may be apertures in time, showing not how the past has come to a head in the present but how the present may become part of a different movement of time, a movement backward into another "reality in the second degree" that will in time fill out and become all too much a part of a world of ordinary vision.

The simian cyborg is neither modern nor medieval, but he does represent the often surreal nature of violence in our time. When change has gotten ahead of conventional political labels, the emerging reality may become evident in small changes that are identified through analogies, as when demonstrators are labeled peasants. As those analogies begin to accumulate, perhaps a corresponding political aesthetic is emerging as well: for example, one in which the apparatus of power can look at once modern and medieval. Admittedly, sometimes costumes are just that, and the surface rarely expresses unerringly what lies below, but we believe that these changes in style can reflect far more troubling changes in political relationships. As only signs of potential futures found among anonymous actors in fleeting events, they may not amount to much. But what if the analogy holds for the state?

Consider figure 34. As if a scene from Middle Earth, faceless legions with body armor and shields are massed in the winter half-light. They stand in crude uniformity, waiting to be unleashed against another peasant revolt. (You can see the protesters in the snowy haze at the back of the picture, as if they were villagers wandering in from *Hunters in the Snow* by Pieter Brueghel the Elder.) Shields up, visors down, the troops will serve their masters obediently and show no mercy to the weak. Such was J. R. R. Tolkien's reconstruction of medieval warfare, and for all his love of the period, he had few illusions about its brutality.

The demonstrations in Kiev produced many similar images, and the winter setting and use of primitive weapons on both sides easily reinforced the sense that this was a world out of a cold, harsh past time.[42] But there are images from Thailand, Israel, Greece, Spain, London, and elsewhere that strengthen the comparisons with medieval costumes. Riot police in particular are often clothed in body armor and full-collared, visored helmets, carrying shields and macelike clubs, advancing en masse or on horseback to battle with ragged civilians. These images capture a dark tendency that is spreading across the globe: what might be called a new feudalism. In place of the egalitarian principles and shared prosperity of the twentieth-century social contract, we see a harsh reassertion of economic power backed by ever-greater investments in security forces. And those forces increasingly look like the private armies of the late medieval period.

Thus a superficial analogy could be documenting a regressive transformation of political power. The surreal photograph can re-

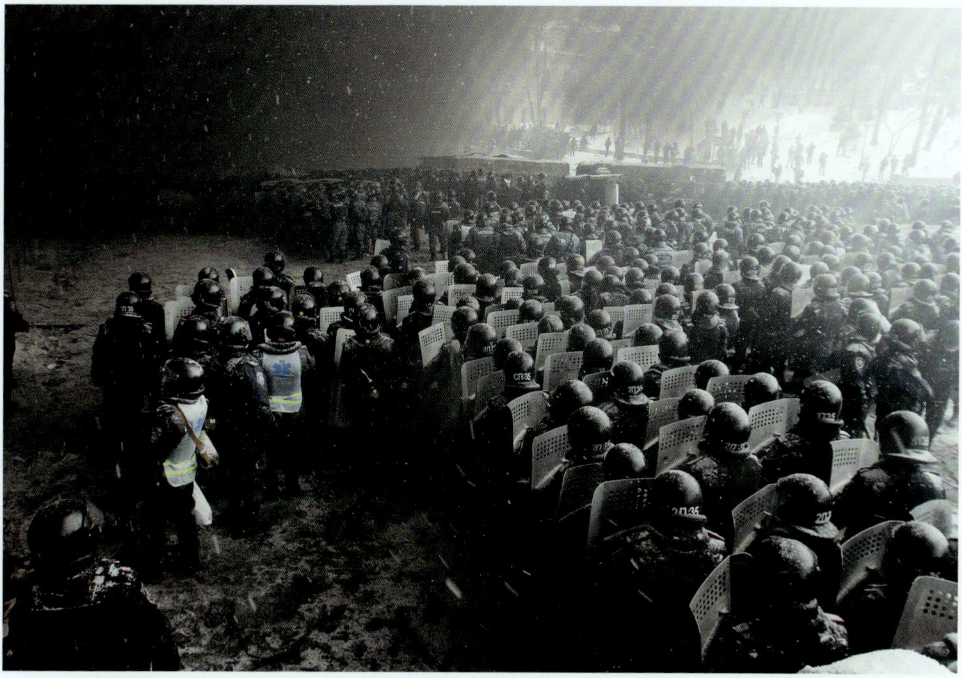

Figure 34. © Anatolii Boiko / AFP / Getty Images.

mind us that time need not be linear, that the past may not have been that long ago, and that the outline of another medieval world may already be present along the edges of the modern nation-state system. Modernity may be riven with ruptures where what was thought to be safely superseded continues to lurk, resurface, or reassert its power. These remnants of the past are likely not the absolute opposite of modern times but something much more capable of displacing and redirecting the course of history.

If such a change is occurring, it remains unclear what the conditions of visibility will be during the transitional period. What is clear is that changes in the use of force are somewhat evident as subtle shifts in the political aesthetic of state power. To take a contemporary example, the removal of all insignia from the Russian invasion of the Crimea in 2014 may be revealing of more than a return to the Great Game or the Cold War. The important point is not only that the invading army was anonymous but that its anonymity was hardly remarked upon, as if it were the most normal thing in the world, or just a small wrinkle in what was otherwise a legible situation. It was a small wrinkle but also a small revelation: if the professional military of a modern state is not expected to be identifiable as such while in full view of the public media, then the modern concept of the state has been degraded. This isn't a question of literal recognition—was that the 184th or the 185th Brigade?—but of the legitimacy of the state's monopoly on force. If soldiers are not wearing insignia, they are partially out of uniform; if they are partially out of uniform, they are that much closer to being private militias, gangs, or thugs. The informality may be justified for partisans battling against conquest or tyranny, because resources are limited, invisibility is necessary, and they disband after victory.[43] But it is definitely an odd thing when the unmarked troops are state troops and the occupying army. Something important has shifted: you still have all that makes state power lethal, but the social contract that went along with that concentration of force has been weakened. The army is still there but is less accountable: still under professional command but lacking legal authority and transparency.

The appearance of the anonymous troops in the Crimea thus suggests how the relationship between the army and society is changing. Think of all those out-of-uniform "contractors"—that is, mercenaries—hired by the US government for work in Iraq, including guard detail for State Department officials. Think also of the increase in special forces and police units that often are not uniformed while deployed. If the state's monopoly on violence begins to adopt the appearance and techniques of stateless violence, then state power is changing. Of course state-sanctioned violence has been anything but a lesson in restraint, but it has been relatively beneficial in comparison with many of the warlord eras in history or any of the natural experiments in anarchy now under way in Mexico, Africa, and the Middle East. The choice apparently is no longer between modern and premodern violence. The visual record suggests that a third kind of force may be emerging, something for which public discussion lacks a vocabulary. But it can be seen.

This line of reasoning obviously moves from the small visual detail, to the wider practice and its conditions of visibility, to speculation about structural change. The limitations are obvious, but it should be clear that the photograph can provide more than both factual information and moral shock. Descriptions of violence (like this one) are abstract, but violence is not abstract. Photography documents what it is and how it works and how it changes whatever it touches, including those who think they are in control. That documentary record is conventional much of the time, like its subject, but it also explores what is happening at the edge of history.

Globalization, excessive capital accumulation, and other structural changes may be leading not to the march of progress but to the breakdown of modernity itself. As the state becomes an economic cartel and loses its monopoly on violence amid ever-greater investments in security, localized power vacuums emerge and have to be filled with some other approach to the use of force. The similarities with medieval military gear correspond with other changes in the same direction, including the destruction of the middle class, corruption of public institutions, hardening of the class structure, comprehensive securitization while the state's monopoly of violence gives way to mercenary armies, and—not least—millions of people being treated as if they had no value beyond their economic utility to those who have consolidated enough power to skim the profits from the labor of the land. As working people have been driven down in the economic order, they also have been driven down in the political process; taking to the streets becomes the only remaining option when the government has been captured by the same elites that are grabbing and hoarding what had been the society's common wealth.

The late-medieval uprisings were the result of conditions that sound all too contemporary: expansion of the income gap between the rich and the rest, corrupt government serving elite greed, massive deficits caused by expensive wars, and environmental changes that degraded everyday life.[44] Yet it remains all too easy, even among those who recognize the underlying lesson of the analogy, to deny its full implication: the riots and the police response are merely matching symptoms of the same disease. As the social order is transformed from a modern to a neofeudal system, riots will become more common while money that could address the causes of the unrest will be poured instead into security. Perhaps it should be no surprise that those security forces are looking more and more like something seen in a distant mirror.

Normalizing Violence

Violence is the ultimate disruption: it violates bodily integrity, the autonomy of the person, and the social order. Despite its ubiquity in television and film, any eruption in most locales is momentous, traumatic: an explosion of destructive impulses that expand outward like shock waves through the social setting. Children flee to another room, bystanders clutch their possessions or companions, authorities react with sirens blaring. Social disruptions call for recontainment and repair, but even so some victims may be lost forever and the damage can continue for generations. It can continue for generations because the society sustains itself despite the abuse, the muggings, the murders and bombings and invasions. As in a fight in a bar on a busy night, the crowd surges away from the conflict to leave a circle of disorder that quickly will be broken up by the bouncers, and then the crowd will flow back into the space to talk or dance as if nothing had happened.

This drive to restore relative peace is far more powerful than we might recognize, and it certainly is a key to species survival. The Hobbesian state of nature is more metaphor than reality, because it doesn't recognize how social cohesion exists alongside self-interest from the beginning, and not only as a second-order stage of human association such as the social contract that cedes power to a sovereign. The attempts to contain violence—to manage it, remedy it, displace it, and resolve conflicts through other means—have been fundamental to human survival. War is crafty, however, and one of the most perverse elements of violence is how it can hijack the processes that would be used to prevent it. There comes to be a fine line between restoring peace and creating a national security state, or between adapting for survival in a war zone and becoming habituated to a ruined civilization.

The normalization of violence occurs in many registers, of course—for example, the way military images have become insinuated into civilian activities. Consider how war analogies pervade the vocabulary of sport: a season is a "campaign"; coaches, quarterbacks, and point guards are "generals"; contests are won or lost "in the trenches"; the field of play is a "war zone." The list goes on, although you will never see a firefight stopped because one of the soldiers has been injured.[45] So it is that military camouflage can become something of a fashion statement, Jeeps and Humvees have become middleclass vehicles, the AR-15 is sold as a hunting rifle, war-themed video games have become a billion-dollar industry, and live simulations like paintball have become minor industries of their own.[46] And then there are the military flyovers at athletic events, identification with the troops in countless advertisements for products having no relationship to combat, the militarization of police practices and crowd control, and the endless supply of action movies that depict war by other means.

Normalization in general is a complex process that occurs in any society, but the complexity and plurality of perspectives of modern societies provide additional resources for both constructing and questioning the taken for granted. Institutions and photography negotiate both complexity and plurality, and these dual capacities come to the fore in images of children. Children are key symbols for several obvious reasons: they are the primary object of socialization, they are vulnerable because wholly dependent, and they will be the adults of the future and thus responsible for society's sustainability. Whether they are being socialized into a war culture is an important question, and one that is foregrounded by many images from the conflict zones of the Middle East and elsewhere.

The trope of "youthful innocence" is a common photojournalistic convention, often marked by photographic representations of children playing as if they were adults. Such images can range from the somewhat ordinary—a young girl selling lemonade to passersby for 10₵ a cup—to the extraordinary: a young boy saluting the passing caisson of his assassinated father. In almost every instance we are invited to imagine the purity and innocence of youth unencumbered by the world of experience, and to hope for a future in which the transition to adulthood can preserve some of their happiness as they assume the full responsibilities of the roles they now are only imitating.

In figure 35 the normative romance of youthful inexperience is transformed into tragedy. The photograph is of a group of "young supporters of the Islamic Jihad movement" marching at a rally in Gaza City "to show solidarity with the Al-Aqsa mosque in Jerusalem." Any sense that the child is playing has been obliterated, and with it

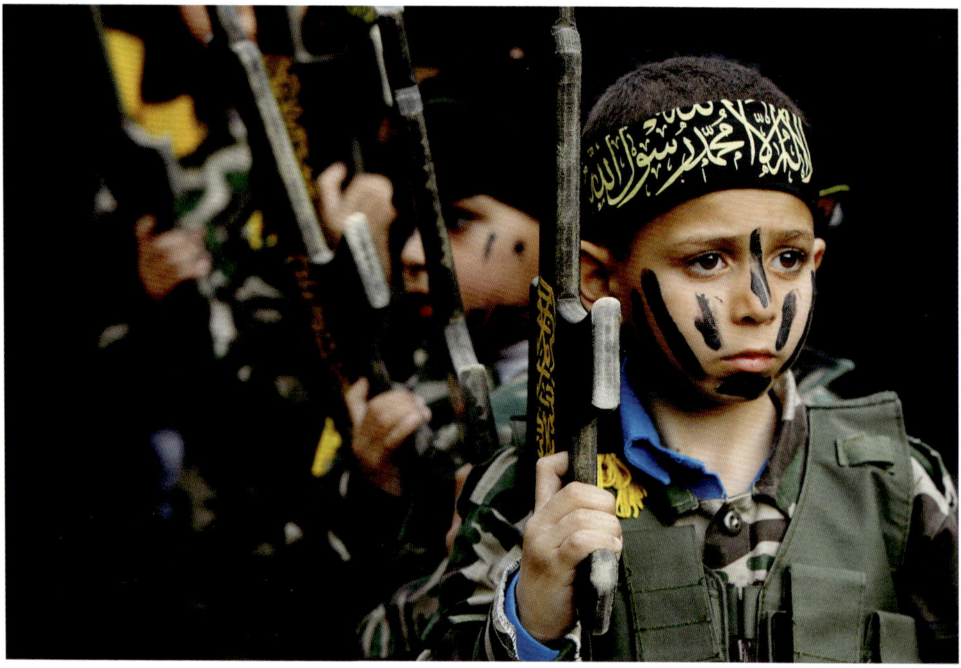

Figure 35. © epa / Ali Ali.

all hope that the next generation can see its way to a better and more peaceful future. The toy guns and uniforms underscore the potential militancy of the image, but they are not the key signifiers of the shift from romance to tragedy. To take the full measure of the symbolic transformation, you have to look at the child's facial expression, especially his eyes, which teeter between being altogether vacant and deadly serious, and in either case are wholly dissociated from our expectations of an idealized world of youthful innocence. The contrast of his childish face and the military uniform and entrainment emphasizes his vulnerability, and so it becomes much easier to think of him as someone already being prepared for ritual sacrifice and not as a child with a future. The contrast of that realization with his modern garb raises the stakes higher yet. Perhaps modern warfare is this civilization's Baal.

Any ambiguity in such photographs from the Middle East is countered by the presumption of sheer otherness from the Western media audience. Within this optic, the image becomes a double indictment: by aligning Gaza with the image of the child soldier, Palestinian society is abusing its children while perpetuating violence that appears increasingly intractable, sure to be repeated endlessly. The implicit contrast goes further, for the professionalized military of the modern state is for adults only, while martial training for adulthood is linked with either primitive coming-of-age rituals or totalitarian regimes. Societies that train children for warfare would therefore not be modern societies or legitimate governments, and thus not deserving the privilege of statehood, and with that a neocolonial mentality has been made part of the background of public culture.

But what if the warrior child lives in one of the advanced nations?

The boy in figure 36 is described as a member of a Junior Reserve Officers Training Corps honor guard participating in a Veterans Day ceremony. Lacking a name, he takes on the quality of an individuated aggregate—an individual cast in the role of a collective.[47] He stands for something more than himself. But what? The answer must lie in the relation between the boy and the tableau. His serious countenance and rigid pose are dwarfed by the large, highly polished helmet, an instrument of war turned to ceremonial purposes. The bright, mirrorlike surface reflects the deeply saturated colors of the national flag that he appears to be holding and that shrouds his head and shoulders, as well as another flag, more difficult to make out, that appears to be in his line of vision. There is no hint of the boy in that reflection, let alone the individual veteran, but there is a connection between the past (behind him) and the future (in front of him) defined only by the national colors. His (and our) present is defined by a direct line from past to future, and the trajectory is, well, fated. He stands at attention while the flag marches on.

The complete appropriation of the child for patriotic display could not be more obvious, but it will be no less effective for that. Like the rest of the patriotic decor, he is there to celebrate the nation defined primarily in terms of a militarized citizenship.[48] All service is represented as military service, and protecting the nation (symbolized by the flag) is the highest calling. As the child is a symbol of both present dependency and futurity, the scene reminds us that the soldiers of today are protecting the children already being prepared to take their place. And we need not worry about his safety: the distance from actual warfare is announced by the brilliant chrome sheen of

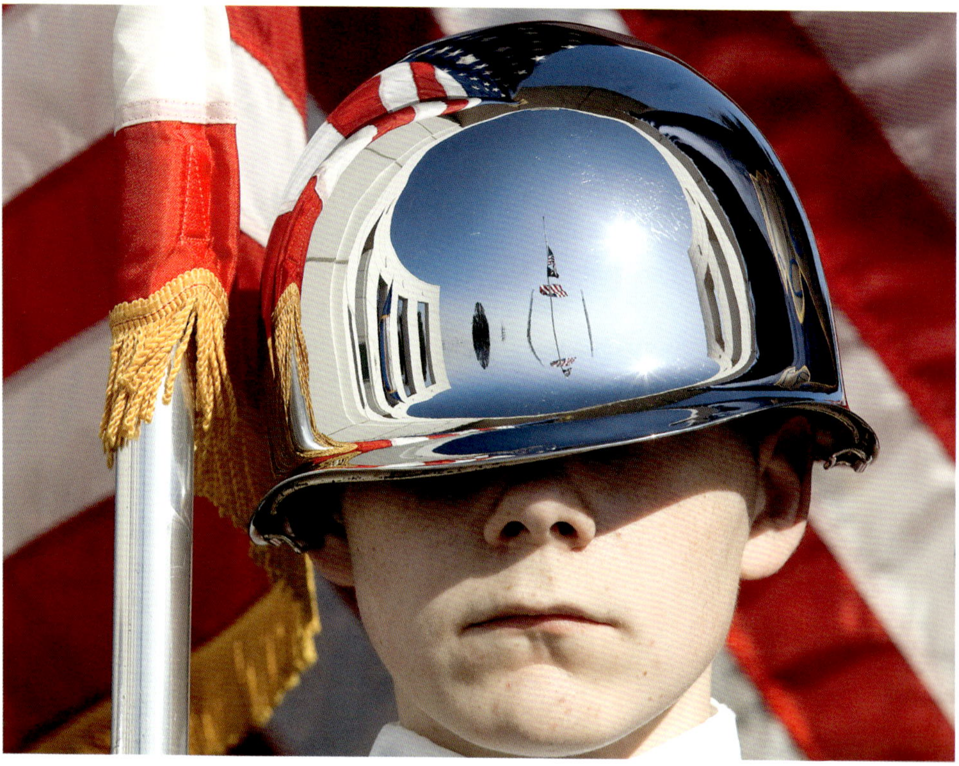

Figure 36. © AP Photo / Nati Harnik.

the helmet. The horror of war cannot be completely forgotten—otherwise there would be no sense of sacrifice and no public virtue to be honored—but it is kept under wraps. Any gap between idealization and reality is managed by the vaguely comic contrast of the flag and helmet with his small size and smooth skin dotted with acne: he's not yet ready, but he will be.

Yet the photograph is not identical with the display. It is not only relaying the ceremony but also framing it for reflective judgment. The framing here is telling: the close-up shot and tight cropping of the image features the boy's face, giving it a presence that would be lost if we were seeing the pageant as a whole. What is overlooked in the spectatorship of institutional spaces (the space reflected on the helmet) is brought into another form of public viewing by the photograph. Still in and about the public, the image reveals tensions between public and private life, the individual and the collective, the present and the future, and one type of citizenship and another.

As in the photograph from Gaza, the boy becomes a highly ambivalent figure. He is trying hard to play a role that has been given to him too early, and it is a strain. He is a portrait more of vulnerability than of future strength: biting one's lip is a long way emotionally from the shouts of exertion in boot camp. The fact that the helmet is too big can be more sad than comic, as he already is overmatched: his brain encased in a carapace of ideology, his growth defined by overlarge and rigid conceptions of duty, masculinity, and national greatness.

These second thoughts are given more depth by the reflective space of the helmet. There we see the national icon and public monument, but distorted into an anamorphic projection. The flag itself is multiplied and diminished, while other fixtures behind it look like reeds and rocks in a deserted lake. The rectilinear stability of the monument is cast into a more plastic art form, while the large flag next to both is bent like one of the dripping clocks in a Salvador Dali painting. The gorgeous blue sky and bright sun are still suffusing the day, but they too are now double images within an image within an image. The patriotic project has been cast into a surreal space, one that makes the surrounding reality seem equally contrived and excessively fantastic.

One of the functions of normalization is to make the excessive appear to be something else: inspiring, noble, worth growing into. The use of the warrior child cements colony and metropol, promising unending war that is worth the sacrifice. Enormous expenditures on military weaponry, unnecessary invasions, and similar exercises in the surreal are retold as idealized abstractions of national pride. A critical response comes not from a competing spectacle but from close attention to the surface of things and how they create a reflective space. When reality is surreal, photography's combination of realism and distortion can be a path to reflective insight.

Such pageantry, whether in the United States or in Gaza, is a top-down affair. There is a second dimension to normalization that operates from the bottom up. This is the space in which ordinary people have to adjust, adapt, and otherwise cope with the material conditions of war. Ways of coping include everything from keeping the kids inside so they don't get shot, to spending many hours each day scavenging for the bare necessities of life, to having to make the hundreds of adjustments needed to live with a loved one who now is severely wounded. Given the relative affluence and norms of privacy in the United States, many of these kinds of domestic adjustments are not seen or easily compartmentalized. In the spreading war zones of the Middle East, Africa, and elsewhere, a more visible change is taking place.

Figure 37's caption reads, "After Shiite fighters seized control of parts of west Beirut, a gunman, right, took a break to drink coffee on a street corner." The image is striking in part because of how it falls between more familiar representations: on one hand, the scenes of urban warfare, whether troops advancing under fire down an empty street or the burning tires and ragged attacks seen in violent political protests; on the other hand, the ordinary scenes of peace, whether in the workplace or out on the street. At once both and neither of these stock images, the photo is almost disorienting, or it should be. The scene is the epitome of a worker's coffee break: a thermos, a smoke, a joke. This could be an image of civilization at its best: making the impersonal curb into a place of conviviality. And look at his feet: loafers, no socks. See the military vest as a life jacket and he could be waiting for his yacht to be put in the water.

But it isn't a life jacket, and that weapon is designed to shoot other people, and the two men are obviously at home in a vicious cycle of sectarian violence. But that cannot be demonized, either. The texture of the photo connotes everyday life across the planet: comfortable pants, the pleasures of private association, and the plastic goods and stylish informality of consumer culture as it is found in every demographic. These guys are typically modern, but they are nonetheless habituated to moving in and out of war on a daily or even hourly basis. We might wonder if they are sitting just around the corner from us.

Although they are recognizably modern, the photo also suggests a conundrum and probably a change in the modern conception of war. On the one hand, modernity has been defined by the state's monopoly on violence and professionalism of the military; both are symbolized by the military uniform. On the other hand, modernity also promotes society (and especially civil society) as the common

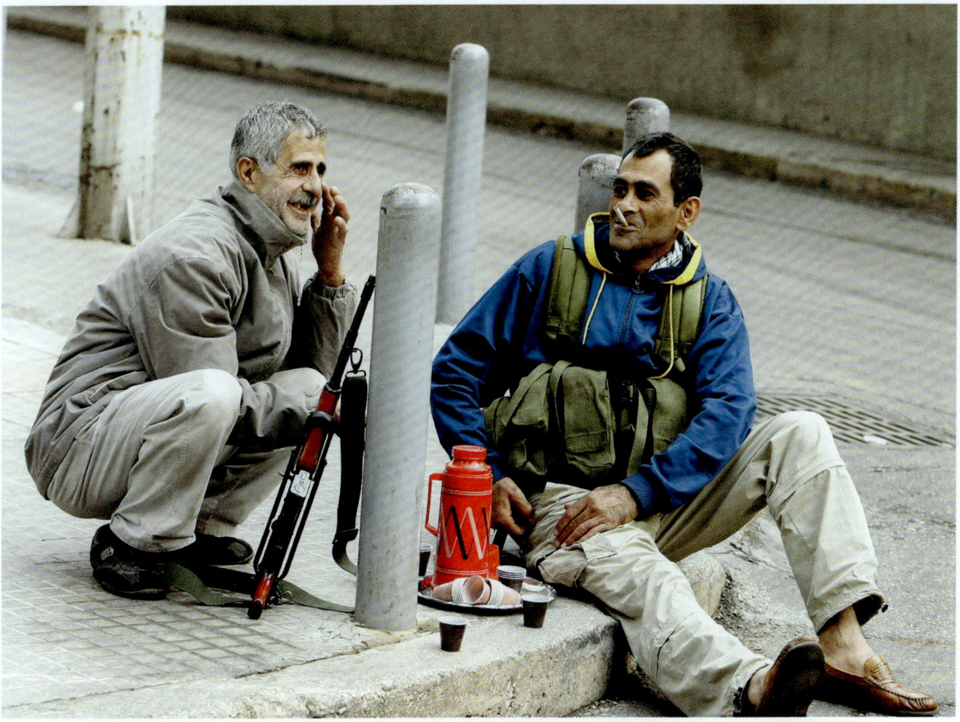

Figure 37. © Ramzi Haidar / AFP / Getty Images.

denominator for all institutions, a remarkable development that voids the need for either castes (including a military caste) or theocratic rule. The many images of civilian fighters that now populate the public space suggest the expansion of one tendency, but only to undermine the other. As rebel fighters go to battle in the latest running shoes or man checkpoints while sitting in office chairs, as special operatives and private mercenaries (both numbering in the many thousands) dress like TV action heroes, and as children play on rusting war materiel that apparently never will be towed away, military and civilian practices become increasingly jumbled together into a newly hybrid society that is both civil and uncivil.

Thus as war between great powers becomes less likely, war continues to spread in another way: by becoming less partitioned off from the rest of society. The borders between town and military base, war zone and neutral zone, humanitarian aid and military occupation become more permeable. Figure 37 captures this sense of normalization. While earlier attempts at the militarization of civil society were unabashedly so, and marked by uniforms—think of the Boy Scouts or the Corps of Cadets at Texas A&M University—now it can happen more subtly, with barely a trace. The question becomes, when will we notice what is but should not be familiar?

Normalization through interpenetration and informality creates new problems of visibility. Conditions of permanent degradation can persist despite media attention because they are mundane rather than dramatic, ordinary rather than exceptional, and involve familiar routines and settings rather than the big stage of history. This distribution of the visible structures a wide swath of press coverage and generally works to maintain the status quo.

One of the key markers of such a distribution is the presence or absence of emergency claims. Sirens, yellow police tape, cordoned-off streets, satellite trucks and other equipment of intensive press coverage: these and similar disruptions and investments create a zone of heightened attention and significance. Such signs are more or less evident as coverage becomes distributed geographically; not surprisingly, coverage typically recedes as events become more distant. Distance might be counted literally or socially—miles can be shortened by ethnic or economic ties, for example—but it is a reliable metric.[49] The problem is that an understandable feature of attention management becomes morally and politically consequential when coupled with the causes and sanctions for violence.

In figure 38 an explosion has taken place in Iraq, or more specifically, as the caption tells the reader, "a series of attacks" have taken place, and yet any sense of urgency in dealing with the situation is altogether missing. Everyday life has been disrupted, to be sure, tragically so with the violent loss of life, but the event is *shown* to be so routine, so commonplace, that its status as a horrifying emergency goes unnoticed and unaddressed. Put simply, the everydayness of the scene, which should alert us to the profoundly precarious condition of the society, actually veils—if not altogether erases—the tragedy before our eyes. The photograph thus reveals a society that has become conditioned to such everyday violence; the problem is that the society in question is not in Iraq.

The photo is particularly revealing in that the terrorist attack in

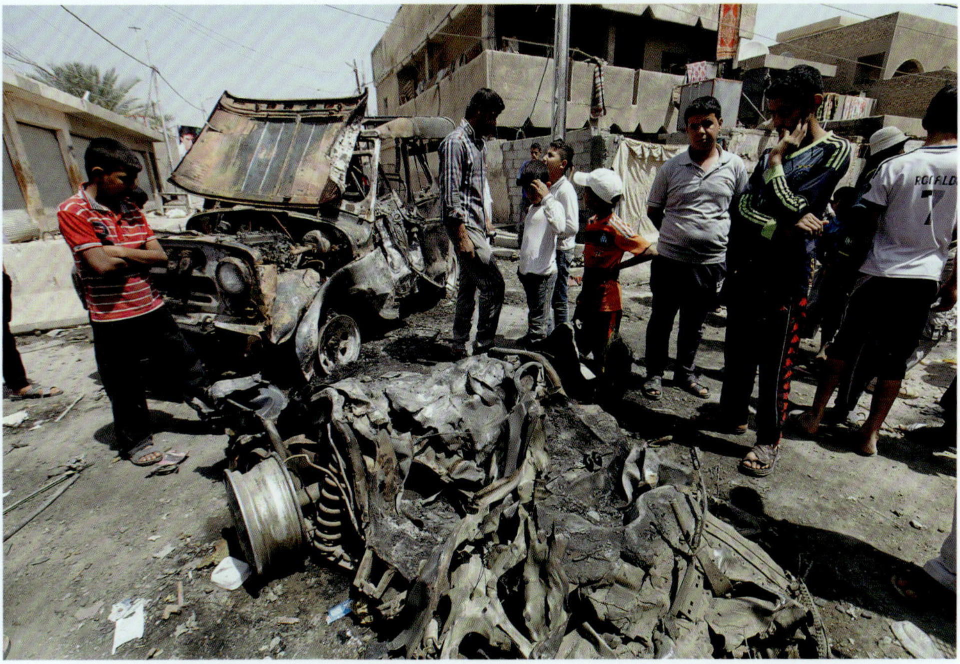

Figure 38. © Reuters / Mohammed Ameen.

Iraq was reported in the *New York Times* on the same day as the lead story on the Boston Marathon bombing. The attack in Boston killed three people and wounded over two hundred others, while in Iraq that day there were "more than 20 attacks around the country" that "killed close to 50 people and wounded nearly 200."[50] The *Times* also had reported in 2011 that suicide bombings had by that time killed over twelve thousand civilians in Iraq, while over thirty thousand had been wounded.[51] Twelve thousand dead: that is the three deaths from Boston multiplied by 4,000, as if you had a Boston Marathon bombing every day for eleven years, and all that in a country with a population one-tenth the size of that of the United States.

That's bad, but it also is just another day in the news for most readers of the *Times.* To really get a sense of the difference, compare figure 38, which is the photo that accompanied the *Times* story, with any of the images from Boston that circulated through US papers. The intensive coverage of the US bombing featured screaming crowds, police leaping into action, emergency personnel and citizens helping the wounded, who were shown as they were bloodied, maimed, and in shock. The photos from Boston all screamed EMERGENCY. They insisted that this event was unique, exceptional, and deserving of an immediate and comprehensive response. Like the pronouncements by the president and other public officials, they all demanded justice for the innocent citizens cut down by a brutal terrorist attack. No longer mere images, they become statements addressed to the viewing public. In Azoulay's terms, they made the suffering of the victims into a political object—that is, an object of collective concern that mandates state action.[52]

By contrast, in the image from Iraq both the violence and any political response are kept off stage. The bombing is portrayed as a nonevent, and thus it never rises to the level of an emergency claim. Instead of action, we see inaction: a burned-out car and jeep are the center of attention, around which kids and adults stand as if wondering how to salvage a part or two. The state is nowhere to be seen. Any suffering is offstage or abstract, and it falls short of meriting a specific political response. The fact of violence is being shown, yet the moral and political context remains largely invisible. The image has all the emotional urgency of a junkyard, and no wonder: there is no trace of the dead and wounded, and those present appear to be bored rather than acting as if they were in any danger. The casualness of the children standing around the metal carcasses suggests that the scene is merely a waning curiosity. It is a portrait of past violence, but violence that is unexceptional. Cars get blown up, just as they get into accidents. Showing only damage to property, lacking pain, suffering, or any other emotional intensity, and suggesting that those at the scene are without any risk of being harmed themselves—this is what happens when a disaster is coded as an event that is *not* an emergency.

That said, the photograph is not merely an accomplice to normalization. It deserves a second look, as a process of thoughtful spectatorship is coded into the image. Some of those in the picture are gazing meditatively at the blasted vehicle. They appear to be looking at the car as a social object, a vehicle of meaning. The car has not been vaporized, so one can still make out its components and purpose, but it has been crushed, mangled, ruined—like Iraq. Parts of it have been destroyed, others burned, all of it stripped of what it needs to be functional. The spectators may be looking as if into a mirror, for they too seem to be both present and immobilized, unable to begin the perhaps futile work of restoring a civil society that is still subject to such bombings. Their thoughts remain unknown to the spectators of the photo, but their behavior can be a model and perhaps a cautionary tale regarding how to look at societies that are being traumatized by violence.

Not every photo is subtle, and we shouldn't fault the coverage of the Boston bombing for doing everything differently: for showing suffering, action, anguish, and much more. And earlier in the war in Iraq there were photos, including some that won awards, that did communicate the violence and terror being wreaked on the people living there. That's the reportage that should be provided. But the United States has from the start abandoned large civilian populations to the horrors of war, and now too often coverage of continuing violence presents it, not as a dramatic disaster requiring an extraordinary response, but as just another day in the life for those accustomed to living in a war zone. The viewer's indifference is not a matter of compassion fatigue but a rational response to coverage that keeps victims below the level of active concern. They have been relegated to the condition of living on the verge of catastrophe. Neither being systematically sacrificed nor adequately protected, they are abandoned to a life of continuing "low-level" violence.

So it is that two forms of normalization converge. It shouldn't be surprising that one response of those trapped there is to treat bombed cars as a part of life. But the more secure spectator might take a moment to realize that all the horror experienced in Boston really is happening elsewhere, and much, much more often. Because the distribution of the visible doubles as a partitioning of emotional and political response, it may help perpetuate cycles of violence.[53] These photos are being taken all around the globe: photos of situations that are not and yet are the same as disasters in one's own society, and that are relegated to a condition of invisibility. When we focus only on the literal facts of the image, habits of denial are perpetuated. This geography of indifference is maintained in part by photography; the question that remains is whether the archive also offers solidarity with those who are suffering.

Seeing Violence

A prevalent topic in professional and public discussions of press coverage is the extent to which the cruelty and physical damage of warfare should be shown: should the public have to view executions, soldiers torturing the wounded, or the bloody mutilation, dismemberment, disembowelment, and decapitation produced by modern weaponry?[54] The examples we've given suggest that much is not shown, yet there always are images that provoke negotiation of the tradeoff between documentation and decorum. Too much imbalance in either direction rightly draws criticism—few want to encourage either pornography or propaganda—while the temptations to shock or to censor are always there. But the topic—and its close relative, the discussion of embedding and other measures to control access and distribution—obscures much of what is needed and available for the representation of violence. Additional images of carnage won't stop the war machine, and photographs already are providing all that is needed to remove any doubt about whether the public ought to be held morally and politically accountable for what is authorized in its name.

The task that remains is not deciding what should be shown but rather understanding the obligations of spectatorship. Linfield puts the point bluntly: "Photojournalists are responsible for the ethics of showing, but we are responsible for the ethics of seeing."[55] To emphasize the point, she then quotes Azoulay's statement that "it is our historic responsibility, not only to produce photos, but to make them speak."[56] One could add as well Michael Herr's comment, uttered in the context of the Vietnam War, that "you were as responsible for everything you saw as you were for everything you did."[57] Our point is that these are not mere dicta but variations on a profound understanding of citizenship that grows out of the nexus of photography and violence in this historical period. Because violence is now shown to the public (even if as a "spectacle"),[58] verbal rationalization can no longer be sufficient, the state is no longer the sole source of authority, and the citizen is placed in a social relationship with those being harmed.[59]

Rather than being disqualified by likely misuses of the image, the spectator has to take responsibility for what is shown: the specific circumstances, operations, and effects of modern violence. That obligation begins with saying "Yes, I have seen that." Where it goes from there need not be specified in every case; to do so may be important, but questions of policy also can limit both moral reflection and creative action. Ultimately, meditative use of the image may be far more important than any supposed "CNN effect."[60]

The meditative response draws many considerations into the image, but it is not an extrinsic process. It begins with the image and proceeds by enlarging the view from image to optic. One not only sees the event recorded but begins to see as the photographer or the subject of the photo was seeing that event, and also how other spectators might see it. Thus photography provides a basis for ethical and political reflection on violence not only by showing its effects but also by bringing us to see it as if in a common world that now irrevocably contains the pain of others. That encounter then can be the basis for a specific type of moral reflection: one that is neither personal nor impersonal, but an intermediate way of being in the world that is at once grounded in the specific event and yet generalized through the public context provided by other spectators. One connection between the two standpoints of being within and looking in on the event is the ways of seeing that are being displayed. The image can show how violence depends on habits of observation that double as forms of blindness, and how it changes the way people see those around them.

Indeed, the presentation of carnage may be a distraction, not least by implying that violence can be seen and understood directly. Violence is more complicated—and war is more cunning—than that. The more profound image, then, may be one that can show violence indirectly, through its traces, and that reminds us how war stains the act of seeing.

It is said that the eyes are the window to the soul. Let's hope that that is not true. The boy in figure 39 is looking into a car not long after mercenaries in the employ of the US government had destroyed the two women in the front seat. Every line of the *Times* story provided indirect evidence of how the US invasion of Iraq had gone out of control. Once again innocents were slaughtered for supposedly threatening "security" forces that shouldn't have been there in the first place. Culpability was displaced to the unholy mix of agencies and companies involved: USAID, a "quasi-independent" agency of the State Department, hired RTI International, which hired Unity

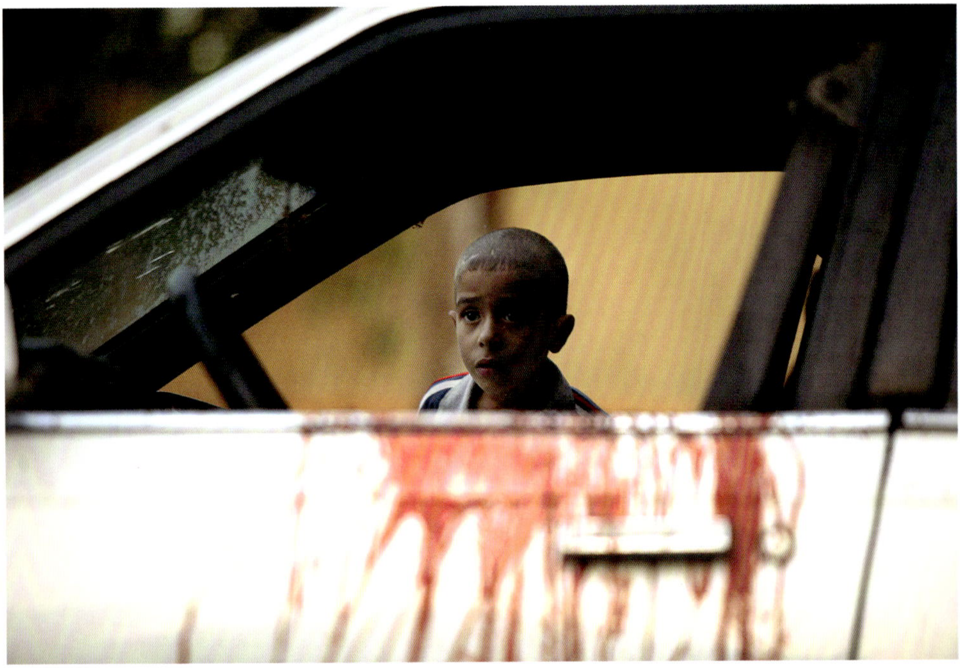

Figure 39. © Joao Silva / The New York Times / Redux.

Resources Group, "an Australian-run company that has its headquarters in Dubai and is registered in Singapore." We should not overlook the language used by the *Times*, which labeled the mercenaries "contractors" in the print edition and "guards" online, both euphemisms.[61]

But all that pales next to the mute testimony given by this photo. The photographer has used the most common elements of visual composition to focus our attention on something extraordinary. We see the boy's face in the center of the picture; he is isolated against a soft-toned background as in studio portraiture; successively tighter framings by the border of the photo, the left side window, and the right side window channel our attention to his expression; his face is soft, his eyes are wide open. His acute vulnerability is accentuated by the contrast with the blurry smear of blood on the metal surface in the foreground. Between the passenger door and the boy lies the interior of the car, now a dark, gory killing pen. He has looked down and seen the stain inside. He looks up, as if for an answer.

The photograph shows us many things, but one achievement is to show seeing—raw seeing, when you cannot necessarily filter out or fully comprehend what you see—and to show how we are affected by what comes in through our eyes.[62] This child has seen the traces of horror within that car without benefit of geopolitical framing or any other adult defense mechanism. And he has been harmed.

As with the rest of the composition, nothing new is involved: think of the many photographs in which we observe people seeing as they look back at the camera in one snapshot after another. We smile for group photos and enjoy reaction shots when birthday gifts are opened. But that isn't really seeing, for everyone knows how to react and no damage is likely to be done. And we're not in a war zone.

Of course the photograph can be faulted: It is the women who were killed, not the child. Young and still living, he has a future despite the violence. In place of the horror of the attack, we see only blood, only a trace of the physical damage, and only after the event has cooled to the extent that a child can come close. The appeal is sentimental, substituting the subjective experience of pity, a cheap emotion anyway, with a call to action. Isn't this photograph another withholding of an emergency claim?

The genius of figure 39 is that it breaks through the conventions that inadvertently but effectively normalize war. Instead of incorporating a mediated experience of the war into the habits of social seeing in private life, this image shows us how seeing, feeling, and being in the world are irrevocably altered by a direct experience of violence. Instead of defining violence in terms of a body count, the photo exposes the psychological damage that can chain out for generations. Instead of the normalization provided by the agencies, abstractions, and euphemisms in the written text, the photograph documents the reverse process: the destruction of the basic requirements for normal life for those trapped in a war zone. In the same manner, instead of keeping the emphasis on "security" and the professional use of force, the photograph shifts the emphasis to spectatorship. The boy mirrors the viewer, who mirrors the boy. By seeing his eyes and his incomprehension, we are to question what we have been seeing. By seeing that he has been harmed, we are to ask how we might have been damaged as well.

One reason that more gore is not needed is that it doesn't address

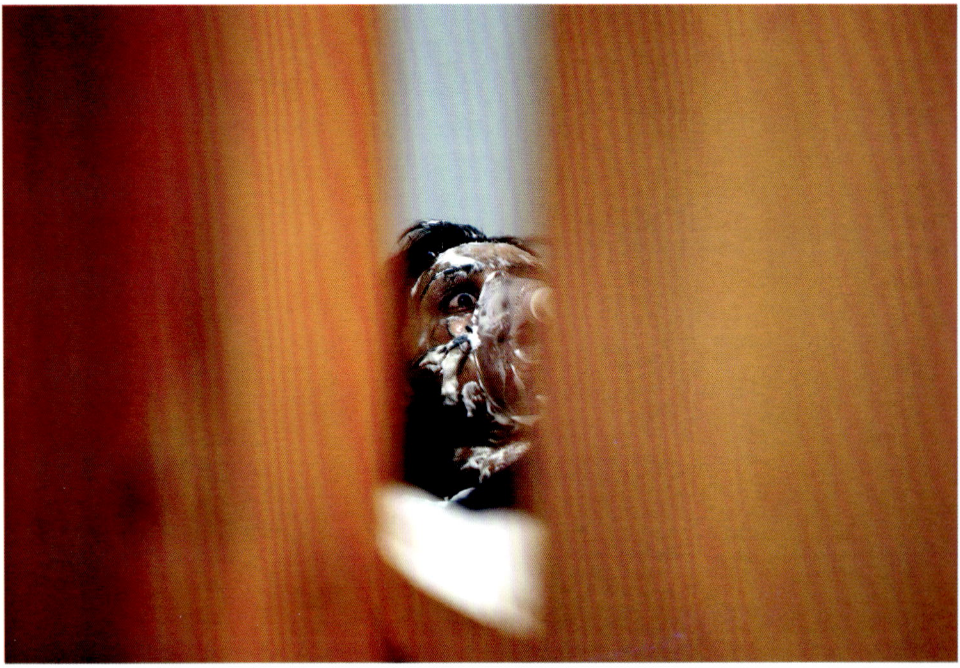

Figure 40. © Reuters / Navesh Chitrakar.

the real problem. Few doubt that war is bloody, but habits of indifference or deferred responsibility are all too common. The problem is not a lack of literal detail or insufficient revulsion or compassion fatigue; the challenge is to activate a complex response that includes emotional identification, acknowledgment of the distance between subject and spectator, and a desire to act nonetheless. So it is that less can be more, as with the tableau in figure 40.

She has seen terror, she is seeing terror, you are seeing terror, we will continue to see terror. The grammar is at once familiar and out of place; we might call it a declension of violence.

The caption said, "A victim, with her eyes wide open, lies on a hospital bed after an attack on a passenger microbus by an unidentified group in Kathmandu." Too many elements of this scenario are all too familiar: civilians being targeted by unknown attackers, institutional support coming after—not before—the carnage, while eyes are wide open yet seemingly unable to see any means to stop the violence.

And not just her eyes: ours are open (and perhaps opened) as well. We see her and we see her seeing, which raises the stakes for photography's promise as a communicative art. It seems that the photograph might channel her seeing directly into ours or, if that connection fails, at least ask what she might be seeing and what we ought to see.

In this case, whatever still holds her eyes in fixed, horrified attention remains invisible to us. All we can see is the terror itself: How it stuns body and soul; how it drives consciousness to a fixed point of horror amid a welter of disorder, confusion, and pain. How she is too transfixed by the damage to even be able to plead for help, much less for an end to the arbitrary slaughter of human beings.

The photograph's intelligence doesn't end there, however, for it starkly highlights how much we don't know simply by seeing. Our vision is limited to a portion of her face, and we see that through a slit in the curtain beside her bed. The narrow aperture is as salient as the face behind it, while the blinds on each side make a thick frame designed to obscure. The message is clear: what you see through the aperture of the camera is not the whole picture.

Too often the full import of that point is misunderstood, even by those who suggest that adequate representation is available otherwise. Better captions, extensive written reportage, historical study, ethnographic immersion—whatever the alternative, the idea is that a corrective is available. Those and other investments are certainly needed, and not just in the war zones, but this photograph goes one better. It says that the whole picture is never available. Pull aside the curtains, and what do you see but the rest of the battered body? Interview the doctors and emergency workers and bystanders and diplomats, and what do you know? One can learn quite a bit, but nothing that will erase her terror. That may be why the oxygen mask is so terrifying: because of the surreal cyborg visage, she seems to have been transformed into something half-bestial, a declension from human to merely animal, from person to prey, and at the mercy of those in the room now instead of those who threw the bomb. Somehow even medical technology, like the technology of the camera, has been co-opted into an apparatus of terror, as if it and not the bomb were harming her. That's not true, but it is one example of how terror works by making the familiar world into an environment of pain and fear.[63]

Of course everything that can be done to help the victim and to understand the situation should be done, but one does need to be wary of the illusion that all distance between the victim and the unharmed can be eliminated.[64] This photo, by contrast, shows us how that distance is part of our experience of her experience. We are able to see that something awful lies beyond mediation, and thus beyond knowledge, and that our experience is mediated. Yet, for all that, the spectator is still put in a relationship with a single bombing victim far away from most of those who will see this photograph. That's why the photo has more than academic interest. You might say that one of the contributions of photography is that it shows how solidarity with others doesn't have to wait on fully sharing or understanding their experience.

The photo shows us terror that is stalking the world today, and it reminds us that many viewers are fortunate enough to see it only at a distance. The close framing of the victim's act of wide-eyed concentration reminds us that she may not be seeing what is in fact in front of her—she could be blind to the room because still back in the blast—and that *we* may not be seeing what is in fact in front of us. Perhaps it suggests that context is needed, but that is settling for too little. She isn't looking at us, but the photograph does ask at least one question on her behalf: Now that you see how she has been changed by the attack, how have you been changed? Who is willing to look terror in the face and to stand with those who continue to suffer?

As Paul Frosh and Amit Pinchevski have noted, "In a world of mass media where all is visible, excuses like 'we did not know' will no longer be acceptable; with media proliferation ignorance can never be used as justification for inaction." They add, however, that it also is naive to assume that "knowing necessarily leads to acting" and that "information entails involvement." Instead, "the question today is not how violence takes place without us knowing about it, but how violence takes place when it is almost impossible not to know about it."[65] As they also note, compassion fatigue and other explanations have arisen to try to account for this gap; one challenge for the contemporary approach to photojournalism is to address the problem without relying on flawed accounts of how the glut of images anesthetizes moral response.[66]

This is not to say that the key to breaking the cycle of violence is simply political will. Any such reductive explanation is inadequate when we are trying to account for what rhetorical potential photography might have. Media experience will never devolve into pure information or direct action without remainder, but an image can confront indifference to make suffering into an object of political concern. At that point one faces a decision to know and perhaps to act. "Action" itself is suspect, however, as there is little that anyone can actually do at any given moment. Some moments matter more than others, such as when in a voting booth or at a demonstration, but public influence can be inchoate much of the time. Moreover, as Wendy Kozol argues, the acts of recognition necessary for ethical action are themselves matters of ambivalence.[67] And as Kozol, Susie Linfield, Lilie Chouliaraki, Sharon Sliwinski, and others have emphasized, admission of the failure of the image to convert inaction to action is a crucial requirement for both ethical and political judgment.[68] None of these statements, however, diminishes the importance of either the image or the spectator.

In this predicament, one response has been to assess the image according to whether it foregrounds the inadequacy of the political system. John Berger's critique of "photographs of agony" is representative:

> The reader who has been arrested by the photograph may tend to feel this discontinuity as his own personal moral inadequacy. *And as soon as this happens even his sense of shock is dispersed*: his own moral inadequacy may now shock him as much as the crimes being committed in the war.
>
> . . . The issue of the war which has caused the moment is effectively depoliticized. The picture becomes evidence of the general human condition. It accuses nobody and everybody.
>
> . . . The next step should be to confront our own lack of political freedom. In the political systems as they exist, we have no legal opportunity of effectively influencing the conduct of wars waged in our name. To realize this and to act accordingly is the only effective way of responding to what the photograph shows. Yet the double violence of the photographed moment actually works against this realization. That is why they can be published with impunity.[69]

This critique obviously has its own problems: like Barthes, Sontag, and others of the time, Berger had no qualms about demeaning other viewers' psychological reactions; in addition, he was skeptical of any media effect short of ideological structuration, while he relied on an idealistic sense of revolutionary politics that seems naive today. Even so, he both identifies a mode of response that can become too comfortable and provides a template for a more critical spectatorship.

We will admit to a susceptibility to displacing blame from actual perpetrators onto the human condition. We note as well that exactly the same path is taken by Sontag in *Regarding the Pain of Others* and other writers on the representation of atrocity.[70] One should beware the temptation to wax philosophical when photography actually is providing an entirely different kind of moral engagement.[71] Linfield stresses the need to refocus on the perpetrators, and that is important, but it is not enough. There is need not only to avoid distraction but also to forge public response to conditions that are systemic and broadly incriminating. Perpetrators can be causes and also symptoms.

This temptation to abstraction is there not only because horror is specifically, viscerally awful to see. It is there because the human condition is there in the photograph, not least as the image always evokes the photographic archive. As Kennedy affirms:

> A key tenet of the visual philosophy of mid-century photojournalism was its commitment to a democratizing vision of human affiliations and an imaginary globalization of conscience: it posited a culture of humanity as a universal ideal and human empathy as a compensatory response to global threats . . . and promoted compassion as a commensurate response to the suffering of distant others. The idealism of that vision would be severely challenged before the century was over, yet its moral currency remains a vital part of photojournalism's DNA.[72]

That sense of photographic humanism also is constructed, but no photograph presents absolute particularity; some feature of the world has been selected because of its representative value. Instead of looking for a transcendental referent, today we might consider that the idea of humanity is itself a figural representation of public spectatorship, and therefore of the predicament of collective action in a modern liberal-democratic society. So it is that public response can be an ethical and political achievement, but only by following a logic that can be slow and precarious: "We" are seeing because the action already is occurring without our direct participation; we personally don't have to become involved and couldn't do much anyway; collective response requires bonding on the basis of more than individual self-interest and thus appears costly and unreliable; the shift from complacency to mobilization is likely to begin as a shift in perception.

That shift in perception is why Berger is correct to focus on the particular structures that are impeding a society's freedom to recognize and diminish its own destructiveness. Censorship is the obvious example but also the least important in the West. Another factor is ideological filtering, which always is present; though never absolutely determinative of the individual image or range of responses, it rightly remains an important object of concern, especially as the ideology of empire becomes intertwined with other processes of globalization and technological change.[73] Photography captures more as well, however. By identifying the conditions of visibility created by the organization of civil society, photography can reveal how political agency is weakened by ordinary practices having no specific political intentions.

The photograph in figure 41 of a coffin being prepared for delivery captures all too well the terrible disconnect between US civilian experience and the costs of the wars in Iraq and Afghanistan.[74] The honor guard are doing everything they can to pay proper respect to their fellow Marine, but nothing can change the fact that the dead are consigned to the cargo hold while not far above them the living go about their business. It is not that those peering out of the windows of the plane are uncaring, but all they see is the family waiting on the tarmac. As accidental spectators of a scene only half visible, they are placed somewhere between incomprehension and not knowing how to respond. And unlike the uniformed guard performing carefully coordinated actions, the passengers are isolated into individual reality compartments, each one firmly separated from the others. The structure of the plane reflects the structure of ordinary life in a liberal society: those things held in common are like baggage thrown together

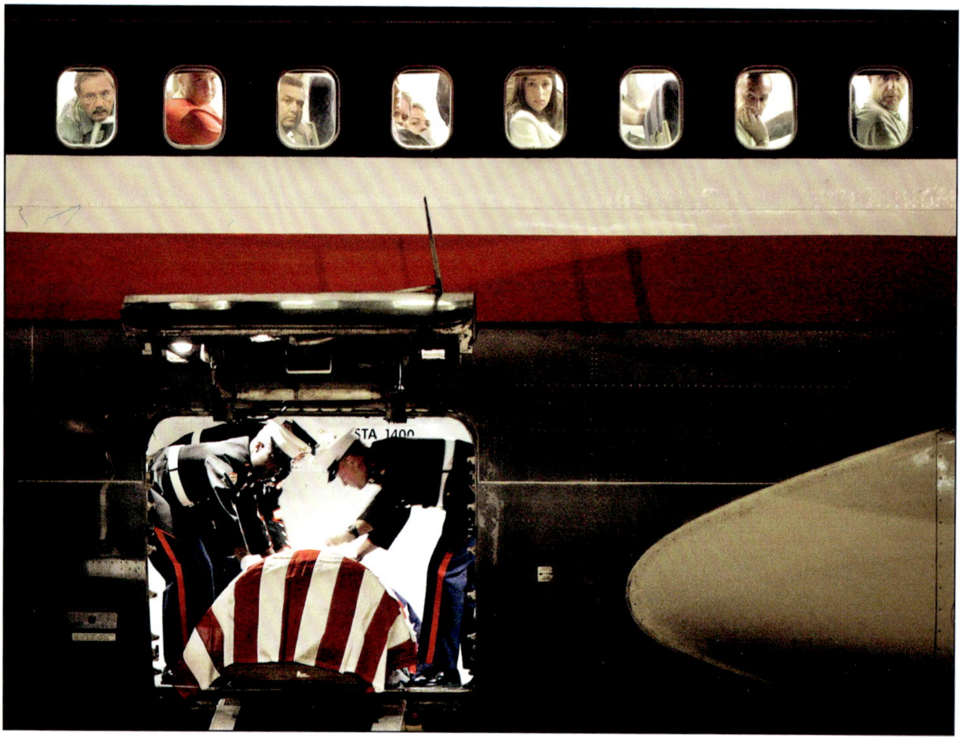

Figure 41. © Todd Heisler / Denver Public Library, Western History Collection.

in the hold while each of us travels to our separate destination, free to choose and not likely to even know what is shared.

The photo is not showing suffering, and yet it is, and other wounds as well. There is no doubt that the casket has a destination, one that will be marked by grief, sorrow, and other manifestations of pain and loss reverberating across family and community. Like the photo of the boy who has looked into the bombed car, this photo suggests that collateral damage extends across societies and generations. Here that damage also is receiving the ritual containment provided by military funerary rites. As in any military funeral, the rites help repair the breach that violence inflicts on the social group, and so also can serve the normalization of war. There are many photographs of funerals and memorial displays of grief, but the pathos of this image comes from showing another kind of containment. The loss marked by the casket is contained by the uniforms and attentive care of the ceremonial guard, while the passengers above are encased in the industrial canister of the plane. They are neatly coordinate—one above the other, neither interfering with the other—but like the axes of plane and casket, also at cross-purposes.

The photograph thus marks another type of loss as well, which is embedded in the image of spectatorship. They look but do not see. Perhaps they had seen the casket, but now it has been removed from sight. In any case they remain immobilized, unable to move without disturbing those next to them, as all are belted into a highly functional system of modern transportation. So they look but cannot act. They also are only temporarily in one place, and they will be dispersing along a hundred different vectors of private activity. They inhabit the structure of civil society rather than a public space. As a group, they are plural (men and women, for example) but also locked into their level of uniformity (white, coach class), with their view strictly limited by the uniformity of the plane's small rectangular windows. The colors of the plane match those of the flag and the honor guard, giving private and public life another dimension of uniformity and a relationship more functional than emotional. The passengers look but cannot connect.

This photograph does not foreground the human condition. Death and incomprehension may be universals, but this is a portrait of a specific social system and how it limits awareness. It demonstrates that the institutions of government and commerce can fit together expertly below the level of public awareness. It models this society's hierarchy of risk now that most military personnel are drawn from the working class, with the middle class able to remain oblivious to the actual costs. It suggests that "freedom" has acquired two very different referents: the personal liberty evident in the small differences and material separation among the passengers, and the wholly abstract value of national sovereignty signified by the flag. This disconnect frames the spectator's gaze: as we see through the lens of "personal liberty" and not also the lens of "a free people," it becomes easy to see the war dead as only individual losses and not as a common diminishment reflecting obligations to one another. (It is important to note that this collective identification does not imply that the war was just, only that the loss of life came within a context of mutual obligation, even if that trust had been betrayed by those holding office.) The photograph documents not a lack of political freedom but rather how it can be channeled and neutralized by the organization of everyday activity. The public may have become blind to what they needed to see, but that doesn't seem to matter when you've got work to do in flight and a tight connection at the next airport. Censorship isn't needed if everyone is too busy.

The habits of a modern liberal society prevent many abuses of power, but the civic spectator may be characteristically incapacitated when it comes to seeing and sharing suffering. And not because she has been looking at too many photographs. The emotional distances built into civil society make it hard to see our complicity in complex processes of aggression, destruction, and exploitation. If that is so, much of the violence in the world will continue to appear to be less painful, extensive, or persistent than it is, while the perpetrators will continue to be able to hide where they always hide: among the rest of us. Fortunately, we are not only looking out the windows of an airliner; a far more important view is provided by the photograph.

Photography documents not only the costs of war but also the reasons we can and cannot see what is happening. Its ubiquity may help to normalize war, but it also can track how war has insinuated itself into the seams of the modern world and is changing in ways that can fracture modernity itself. Rather than presume censorship or mystify war as an experience beyond representation, the public should face up to the fact that all it needs to know is already being shown. Instead of treating photographers as "moral menials" doing the dirty work of public representation, the public should consider why, time after time after time, it has to be shown images that document, argue, challenge, shock, or plead.[75]

Images of violence are a characteristic part of modern society, but so is the violence that they depict. The problem is not the presence of the images but the processes by which modern citizens become habituated to the specific characteristics of violence in their own time. It is a common experience to look back and say, "How could they [a previous generation] have stood for that? Sixteen million dead; seventy million dead: surely *we* wouldn't do that." No, not that . . . But what about the violence that has mutated and adapted to destroy modernity's promise for so many millions of people? The scandal is not only in the numbers themselves but also in the extent to which they could have been avoided.

The processes of normalization go far beyond photography; photography contributes to habituation but also confronts it. Modernity is producing both an overall reduction of violence and continued acceptance of high levels of military expenditure across the board as well as terrible destructiveness in specific areas. It is as if there were zoning laws for violence, and so there are. Given that distribution, photography can be the difference between seeing what is happening and not having to look at all.

Humanity among the Ruins

It is understood that one of the challenges, and responsibilities, of photojournalism is to capture "the decisive moment": that instant when intention becomes action or action becomes effect to define an event and perhaps change the course of history. This encounter with history's eventfulness is not the only task facing either the photographer or the viewing public. Another, perhaps equally daunting responsibility is to ask how photography can represent history's longer, more repetitive patterns. What happens when suffering is prolonged, destruction becomes routine, war is normalized, and searing images turn into genres of catastrophe?

Figure 42's photograph from Aleppo is one answer to this predicament. It is another scene from Rubble World; images of wrecked urban neighborhoods in Syria have become so common that Reuters has gathered some of them into a slide show.[76] We need to admit to the frequency and redundancy of these images. We need to grasp that war is now business as usual for too many people, and that no photograph is likely to change that.

So what can a photograph do? Perhaps it can show us how much is at stake and how much already has been lost. It may have become too easy to see wrecked concrete as another occasion for urban renewal, or to see a broken city as merely a reason for pulling up the drawbridge, or to accept the repetitiveness of the news as a reason to pay less attention rather than become more troubled. Figure 42 challenges all of that and more.

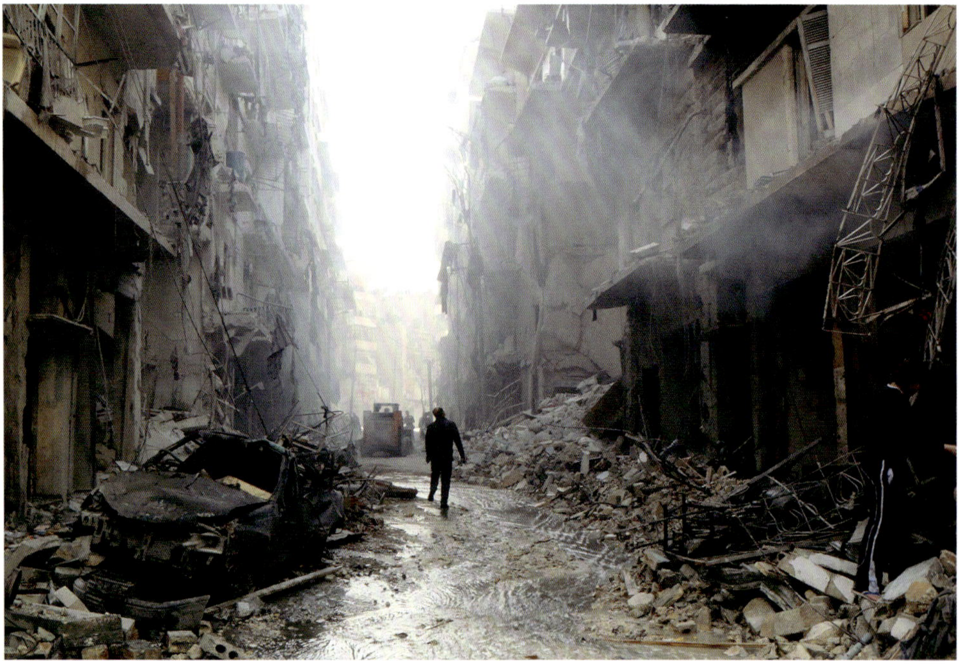

Figure 42. © Reuters / Hosam Katan.

Admittedly, this image has a markedly aesthetic quality, but that is precisely how it becomes capable of making an important political statement. The dark ruins on either side contrast with a stream of light flowing from the hazy shaft of space in the background to the muddy sheen of gray roadway in the foreground. It seems that one can move through this space, albeit slowly and carefully, but there is little chance that one could live there. And yet people will live there.

Perhaps the figure in the right foreground is from the neighborhood. He is looking into the building as if looking for someone or something. He might stand for the usual photographic subject: shown as he would appear to us on the street, detailed (e.g., white shirt, dark sweater, dark workout pants, white stripe) yet anonymous, acting in respect to his immediate circumstances and looking with either an ordinary or an instrumental gaze. The same orientation applies to those working with the skid steer loader in the background. They are figures in context, and their looking is directed by their work. By working to clear the war-torn street they represent more than one virtue, but they are not yet civic spectators. The instrumental gaze looks for information that will never be sufficient to allow us to comprehend the patterns of destructiveness that are wreaking havoc in what once were civil societies.

And so we get to the figure in the middle, and the task of seeing him as an allegorical figure. Of course he could be looking on behalf of a specific interest: Will the wreckage above break loose to fall on those below? Should the buildings be repaired or razed? But something about his posture suggests a more profound openness, as though he were taking in the sheer scale of the wreckage. He seems to gaze in stunned amazement, absorbing the enormity of the change being revealed. Where once neighbors looked down on the street as they conversed on the balconies, now he looks up at those ruined choirs in silence. Instead of seeing what has been damaged, he begins to sense that the city has been blasted into another, surreal reality. He stands on the precipice of the sublime, encountering forces that invoke awe while exceeding human comprehension. His contemplative gaze is underscored by the glint of light on his glasses and the fact that we see him from behind, in darkened clothing. (In some reproductions one can see only the silhouette of a human being.) No ascriptive marker is provided: you cannot limit his identity to Freedom Fighter or Aid Worker or Scavenger or Resident, or adopt the pragmatic optics that would come with those roles. Instead he is somewhat out of context because of how he is seeing: he has become a stranger in his own world, made so by witnessing the unmaking of that world. As his identity becomes abstracted from the familiar characters, circumstances, and reassurances of the news, he becomes a philosophical figure: the Existential Subject who, with his society in ruins and only empty space for a god, now has no choice but to consider how civilization and barbarism are two sides of the same thing. The photograph reveals not only what has happened but also how the city was always on the verge of desolation.

The war in Syria has led to a cascade of sectarian violence throughout the region while activating America's imperial reflex. Add to that the many wars periodically erupting across Africa, the drug wars in Latin America, land grabs and militarization in Eurasia, military suppression of indigenous peoples, minorities, and dissidents around the globe . . . If any of this is to stop, something more than another decisive moment is needed. The pressure for peace will have to be as it always has to be: slow and wide and insistent and then more insistent. If that is to become a decisive process, it will require habits of representation and spectatorship to match.

As the public image prompts a distinctive mode of spectatorship, it requires admitting to how we settle for circumstantial information rather than the knowledge that is needed for real change. And it will require that we look again and again in stunned amazement at what humans can do to one another. Neither amazement nor estrangement is the goal, however. The obscure figure staring amid the ruins can stand for the civic skill of contemplative engagement with the world as it is.

Even so, humanism alone is not enough. The question remains, what, or who, is still missing? The intersection of photography and violence exposes some of the gaps in a society's relationship to its ideals. What is needed are citizens who are willing to take responsibility for what they see. Spectators who are willing to be changed by seeing, to see themselves as part of the same community as the victims and as part of the same community as the perpetrators. Spectators who will decide that violence can be reduced and ask what in their lives is preventing that from happening. These are not easy expectations, and many people have the option of avoiding them. That decision is not innocent. As long as the obligation of seeing is taken lightly, the procession of bodies and treasure brought to the altar of war will continue to be modernity's most unnecessary spectacle.

CHAPTER SEVEN

THE ABUNDANT ART

Modern societies are marked by astonishing levels of prosperity, purchased at the cost of enormous resource depletion. Likewise, the achievements of modern technological and economic development create untold abundance, yet the distribution of that wealth creates wrenching disparities that condemn many to having too little while working for those who have too much. Both justice and sustainability require a better understanding of the relationships between technology, scarcity, and the abundant life. If not, the arc from Neolithic scarcity to modern prosperity to scarcity without hope seems inevitable.

Because photography is a distinctively modern technology, it is deeply entangled in problems of scarcity and abundance. Criticism of the medium has adhered to an economic model of overproduction: by flooding society with images, photography has cheapened everything from image making to reality itself, while at the same time increasing competition for attention and emotional bonding to the point that those resources become exhausted. The same concerns also are voiced today about social media, which supposedly generate far too much media activity while starving social and personal relationships. This conventional anxiety retains special force with photography because of the uncanny resemblance between image and reality and the ease and extent to which images are created, copied, and circulated.

Susan Sontag sounded the characteristic warning: "The omnipresence of photographs has an incalculable effect on our ethical sensibility. By furnishing this already crowded world with a duplicate one of images, photography makes us feel that the world is more available than it really is."[1] One type of excess, the proliferating images of technological reproduction, fuels another one, the emotional expansiveness of "feeling," which creates a third, the imaginary availability of a world that "really" is not easily available. So it is that "industrial societies turn their citizens into image-junkies"; excess, it seems, is the most powerful opiate, breeding dependency, delusion, and dysfunction. As digital technologies now mediate every dimension of everyday life, the warning seems all the more prophetic: photography is inherently excessive, "the most irresistible form of mental pollution," and for that reason dangerous.

Although this anxiety is not baseless, we believe that it is misleading. The concept of "excess"—"the state of exceeding or being in greater quantity or degree than is usual or necessary" —along with its corresponding assumption of a redemptive asceticism, is not the best means for thinking about photography's proliferation.[2] What is needed instead of warnings about "the image world," the "flood" or "deluge" of images, and similar figures of overwhelming displacement is a reconsideration of how photography is valuable precisely because it is an abundant art.[3] By rethinking excess through the lens of "abundance"—"superfluity, more than sufficient supply; plentifulness . . . generosity, liberality"—one can move beyond mistaken conceptions of photography and public spectatorship.[4]

Rather than describing photography as an example of modernity's drive to overproduction, we submit that it provides an opportunity to rethink questions of abundance and scarcity that are central to the sustainability of modern civilization.[5] Does the proliferation of images make understanding appear easier than it is, or could it reveal something about the world? Was the world already too crowded, or does photography reveal how little was being seen before and how much is being wasted? Is image abundance the problem, or could it be a resource for combating regimes of artificial scarcity? We hope to suggest that instead of overwhelming consciousness, the image world can be one way that nature becomes aware of itself; that instead of reproducing a myth of unending prosperity haunted by specters of catastrophe, perhaps photography provides a way of thinking about modern sustainability; and that instead of an antidemocratic social contract coercively backed by assumptions of scarcity, perhaps the civil imagination of photography might offer a different model for democratic association on behalf of the abundant life.

Billions and Billions of Images

The numbers are staggering. By 2013 over two hundred thousand photos were being uploaded to Facebook every minute, and that rate continues to climb along with additional activity on Flickr, Tumblr, Instagram, Snapchat, e-mail, and other platforms.[6] In 2014, ninety million cameras and two billion smartphones and tablets with cameras were purchased, to add to the billions already in hand.[7] These figures also are misleading, as they only begin to capture the extent of the image world. Think of the photographs in endless advertisements as they appear across every conceivable surface, and in every edition of every newspaper, magazine, and online news site, and on the almost one billion other websites, and on the fridge and at your desk . . . Photography has been woven into every part of the social fabric, and to experience modern life is to be awash in images.

The current numbers reflect a process of acceleration, but the proliferation of images was evident from the nineteenth century. Worries about photography's displacement of the real were grounded in experience: it was obvious that images could be reproduced much more easily than other things and that images were being made of every visible thing. Instead of one image, a torrent of images. Instead of one world, a constantly expanding jumble of copies of this and that, ubiquitous but uneven, unwieldy, overwhelming, piling up like the wreckage before Benjamin's angel of history. Photography both exemplifies and fuels the incredible productivity and expansiveness of modernity, while suggesting that the end result can only be chaotic.

But even this focus on productivity is misleading, as the realm of possible experience is far, far greater yet. As Paul Feyerabend reminds us, "The world we inhabit is abundant beyond our wildest imagination. There are trees, dreams, sunrises; there are thunderstorms, shadows, rivers; there are wars, flea bites, love affairs; there are the lives of people, Gods, entire galaxies."[8] To focus on images alone is a form of hubris—and shortsighted. From the smallest variation in gesture to the vast expanses of space and time, human comprehension can encompass neither the endless particularity of the surface of things nor the extreme variations in scale that define the physical world, to which we add the subjective experiences of all the people inhabiting the many worlds of human association, experiences that we try to communicate through a constant chatter of words and images that cannot begin to represent all that they supposedly encompass.

As Feyerabend quickly adds, human consciousness can exist at all because "only a tiny fraction of this abundance affects our minds. . . . A superconscious organism would not be superwise, it would be paralyzed."[9] Nor is this limited to cognition. As George Eliot noted, "If we had a keen vision and feeling of all ordinary human life, it would be like hearing the grass grow and the squirrel's heart beat, and we should die of that roar which lies on the other side of silence. As it is, the quickest of us walk about well wadded with stupidity."[10] Both thinking and feeling have to be buffered to keep out the roar of reality, and the elements of both thought and communication have evolved for that purpose. Words, syntax, numeracy, imagery: these and other tools are valuable both for what they show and for what they do not show. That said, images are often expected to provide a sense of particularity that has been elided by other, more abstract media. At that point, each individual image is suspect for providing too little of the world, while the archive can be faulted for overwhelming our ability to select, judge, or respond rationally. Although these dangers exist, they occlude another capability, which is how image and archive can balance the dangers of abstraction and indifference.

This relationship between overproduction and abstraction is already captured in modern design. The strong emphasis on formal simplicity, rectilinear structure, streamlined surfaces, and absence of decoration provides a comprehensive minimizing to counteract the incredible profusion of industrialized production. A world saturated with products appears less cluttered through techniques that reduce visual noise and encourage efficient substitution and stacking. The rationalizing and smoothing of the built environment may have another function as well: an architectural disenchantment that through standardization purges any locale of mystery or immanence. As Charles Taylor has summarized the point (following Max Weber), "One of the central features of Western modernity, on just about any view, is the progress of disenchantment, the eclipse of the world of magic forces and spirits."[11] Modern society becomes profoundly secularized. Paddy Scannell puts the point bluntly: "It was not God that was killed in the course of modernization but the world."[12] For all the benefits of secularization—and they are extensive—it also is a radical simplification that denies more parochial resources for acknowledging the full extent of reality, and for crafting a sense of being in right relationship with a world that vastly exceeds individual understanding.

This radical undermining of traditional mentalities persists even as it has become a flash point for cultural conflict both within states and at the edges of the Western system. In fact, it has produced a need for magical thinking, which is evident in everything from the daily fare in television and advertising to market ideology.[13] (Again, focusing on photography's capacity for enchantment misses the mark in respect to where illusion really thrives.)[14] What is important, however, is not assessing levels of delusion but rather considering how spiritualism can involve a recognition or homage to abundance. Whatever else the imp, sprite, nymph, angel, or god may be, it signifies the excessive nature of reality that always eludes human comprehension. In a world without spirits, something else has to provide that sign; if not, then humans truly will be alienated from reality.

But isn't photography limited to the natural world, not the supernatural? Spirit photography is now a historical oddity, and few will say that God can be photographed.[15] The production of any visual semblance or likeness of divinity is anathema in some faiths, and in at least one not even the name should be seen in full. More secular thinkers could add that the cosmos is enormous, with much of it beyond the sliver of the electromagnetic spectrum visible to the human eye. The universe is big, humans are small; get over it and get on with the practical business of living in this world. One day at a time in the here and how, where it is hard enough to see your way to the end of the week, much less across the endless, expanding vastness for ever and ever. Really, who has time for that?

Well, some do. The monks in figure 43 are looking into the night sky of a lantern festival in northern Thailand. There is something important to see here, even if one doesn't know the full meaning of the festival, the specific religious practice of the monks, where the lanterns came from, or just about anything else specific to this scene. Our interpretive clue comes from Buddhist texts such as the Lotus Sutra, which provide many recitations of the vastness, richness, and

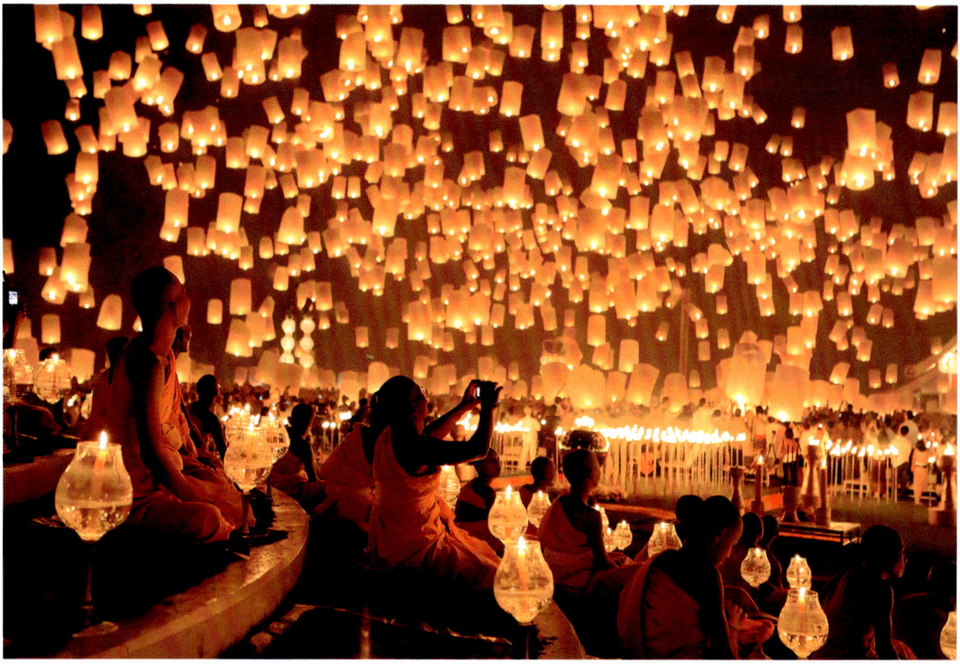

Figure 43. © Frans Jo - Imageenation / Getty Images.

endlessness of the Buddha worlds: "innumerable hundreds of thousands of billions" of them, each showing "bodies as innumerable and numberless as the sands of hundreds of thousands of millions of billions of Ganges," extending for "innumerable tens of millions of billions of eons," and that is only one small part of the teaching.[16] One tiny fragment of the immeasurable Dharma of the innumerable millions of billions of Buddha worlds, but still glorious.

Radiant, you might say, like a thousand (million billion) lights in the sky. We have no doubt that the monks know that they are looking at lanterns, and we expect that they are enjoying them much as anyone would, that is, for the sheer delight created by the visual spectacle. But perhaps some of them are seeing more as well—seeing through teachings and ritual practices that have developed the human ability to discern the universal radiance that lies beyond the range of ordinary vision. Religion and science alike draw on and extend this larger power of perception—not always, of course, but enough to give us hints of what more could be known or experienced. Stated otherwise, this photograph illuminates a relationship between seeing a lantern and seeing the eternal radiance of being; that relationship is what we have been calling imagination.

Photography, by fusing reality and the imagination, can be another way to extend that power of perception, or at least to hint at what more could be done when it teams up with the right ritual or the right telescope. But even though such images are familiar enough, they often come wadded in spiritual denial. We see them as images of something, instead of understanding them as signs of things unseen.[17] This claim need not be mystical: it is instead an imaginative arc traced from the photograph to the photographic archive, and then from the archive, as if it were but one photo, to the reality that includes and exceeds what has been shown. Or perhaps one might consider how photography is not about objects, and sense what is suggested by figure 43: that not only a festival or the night sky but all of reality is glittering with the same connecting, enveloping, awakening energy.

This photograph is important not only for its reflexive luminosity but also for capturing small signs of everyday behavior amid the heavenly spectacle. No one is prostrate, the monks exhibit various attitudes from delight to curiosity to inattentiveness, and the spectators in the crowd mill about as they typically do. Like those in the image itself, we are in the presence of both a moment of wonder and the ordinary habits of everyday life. As Jane Bennett observes, that is the place of enchantment: "to be enchanted is to be struck and shaken by the extraordinary that lives amid the familiar and the everyday." As she also notes, this can be an ethical encounter that requires imagination, which "energizes us with alternatives, with the power of the new and startling and wonderful."[18]

Which is precisely when many people whip out their cameras, like that monk in the middle of the photo. As he is the central figure, he would seem to be the primary subject of the photograph and one that sets up the standard critique. It is not enough for him to be in the presence of the marvelous event, it seems; he has to buffer it with the camera, producing an image-token of participation that already is displacing the event itself. This contrast between the enveloping experience and the tiny rectangle of his viewfinder is damning: instead of opening himself to an authentic experience of the reality that is present to him, he looks at an image, a secondary reality that is a tiny fragment of the whole. His mistake of becoming blinkered by the technology of the camera is multiplied by others doing the same: perhaps the monk on his right is checking his device, while other cameras are part of the visual noise of the crowd.

But that critique features only a small slice of the virtual experience. We think the photograph shows much more, including a world in which the camera is one form of spectatorship among others that all are part of the event itself. Look again, and note how easily the cameras fit in to what is, after all, a festival of lights, and how they are not dominant. They are bits of light added to the spectacle, and because the monk with the camera is a bit off center, the spectacle as a whole remains the central interest. The light of his viewfinder is matched by the glint off his glasses (an optical technology exempt from critique), while both devices are distinct from his exposed head and hands, while the many swatches of lights are balanced by areas of darkness. The scene is a study in multiple complementarities, not hard contrasts. The camera phone that is lifted up will again be set down, just as the continual shifting of attention by and among the monks is a part of the ceremony itself. And if some of them find the crowd more intriguing than the lights, isn't that also part of the story? Equally important, the lanterns are not only in the sky but already all around the monks—among them and surrounding them, largely unnoticed yet part of the celebration. The lesson to be learned might be that a camera can get in the way of seeing, but really? Consider instead how the photograph shows that luminosity envelops us, that it always exceeds our limited powers of perception, that there are multiple ways to experience it, and that the choices available involve many possible encounters that reflect the dynamics of light and darkness, perception and mediation, individuals and groups, quotidian habits and moments of awe, and much else that is part of any path to enlightenment.

As imagination is an act of extraordinary seeing, enchantment might be a representative moment for reconsidering photography's relationship to the world. Could heaven and earth, secular and spiritual, ritual and routine, ordinary and miraculous be mirror images of each other? The lamps extend imaginatively to the stars, and the tableau on the ground extends around the bend of the scene and through the horizon as if following the curve of the earth to the curve of spacetime. The lamps are radiant, but so is everyone and everything else. Photography is always grounded in the mundane world, but that world now is being transformed into a world overflowing with energy and meaning. Even the careful spacing between the monks becomes richly evocative, not empty but full of potential, as if each speck of space or time could contain innumerable Buddha worlds, each one a universe as abundant as our own.

Photography and Philosophy

If there can be a philosophy of abundance, then photography is one of its media and its representative art. Such a philosophy unlocks photography from artificial constraints on what an image can mean or should do, and it offers a means for exploring and expanding the conception of the world as defined by abundance more than scarcity. Too often those suspicious of photography are holding out for a conception of meaning as a scarce resource, something to be won in a zero-sum game between reason and other human faculties. By contrast, photography reveals a different conception of meaning: one that is multifold, plural, continually being augmented and altered through production that is excessive and necessarily so. To mark the cultural significance of this orientation, Martin Jay has suggested—approvingly—that photography "has served to re-enchant the world." Jay labels this orientation a "magical nominalism": photography evokes a world that is "more than the categories we impose on it, more than the meanings we impute to it . . . a world that somehow stubbornly thwarts all of our best—or is it worst?—efforts to disenchant it."[19] As others have suggested, getting beyond the critiques of mythology and then of enlightenment itself can lead to the realization that there are, "in the modern age, *fully secular and deliberate* strategies for reenchantment, of which (to put the point another way) no one, however hard-bitten he or she may be, need feel ashamed."[20] Actually one need not insist on secular purity nor hold out for explicit deliberativeness, given that what photography affords us comes from its entanglement with ordinary life.

Photography's abundance is a material condition, the principal means by which it makes a common world, and a way of being with others in that world. That abundance includes the many practices of image production, sharing, and spectatorship that generate photographs, but it has a cultural weight by itself as well. Because of the omnipresence of this museum without walls, one is always in an aesthetic space dedicated to seeing others, and to seeing them as both typified and unique, strangers and equals, near and far, present and absent, and continuously moving through time. This space, which becomes continuously expansive and collapsible, creates a political geography having at least three dimensions: reproduction of conventional demarcations; an egalitarian imaginary in which anything can merit the full attention of global spectatorship; and a sense of a continuously unfolding world that is inherently excessive, beyond representation itself. Perhaps equally important, spectatorship remains secular in a significant sense even as it opens itself to imaginative expression: as photography points toward the boundlessness of reality, it also makes it so continuous with ordinary life that it need not become a source of terror requiring worship and sacrifice. What is denigrated as a lack of context is also the source of what might be (noting the irony) a naive cosmopolitanism. The abundant world is one that is both too capacious and too familiar to be constantly threatening.

Most important, the archive creates a continuously unfolding process of spectatorship. As Ariella Azoulay notes, "The event of photography is subject to a unique form of temporality" that is made up of an ever-expanding series of encounters.[21] As images are seen again and again—the same images, similar images, other images, by more and more people, again and again—the habitus of photography becomes a place where images and the image world as a whole are continuously developing through use as they circulate beyond local boundaries, being taken up by others here and there, and then again somewhere else, and again and again. This is another dimension of abundance: an open-ended process of circulation that contains a multitude of spectators, each one having a distinctive encounter while also aggregating into multiple patterns of response. As Michael Warner observes, this is one of the characteristics of a public culture, that is, a culture created through open circulation: "Public discourse, in the nature of its address, abandons the security of its positive, given audience. It promises to address anybody. It commits itself in principle to the possible participation of any stranger."[22] Many photographs are not intended for public circulation, but circulation has become the ground of photography, a social fact that is reinforced by the understanding that any photograph is inherently accessible. Because it shows what can be seen, it is open to view unless withheld from view; because it can be reproduced repeatedly, it is easily shared. Thus photography presumes a capacious sense of audience, and with that of photographic meaning. The photograph is not merely an object but an object in circulation; whether that is actual or potential circulation need not matter. The public world of photography is necessarily continuous, unrestricted, sure to contain many different responses, including objectionable responses. It will include channels of consensus and eddies of controversy, but the succession of images is unending.

This continuing series of encounters is very close to Feyerabend's example of the abundance evident in ordinary experience: "The simplest human action varies from one person and occasion to the next—how else would we recognize our friends only from their gait, posture, voice, and divine their changing moods?"[23] Abundance is a feature of intimacy—close knowledge of and affection for another is not possible without it, and then creates more of it. Of course scarcity is a frequent and often painful fact of life in intimate relationships, and yet one that can be overcome through discovery of other reservoirs of plentitude, and that breakthrough is intimacy in action. A capacity for something *like* intimacy in collective association may be an unexpected benefit of photography's close encounter with the decor, postures, and expressions of everyday life. Looking at a photograph can always be faulted for being only a semblance of the unique, authentic, profound emotional relationship that can be fully experienced in private life, but the public image offers something else as well. Continuous exposure to the habits, moods, and trials of others teaches not only that scarcity haunts the smallest details of getting through the day but also that every day is filled with people and energies that exceed every limit but one. As collective association acquires some of the intimacy of private life, it also acquires a sense of abundance not limited to our meager knowledge of each other as individuals. All can share in a virtual world that displays countless possibilities for seeing, thinking, and acting together.

More important still, the full implication is that any scarcity should only be temporary, something to be remedied or compensated for by better use of the richness of a world in which so much is given. Thus a philosophy of abundance is not a deluded denial of real scarcity but an ethical standpoint for freeing people from the many forms of hoarding. Even when documenting want and other privation, the photograph implies that these deficiencies are not necessary. In the photograph of social deprivation, moral pressure is supplied in part by the abundance both absent and present. Even when seeing abject poverty, one sees bodies, social relationships, tools, shelters, gestures of assistance, all of which are markers of enormous human potential. Often a patterned cloth or bracelet or some other decoration is visible, as yet another sign of social energy and organization that could be tapped. And not least, the camera is there, and with that the system of photo distribution and all that it draws on and connects. Documentary witness is again and again a critique of social distribution, as both the presence and the content of the image are testimony that scarcity is unnecessary and immoral amid a larger abundance that could sustain enough for all.

This conception of an abundant world is maintained by all photography. Again, whatever the particular composition of the individual photograph of scarcity, the entire archive represents an abundant world. A world having endless numbers of hills, valleys, sunrises; a world of natural and social energies that could be continuously renewable; a world of images that capture and share this abundance. The archive also provides a basis for knowing that world in its complexity and richness: through the specialized optical technologies of scientific research, the dedicated witnessing of documentary photography and photojournalism, and even the conventional reproductions of snapshot photography and other popular genres.

To suggest the importance of the archive and the difference that comes from defining photography as a medium for highlighting the richness of the world, we might want to reconsider the genre of landscape photography.[24] There is no doubt that landscape photography is popular, but is it really *important*? When people take photography seriously, they almost always are doing so to focus on the people who are being shown. War, poverty, politics, sports—whatever the subject, the point is to show what people are doing and experiencing. They are shown in specific circumstances, but there is no doubt that *who* matters more than *where*. Why should an empty vista matter?

Perhaps because it is never empty.

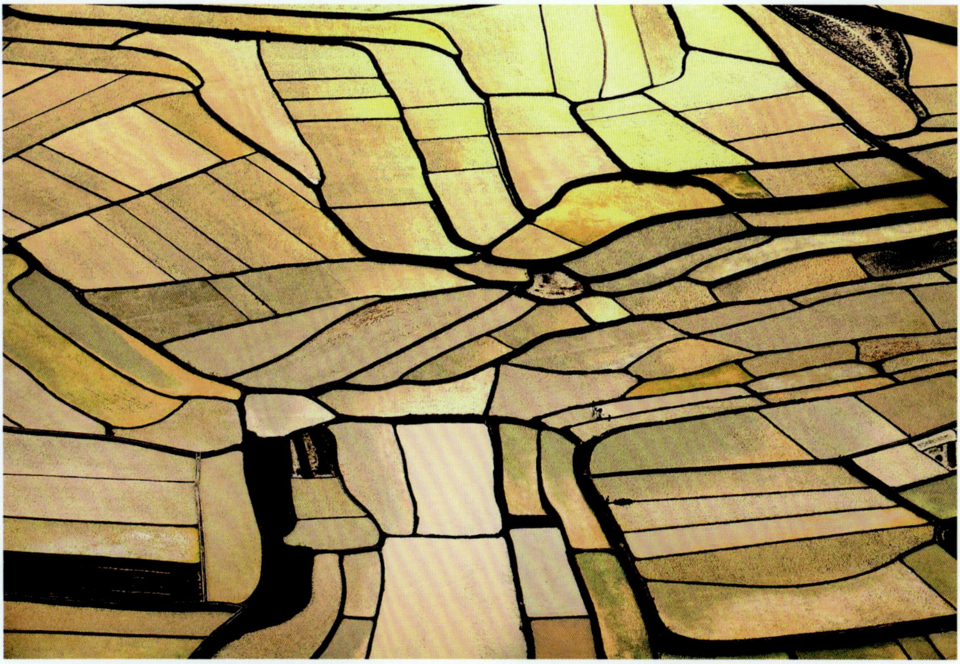

Figure 44. © Xinhua / Landov.

The land in figure 44 undulates slowly and smoothly, almost as if a musical composition. The liquid flow of light over a hill, and the ease with which the earth exceeds human scale, suggests vast continuities across time and space. The exquisitely fitted paddy fields seem to have followed the same processes: they are the result of many generations of careful agriculture, and if their beauty cannot be appreciated fully from the ground they are no less artfully wrought for that.

Like any garden, most landscapes reflect human engineering of one sort or another—not least the framing and other artistry provided by the camera. The landscape could be a subtle exercise in narcissism: humans can pretend that they are looking at nature while actually admiring their own reflection. Or these photos could be another form of vanity, suggesting an easy harmony between humanity and nature (and perhaps nature's God). Such photos rarely feature nature's harshness, and in any case the camera will not let you feel how cold the desert gets at night or how flies can drive you mad. But that is not the lesson to be learned here.

Nor is it enough to note how landscape photography has been an important resource for the environmental movement. To be sure, many civilizations have driven themselves to environmental catastrophe, but this civilization's descent can be photographed, and so one modern technology might provide some leverage against the inertia of resource depletion.[25] From Ansel Adams's portraits of Yosemite to the "Earthrise" on the cover of the *Whole Earth Catalog* to the successive *Sierra* magazine covers to the many documentaries of environmental degradation, landscape photography has been a powerful means for political advocacy on behalf of a planet that cannot speak for itself. At some point, however, environmentalism overwrites the images; they become merely means to a pragmatic end, rather than something also capable of guiding other forms of reflection. We want to suggest one such alternative, one that is consistent with an environmental ethos but not the same thing.

Whatever else it is, the landscape photograph can be an image of abundance. Whether capturing the lush density of a rain forest or the traces of wind on a barren sand dune, the landscape shows a world that is immensely larger, more interconnected, more amazing than anything any human society will ever make. Which may be why, in a secular society, there is such immense popular demand for sunrises, golden fields of wheat, shimmering vistas, and other examples of the immense energy flowing across the planet every day. These images put the spectator in a relationship with an abundant earth, which can be a source of promise amid all the smaller scarcities of time, money, attention, and so forth that one deals with throughout the day. Instead of a spirit of the place, the image on the desktop or photograph on the wall can provide a similar connection to vital energies.

None of this denies the role of scarcity in nature or human affairs. Indeed figure 44 can be seen as a subtle meditation on how to build a sustainable relationship with scarcity on behalf of abundance. That said, there are good reasons in this case to ask whether the aesthetic values are misleading in respect to the political and economic provenance of the photograph. The photo would not have been taken by a farmer, and it is of an area that had been undergoing severe drought for several years; thus the image could fit in with Chinese government propaganda to the effect that there is nothing to worry about in Donglan County. One also might see imperfect property rights, land divided and subdivided over time as families grow, and very low productivity from manual labor in a system that kept peasants poor during a century of enormous increases in rural productivity and prosperity elsewhere. Yet this golden image of the sun's ever-streaming energy could underwrite negotiations of land use, highlighting how scarcity is a byproduct of human organization.

The dangers of being blinded by abundance are discussed below, but in the interim we should emphasize that complaints about overconsumption do not qualify as a sufficient account of abundance, as they presume a more beneficial scarcity. Although that concern applies when buffering the roar of the world, in other contexts it can have unstated implications that are decidedly antidemocratic. By contrast, the critical edge to an ethics of abundance is the supposition that there always can be enough, if one is willing to find it and share it. This is not a denial of natural limits such as mortality, but there always is more time than you think; or if you are running out of time, more money that could be spent or more love that could be expressed; or if you are running out of money or love, other people who could be called on for help; or if you are running out of people, other sources of spiritual support or insight; and so forth—and the "and so forth" is part of the story. In respect to photography itself, there always can be another image; or if not another image, something new to be seen in the ones we have; or if nothing new can be seen, another interpretation becomes possible; or if interpretation is exhausted, then other spectators can be included; and so forth. More to the point, there already have been such images, and there already are such reservoirs of time, money, love, people, and spirit. And when there really is not enough, then neither nature nor the image world is at fault. Instead responsibility lands squarely on those who have used or hoarded the resources needed, and especially on those who have created artificial scarcity in order to hold power over others.

This ethic of abundance is necessarily democratic, in two senses. First, it is sustained by photography's democratic sweep and uptake. Calls for recognizing the abundant life go back deep into the history of religion, but they can acquire a specifically democratic inflection because of how photography has recorded vernacular life and been taken up so thoroughly into the lifeworld of democratic societies. In the image world of photography, abundance comes not from a single, distant source on high but through the incredible proliferation of ordinary things, and it is recognized not through the monumental work of art but through the continuous reproduction of everyday life—say, through two hundred thousand photos being uploaded every minute. As Sontag recognized (and disliked), this profusion of images is an act of democratic leveling—all values are given equal footing, all perspectives can be expressed, all lifestyles acknowledged.[26] Of course life remains transversed with distinctions and hierarchies, and photography is used to reinforce all of them, but that social complexity now has to happen within a habitus in which hierarchy is not automatically sovereign. Likewise, this is not simple relativism but a condition of egalitarian access to the image and unavoidable pluralism in both what is shown and the range of responses. The oversupply of images testifies to a common world in which there should be room for everyone.

Abundance is a democratic concept in a second sense as well. The abundant life is by definition not something for the few and the very few. Abundance has to be abundant, not hoarded. By contrast, authoritarian regimes (and their wannabe leaders in democratic societies) put great stock in scarcity: actual or impending scarcity is always the basis of authoritarian measures, which are claimed to be necessary in order to avoid the loss of security, liberty, and other goods and essential resources. The democratic alternative is to share those goods and so to define them as part of the common life that should be available to all, rather than to withhold them on behalf of an artificial scarcity that justifies concentrations of power.

One irony is that democratic societies can be a serious threat to environmental sustainability, particularly as they are yoked to robust capitalist economies oriented toward expansion by increasing consumer consumption. This global expansion of prosperity is creating systemwide problems of resource depletion, environmental degradation, and climate change. (Yes, there can be real scarcity, especially when humans are ignorant of or indifferent to other forms of abundance.) Therefore, one of the challenges for an ethic of abundance is to account for its relationship, positive and negative, to environmental sustainability. As it turns out, that is not the only problem it faces, but it is a big one.

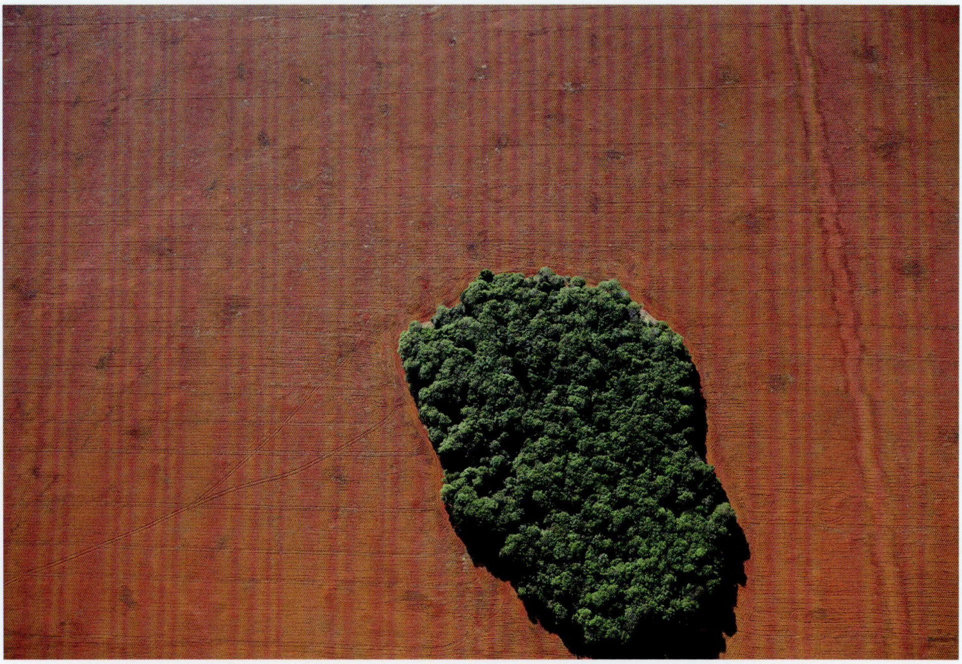

Figure 45. © Damon Winter / The New York Times / Redux.

Too Much of a Good Thing?

You might wonder what you are seeing in figure 45. Look closely, and you will see a clump of trees. Some might also recognize the even rows of high-tech monocultural agriculture stretched across the plain. Now we've given too much away, as you also could have seen a clump of mold or cells bunched together in some microscopic field. Beneath the surface one might also "see" some more elemental social form such as herd animals pressing together for warmth or even a raft adrift in a barren sea. Whatever it is, it is visually striking: one blot of rich green on a uniformly reddish-brown background etched with small modulations in black. Scale becomes elastic while form and color dominate in any register. There is something basic here, but what?

Perhaps some context would help. The caption in the *New York Times* read: "Small islands of forest dot the landscape of farms and ranches, fulfilling regulations to maintain percentages of native forest on agricultural properties. Driven by profits derived from fertile soil, the region's dense forests have been aggressively cleared over the past decade, and Mato Grosso is now Brazil's leading producer of soy, corn and cattle, exported across the globe by multinational companies."[27] So it is a photograph of trees in a field—specifically, of trees saved to maintain a forestation quota in a field of soybeans produced for the international commodity markets. The additional information and the political subtext are helpful, but a problem remains. Note how the photo's ambiguity in scale is also present in the text. We are seeing something "small" and also something that extends "across the globe." The *Times* story emphasizes the tension between localized benefits and global costs.[28] Life might be simple if one could focus exclusively on one dimension or the other: manage the forests for the planet or allow economic development wherever possible. But, of course, the problem is that both are needed. What were called "profits" are also jobs, and also cheap food in a world where hundreds of millions of people still are not fed adequately. One has to be able to see both locally and globally, a bifocal vision that itself does not come cheap.

Some might argue that the picture is unfair. It looks as if only the trees are natural, whereas in a few months the entire field also would be a vibrant green. The photo is not so much fair or unfair, however, as it is profound. It captures something essential, a sense of what is at stake. That small island of trees can stand in for everything from a tiny cell to the planet itself, and the point is always the same: no matter what the scale, life on earth is a small, precious island amid a void. That void, however, is not a reassertion of scarcity as the ultimate horizon but a cue for an even larger framework. Theism is the obvious example, but in our case that framework is dialectical: abundance and scarcity are two poles of a productive tension within human consciousness because consciousness is grounded in material conditions of existence.

The photo also captures a dialectical relationship between two different kinds of resource management: the high-modernist, industrial-scale agribusiness of the fields and the scene as a whole, and low-impact sustainability under the canopy of the Amazonian forest (something no longer possible in the scrap of forest remaining in the picture, an intuitive loss that gives the image some of its moral force). Each contains a different ratio between abundance and scarcity. In the original forest, the environment is astonishingly lush, but it supports only very small populations of human beings. When the land is stripped bare and production depends on external inputs of machines, fuel, and fertilizer, many of the original species—and peoples—are destroyed, but monocultural productivity soars and the environment can support far larger populations.

The image is ironic as well: trees having no need of human intervention evoke something like sympathy, whereas the field is an achievement of human productivity that evokes a sense of sterility. But, of course, one cannot simply reverse the equation. The fields will wither if carbon dioxide levels get out of whack, and the deeper irony is that as commodity cropping produces excesses that are then funneled into processed foods, what feeds us can kill us. Indigenous peoples in the Amazon basin learn to discriminate carefully between poisons, medicines, and foods in the forest, and moderns need to learn to do the same in respect to their remaking of the forest. In each case one needs to learn to see, but not in the same way.

In this case the photograph provides one lesson in how to see modern development: as if cultured for observation, both up close and from a distance, on behalf of sustainable growth and capable of extinction. By seeing abundance and scarcity as reciprocal bases for interpretation, one becomes equipped to address problems in both the image world and the world it represents. That does not become a commitment to endorsing resource addiction, gluttonous oil consumption, or other dysfunctional or unsustainable habits that harm individuals, society, and the environment. It would involve considering how scarcity is both a natural and an artificial condition, and how exceeding limits can lead to both newfound abundance and catastrophe. (Too much of anything can kill, while scarcity can be a boon to improvement, as with the constitutive scarcity of sports and some other competitive events.) There are dangers of abundance in both the virtual and the material worlds, but they need to be seen in a dialectical relationship with problems of scarcity, rather than in respect to fantasies of moderation or ascetic propriety. Too often those who fault overproduction have no conception of the stoop labor and chronic shortages it replaced, and those who fault the profusion of images have little recollection of how blinkered, deluded, and mean people can be when they have no sense of a wider world and no encounter with other ways of living.

That said, there are some concerns that need to be acknowledged. The first was suggested by the questions of land use and perspective in figure 44: a celebration of abundance, particularly through the enjoyment of natural beauty, can become a distraction from serious economic and political problems wrought by the powers that be. As this is one of the central tenets of the old paradigm, it needs only to be mentioned here; we really cannot avoid that critical wariness now, and it is one of the elements of contemporary citizenship. As others have argued, however, one should not fault aesthetics or photography tout court or assume that either one is rightly ascetic.[29]

A second and related question is whether abundance hasn't already been made into a means of social control. The specific concern here is with the role that consumerism plays in modern societies. Surely the most immediate experience of abundance for many people in the most prosperous countries is the abundance of commercial goods. Supermarkets and restaurant chains, malls and outlet malls, items stacked to the ceiling at the big box stores, vending machines everywhere, and the giant online emporium at your fingertips—the abundant world appears to be a commercial world, prewrapped for your convenience, and don't count the cost. Add to this the constant advertising across all media, and critical concerns about the modern phantasmagoria appear all too prescient. Citizens are being turned into consumers simply by looking at things they cannot avoid seeing, while everyone becomes increasingly disposed to believe that the market economy can meet any need.[30] Indeed Anne Norton has argued that shopping has become a popular enactment of liberalism, which promotes individual choice and makes the availability of consumer goods "an index of freedom."[31] What is most distinctive about her analysis, however, is that she sees this mentality not as a false consciousness but as an already ambivalent awareness of both freedom and compulsion; furthermore, she argues that "the virtue of democracy lies in its desire for more" and that popular culture is a continuous expression of "the desire for more things, more knowledge, more sensation, more speech, more forms for the self, more time, more power, more rights, more justice."[32]

One need not agree with this highly optimistic alignment of capitalism, liberalism, and democracy to acknowledge that it contains an important insight. Although the drive for abundant life can be captured, distorted, misdirected, exploited, and limited by a culture of consumer consumption, it also works through that culture, which actually has more resources for realizing the good life than those it promotes. The key to evaluating the role of photography or any other medium is to consider how the dominant images of abundance are both limiting and empowering, diversions and examples of an important drive, tokens of compulsion and refusals of artificial limits. And, of course, one antidote to the obvious constrictions and delusions is more images, more visions, other forms of excess beyond those that can be commodified.

A far more insidious danger could be that a philosophy of abundance could suggest that particular individuals or peoples are dispensable, as their labor or other contribution or way of being in the world could always be replaced. Such claims are another example of how anything can be misused, but they are more peculiar still, for typically calls to the abundant life have come from figures who insisted on human dignity: Buddha, Confucius, Hillel, Jesus, and other sages did not use the modern vocabulary of individual rights, but their commitment to the inherent value of the individual person is unmistakable.[33] The importance of this association is twofold. First, it reminds us that no one value should dominate all discussions and that ethics and politics alike require continuous attention to a host of values and other goods, not least in our time the commitment to human rights. If wealth of any sort is to be displayed and celebrated, it must be to support rather than be at the expense of other values. Second, the values of human dignity and creativity are not ancillary to a philosophy of abundance but central to its development. A denial of human autonomy and dignity occurs whenever an individual is treated as only a means to an end, to be valued only in that regard and disposable otherwise. That treatment becomes thinkable only in conditions of scarcity, and it then transforms one kind of scarcity into another—for example, a deficit of labor is replaced by the multiple impoverishments of slavery. The vision of an abundant life is a promise to those who have been denied, not those who already have it. It is an abundance across all dimensions of human life, including the subjective and spiritual. It is inclusive and cooperative rather than exclusive and possessive: something that can be had only by sharing.

Abundance and Terror

Photography's reproduction of abundance is not all sunrises and birthday parties. Evil is known by its excess, and the ability to confront evil draws on a similar capacity to rupture our boundaries of emotional complacency. Consider how a single photo, figure 46, draws on a darker sense of abundance.

The caption reads, "The human remains are seen during the exhumation of a Stalinist-era mass grave on the military cemetery in the heart of the Polish capital Warsaw. May 13, 2013. The grave is believed to contain the remains of around 200 victims of a post-war campaign of communist terror." Perhaps the victim was screaming at the moment of death, but the gaping jaw could be an accident of decay or excavation. Perhaps the lost individual will be identified, and perhaps the family can be notified. Perhaps the remains will have forensic value, and maybe some remnant of justice can yet be done.

And none of these assessments can mute the emotional excessiveness of the image. The accidents of time have produced a howling, shrieking cry of pain and rage. The body emerging from the earth is still shrouded with dust, as if still more ghost than material thing. The immobility of being long buried is still binding the corpse, but it seems to be straining to be released, to rise up in glorious, savage revenge. A revenge that will never come, as instead it will be interned again in a bureaucratic process constrained by a decided imbalance of power.

In like manner, the power of the image may be channeled into symbolism: there lies the Past, or Terror, or the Human Condition. Whatever their limitations, such things do need to be said. Skull imagery suggests comparisons with the memento mori of art history, but the brutal truth of modern remembrance is that these victims did not have to die so soon. We cannot help but think—or hope—that this image might haunt whatever idea is brought to it; that it might arise again in the night or at an odd moment, and that it might disturb, trouble, bring one perhaps to tremble for this lost soul. As it does so, a deeper form of testimony begins to emerge: the photo-

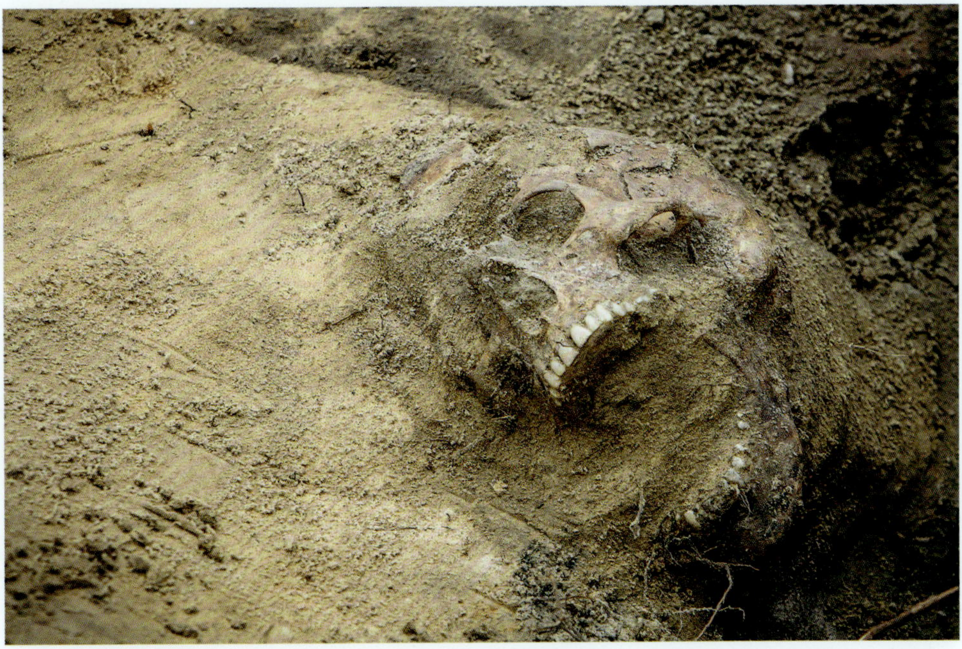

Figure 46. © Wojtek Radwanski / AFP / Getty Images.

graph documents how evil is a perversion of abundance. How it kills beyond reason or measure; how it unleashes the worst elements in human nature and rewards the most vicious thugs in any society; how it makes the tortured body into a landscape of pain. The skull becomes not only the trace of a victim but also a sign of the predator. An abundant world can be turned against itself, perhaps too easily: "abundance and chaos are different aspects of one and the same world."[34] As Elaine Scarry has warned, the most awful intention of the torturer is to make the objects and places of the ordinary world, in all its quotidian presence and continuity, into a continuous experience of terror.[35] The abundant life has to be one that can resist such attempts at diabolical transformation.

One hope is that photography's compact with overproduction and excessive saturation of the image world can equip people to resist cruel forms of excess. To do so, photographer and spectators alike will have to become increasingly capable of moving between image and archive, between the decisive encounter and the assurance that there always can be a world that is wider than the prison or killing field. As one example of that, consider how the howling skull might evoke a macabre spirit world, and with that might be an act of resistance against terror and violence. As we imagine it howling, the skull evokes all those lost to violence—the multitude who were murdered, starved, or destroyed otherwise by hatred and greed. An abundant world is a world filled with death but also redeemed by the memory of those who have died. Just as the act of exhumation creates a more crowded—and more emotional—world, so does looking at an image to bring back the spirits of the dead. One form of excess (the skull) activates another (the spirit world of history's victims), and as they crowd into the present they become a cloud of witnesses.

This sense of abundance can be a political commitment because of how it refuses the reduction to bare life. That concept exemplifies how scarcity can be an artificial condition created and managed for domination; by contrast, the optic of abundance always sees what else is also there or could be there.[36] A salient comparison is provided by the iconography of Holocaust memorials displaying shoes, watches, and other items of everyday life that were confiscated from the victims. The crucial statement comes from the display of an excessive accumulation of these ordinary objects. That tragic abundance transforms perception to recognize the enormity of the crime of genocide: instead of seeing merely signs of fashion or routine or uniformity or individuality in these social objects, one is confronted with the extraordinary richness of the lives that were destroyed. Every domestic item and routine, every second of every day, the myriad experiences that filled up those spaces and hours continuously—by re-creating the overlooked abundance of everyday life, the memorial recalls the unsung plentitude of a people living together. The photographic archive does the same: the abundance of vernacular life stands in contrast to all that was stolen, wasted, damaged, denied, and destroyed.

The Ongoing Revelation of the World

The encounter with evil is only the most extreme of the places where photography, because of its capability as an abundant art, can reveal something about the world. This capacity involves more than recording, and it extends beyond problems of representation. Although any image is of course askew from the reality it depicts, the archive of images becomes much more than accumulated distortion. (Language works the same way.) The archive as a whole can be turned and folded to let light shine through on some of the most tragic features of history: a history of lost messages, lives, futures. That is, the abundance of the image world reveals something about the real world, and perhaps the deepest challenge of photography is to figure out what that is.

One point of departure is to pay attention to beauty, for it is one of the most important filters that we use to discern the essential sound within the roar of reality. Consider figure 47. Beautiful, isn't it? And beautifully engineered: the sleek design, the precisely machined pleats in the undulating surface that transfers energy as the strong prow slices through the water—these are the marks of technological prowess taken to near perfection.

Or would be, if it were a machine. Instead you are looking at a whale opening its jaw to channel water and krill into its feeding pouch. But are you really seeing what has just been described? We still do not quite see an animal feeding. We see an elegantly complex shape that is further distinguished by a waveform flowing along a stunning array of parallel lines. We see an astonishing combination of strength and suppleness, something that is at once a model of precision and completely organic. The structure is both a bold assertion, a statement rising above the uniformly horizontal surface of the sea, and yet profoundly a part of its environment, so deeply adapted that it embodies a larger harmony. And it is both completely functional and seemingly so uniquely itself that it could be a work of art.

We don't mean to rhapsodize, but words do come up a bit short when one comments on this photograph. Or at least it is fair to say that our abilities as writers do not begin to match the beauty evident in the image. The point is not simply to marvel, however. Awe and similar emotions are not only appropriate but also necessary to understand what is before our eyes, but that is not enough. This photograph provides an opportunity to reflect on how visual media provide aesthetic resources for seeing how nature works and how human beings might live in closer harmony with natural processes. Lyle Rexer places the idea at the center of photography: "There is a

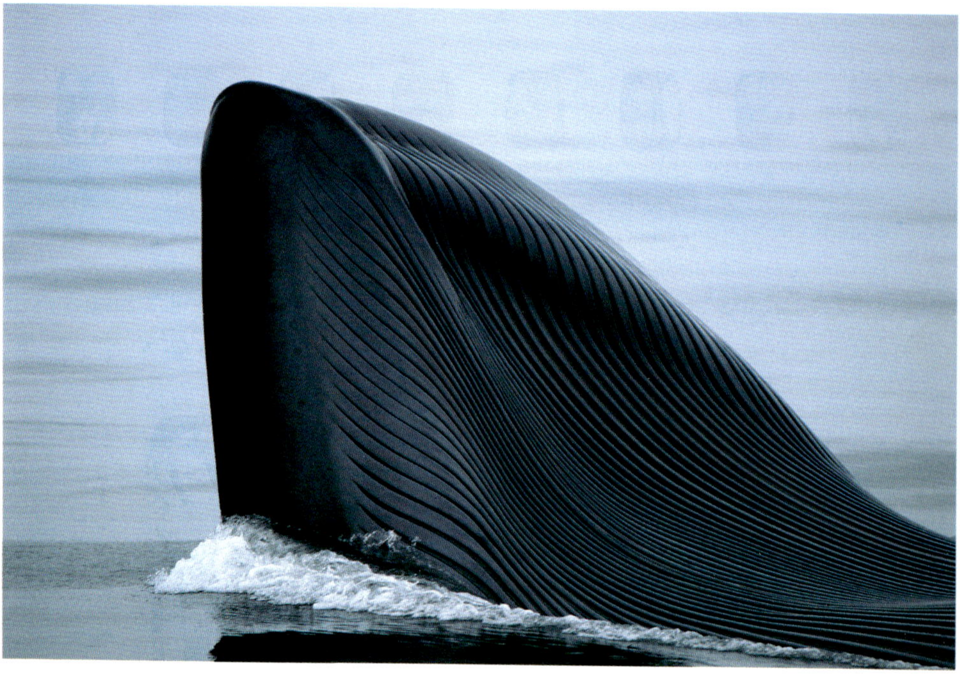

Figure 47. © Hiroya Minakuchi / Minden Pictures.

conviction that experience manifests deep unities that are not logically or immediately perspicuous. . . . We feel throughout the history of photography a chafing at its limits, an impatience with mere visuality, and a wish for some more intimate expression of the world's relation—but one somehow made available through the eyes."[37]

The reconsideration of visual form may be the most profound dimension of the paradigm shift that is under way in thinking about photography. Both the broad field emphasis on literal reference and the avant-garde disdain for formalism prohibited recognition of how photography draws on and contributes to the relationships between artistic form, the disclosure of the world, and social organization. Although, as Rexer suggests, larger conceptions of the medium were always available at least in part, now enough ground has shifted technologically and culturally to see photography as not a copy of the world but something *like* a copy. As Kaja Silverman states boldly, photography is "the world's primary way of revealing itself to us—of demonstrating that it exists, and that it will forever exceed us." Silverman redefines the most fundamental sense of the medium as the revelation of a "vast constellation of analogies," which are "the authorless and untranscendable similarities that structure Being." Where some have worried about social and cultural leveling, and others celebrated a political equality created by the camera, Silverman points toward the deep structure of plenitude that holds everything in relation. "It is only through this interlocking that we ourselves exist. Two is the smallest unit of Being."[38] Two, not one; relationship, not singularity; reality and image, not reality alone; original and copy, not original alone; matter and form, not matter alone.

One might go so far as to say that perhaps the abundance of photography depends not on the medium's reality principle but on its development of artistic form. The point isn't that there's a big world out there but rather that photography's peculiar combination of mimesis and abstraction allows the plenitude, energy, and interdependence of the cosmos to emerge within the spectrum of human visibility. By achieving formal awareness within a mimetic art—as is done explicitly with double images, silhouettes, aerial views, or close framing—photography is able to connect one's sense of a material world with a much larger sense of world formation. We should add that the same logic applies to estrangement from that world. Formal continuity, or felt analogy, need not come at the expense of social critique; but critique is not achieved merely by returning to a material base. Instead, photography might offer an aesthetic experience that is both playful and serious, capable of moral extension because of how it already combines representational identification and analogical inference.[39]

Photography's use of form also marks the plenitude of the world through a continuous communication of potential energy. We have drawn on this capability already in several senses: the photograph implies subsequent movement both natural and social (as with gravity or the gesture); it refers to an ongoing eventfulness outside of itself (often marked as context or narrative); the image can be selected, discarded, lost, found, stored, carried about, circulated, repurposed, and otherwise moved around; it requires interpretation that of necessity remains open to multiple points of view and imaginative projections; and it is part of modernity's continuous unfolding. One might say that there are no still photographs. Or that the apparent immobility of the photograph is one way that it operates as a small language: by not being in motion, it provides a better basis for communicating some facets of motion, such as a sense of potential energy.

This capability is most evident in the articulation of form, once form is understood to be, like the photograph itself, arrested movement. As Henri Focillon has argued, form is motion, change, generation, both the concentration and the release of "the reality of an immense number of possibilities."[40] It is "as a kind of fissure through which crowds of images aspiring to birth may be introduced into some indefinite realm—a realm which is neither that of physical extent nor that of pure thought"; so it is that "a work of art is motionless only in appearance."[41] As Hilton Kramer summarized, "Form is therefore not primarily line and color, it is a dynamic organization that brings into play the concrete texture of the world as the sum of the body's reactions to that which surrounds it."[42] These claims apply with special force to photography, particularly because of how its materiality—which always is part of any form[43]—is relatively smooth, frictionless, and otherwise suited to instantaneous transmission and audience uptake. The photograph is a space between physical reality and pure thought, and each image is but one of a plenitude of images waiting to be released, all of them oriented, for better or worse, toward the spectator living in a continuously unfolding present.

Stated otherwise, photography's development as an abundant art does not consist of piling up particular details of the world. It is not merely the reminder that the world is full of things: this fork, that spoon, the dustpan left in the corner. Such particularity can be vitally important for several reasons, but it need not be an end in itself. That may be the insight behind the idea that images can be so much clutter producing an image world that is overly crowded, claustrophobic, or chaotic. Details without design need not be edifying, and as we noted above, one can become lost amid the phenomenal deluge of continuous experience. The details become important as they reveal or activate specific ways of being in the world, especially as they call the spectator to enter into a common life. This sense of abundance was captured with Emerson's celebration of a new aesthetic for his democratic society:

> I embrace the common, I explore and sit at the feet of the familiar, the low. Give me insight into to-day, and you may have the antique and future worlds. What would we really know the meaning of? The meal in the firkin; the milk in the pan; the ballad in the street; the news of the boat; the glance of the eye; the form and the gait of the body;—show me the ultimate reason of these matters; show me the sublime presence of the highest spiritual cause lurking, as always it does lurk, in these suburbs and extremities of nature; let me see every trifle bristling with the polarity that ranges it instantly on an eternal law; and the shop, the plough, and the ledger, referred to the like cause by which light undulates and poets sing;—and the world lies no longer a dull miscellany and lumber-room, but has form and order; there is no trifle; there is no puzzle; but one design unites and animates the farthest pinnacle and the lowest trench.[44]

Although predating the invention of photography, this passage could serve as a manifesto for the technology's artistic and political capabilities. Where the critics of abundance see the image world as only "a dull miscellany and lumber room," Emerson points instead to a deeper relationship between sheer particularity and the beauty to be found in ordinary experience and the common life. The abundant world is a common world, one that has its own dignity, integrity, intimacy, and transcendental aura. The news of the boat and glance of the eye are not distractions from a higher calling but are where art and experience should intersect. What was announced as an American ethos when America was seen (e.g., by Tocqueville) as the leading edge of modern democratization now appears as the inheritance of a global society created in part by the circulation of images.

The philosophy of abundance was never merely American, however, just as it was not waiting for photography to spring full born into the world. Every era, every religion, every society includes this affirmation of the world, and each works out aesthetic designs or ideas to articulate a relationship between particularity and expansiveness. What modernity, via photography, has done is create a realm of virtual experience so comprehensive and accessible that abundance can, like the image itself, become a form that seemingly is "henceforth divorced from matter."[45] Money has come to the same thing, and we know the benefits and dangers of that, but photography is both less fungible and less suited for hoarding. The excess of images performs an excess of things and suggests that wealth could be available anywhere. The global proliferation of an image world changes abundance from one end of an economic hierarchy into something already available in any locale—at least until it is denied. If reality appears to be endlessly generative, and if the small details of the common can be radiant with larger energies, one cannot help but ask why that potential is not more fully realized. Photography releases abundance from wealth and religion alike to become an idea that can be applied to any circumstance, however far that place might seem from conventional sources of value.

This commitment to illuminating the commonplace is the aesthetic of realism, and a realism that requires an active imagination. It is the imagination that calls us to see the connection between a "trifle" and "the polarity that ranges it instantly on an eternal law," or (more prosaically) that makes the connection between surface details and larger patterns, and between actual circumstances and possible worlds. It does not require Emerson's level of exuberance or his specific sense of transcendental unity, although these are examples of how one can appreciate an abundant world and articulate a mode of generalization and critique that doesn't depend on a simplistic conception of direct representation. It does suggest that if one is seeing photographs only as records of particularity, only as sources of information, then one is not seeing photographically. Emerson's vision could just as well be labeled immanent, for he is suggesting a grounded sense of abstraction that does not leave behind the phenomenal world. Like photography, his aesthetic does not transform surface particularity into immaterial implication, yet it is a mode of seeing larger continuities nonetheless. Emerson's vision offers a sense of how the common world—that is, the world of ordinary objects as they can be seen—offers intimate expression of a larger reality, one that does not leave behind present encounters and obligations. Because it remains grounded in the small detail, that seeing is also a relational encounter: one sees by entering into the embodied experience of everyday life and then discerning a larger pattern through that experience.

This mode of seeing becomes particularly important in a society beset with programs of radical simplification. Authoritarian social engineering and draconian models of free-market competition are the largest and most dangerous examples of how schemes of abstraction can become recipes for disaster.[46] Photography can counter with local knowledge grounded in particularity, a richer and more supple sense of visual forms to extend the civic imagination, and a vision of plenitude that provides an ethical challenge to regimes built on artificial scarcity. At this widest circumference, photography and an ethic of abundance offer an alternative to any example of excessive abstraction. In place of the blank canvas, a return to figural representation. In place of top-down development, the view from below. In place of economies of scale, a look into the small worlds that would be deemed expendable. In place of monocultural uniformity, an aesthetic of form and texture that allows for continuous variation within larger patterns of sustainability.

To heighten the contrast between abundance and radical simplification, consider how the images in this chapter feature only partial legibility. Seeing is not synonymous with knowing, yet seeing is being activated nonetheless. More to the point, the optic being offered develops a dialectical relationship between seen and unseen, subject matter and content, perception and understanding, as these are themselves variations on scarcity and abundance. You see not enough, because there is more to be discerned; you see simple forms, which signify larger processes; you experience emotions of awe or terror, which come from exceeding a limit. Because this abundant art has necessarily complicated relationships with both material excess and formal simplicity, one can consider how these entanglements reflect a world in which abundance and scarcity are often paradoxically intertwined. Because photography is so much more than an archive of fragments, photographic spectatorship has to include a dialectical mentality that can consider how extremities are each implicated in the other and perhaps capable of triggering deeper transformations of consciousness.

No wonder photography is a modern technology. Modernity has discovered and created astonishing levels of prosperity, only to also precipitate a great die-off of other species. The misuse of abundance creates real scarcity, while illusions of scarcity restrict abundance from those who deserve and need it. What is needed, perhaps, is additional thinking about how the world is an abundant world, but paradoxically so. Abundance can create scarcity, yet richness also is found in simplicity. Just as the oversaturation of the virtual world can reveal something about the material world, so can visions of simplicity reveal something about the abundant life. Most important, these are not acts of empirical investigation but modulations in our relationships with nature and one another. Although the discovery of riches can lead to hubris, understanding the real source of wealth may lead to wisdom.

The Reflective Moment

Perhaps no reconsideration of the deluge of images should invite closure. In fact, we need to open up the discourse of photography to better encompass the wide ambit of the medium. This change need not dislodge critical awareness of the dangers of media enthrallment, but it does identify a potential gift of the photographic habitus that is too often overlooked or denigrated. The purpose is not to reenchant the world but to engage with a world that is profoundly abundant. This world is at once real and virtual, political and aesthetic, active and passive—and sure to exceed these and other binaries that have bedeviled thinking about photography. Thus rather than defining the image as too little while declaring that the archive is too much, one might consider how abundance and scarcity are a representative dialectic for thinking photographically—and for developing creative responses to some of modernity's more intractable problems such as resource sustainability and the reproduction of violence.

Instead of looking for how an image might create a decisive effect, there is need to consider how this medium of abundance makes specific capabilities for reflection available to ordinary people. Whether seeing the exquisite jewelry of a raindrop hanging from a leaf or feeling one's smallness beneath the stars strewn across the night sky, the spectator can sense that the visible world is but a small part of a richly encompassing reality. And if most people do not articulate those thoughts as such, they can enter into that modality anytime they look at the images adorning their computer screens and other surfaces of the everyday world. Of course, distraction is always pos-

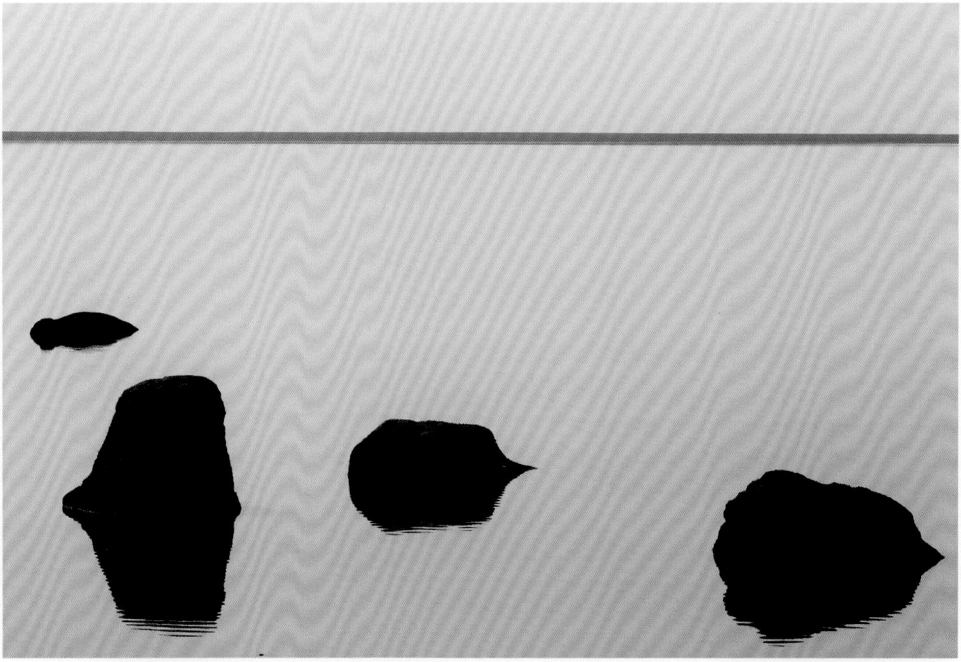

Figure 48. © Reuters / Lucas Jackson.

sible and sentimentality is a likely habit. At the same time, the continuous rearticulation of an abundant world offers an orientation toward reality that is neither explicitly thoughtful nor thoughtless but rather a mode of perception that is open to an encounter with plenitude. What it is and what it can be are not yet obvious, but surely there are images that can help us understand what is being shown.

Beauty in a photographic image can distract and displace, but it also can be a mode of reflection. Whatever the controversy or conflagration, in nature's time all will be peaceful again. For precisely that reason, human beings should strive to preserve the earth that will outlast them and to create societies that can work in concert with nature rather than in the pursuit of dominion. The abundant life is ours for the having, but only if we realize how precious it really is.

The richness of the image world is but one example of a much larger reality, one that extends both outward and inward. As Jay suggests, the image world provides evidence of another world "that has not entirely lost its capacity to inspire awe, wonder and humility."[47]

And perhaps even serenity. Not because all will be quiet in the end, but because everything that is needed for a just, sustainable society is already available for those who are willing to see and share. Photography prompts us to consider how the still image mirrors unseen radiance, and how the ever-expanding archive promises a world that has enough for everyone.

NOTES

Chapter One

1. Ellis Cashmore, *Celebrity/Culture* (New York: Routledge, 2006); Anne M. Cronin, *Advertising Myths: The Strange Half-Lives of Images and Commodities* (New York: Routledge, 2004); Anne Rothe, *Popular Trauma Culture: Selling the Pain of Others in the Mass Media* (New Brunswick, NJ: Rutgers University Press, 2011); Gregory Button, *Disaster Culture: Knowledge and Uncertainty in the Wake of Human and Environmental Catastrophe* (Walnut Creek, CA: Left Coast, 2010); and the Spring 2014 special issue of *Public Culture*, "Visualizing the Environment," guest edited by Allison Carruth and Robert P. Marzec.
2. Susan Sontag, *On Photography* (New York: Picador, 1977), 3.
3. See Martin Heidegger, "The Age of the World Picture," in *The Question concerning Technology, and Other Essays*, trans. William Lovitt (New York: Garland, 1977), 115–54.
4. Peter Sloterdijk, *Critique of Cynical Reason* (Minneapolis: University of Minnesota Press, 1988).
5. See Peter Arnett, "Eyewitness to History," in *Flash! The Associated Press Covers the World*, ed. Vincent Alabiso, Kelly Smith Tunney, and Chuck Zoeller (New York: Henry N. Abrams, 1998), 15–24; Ariella Azoulay, *The Civil Contract of Photography* (Cambridge, MA: MIT Press, 2012) and *Civil Imagination: A Political Ontology of Photography*, trans. Louise Bethlehem (London: Verso, 2012); Claude Hubert Cookman, *American Photojournalism: Motivations and Meanings* (Evanston, IL: Northwestern University Press, 2009); Kevin Michael DeLuca and Jennifer Peeples, "From Public Sphere to Public Screen: Democracy, Activism, and the 'Violence' of Seattle," *Critical Studies in Media Communication* 19 (2002): 125–51; Robert Hariman and John Louis Lucaites, *No Caption Needed: Iconic Photographs, Public Culture, and Liberal Democracy* (Chicago: University of Chicago Press, 2007); Fred Ritchin, *Bending the Frame: Photojournalism, Documentary, and the Citizen* (New York: Aperture, 2013); Alan Trachtenberg, *Reading American Photographs: Images as History, Mathew Brady to Walker Evans* (New York: Hill and Wang, 1989); and David Campbell's blog, http://www.david-campbell.org/.

6. Kenneth Burke, "Literature as Equipment for Living," in *The Philosophy of Literary Form: Studies in Symbolic Action* (Berkeley: University of California Press, 1973), 293–304.
7. C. Wright Mills, *The Sociological Imagination* (New York: Oxford University Press, 1959), 38.
8. Sontag, *On Photography,* 138–39.
9. Examples from Sontag's *On Photography*: "Only that which narrates can make us understand" (23); "Nobody demands that photography be literate" (31); "Unlike the fine-art objects of pre-democratic eras, photographs don't seem deeply beholden to the intentions of an artist" (53); "The only prose that seems credible to more and more readers is not the fine writing of someone like Agee, but the raw record. . . . There is a rancorous suspicion in America of whatever seems literary, not to mention a growing reluctance on the part of young people to read anything, even subtitles in foreign movies and copy on a record sleeve, which partly accounts for the new appetite for books of few words and many photographs" (74); "The proliferation of photographs is ultimately an affirmation of kitsch" (81); "Hence, its longstanding quarrel with art, which (until recently) meant the results of a discriminating or purified way of seeing, and a medium of creation governed by standards that make genuine achievement a rarity" (129); "Photography is the most successful vehicle of modernist taste in its pop version, with its zeal for debunking the high culture of the past" (131); "The traditional fine arts are elitist: their characteristic form is a single work, produced by an individual; they imply a hierarchy of subject matter in which some subjects are considered important, profound, noble, and others unimportant, trivial, base. The media are democratic" (149). The comparison continues in *Regarding the Pain of Others* (New York: Picador, 2003), usually to highlight photography's capacity to shock or persuade, which now is granted some value for moral response, but meaning remains a property of "words"; see, e.g., 26, 28–29.
10. Susie Linfield, *The Cruel Radiance: Photography and Political Violence* (Chicago: University of Chicago Press, 2010), 68.
11. Note, for example, Azoulay's discussion of how the French government purchased the patent rights for photography and transformed the invention into "common property." Azoulay, *Civil Contract of Photography*, 153–55. More recently, consider the exhibition *Democratic Camera, Photographs and Video, 1961–2008* that premiered at the Whitney Museum of American Art in 2008. The catalog is available as *William Eggleston, Democratic Camera, Photographs and Video, 1961–2008* (New York: Whitney Museum of American Art, 2008).
12. For detailed accounts of photography—and photojournalism in particular—as a democratic medium, see Michael L. Carlebach, *The Origins of Photojournalism in America* (Washington, DC: Smithsonian, 1992) and *American*

Photojournalism Comes of Age (Washington, DC: Smithsonian, 1997); Bonnie Brennen and Hanno Hardt, eds., *Picturing the Past: Media, History, and Photography* (Champaign: University of Illinois Press, 1999); Julianne H. Newton, *The Burden of Visual Truth: The Role of Photojournalism in Mediating Reality* (New York: Routledge, 2000); and Cookman, *American Photojournalism*. For more general accounts of the news as a social form, see Michael Schudson, *Discovering the News: A Social History of American Newspapers* (New York: Basic Books, 1978); Gaye Tuchman, *Making News: A Study in the Construction of Reality* (New York: Free Press, 1978), 47–58.

13. For overviews of the theoretical and ideological controversies, see George A. Kennedy, *Classical Rhetoric and Its Christian and Secular Tradition from Ancient to Modern Times*, 2nd ed. (Chapel Hill: University of North Carolina Press, 1999).

14. See Theodor Adorno, "Culture Industry Reconsidered," *New German Critique* 6 (Autumn 1975): 12–19; Theodor W. Adorno and Max Horkheimer, *Dialectic of Enlightenment* (New York: Verso, 1997). See several Walter Benjamin pieces, all in *The Work of Art in the Age of Its Technological Reproducibility, and Other Writings on Media,* ed. Michael W. Jennings, Brigid Doherty, and Thomas Y. Levin (Cambridge, MA: Belknap / Harvard University Press, 2008): "Little History of Photography," trans. Edmund Jephcott and Kingsley Shorter, 274–98; "Letter from Paris 2: Painting and Photography," trans. Edmund Jephcott, 299–311; "The Work of Art in the Age of Its Technological Reproducibility, Second Version," trans. Edmund Jephcott and Harry Zohn, 19–55. Also see Bertolt Brecht, *War Primer*, trans. and ed. John Willett and Ralph Manheim (London: Libris, 1998); Max Horkheimer, "Art and Mass Culture," in *Critical Theory: Selected Essays*, trans. Matthew J. O'Connell (New York: Seabury, 1972), 273–90; Siegfried Kracauer, *Theory of Film: The Redemption of Physical Reality* (New York: Oxford University Press, 1960). For a survey of the role that aesthetics played in the Frankfurt School, see Martin Jay, *The Dialectical Imagination: A History of the Frankfurt School and the Institute of Social Research, 1923–1950* (Berkeley: University of California Press, 1973), 173–218.

15. Susan Sontag is the primary channel for the hermeneutics of suspicion that emerged out of the Frankfurt School, most notably in *On Photography*, and we will have more to say about her shortly, but one can find a similar iconoclasm throughout twentieth-century intellectual culture. The fullest history of this critical attitude is worked out in Martin Jay, *Downcast Eyes: The Denigration of Vision in Twentieth-Century French Thought* (Berkeley: University of California Press, 1993). See also David Michael Levin, ed., *Modernity and the Hegemony of Vision* (Berkeley: University of California Press, 1993). Our primary concern is with how this attitude manifests in those authors defining what might be called the conventional twentieth-century discourse on photography, including most prominently Roland Barthes, *Image-Music-Text*, trans. Stephen

Heath (New York: Hill and Wang, 1977), 15–78. and *Camera Lucida: Reflections on Photography*, trans. Richard Howard (New York: Hill and Wang, 1981); John Berger, *Ways of Seeing* (New York: Penguin Books, 1990), *About Looking* (New York: Vintage: 1991), *Understanding a Photograph* (New York: Aperture, 2013), and, with Jean Mohr, *Another Way of Telling* (New York: Pantheon Books, 1982); Victor Burgin, *In/Different Spaces: Place and Memory in Visual Culture* (Berkeley: University of California Press, 1996); Guy Debord, *Society of the Spectacle* (Detroit, MI: Black and Red, 1983); Rosalind E. Krauss, *The Optical Unconscious* (Cambridge, MA: MIT Press, 1994) and "Reinventing the Medium," *Critical Inquiry* 25 (1999): 289–305; Martha Rosler, "In, Around, and Afterthoughts (On Documentary Photography)," in *The Contest of Meaning: Critical Histories of Photography*, ed. Richard Bolton (Cambridge, MA: MIT Press, 1992), 303–42, and *Decoys and Disruptions: Selected Writings, 1975–2001* (Cambridge, MA: MIT Press, 2004); Allan Sekula, "Traffic in Photographs," *Art Journal* 41 (1981): 15–25, "The Body and the Archive," *October* 39 (1986): 3–64, "Dismantling Modernism, Reinventing Documentary (Notes on the Politics of Representation)," *Massachusetts Review* 19 (1978): 859–83, and "On the Invention of Photographic Meaning," in *Thinking Photography*, ed. Victor Burgin (London: Palgrave Macmillan, 1982), 84–109; Carol Squiers, *The Critical Image: Essays on Contemporary Photography* (London: Lawrence and Wishart, 1991); Abigail Solomon-Godeau, *Photography at the Dock: Essays on Photographic History, Institutions, and Practices* (Minneapolis: University of Minnesota Press, 1991) and "Photography after Art Photography," in *Art after Modernism: Rethinking Representation*, ed. Brian Wallis (New York: New Museum of Contemporary Art, 1984), 73–86; John Tagg, "The World of Photography or Photography of the World?" *Camerawork* 6 (1977): 8–9, "The Currency of the Photograph," *Screen Education* 28 (1978): 45–67, *The Burden of Representation: Essays on Photographies and Histories* (Minneapolis: University of Minnesota Press, 1993), *Grounds of Dispute: Art History, Cultural Politics and the Discursive Field* (Minneapolis: University of Minnesota Press, 1992), and *The Disciplinary Frame: Photographic Truths and the Capture of Meaning* (Minneapolis: University of Minnesota Press, 2009). See also Richard Bolton, ed., *The Contest of Meaning: Critical Histories of Photography* (Cambridge, MA: MIT Press, 1989).

16. Sabine T. Kriebel identifies some of the differences within the critical discourse in "Theories of Photography: A Short History," in *Photography Theory*, ed. James Elkins (New York: Routledge, 2007), 3–49.

17. See Dora Apel, *War Culture and the Contest of Images* (New Brunswick, NJ: Rutgers University Press, 2012); Azoulay, *Civil Contract of Photography* and *Civil Imagination*; Geoffrey Batchen, *Burning with Desire: The Conception of Photography* (Cambridge, MA: MIT, 1997); Susan Buck-Morss, "Visual Studies and Global Imagination," in *The Politics of Imagination*, ed. Chiara Bottici and Benoit Challand (Abingdon, Oxon, UK: Birkbeck Law Press, 2011); David Campbell, "Atroc-

ity, Memory, Photography: Imaging the Concentration Camps of Bosnia—the Case of ITN versus Living Marxism, Part I," *Journal of Human Rights* 1 (2002): 1–33, "Atrocity, Memory, Photography: Imaging the Concentration Camps of Bosnia—the Case of ITN versus Living Marxism, Part II," *Journal of Human Rights* 1 (2002): 143–72, and "Salgado and the Sahel: Documentary Photography and the Imaging of Famine," in *Rituals of Mediation: International Politics and Social Meaning*, ed. Francois Debrix and Cindy Weber (Minneapolis: University of Minnesota Press, 2003); Lilie Chouliaraki, *The Ironic Spectator: Solidarity in the Age of Post-Humanitarianism* (Cambridge, UK: Polity, 2013); Geoff Dyer, *The Ongoing Moment* (London: Little, Brown / Abacus, 2005); Jae Emerling, *Photography: History and Theory* (New York: Routledge, 2012); Cara Finnegan, *Making Photography Matter: A Viewer's History from the Civil War to the Great Depression* (Urbana: University of Illinois Press, 2015); Liam Kennedy, *Afterimages: Photography and US Foreign Policy* (Chicago: University of Chicago Press, 2016); Wendy Kozol, *Distant Wars Visible: The Ambivalence of Witnessing* (Minneapolis: University of Minnesota Press, 2014); Susie Linfield, "Every Photo an Archive," *The Nation*, April 17, 2008, and *Cruel Radiance*; Nicholas Mirzoeff, *Watching Babylon: The War in Iraq and Global Visual Culture* (New York: Routledge, 2005) and *The Right to Look: A Counterhistory of Visuality* (Durham, NC: Duke University Press, 2011); W. J. T. Mitchell, *Picture Theory* (Chicago: University of Chicago Press, 1994), *What Do Pictures Want?: The Lives and Loves of Images* (Chicago: University of Chicago Press, 2005), and *Cloning Terror: The War on Images, 9/11 to the Present* (Chicago: University of Chicago Press, 2011); Margaret Olin, *Touching Photographs* (Chicago: University of Chicago Press, 2012); Griselda Pollock, *Psychoanalysis and the Image: Transdisciplinary Perspectives* (Oxford: Blackwell, 2006), *After-Affects/After-Images: Trauma and Aesthetic Transformation in the Virtual Feminist Museum* (Manchester, UK: Manchester University Press, 2013); Jacques Rancière, *The Future of the Image*, trans. Gregory Elliott (London: Verso, 2009), *Dissensus: On Politics and Aesthetics*, trans. Steven Corcoran (New York: Continuum, 2010), and *The Emancipated Spectator* (London: Verso, 2011); Mark Reinhardt, "Picturing Violence: Aesthetics and the Anxiety of Critique," in *Beautiful Suffering: Photography and the Traffic in Pain*, ed. Mark Reinhardt, Holly Edwards, and Erina Duganne (Chicago: University of Chicago Press, 2007); Fred Ritchin, *In Our Own Image: The Coming Revolution in Photography*, 2nd ed. (New York Aperture, 2006), *After Photography* (New York: W. W. Norton, 2010), and *Bending the Frame: Photojournalism, Documentary, and the Citizen* (New York: Aperture, 2013); John Roberts, *The Art of Interruption: Realism, Photography, and the Everyday* (New York: St. Martin's, 1998), and *Photography and Its Violations* (New York: Columbia University Press, 2014); Sharon Sliwinski, "On Photographic Violence," *Photography and Culture* 2 (2009): 303–315, and *Human Rights In Camera* (Chicago: University of Chicago Press, 2011); Shawn Michelle Smith, *At The Edge of Sight: Photography and the Unseen* (Durham, NC:

Duke University Press, 2013); David Levi Strauss, *Between the Eyes: Essays on Photography and Politics* (New York: Aperture, 2005), and *Words Not Spent Today Buy Smaller Images Tomorrow: Essays on the Present and Future of Photography* (New York: Aperture, 2014); Barbie Zelizer, *About to Die: How News Images Move the Public* (New York: Oxford University Press, 2010).

18. Thomas S. Kuhn, *The Structure of Scientific Revolutions*, 2nd ed., International Encyclopedia of Unified Science 2 (Chicago: University of Chicago Press, 1962).
19. For overlapping examples of other (and we would say kindred) calls for reformatting the discourse of photography, see Batchen, *Burning with Desire*, 2–21, and Emerling, *Photography*, 1–41.
20. "The book [*On Photography*] remains astonishingly incisive, and has been immensely influential on the thinking of other photography critics—and immensely influential, too, in setting a certain tone of photography criticism" (Linfield, *Cruel Radiance*, 5).
21. Neal Ascherson, *Los Angeles Times Book Review*, August 26, 1990, 10. A list of translations through 1992 is provided by Leland Poague and Kathy A. Parsons, *Susan Sontag: An Annotated Bibliography, 1948–1992* (New York: Garland, 2000), 80–82.
22. Linfield (*Cruel Radiance*, 98–99) is one of the very few who have taken Sontag to task following the publication of *Regarding the Pain of Others*.
23. Sontag, *Regarding the Pain of Others*, 105.
24. Ibid., 6, 85, 115, 86, 81, 27, 26, 23, 89.
25. Ibid., 42, 47, 60, 72, 18, 78.
26. Ibid., 84, 79, 101, 102, 117, 103.
27. Mark Reinhardt has noted as well how Sontag remained trapped within her original conceptual vocabulary. See Reinhardt, "Picturing Violence," 27.
28. This combination of error and critique is evident in the reception of the book. A significant number and range of commentators excoriated *On Photography* for problems we identify and others as well; see, for example, the reviews listed in Poague and Parsons, *Susan Sontag*, 481–88. At the same time, the book's success and classroom use were evidence of its critical value.
29. W. J. T. Mitchell captures the hermeneutical shift that is needed when he contrasts the conventional "myths" of visual culture with his own "countertheses," especially in this sense: instead of assuming that "visual culture consists of 'scopic regimes' and mystifying images to be overthrown by political critique. . . . the political task of visual culture is to perform critique without the comforts of iconoclasm" (Mitchell, *What Do Pictures Want?*, 343–44). Susan Buck-Morss makes the same point in her call for a shift from the Marxian critique of appearances to an aesthetics that considers the image "as a key, rather than a hindrance to understanding. . . . One risks falling victim to the illusions of the society as spectacle, but the risk is worth the promise of illumination" ("Visual Studies in Global Imagination," 223).

30. Trevor Paglen, “Is Photography Over?,” *Still Searching*, March 3, 2014, http://blog.fotomuseum.ch/2014/03/i-is-photography-over/.

31. Any current attempt to define photography should emphasize the futility of the task. As David Campbell states, “I am increasingly struck by the difficulty even of talking about photography generally. To use the term as an all-encompassing concept seems pretty much impossible. After all, what, if anything, connects stock photography, fashion photography, art photography, news photography, conceptual photography, documentary photography, amateur photography, forensic photography, vernacular photography, travel photography, and any other sort of photography?” David Campbell, “Afterword: Abundant Photography, Discursive Limits, and the Work of Images,” in *The Versatile Image: Photography, Digital Technologies, and the Internet*, ed. Alexandra Moschovi, Carol McKay, and Arabella Plouviez (Louvain, Belgium: Leuven University Press, 2013), 265. Asko Lehmuskallio elaborates the point:

> A search for “photography” in the *Oxford Reference Premium Collection*, a digital compendium of dictionaries and encyclopedias, yields 3,741 entries, while a search for “photograph” finds 8,491. *A Dictionary of Physics, Encyclopedia of Semiotics, The Oxford Companion to the Body* and *The New Oxford Companion to Literature in French* are only some of the titles that provide entries for “photography,” entries that tend to emphasize aspects of photography that are important in terms of physics, semiotics and the body or literature in French, respectively, among many others. Somewhat surprisingly, *The Oxford Companion to the Photograph*, published in 2006, does not have an entry for “photography” or for “photograph.” This may have to do, at least in part, with the digital revolution discussed in the book’s introduction, which has changed photographic practice in multitudinous ways. (Asko Lehmuskallio, “Everyday Digital Photography and Simulative, Heuristic, and Layered Photographs,” in *Digital Photography and Everyday Life: Empirical Studies on Material Visual Practices*, ed. Asko Lehmuskallio and Edgar Gómez Cruz [New York: Routledge, 2016])

See also the marvelous book by Mishka Henner, *Photography Is* (Manchester, UK: Author, 2012), which lists over three thousand statements about photography. This abundance of definitions, along with the proliferation of digital technologies, motivates some to declare an era “after photography” or “postphotography.” Fred Ritchin, *After Photography* (New York: W. W. Norton, 2010); Robert Shore, *Post-Photography: The Artist with a Camera* (London: Laurence King, 2014). These, too, are definitional claims, and so it seems that definitions, however partial they may be, remain useful—at least if they are oriented toward understanding specific domains of practice. Our definition in this volume is provided as a very provisional point of departure for understanding the public image as it is a medium for identity, thought, and action. It obviously does not apply to many other photographic practices, and particularly to the extensive use of photography in science, technology, engineering, and biomedical disciplines. Perhaps the day is coming when a new definition, starting from new assumptions, can encompass the full realm of photographic practices without being merely general. In any case, we hope our narrower approach proves useful in respect to understanding photography and public culture.

32. Brian Ratliff, "Outsider Whose Dark, Lyrical Vision Helped Shape Rock 'n' Roll," *New York Times*, October 27, 2013, http://nyti.ms/19zyQJN.
33. Chouliaraki's *Ironic Spectator* emphasizes the importance of theatricality for moral education and the self-constitution of the public.
34. Note that we often use the terms *civic spectator* and *public spectator* interchangeably. They can resonate differently in scholarly literatures and public discourse, and occasionally one term is more apt than the other, but we find that both contribute to understanding modern society, politics, and culture.
35. Rancière, *Emancipated Spectator*, 17. Note also this political implication: one can move beyond a liberal model of citizenship that defines civic capacities primarily in terms of reason, verbal agency, and direct action to influence policy. This ideal still has value, but it also has become increasingly brittle and unable to adapt to changes in mediated collective association. A more pliant model also includes affect, visual engagement, and gradual shifts in norms instead of abrupt action.
36. Azoulay, *Civil Contract of Photography*, 95–97, and *Civil Imagination*, 29–125, esp. 67–68.
37. See DeLuca and Peeples, "From Public Sphere to Public Screen"; Cara A. Finnegan and Jiyeon Kang, "'Sighting' the Public: Iconoclasm and Public Sphere Theory," *Quarterly Journal of Speech* 90 (2004): 377–402; Jürgen Habermas, *The Structural Transformation of the Public Sphere: An Inquiry into a Category of Bourgeois Society*, trans. Thomas Burger and Frederick Lawrence (Cambridge, MA: MIT Press, 1989); Benjamin Lee, "Going Public," *Public Culture* 10 (1993): 165–78; Anna McCarthy, *Ambient Television: Visual Culture and Public Space* (Durham, NC: Duke University Press, 2001); Anthony Pollock, "Neutering Addison and Steele: Aesthetic Failure and the Spectatorial Public Sphere," *ELH* 74 (2007): 707–34; Rancière, *Emancipated Spectator*; and Donald J. Newman, ed., *The Spectator: Emerging Discourses* (Cranbury, NJ: Associated University Presses, 2005). See also Jeffrey Edward Green, *The Eyes of the People: Democracy in an Age of Spectatorship* (Oxford: Oxford University Press, 2010).
38. Nicolai Ouroussoff, "New Look for the New Museum," *New York Times*, November 30, 2007, http://www.nytimes.com/2007/11/30/arts/design/30newb.html.
39. We define liberalism and democracy in *No Caption Needed*, 14–17, and argue that iconic photographs often mediate the tension between these two princi-

ples of modern social organization. Briefly, a liberal-democratic polity is committed to both majority rule and the autonomy of the individual person.

40. Mitchell, *What Do Pictures Want?*, 336–56.
41. "Looking" is by no means a politically innocent category, and we will have more to say about this subsequently. See Mirzoeff, *Right to Look*, and Catherine A. Lutz and Jane L. Collins, *Reading "National Geographic"* (Chicago: University of Chicago Press, 1993), esp. 15–118, 187–216. Surveillance, of course, can operate in multiple registers. On one hand, we have Jeremy Bentham's notion of the "Panopticon" made popular by Michel Foucault in his characterization of a disciplinary society in which surveillance serves a policing function. On the other hand, we have Jane Jacob's notion of "natural surveillance" that relies on people observing what is taking place in public, often assisted by urban planning that features landscapes, lighting, and other architectural designs to facilitate civic sight and security. The conventional paradigm has aligned photography entirely with the former—e.g., Sekula, "The Body and the Archive"—whereas we believe that Jacobs's "natural surveillance" applies more often and especially in photojournalism. See Michel Foucault, *Discipline and Punish: The Birth of the Prison*, trans. Alan Sheridan (New York: Vintage Books, 1979), esp. 195–230; Jane Jacobs, *The Death and Life of Great American Cities* (New York: Random House, 1961), 29–142, 372–91.
42. Pierre Bourdieu, *Distinction: A Social Critique of the Judgment of Taste*, trans. Richard Nice (Cambridge, MA: Harvard University Press, 1984).
43. Pictures of the Day, April 9, 2009, http://www.nytimes.com/slideshow/2009/04/09/nytfrontpage/20090409POD_14.html.
44. Roland Barthes, "The Reality Effect," in *The Rustle of Language*, trans. Richard Howard (Berkeley: University of California Press, 1986), 148.
45. See W. J. T. Mitchell, *Iconology: Image, Text, Ideology* (Chicago: University of Chicago Press, 1986).
46. Daniel Boorstin, *The Image: A Guide to Pseudo-events in America* (New York: Harper and Row, 1961); Neil Postman, *Amusing Ourselves to Death: Public Discourse in the Age of Show Business* (New York: Penguin Books, 1986). Postman had favored new media in the 1960s but later turned against them with a convert's zeal.
47. This claim is an adaptation of the argument regarding print media made by Benedict Anderson, *Imagined Communities: Reflections on the Origin and Spread of Nationalism* (London: Verso, 1991), and expanded theoretically by Charles Taylor, *Modern Social Imaginaries* (Durham, NC: Duke University Press, 2004). For a superb study of how the modern mass public was created through institutions of collective spectatorship, see Vanessa R. Schwartz, *Spectacular Realities: Early Mass Culture in Fin-de-Siècle Paris* (Berkeley: University of California Press, 1998). Danielle Allen makes a similar point in her argument that citizens "must imagine themselves as part of a 'whole' they cannot see":

Talking to Strangers: Anxieties of Citizenship since Brown v. Board of Education (Chicago: University of Chicago Press, 2004), 17. The key point is that photojournalism enables citizens to imagine a relationship to strangers they *can* see, and thus raises the stakes of what it means to recognize oneself as part of a body politic.

48. For a remarkable exhibition on the relationship between individuation and image replication in modern consumer societies, see Hans Eijkelboom, *People of the Twenty-First Century* (London: Phaidon, 2014).
49. Hariman and Lucaites, *No Caption Needed*, 8.
50. See Louis Kaplan, *The Strange Case of William Mumler, Spirit Photographer* (Minneapolis; University of Minnesota Press, 2008); Tom Gunning, "Phantom Images and Modern Manifestations," in *Fugitive Images: From Photography to Video* (Bloomington: Indiana University Press, 1995), 42–71; and John Durham Peters, "Phantasms of the Living, Dialogues with the Dead," in *Speaking into the Air: A History of the Idea of Communication* (Chicago: University of Chicago Press, 1999), 137–76.
51. Mitchell, *What Do Pictures Want?*, 336–56.
52. David Michael Levin, ed., *Modernity and the Hegemony of Vision* (Berkeley: University of California Press, 1993), 4.
53. Plato, *Republic* 514–18b, trans. Paul Shorey in *Plato: The Collected Dialogues, including the Letters*, ed. Edith Hamilton and Huntington Cairns (Princeton, NJ: Princeton University Press, 1961).
54. Ibid., 517b, 517d; the allegory is identified at 517a.

Chapter Two

1. For methods of visual interpretation see, e.g., Gillian Rose, *Visual Methodologies: An Introduction to Researching with Visual Materials*, 3rd ed. (London Sage, 2012) and the companion website, http://www.sagepub.com/rose/home.htm; Terry Barrett, *Criticizing Photographs: An Introduction to Understanding Images*, 5th ed. (New York: McGraw-Hill, 2011); Marita Sturken and Lisa Cartwright, *Practices of Looking: An Introduction to Visual Culture*, 2nd ed. (New York: Oxford University Press, 2009); Gunther Kress and Theo van Leeuwen, *Reading Images: The Grammar of Visual Design*, 2nd ed. (New York: Routledge, 2006). Rose argues for better use of the available methods via a shift from representational to performative conceptions of visual culture: "On the Relation between 'Visual Research Methods' and Contemporary Visual Culture," *Sociological Review* 62 (2014): 24–46.
2. Readers should be careful with our allusion to Susan Sontag's *Against Interpretation* (New York: Farrar, Straus and Giroux, 1966). Had she applied her argument there to photography, the result could have been very different. That did not happen, perhaps because she saw photography as a medium rather than

an art and as inherently mimetic. That said, *Against Interpretation* remains relevant to discussions of critical method, not least our own, while nonetheless restating modernist binaries (e.g., between art and interpretation) that need to be set aside if one is to achieve the shared goals of paying "more attention to form in art" in order "to *see* more, to *hear* more, to *feel* more" (12, 14, emphasis in the original).

3. Norms of objective representation have been central to the professional codes of photojournalism, including the National Press Photographers Association Code of Ethics, the Associated Press's definition of "News Values," and the editorial policies and standards one finds at Reuters, the Poynter Center, and elsewhere. Due to the conversion to digital technologies and the corresponding democratization of image production, these norms now are at the center of frequent debates among both professionals and the public; for example, images were disqualified from the 2015 World Press Photo Competition for "excessive" postprocessing. The controversies occur for good reasons: because codes need to be reexamined periodically and especially in respect to relevant changes in technology and society; the values themselves are socially constructed, essentially contested, and not entirely consistent or comprehensive; standard practices and some highly esteemed photographs don't follow the prescriptions, and some highly respected photographers have explicit artistic and political commitments that require more leeway; successful professional practice will require bending the codes when they reflect unrealistic epistemological, aesthetic, and political assumptions; and rules for production are not sufficient to account for the full range of reception and the values of spectatorship. It becomes apparent that objectivity is an important value—and one containing rather arbitrary customs. Changes such as eliminating the photographer's shadow in the image are not allowed, yet shifting from color to black and white is thought *not* to alter the "literal reality" of the event photographed. (See David Campbell, *Integrity of the Image: Current Practices and Accepted Standards Relating to the Manipulation of Still Images in Photojournalism and Documentary Photography*, World Press Photo Academy, November 2014, http://www.worldpressphoto.org/sites/default/files/upload/Integrity%20of%20the%20Image_2014%20Campbell%20report.pdf.) What is needed is neither to scrap the standards nor to insist on bright-line enforcement, but rather to recognize that the debates reflect the need for a richer conception of the work that photography does for public culture. Fortunately, and as another example of the paradigm shift that is under way, many professionals are recognizing the importance of moving past prior clichés about documentary truth to understand the productive relationships between realism and aesthetics. David Campbell discusses these changes in "Securing the Credibility of Photojournalism: New Rules from World Press Photo," *LensCulture*, [November 2015], https://www.lensculture.com/articles/david

-campbell-securing-the-credibility-of-photojournalism-new-rules-from-world-press-photo. Campbell promotes the emerging consensus that "photography is an interpretive process," that aesthetics is "an indispensable part" of photographic representation, and that the integrity of the image can be secured through pragmatic verification processes.

For the professional codes of photojournalistic ethics, see National Press Photographers Association Code of Ethics, https://nppa.org/code_of_ethics; Associated Press Code of Ethics for Photojournalists, http://www.csus.edu/indiv/g/goffs/135%20photojournalism/Associated%20Press%20ethics%20code.pdf; Reuters, "A Brief Guide to Standards, Photoshop, and Captions," http://handbook.reuters.com/?title=A_Brief_Guide_to_Standards,_Photoshop_and_Captions; and the Poynter Center, "Hot Tips for Writing Photo Captions," http://www.poynter.org/uncategorized/1753/hot-tips-for-writing-photo-captions/. For recent public debates regarding what is acceptable and what is not in altering the photojournalistic image, see Scott Alexander, "Processing the News: Retouching in Photojournalism," *American Photography*, November 10, 2014, http://www.americanphotomag.com/processing-news-retouching-photojournalism; and "Debating the Rules and Ethics of Digital Photojournalism," Lens: Photography, Video and Visual Journalism, *New York Times,* February 17, 2015, http://lens.blogs.nytimes.com/2015/02/17/world-press-photo-manipulation-ethics-of-digital-photojournalism/?_r=1. For a carefully considered discussion of the problem of manipulation, see David Campbell, "Why Does Manipulation Matter?," February 24, 2015, https://www.david-campbell.org/2015/02/24/why-does-manipulation-matter/. For examples of the debates regarding the manipulation of images, see Steve Myers, "AP Drops Freelance Photographer Who Photoshopped His Shadow out of Image," Poynter@40, July 11, 2011, http://www.poynter.org/news/mediawire/138728/ap-drops-freelance-photographer-who-photoshopped-his-shadow-out-of-image/; Matthias Krug and Stefan Niggemeier, "Enhanced Reality: Exploring the Boundaries of Photo Editing," Spiegel Online International, May 8, 2013, http://www.spiegel.de/international/world/growing-concern-that-news-photos-are-being-excessively-manipulated-a-898509.html; "AP Severs Ties with Photographer Who Altered Work," *AP Archive*, January 22, 2014, http://www.ap.org/Content/AP-In-The-News/2014/AP-severs-ties-with-photographer-who-altered-work; and Michael Zhang, "Vietnamese Photojournalist Apologizes for 'Shopped War Photo," *PetaPixel*, June 17, 2015, http://petapixel.com/2015/06/17/vietnamese-photojournalist-apologizes-for-shopped-war-photo/.

4. The larger argument here includes shifting from "studying journalism not as a demarcated culture of production disseminating texts but as interspersed cultures of circulation": Henrik Bødker, "Journalism as Cultures of Circulation," *Digital Journalism* 3 (2015): 103. See also Benjamin Lee and Edward LiPuma, "Cultures of Circulation: The Imaginations of Modernity," *Public*

Culture 14 (2002): 191–213. We also appreciate Mishka Henner's description of her book *Photography Is* (Manchester, UK: Author, 2012): "*Photography Is* presents more than 3,000 phrases that define one of the most democratic and ubiquitous of all art forms. Mirroring the ambiguous and untrustworthy nature of photographs themselves, each phrase in this book has been torn from the context in which it originally appeared. The result is contradictory and chaotic, frustrating and insightful. In short, it is photography, without photographs" (book description at http://www.mishkahenner.com/filter/bookshop/Photography-Is-10).

5. Fred Ritchin, *Bending the Frame: Photojournalism, Documentary, and the Citizen* (New York: Aperture, 2013). See also *After Photography* (New York: W. W. Norton, 2009).
6. Plato, *Phaedrus* 274e–276a, trans. R. Hackforth, in *Plato: The Collected Dialogues*, ed. Edith Hamilton and Hunting Cairns (Princeton, NJ: Princeton University Press, 1971).
7. Susan Sontag, *On Photography* (New York: Picador, 1977), 24.
8. We are borrowing and repurposing this phrase from John Tagg, *The Burden of Representation: Essays on Photographies and Histories* (Minneapolis: University of Minnesota Press, 1993). Tagg's book is a sophisticated analysis of the construction of the evidentiary status of the photograph, and of how that status has been structured by relations of power. Roger Silverstone also uses the term and provides something like a core commitment: "to provide and then respond to the resources for judgment which alone enable a degree of reflexivity sufficient, one would hope, for an effective engagement with the world" (*Media and Morality: On the Rise of the Mediapolis* [Cambridge, UK: Polity, 2007], 53). Silverstone assumes that the burden (and corresponding failures) should be carried by all media, while we point out that newer media and visual media are singled out for ethical scrutiny while others are given a pass, which inevitably increases disappointment while reducing accountability and inhibiting understanding.
9. Sontag, *On Photography*, 21–22.
10. On the role that photography plays in the reproduction of family, see Julia Hirsch, *Family Photographs: Content, Meaning and Effect* (New York: Oxford University Press, 1981); Jo Spence and Patricia Holland, eds., *Family Snaps: The Meaning of Domestic Photography* (London: Virago, 1991); Marianne Hirsch, *Family Frames: Photography, Narrative and Postmemory* (Cambridge, MA: Harvard University Press, 1997); Marianne Hirsch, ed., *The Familial Gaze* (Hanover, NH: Dartmouth University Press, 1999); and Andrea Noble, "Family Photography and the Global Drama of Human Rights," in *Photography: Theoretical Snapshots*, ed. J. J. Long et al. (London: Routledge, 2009), 63–79.
11. See Jack Goody, introduction to *Literacy in Traditional Societies*, ed. Jack Goody (New York: Cambridge University Press, 1968), 1–26, and *The Logic of Writing*

and the Organization of Society (Cambridge: Cambridge University Press, 1986). As Goody summarizes, "Writing is critical in the development of bureaucratic states" (*Logic of Writing*, 91).

12. See Allan Sekula, "The Body and the Archive," in *The Contest of Meaning: Critical Histories of Photography*, ed. Richard Bolton (Cambridge, MA: MIT Press, 1992), 343–89. The point is not that photography hasn't been appropriated for social control but that focusing on its role there occludes a much larger background of textual practices, such that only the lesser medium is saddled with the burden of media complicity.
13. On the history of the hypodermic model, see Deborah Lubken, "Remembering the Straw Man: The Travels and Adventures of *Hypodermic*," in *The History of Media and Communication Research: Contested Memories*, ed. David W. Park and Jefferson Pooley (New York: Peter Lang, 2008), 19–42.
14. For the classical idea, see Gorgias, *Encomium on Helen* 14, in *The Older Sophists: A Complete Translation by Several Hands of the Fragments in "Die Fragmente der Vorsokraticker" Edited by Diels-Kranz with a New Edition of Antiphon and of Euthydemus*, ed. Rosamond Kent Sprague (Columbia: University of South Carolina Press, 1972), 50–54; Gorgias, *Encomium of Helen*, trans. Brian R. Donovan, http://www.classicpersuasion.org/pw/gorgias/helendonovan.htm.
15. Ariella Azoulay identifies similar features in a "phantasmagoric model" of spectatorship that underlies the conventional critique of photography, in *The Civil Contract of Photography* (New York: Zone Books, 2008), 192; we pick up this argument regarding the representation of violence in chapter 6.
16. On the variability of textual meaning, see Stanley Fish, *Is There a Text in this Class? On the Authority of Interpretive Communities* (Cambridge, MA: Harvard University Press, 1982).
17. John Edwin Mason, "Déjà Vu All Over Again: James Estrin and 'The Tsunami of Vernacular Photographs,'" *Documentary, Motorsports, Photo History*, September 9, 2012, http://johnedwinmason.typepad.com/john_edwin_mason_photogra/2012/09/estrin-deja-vu.html.
18. Jürgen Habermas, *The Structural Transformation of the Public Sphere: An Inquiry into a Category of Bourgeois Society*, trans. Thomas Burger and Frederick Lawrence (Cambridge, MA: MIT Press, 1989). See also Robert Hariman and John Louis Lucaites, *No Caption Needed: Iconic Photographs, Public Culture, and Liberal Democracy* (Chicago: University of Chicago Press, 2007), 41; Michael Warner, *Publics and Counterpublics* (Cambridge, MA: Zone Books, 2005).
19. Errol Morris, *Believing Is Seeing (Observations on the Mysteries of Photography)* (New York: Penguin Press, 2011).
20. There is a great deal of scholarship and art on this topic. Recent examples of both are included in Alexandra Moschovi, Carol McKay, and Arabella Plouviez, eds., *The Versatile Image: Photography, Digital Technologies, and the Internet* (Louvain, Belgium: Leuven University Press, 2014). See also Martin Lister,

ed., *The Photographic Image in Digital Culture,* 2nd ed. (New York: Routledge, 2013); Jonas Larsen and Mette Sandbye, eds., *Digital Snaps: The New Face of Photography* (London: I. B. Tauris, 2014). The burgeoning literature on digital journalism includes Zeynep Devrim Gürsel, *Image Brokers: Visualizing World News in the Age of Digital Circulation* (Berkeley: University of California Press, 2016); Mette Mortensen, *Journalism and Eyewitness Images: Digital Media, Participation, and Conflict* (New York: Routledge, 2015); Dominic Boyer, *The Life Informatic: Newsmaking in the Digital Era* (Ithaca, NY: Cornell University Press, 2013); Pablo Boczkowski, *News at Work: Imitation in an Age of Information Abundance* (Chicago: University of Chicago Press, 2010).

21. David Campbell identifies both the persistence of the conventional distinction between news and advocacy and the case for a more nuanced understanding of documentary witnessing. "Photojournalism, Advocacy, and Change," April 30, 2015, https://www.david-campbell.org/2015/04/30/photojournalism-advocacy-change-marcus-bleasdale-human-rights-watch-central-african-republic/.
22. Sontag states that "the photograph is like a quotation, or a maxim or proverb" (*Regarding the Pain of Others* [New York: Picador, 2003], 22) and that "a photograph could also be described as a quotation, which makes a book of photographs like a book of quotations," and that "the taste for quotations (and for the juxtaposition of incongruous quotations) is a Surrealist taste" (*On Photography*, 71, 75). Obviously her attitude and conclusions regarding these comparisons are very different from our own. For a largely tacit but nuanced comparison of the two media forms, see Martha Rosler, "Notes on Quotes," in *Decoys and Disruptions: Selected Writings, 1975–2001* (Cambridge, MA: MIT Press, 2004), 133–48.
23. Gary Saul Morson, *The Words of Others: From Quotations to Culture* (New Haven, CT: Yale University Press, 2011) and *The Long and Short of It: From Aphorism to Novel* (Palo Alto, CA: Stanford University Press, 2012).
24. André Malraux, *Museum without Walls*, trans. Stuart Gilbert and Francis Price (London: Secker and Warburg, 1967), 9.
25. Not everyone will share our assessment of the value of this virtual space. Most notably, Sontag declared that "whatever the moral claims made on behalf of photography, its main effect is to convert the world into a department store or museum-without-walls in which every subject is depreciated into an article of consumption, promoted into an item for aesthetic appreciation" (*On Photography*, 110).
26. For a brilliant discussion of this idea, see John Durham Peters, *Speaking into the Air: A History of the Idea of Communication* (Chicago: University of Chicago Press, 1999).
27. Barbie Zelizer, "How Communication, Culture, and Critique Intersect in the Study of Journalism," *Communication, Culture and Critique* 1 (2008): 86–91.

28. Key theoretical statements include Habermas, *Structural Transformation of the Public Sphere*; Benedict Anderson, *Imagined Communities: Reflections on the Origin and Spread of Nationalism* (London: Verso, 1991); Charles Taylor, *Modern Social Imaginaries* (Durham, NC: Duke University Press, 2004); Sharon Sliwinski, *Human Rights In Camera* (Chicago: University of Chicago Press, 2011). Work on the reproduction of nations and nationalism is wide and far ranging, but particularly good examples include Alex Trachtenberg, *Reading American Photographs: Images as History, Mathew Brady to Walker Evans* (New York: Hill and Wang, 1990); James Guimond, *American Photography and the American Dream* (Chapel Hill: University of North Carolina Press, 1991); Andrea Noble, *Photography and Memory in Mexico: Icons of Revolution* (Manchester, UK: Manchester University Press, 2010); Blake Stimson, *The Pivot of the World: Photography and its Nation* (Cambridge, MA: MIT Press, 2006); Karen Strassler, *Refracted Visions: Popular Photography and National Modernity in Java* (Durham, NC: Duke University Press, 2010); and Elizabeth Edwards, *The Camera as Historian: Amateur Photographers and Historical Imagination, 1885–1918* (Durham, NC: Duke University Press, 2012). Of course, not all imagined communities are admirable, nor equally beneficial for all concerned. For work that intersects with questions of imperialism and empire, particularly in the context of race, see Laura Wexler, "Techniques of the Imaginary Nation: Engendering Family Photography," in *Race and the Production of Modern American Nationalism*, ed. Reynolds J. Scott-Childress (London: Routledge, 1999), 359–82; Laura Wexler, *Tender Violence: Domestic Visions in an Age of U.S. Imperialism* (Chapel Hill: University of North Carolina Press, 2000); Carol J. Williams, *Framing the West: Race, Gender, and the Photographic Frontier in the Pacific Northwest* (New York: Oxford University Press, 2003); Deborah Poole, *Vision, Race, and Modernity: A Visual Economy of the Andean Image World* (Princeton, NJ: Princeton University Press, 1997); and Martin Berger, *Sight Unseen: Whiteness and American Visual Culture* (Berkeley: University of California Press, 2007). See also Christopher Pinney, *Camera Indica: The Social Life of Indian Photographs* (Chicago: University of Chicago Press, 1997); and Christopher Pinney and Nicolas Peterson, eds., *Photography's Other Histories* (Durham, NC: Duke University Press, 2003).

29. Readers should be aware that what they see will depend on the technology they are using: the print and several digital versions of these images need not look the same, and can vary further depending on the device and the lighting, and in every case will not show as much as the high-resolution files that we received when obtaining permissions for the photographs. Thus, viewer experience will vary even at this initial level of the photographic encounter. The same holds for captions and related information about the photograph. The available documentation for news photographs can be unreliable, incomplete, or biased, while captions can vary between photographer, agency, print and digital versions of the same newspaper, and subsequent publications.

These variations can be highly consequential or largely irrelevant, depending on the context. Much of the time, civic spectatorship accommodates them easily, and they provide another example of how features of all media use can become more evident in a digital environment. In general, they confirm our argument that written documentation should not be seen as the essential anchor of photographic meaning across the board.

30. Howard Becker, "Photography and Sociology," *Studies in the Anthropology of Visual Communication* 1 (1974): 4. Reprinted without the photographs in *American Ethnography Quasimonthly,* http://www.americanethnography.com/article.php?id=69#.Unvj8ihOjd5. Paul Frosh notes that the habit is most ingrained "within the image-crowded field of consumer culture," where "most photographs are not gazed at but glanced at or *overlooked*. In fact, photographs are doubly overlooked, literally and metaphorically: they are scanned within the onward movement of the glance, but they are also taken for granted. . . . And there is almost always another photograph ready to receive and deflect our distracted look." Paul Frosh, *The Image Factory: Consumer Culture, Photography and the Visual Content Industry* (New York: Berg, 2003), 110 (emphasis in the original).

31. One could say that the slide shows provide a reprise of that signature event of midcentury photography, the *Family of Man* exhibition. That description is as good a fault line as any for the current paradigm shift. Perhaps because of its considerable popularity, the exhibition was excoriated by twentieth-century critics, while one of the signs of the current sea change is revisionary appreciation of how it worked athwart and somewhat against the political and cultural hegemonies of the time. Histories of the critical reception include Eric J. Sandeen, *Picturing an Exhibition: "The Family of Man" and 1950s America* (Albuquerque: University of New Mexico Press, 1995); Monique Berlier, "*The Family of Man:* Readings of an Exhibition," in *Picturing the Past: Media, History, and Photography,* ed. Bonnie Brennen and Hanno Hardt (Urbana: University of Illinois Press, 1999); Lili Corbus Bezner, "Subtle Subterfuge: The Flawed Nobility of Edward Steichen's *Family of Man,*" in *Photography and Politics in America: From the New Deal into the Cold War* (Baltimore: Johns Hopkins University Press, 1999), 120–74; Jean Back and Viktoria Schmidt-Linsenhoff, eds., *The Family of Man, 1955–2001* (Marburg, Germany: Jonas Verlag, 2004); Louis Kaplan, "Photo Globe: The Family of Man and the Global Rhetoric of Photography," in *American Exposures: Photography and Community in the Twentieth Century* (Minneapolis: University of Minnesota Press, 2005), 55–79; Rob Kroes, *Photographic Memories: Private Pictures, Public Images, and American History* (Hanover, NH: Dartmouth College Press, 2007), 99–128. The most influential critiques probably were Roland Barthes, "The Great Family of Man" (1957), in *Mythologies* (New York: Hill and Wang, 1972), 100–102; Allan Sekula, "The Traffic in Photographs," *Art Journal* 41 (1981): 15–25, reprinted in *Modernism*

and Modernity, ed. Benjamin H. D. Buchloh, Serge Guilbaut, and David Solkin (Halifax: Nova Scotia College of Art and Design, 1983), 121–54, and *Photography against the Grain: Essays and Photo Works 1973–1983* (Halifax: Nova Scotia College of Art and Design, 1984), 77–101. Recent revisionary accounts include Ariella Azoulay, "*The Family of Man*: A Visual Universal Declaration of Human Rights," in *The Human Snapshot*, ed. Thomas Keenan and Tirdad Zolghadr (Feldmeilen, Switzerland: LUMA Foundation, 2013), 19–48; Fred Turner, "*The Family of Man* and the Politics of Attention in Cold War America," *Visual Culture* 24 (2012): 55–84; Sarah E. James, "A Post-Fascist Family of Man? Cold War Humanism, Democracy and Photography in Germany," *Oxford Art Journal* 35 (2012): 315–36; Stimson, *Pivot of the World*, 59–103; Viktoria Schmidt-Linsenhoff, "Denied Images: The Family of Man and the Shoah," in *Family of Man*, ed. Back and Linsenhoff, 81–99. For continued critique, see the essay by Abigail Solomon-Godeau in the same volume: "*The Family of Man*: Refurbishing Humanism for a Postmodern Age."

32. Susan Buck-Morss, "Visual Studies in Global Imagination," in *The Politics of Imagination*, ed. Chiara Bottici and Benoît Challand (Abingdon, Oxon, UK: Birkbeck Law Press, 2011), 228–29. The transcript of the original lecture is online at Susan Buck-Morss, "Visual Studies and Global Imagination," http://susanbuckmorss.info/text/visual-studies-and-global-imagination/. See also Ariella Azoulay, "What Is a Photograph? What Is Photography?" *Philosophy of Photography* 1 (2010): 9–13.

33. Roland Barthes, "The Photographic Message," in *Image, Music, Text*, trans. Stephen Heath (New York: Hill and Wang, 1977), 19. This distinction can be misused, as when connotation is thought to be a merely subjective dimension of meaning, even though Barthes was emphatic that some of the connotative meaning is deeply embedded in the image, not least because the image always is produced within the historically specific collective practices known as culture. For nuanced use of the distinction, see Barbie Zelizer, "The Voice of the Visual in Memory," in *Framing Public Memory*, ed. Kendall R. Phillips (Tuscaloosa: University of Alabama Press, 2004), and *About to Die: How News Images Move the Public* (New York: Oxford University Press, 2010). For a prescient argument, albeit one limited by the focus on advertising, see Pierre Bourdieu et al., *Un art moyen: Essai sur les usages sociaux de la photographie*, 2nd ed. (Paris: Minuit, 1965), 215–17. The point here is not that the denotation-connotation distinction per se is objective or sufficient but rather that Barthes's use of it captures how photographic meaning is internally disjunctive and therefore radically plural. For the record, we don't think the distinction is dispositive across the board, and see Daniel Chandler, *Semiotics: The Basics*, 2nd ed. (New York: Routledge, 2007), 137–42, for a succinct review of relevant issues.

34. Barthes, "Photographic Message," 18. Jens Kjeldsen captures the distinction neatly: "Verbal utterances provide, in principle, *unambiguous, but thin informa-*

tion," while "pictures, in principle, are *ambiguous but rich in information*" ("The Rhetoric of Thick Representation: How Pictures Render the Importance and Strength of an Argument Salient," *Argumentation* 29 [2015]: 199–200 [emphasis in the original]).

35. Campbell, *Integrity of the Image*, 7–9.

36. Brian Massumi, *Parables for the Virtual: Movement, Affect, Sensation* (Durham, NC: Duke University Press, 2002), 138 (emphasis in the original). Massumi is concerned primarily with writing, and some adjustments may need to be made for images, but we believe he has hit on a vital point. Note also his claim that "nothing is more destructive for the thinking and imaging of the virtual than equating it with the digital" (137). The claim, not least because of its Deleuzian underpinnings, should not be used to dismiss the expansion, complexity, and transformative potential of digital technologies or vernacular media practices, but it does suggest an important caution against a narrow focus on digitization that would exclude much of the virtual world of public culture.

37. W. J. T. Mitchell, "Realism and the Digital Image," in *Critical Realism in Contemporary Art: Around Allan Sekula's Photography*, ed. Jan Baetens and Hilde Van Gelder (Louvain, Belgium: Leuven University Press, 2006), 18. Mitchell's essay is a superb discussion of the misplaced anxieties regarding digital photography, on behalf of a more engaged development of the medium toward "Truth, Justice, Being, and 'the Real' Itself" (25). See also Hilde Van Gelder and Helen Westgeest, *Photography Theory in Historical Perspective: Case Studies from Contemporary Art* (Chichester, West Sussex, UK: Wiley-Blackwell, 2011), 7–9, and Peter Osborne, "Infinite Exchange: The Social Ontology of the Photographic Image," *Philosophy of Photography* 1 (2010): 59–68.

38. Much of the work on digital photography focuses on vernacular practices. See, e.g., Asko Lehmuskallio and Edgar Gómez Cruz, eds., *Digital Photography and Everyday Life: Empirical Studies on Material Visual Practices* (New York: Routledge, 2016). Digital technologies also have prompted strong reconsideration of the materiality of the image—and often (and not ironically, we would add) to valorize the material instantiation above other conceptions of the image. See Gillian Rose and Divya P. Tolia-Kelly, eds., *Visuality/Materiality: Images, Objects, and Practices* (Burlington, VT: Ashgate, 2012); Elizabeth Edwards, "Objects of Affect: Photography beyond the Image," *American Review of Anthropology* 41 (2012): 221–34. For some research, the focus on materiality will be the key to insight and understanding. We are assuming that there still is need for consideration of how public image circulation and reception require and reproduce a relatively dematerialized conception of the image, and with that a corresponding approach to image interpretation.

39. Lehmuskallio develops the distinction between simulative, heuristic, and layered images on behalf of a carefully expanded conception of photogra-

phy in "Everyday Digital Photography and Simulative, Heuristic, and Layered Photographs," in *Digital Photography and Everyday Life*, ed. Lehmuskallio and Gomez.

40. Melanie Bühler, "Online Image Behavior, Where Photographs Live Today," *Still Searching* blog, Fotomuseum Winterthur, April 8, 2015, http://blog.fotomuseum.ch/2015/04/3-online-image-behavior-where-photographs-live-today/.
41. Fred Ritchin, *After Photography* (New York: W. W. Norton, 2009), 73–75.
42. Mitchell, "Realism and the Digital Image," 18.
43. Ibid., 18–19.
44. David Campbell, "Afterword: Abundant Photography, Discursive Limits, and the Work of Images," in *Versatile Image*, ed. Moschovi, McKay, and Plouviez, 266–67.
45. Wendy Kozol, *Distant Wars Visible: The Ambivalence of Witnessing* (Minneapolis: University of Minnesota Press, 2014).
46. W. J. T. Mitchell, *What Do Pictures Want? The Lives and Loves of Images* (Chicago: University of Chicago Press, 2005), 336–56.
47. On divergences and continuities between the global north and south, see Dilip Parameshwar Gaonkar, ed., *Alternative Modernities* (Durham, NC: Duke University Press, 2001), and "On Cultures of Democracy," *Public Culture* 19 (2007): 1–22.

Chapter Three

1. Siegfried Kracauer, *Theory of Film: The Redemption of Physical Reality* (New York: Oxford University Press, 1960), 3. Today many speak of media constraints and affordances to make the same point.
2. Ibid., 11–12.
3. Ibid., 13.
4. Ibid., 16. Note that Kracauer's writing on photography included both passionate criticism of its displacement of critical reason and hope regarding its revolutionary potential. This ambivalence need not be debilitating, and it doesn't compromise his theoretical insights regarding the composition of photographic meaning. In any case, our basic point here echoes Patrick Maynard's observation that "Kracauer also argues explicitly against perhaps the most harmful false dichotomy in the history of talk about photography, pointing out that its realist recording powers are fully consistent with its being highly interpretive, even self-expressive." Patrick Maynard, *The Engine of Visualization: Thinking through Photography* (Ithaca, NY: Cornell University Press, 1997), 11. Some would push the point further. For example, Heinrich Schwarz recognized the same two principles but gave the greater importance to creative artistry: *Art and Photography: Forerunners and Influences*, ed. William E. Parker (Layton, UT: Peregrine Smith Books, 1985). An important demonstration that

the photographic image is inherently crafted is provided by Joel Snyder and Neil Walsh Allen, "Photography, Vision, and Representation," *Critical Inquiry* 2 (1975): 143–69.

5. The term is from Rosalind Krauss, "Reinventing the Medium," *Critical Inquiry* 25 (1999): 289–305. Our sense of heterogeneity includes the multiple "semiotic transcriptions" that are layered within any image and throughout its reception; see Robert Hariman and John Louis Lucaites, *No Caption Needed: Iconic Photographs, Public Culture, and Liberal Democracy* (Chicago: University of Chicago Press, 2007), 34–35. We also follow the maxim by W. J. T. Mitchell that "all media are mixed media" (Mitchell, *What Do Pictures Want? The Lives and Loves of Images* [Chicago: University of Chicago Press, 2005], 343.) Contra the insistence in modernism on the optimization of the unique features of each medium in isolation from all other practices, a postmodern approach can acknowledge some media specificity but as part of more comprehensive processes of social interaction. Furthermore, the media specificity of photography is necessarily hybrid, which is one reason it cannot be fully understood within modernist aesthetics. Although we follow Krauss and others who developed the critique of photography through a break with modernism, we want to move away from making ideology critique the default mode of analysis, and we want to revive commitments both to photography's relationship to reality and to its use of form. As Mary Ann Doane has demonstrated, media specificity itself can change with other developments in technology and historical context (Doane, "Indexicality and the Concept of Medium Specificity," in *The Meaning of Photography*, ed. Robin Kelsey and Blake Stimson [Williamstown, MA: Sterling and Francine Clark Art Institute; New Haven, CT: Yale University Press, 2008], 3–14). See also Snyder and Allen, "Photography, Vision, and Representation," who conclude with an eminently clear and sensible brief for critical pluralism. The full extension of the postmodern position denies that photography is a medium at all; see Raphaël Pirenne and Alexander Streitberger, eds., *Heterogeneous Objects: Intermedia and Photography after Modernism* (Louvain, Belgium: Leuven University Press, 2013). That work is centered on art photography, whereas our interest in public communication is better served by staying with the more familiar concept of relatively discrete though intertwined media.
6. Our understanding of the nature and significance of the hermeneutical circle begins with Hans-Georg Gadamer, *Truth and Method*, 2nd ed., trans. Joel Weinsheimer and Donald G. Marshall (New York: Continuum, 1993), 291–95.
7. Maynard, *Engine of Visualization*, 86. The dissociation between imagination and industry paralleled the dissociation between art and society manifest in the nineteenth-century emergence of British Romanticism as well as German Idealism. See Raymond Williams, *Culture and Society, 1780–1950* (New York: Harper & Row, 1958), 30–48; and Richard Kearney, *The Wake of Imagination: Toward a Postmodern Culture* (London: Routledge, 1988), 181–187.

8. Maynard, *Engine of Visualization*, 83–85.
9. Jae Emerling, *Photography: History and Theory* (New York: Routledge, 2012), 15. Although we do not want to overstep in suggesting affinities with Emerling's highly sophisticated discussion of photography theory, several correspondences are especially important, including (a) moving beyond a polarized standoff between formalism and social critique (6, 13); (b) developing a discourse that can better understand photography because it is capable of both critique and admiration (6, 13); and (c) doing so by moving beyond an "overly instrumental" conception of the image to one that experiences "the *image as an image*" (34, 36, emphasis in the original; cf. Hariman and Lucaites, *No Caption Needed*, 46–47).
10. See, e.g., Joel Snyder, "Res Ipsa Loquitur," in *Things That Talk: Object Lessons from Art and Science*, ed. Lorraine Daston (New York: Zone Books, 2008), 195–222; and Elizabeth Edwards, *The Camera as Historian: Amateur Photographers and Historical Imagination, 1885–1918* (Durham, NC: Duke University Press, 2012), 78–90.
11. William Henry Fox Talbot, *The Pencil of Nature* (1844–46), Project Gutenberg, August 16, 2010, http://www.gutenberg.org/files/33447/33447-pdf.pdf.
12. Louis Jacques Mande Daguerre, "Daguerréotype" (1838/39), trans. Beaumont Newhall, http://www.daguerreotypearchive.org/texts/M8380001_DAGUERRE_BROADSIDE_FR_1838.pdf.
13. *Cosmos*, July 14, 1854, 42–43, quoted in André Jammes and Eugenia Parry Janis, *The Art of French Calotype* (Princeton, NJ: Princeton University Press, 1983), 247.
14. Charles Baudelaire, "The Modern Public and Photography," from "The Salon of 1859: Letters to the Editor of the *Revue Française*," in *Art in Paris, 1845–1862: Salons and Other Exhibitions Reviewed by Charles Baudelaire*, ed. and trans. Jonathan Mayne (London: Phaidon, 1965), 151, 154, 155.
15. Baudelaire was mistaken, however, regarding the richness and effects of the French public's delight in photography and other media that combined appeals to realism and amusement. For an excellent account of the role of public displays in the development of modern mass culture, see Vanessa R. Schwartz, *Spectacular Realities: Early Mass Culture in Fin-de-Siècle Paris* (Berkeley: University of California Press, 1999). For a cultural history of realism in the United States that gives considerable attention to photography, see Miles Orvell, *The Real Thing: Imitation and Authenticity in American Culture, 1880–1940* (Chapel Hill: University of North Carolina Press, 1989).
16. Oliver Wendell Holmes, "The Stereoscope and the Stereograph," *Atlantic Monthly,* June 1, 1859, http://www.theatlantic.com/magazine/archive/1859/06/the-stereoscope-and-the-stereograph/303361/.
17. See Mary Warner Marien, *Photography: A Cultural History* (New York: Harry N. Abrams, 2002), 172–98, 256–66.

18. Walter Benjamin, "The Work of Art in the Age of Its Technological Reproducibility, Second Version," trans. Edmund Jephcott and Harry Zohn, in *The Work of Art in the Age of Its Technological Reproducibility, and Other Writings on Media*, ed. Michael W. Jennings, Brigid Doherty, and Thomas Y. Levin (Cambridge, MA: Belknap / Harvard University Press, 2008), 28 (emphasis in the original).
19. Ibid., 42 (emphasis in the original). As numerous commentators have noted, sometimes with little influence, Benjamin's work on the relationships between aesthetics, politics, and media is far more subtle than is suggested by this pronouncement, which, despite its accuracy at the time, has become dated while also occluding Benjamin's interest in photography's emancipatory capabilities.
20. See Marien, *Photography*, 247–54; Alma Davenport, *A History of Photography: An Overview* (Albuquerque: University of New Mexico Press, 1991), 136–37, 163–69; Eleanor M. Hight, *Moholy-Nagy: Photography and Film in Weimar Germany* (Wellesley, MA: Wellesley College Museum, 1985), esp. 15–18, 26–34, 42–45, and the analysis of his photograms, camera photography, and photomontages, 48–121. The only other tradition for discussing art and politics as intertwined practices had been the discourse of rhetoric, which had fallen into near oblivion.
21. John Roberts notes the exhaustion and, in the United States, a corresponding turn away from "the political legacy of the 1930s" to rewrite modern art "from an avowedly revisionist, depoliticized position." *The Art of Interruption: Realism, Photography and the Everyday* (Manchester, UK: Manchester University Press, 1998), 115–16.
22. The claim here is not that photographers had been co-opted. To take but one example, photographers were providing courageous witness to the struggle for civil rights, but neither public nor academic discourses about photography were close to recognizing the political significance of the medium. For later work that corrects the earlier deficiency, see Erina Duganne, *The Self in Black and White: Race and Subjectivity in Postwar American Photography* (Hanover, NH: Dartmouth College Press, 2010); Maurice Berger, *For All the World to See: Visual Culture and the Struggle for Civil Rights* (New Haven, CT: Yale University Press, 2010); Elizabeth Abel, *Signs of the Times: The Visual Politics of Jim Crow* (Berkeley: University of California Press, 2010); Leigh Raiford, *Imprisoned in a Luminous Glare: Photography and the African American Freedom Struggle* (Chapel Hill: University of North Carolina Press, 2011); Martin A. Berger, *Seeing through Race: A Reinterpretation of Civil Rights Photography* (Berkeley: University of California Press, 2011); Nicole Fleetwood, *Troubling Vision: Performance, Visuality, and Blackness* (Chicago: University of Chicago Press, 2011).
23. Roland Barthes recognized as much. "Mad or tame? Photography can be one or the other: tame if its realism remains relative, tempered by aesthetic or empirical habits (to leaf through a magazine at the hairdresser's, the dentist's);

mad if this realism is absolute and, so to speak, original, obliging the loving and terrified consciousness to return to the very letter of Time." *Camera Lucida: Reflections on Photography,* trans. Richard Howard (New York: Farrar, Straus and Giroux, 1981), 119.

24. Susan Sontag, *On Photography* (New York: Picador, 1977), 69.
25. Ibid.
26. Chapter 4 of *On Photography* is a discussion of the relationship between the two principles, a discussion that unfortunately ends with a scathing dismissal of photography (110–12) and also of humanism because it "masks the confusions about truth and beauty underlying the photographic exercise" (112).
27. Maynard aptly summarizes the discourse of "reputable opinions" by Sontag, Berger, and other representative figures of the old dispensation as geared toward reification, dualism, and essentialism: "the conception of a topic in terms of substantives, 'things'—in fact, *two* kinds of things . . . on one side there is 'the photograph'' (click); on the other 'reality' (THUD). . . . [and then] a search for the essences (drawn from impressions of a few instances) of one or the other member of this pair of things, as well as for an essential relationship between them, from which perceptions are to flow" (*Engine of Visualization,* 14–15). We would add that the problem is not being "philosophical" rather than empirical and historical, as Maynard suggests, but rather lacking a better method of interpretation. In any case reification, dualism, and essentialism are not the way to go, especially when fueled by an attitude of disdain for ordinary people.
28. The relationship between advertising and other photography is a sure test of one's attitude toward the medium as a whole. As Paul Frosh explains, the stock images of advertising work precisely by blending realism and imagination, to move from "the conventional reproduction of the *actual*—whose temporality is past continuous, invoked as experience, habit and memory—with the persuasive simulation of the *possible*—whose temporality is future, invoked as dream and desire"; *The Image Factory: Consumer Culture, Photography and the Visual Content Industry* (New York: Berg, 2003), 99. They can do this, however, because they merely amplify the capacity of all photography and other media as well. Advertising is distinguished from news photography not by its transference from the real to the ideal or its future orientation, but by how these features are developed within the specific cultural formats and commercial practices that have come to define advertising as both a business and a mode of spectatorship. Among these differences, as Guy Debord (*Society of the Spectacle* [Detroit, MI: Black and Red, 1983]) and others note, is the additional transformation of that future orientation into the mythic timelessness that is a modality of modern consumption (there are no clocks on public display in stores). Frosh provides an important addition by noting that this time out of time is created through the repetitive citation of the image, rather

than the image per se (166–67). The key consideration from our perspective is whether this particular use is taken as representative of the medium. Either one can denigrate all photography—or any photographic artistry—for being continuous with the advertising's manufacturing of desire contrary to reality and the best interests of the spectator, or one can consider how advertising is but one of several quite different developments of media capabilities, and how there may also be unintended positive correspondences that develop across the larger archive. Advertising traffics in desire, but so does justice; advertising pitches spectatorship toward the future, but so does democracy; in each domain photography provides images of vernacular life that require various modes of visual literacy.

29. John Tagg, *The Burden of Representation: Essays on Photographies and Histories* (Minneapolis: University of Minnesota Press, 1993), 182–83.
30. Note that we are not critical of these methods and movements tout court, for they have been vital sources for our own work. The critique here is that a historically specific development in respect to photography produced both fifty years of important work and serious misrecognition of how photography functions as a public art. The paradigm did what it could do and now needs to be changed, even as all of its methods will continue to be available in the new constellation that eventually emerges.
31. Martin Jay, *Downcast Eyes: The Denigration of Vision in Twentieth-Century French Thought* (Berkeley: University of California Press, 1993), 130.
32. Fredric Jameson, *Signatures of the Visible* (New York: Routledge, 1992), 1.
33. David Levi Strauss notes that "one measure of the success of this critique is the extent to which its assumptions and conclusions were accepted and absorbed into mainstream writing about photography." *Between the Eyes: Essays on Photography and Politics* (New York: Aperture, 2005), 5.
34. Hariman and Lucaites, *No Caption Needed.*
35. Sontag suggests that it is the default mode for all photographic spectatorship: "Everyone is a literalist when it comes to photographs." *Regarding the Pain of Others* (New York: Picador, 2003), 47. Jonathan Crary points to the ethical motive behind literalism, and to the complications that arise in that regard: *Techniques of the Observer: On Vision and Modernity in the Nineteenth Century* (Cambridge, MA: MIT Press, 1990).
36. Errol Morris, *Believing Is Seeing (Observations on the Mysteries of Photography)* (New York: Penguin Books, 2011).
37. Kathryn Schulz, "Errol Morris Looks for the Truth in Photography," *New York Times Sunday Book Review*, September 1, 2011, http://www.nytimes.com/2011/09/04/books/review/believing-is-seeing-by-errol-morris-book-review.html?_r=2&.
38. Aristotle, *Metaphysics* 980a, trans. W. D. Ross, *The Basic Works of Aristotle* (New York: Random House, 1941).

39. See Peggy Phelan, "'In the Valley of the Shadow of Death': The Photographs of Abu Ghraib," in *Violence Performed: Local Roots and Global Routes of Conflict,* ed. Patrick Anderson and Jisha Menon (New York: Palgrave-Macmillan, 2009), 374–76. Liam Kennedy points out that "Morris's argument that 'believing is seeing' has value in foregrounding the role of 'ideological dispositions'" (*Afterimages: Photography and U.S. Foreign Policy* [Chicago: University of Chicago Press, 2015], 165). One can indeed use it that way, although that is not the route taken by the literalist.
40. Jörg Colberg, private correspondence with the authors, August 11, 2014.
41. Ariella Azoulay, *The Civil Contract of Photography* (New York: Zone Books, 2008), 109–10.
42. We borrow the phrase "imagined communities" from Benedict Anderson, *Imagined Communities: Reflections on the Origins of Nationalism* (London: Verso, 1991), although we see its scope as broader than the social construction of nationalism.
43. Samuel Taylor Coleridge, *Biographia Literaria, or Biographical Sketches of My Literary Life and Opinions* (New York: E. P. Dutton, 1975), 50, 167. The distinction was emphasized by I. A. Richards, Wallace Stevens, and other leading figures in mid-twentieth-century literary study.
44. Sharon Sliwinski, *Human Rights In Camera* (Chicago: University of Chicago Press, 2011).
45. Hariman and Lucaites, *No Caption Needed*, 208–42.
46. Roland Barthes, "The Photographic Message" and "The Rhetoric of the Image," in *Image, Music, Text*, trans. Stephen Heath (New York: Hill and Wang, 1977), 15–31, 32–51.
47. Scott McCloud, *Understanding Comics: The Invisible Art* (New York: HarperCollins / William Morrow, 1993), 67 (emphasis in the original). Italicized words in this quotation are in boldface in the original volume, which uses comic-book design conventions.
48. Our understanding of intentionality is indebted to Michael Carrithers, *Why Humans Have Cultures: Explaining Anthropology and Social Diversity* (New York: Oxford University Press, 1992), especially chap. 4, "The Anatomy of Sociality." See also H. P. Grice, "Utterer's Meaning and Intention," *Philosophical Review* 78 (1969): 147–77.
49. As John Berger notes, the simplest denotative message in any photograph is "I have decided that seeing this is worth recording." Berger, *Understanding a Photograph*, ed. Geoff Dyer (New York: Aperture, 2013), 25. Unfortunately, Berger becomes excessively reductionist when he also claims that "the formal arrangement of a photograph explains nothing. . . . Composition in the profound, formative sense of the word cannot enter into photography." (Note, in Maynard's terms [*Engine of Visualization*], the intertwined reification, dualism, and essentialism in this argument.) By contrast, we believe that the

reality coded into the photograph cannot be fully apprehended if the artistic principle has been disabled. For a detailed demonstration of how form implicates meaning in visual imagery, see Gunther Kress and Theo van Leeuwen, *Reading Images: The Grammar of Visual Design*, 2nd ed. (New York: Routledge, 2006).

50. Hannah Arendt, *The Human Condition,* 2nd ed. (Chicago: University of Chicago Press, 1998), 198.

51. See also John B. Thompson's call for "a new kind of publicness which consists of what we may describe as *the space of the visible*: it is the non-localized, non-dialogical, open-ended space of the visible in which mediated symbolic forms can be expressed and received by a plurality of non-present others." *The Media and Modernity: A Social Theory of the Media* (Stanford, CA: Stanford University Press, 1995), 245 (emphasis in the original).

52. Roger Silverstone, *Media and Morality: On the Rise of the Mediapolis* (Cambridge, UK: Polity, 2007), 32.

53. "If we did not have a practical sense of what publics are . . . we could not produce most of the books or films or broadcasts or journals that make up so much of our culture; we could not conduct elections or indeed imagine ourselves as members of nations or movements. Yet publics exist only by virtue of their imagining. They are a kind of fiction that has taken on life, and a very potent life at that." Michael Warner, *Publics and Counterpublics* (New York: Zone Books, 2002), 8.

54. Barbie Zelizer, *About to Die: How News Images Move the Public* (New York: Oxford University Press, 2010), 6–8, 318–20.

55. As Lilie Chouliaraki states, "Theatrical spectatorship mobilizes the faculty of imagination—namely our capacity to see the world from other people's standpoints as well as our capacity to imagine how we might act on these others' predicament" (*The Ironic Spectator: Solidarity in the Age of Post-Humanitarianism* [Cambridge, UK: Polity, 2013], 23). Note how Chouliaraki integrates the second and third dimensions of the imagination: recognition of interpersonal intentionality leads to the higher intentionality of moral and political needs. This connection might be one of photography's stronger capacities. See also Tracy Davis, "Theatricality and Civil Society," in *Theatricality*, ed. Tracey Davis and Thomas Postlewait (Cambridge: Cambridge University Press, 2003), 127–55.

56. Kracauer draws on Marcel Proust, Paul Strand, and Edward Weston to argue that "the photographer's selectivity is of a kind which is closer to empathy than to disengaged spontaneity. He resembles perhaps most of all the imaginative reader intent on studying and deciphering an elusive text." Kracauer, *Theory of Film*, 16.

57. For discussion of these changes, see in particular Fred Ritchin, *After Photography* (New York: W. W. Norton, 2009) and *Bending the Frame: Photojournalism, Documentary, and the Citizen* (New York: Aperture, 2010). For one example

of how professional photographers are thinking about the blurred genres, see Nina Berman, "Object Lessons," *Columbia Magazine,* Spring 2014, http://magazine.columbia.edu/print/1511. Note that where Ritchin, Berman, and many other commentators are focused primarily on changes in production and circulation, our work is oriented primarily toward reception—that is, toward encouraging models of interpretation that can extend photography's contribution to public life.

58. W. J. T. Mitchell, "Realism and the Digital Image," in *Critical Realism in Contemporary Art: Around Allan Sekula's Photography*, ed. Jan Baetens and Hilde Van Gelder (Louvain, Belgium: Leuven University Press, 2006), 15.

59. Jan Baetens and Hilde Van Gelder claim that "realism is making a solid comeback, both in the art world and in society at large." A corresponding redefinition of the term includes shifting from mechanical mimesis to "the invention of new ways of representing the real," shifting "from the art-object to the attitude of the reader or the spectator," and shifting from a period style to multiple articulations of the concept. They also feature photography, "because of its causal relationship to reality (its indexicality)," as the premier medium for revealing and critically reflecting on social reality (*Critical Realism*, 7–9). We believe a renewed realism also includes, as they admit sotto voce, reducing the modernist opposition between formalism and social critique.

60. Roberts, *Art of Interruption*, 5. Although adapted to our own project, our understanding of the history and major themes of photographic realism is indebted to Roberts's work.

61. John Dewey's discussion of the communicative capacity of works of art provides one account of how a public art functions in this regard. For example, "the presence of common or general factors in conscious experience is an *effect* of art," and "works of art are means by which we enter, through imagination and the emotions they evoke, into other forms of relationship and participation than our own" (*Art as Experience* [New York: Capricorn Books / G. P. Putnam's Sons, 1934], 286, 333). As Roberts elaborates, "The very act of engaging with a work of art creates sociality. Again we are in the realm of the intersubjective: the human subject of the vivid artwork should act as a call to the humanity of the spectator" (*Art of Interruption*, 77). As he also notes, in the realist tradition this engagement is an encounter across class lines to highlight how humanity is distorted by unjust social relations and harmful distributions of resources.

62. Roberts, *Art of Interruption*, 36.

63. Ibid., 187.

64. On the role of fantasies of power in the hidden transcripts of both dominant and subaltern groups, see James C. Scott, *Domination and the Arts of Resistance: Hidden Transcripts* (New Haven, CT: Yale University Press, 1990).

65. Thompson emphasizes "the significance that *struggles for visibility* have come

to assume in the social and political life" of mediated societies (*Media and Modernity*, 247 [emphasis in the original]).

66. Katherine Boo, "Staring Down Stereotypes: Writing about Poverty in America," *Berlin Journal* 14 (2007): 50–55; Sieglinde Lemke, "Facing Poverty: Towards a Theory of Articulation," *Amerikastudien / American Studies* 55 (January 1, 2010): 95–122.
67. On the importance of developing representational practices that allow the subject to speak, see Paula Rabinowitz, *They Must Be Represented: The Politics of Documentary* (New York: Verso, 1994). To address this deficit in the documentary work that includes figure 5, photographer Aaron Huey and *National Geographic* established the Pine Ridge Community Storytelling Project, http://ngm.nationalgeographic.com/2012/08/pine-ridge/community-project.
68. Andrew Katz, "Why We Look Again: Aaron Huey at Pine Ridge," *Time*, Lightbox, May 28, 2013, http://time.com/3799842/why-we-look-again-aaron-huey-at-pine-ridge/#1; Aaron Huey, "America's Native Prisoners of War," TEDxDU, University of Denver, May 2010, http://www.ted.com/talks/aaron_huey; Eric Becker, *Honor the Treaties* (short film), 2012. http://vimeo.com/47043218.
69. Michael Shapiro, in a superb account of the realist aesthetic in Richard Avedon's *In the American West*, sets that work against the scripted representations that "accompanied and helped legitimate the westward expansion of white Europeans on the North American continent." This "landscape view of the West . . . helped promote public willingness to support a policy of conquest, settlement, and exploitation" and continues to hide "the human costs associated with working in the West's less pleasant and less remunerative work sites." Avedon's portraits of miners, bartenders, and other workers overturned that pastoral tradition to confront the "silences" endemic to both administrative and photographic practices rationalizing conquest and control of the region. Since then, many have followed in Avedon's steps while the landscape tradition has both continued on its own terms and been reworked for environmental advocacy and other causes. We see figure 5 as yet another reworking of prior conventions to speak amid the silences of governmental and cultural practices. Michael J. Shapiro, *The Politics of Representation: Writing Practices in Biography, Photography, and Policy Analysis* (Madison: University of Wisconsin Press, 1988), 154–61.
70. Our commentary here is greatly indebted to Janna Soeder for both her bibliographic help and her critical insights regarding the problems of Native American representation.
71. The white settlement is discussed in two posts (and comments) at nocaptionneeded.com: "Emptiness at the Center of the Nation," http://www.nocaptionneeded.com/2008/06/emptiness-at-the-center-of-the-nation/, and "When Is a Flag Not a Prop?" http://www.nocaptionneeded.com/2008/06/when-is-a-flag-not-a-prop/.

72. Sontag, *Regarding the Pain of Others*, 125–26. Susie Linfield replies that "this is a remarkable statement, and remarkably wrong": Susie Linfield, *The Cruel Radiance: Photography and Political Violence* (Chicago: University of Chicago Press, 2010), 99. See also our discussion of photographic humanism in chapter 6.
73. "Caught in the Oil," The Big Picture, *Boston.com*, June 3, 2010, http://www.boston.com/bigpicture/2010/06/caught_in_the_oil.html.
74. Daniel Gilbert and Justin Scheck, "BP Is Found Grossly Negligent in Deepwater Horizon Disaster," *Wall Street Journal*, September 4, 2014, http://online.wsj.com/articles/u-s-judge-finds-bp-grossly-negligent-in-2010-deepwater-horizon-disaster-1409842182.
75. Sontag, *Regarding the Pain of Others*, 81.
76. Sontag, *On Photography*, 85.
77. *Nature* is a contested term in a number of disciplines, and rightly so. Although we recognize the limitations (or obsolescence) of the concept, we also believe that it still retains some value, not least in respect to political decisions that should not longer be avoided. The argument for continued and careful use of the concept includes Jedediah Purdy, *After Nature: A Politics for the Anthropocene* (Cambridge MA: Harvard University Press, 2015).
78. Ariella Azoulay, *Civil Imagination: A Political Ontology of Photography* (London: Verso, 2012), 3.
79. Ibid., 3–9, 69–88.
80. Ibid., 18.
81. Ibid., 121.
82. Examples include the essays in Chiara Bottici and Benoît Challand, eds., *The Politics of Imagination* (New York: Birbeck Law Press, 2001), which "all share the idea that we should go beyond the restricted view of imagination as mere fantasy" (3).
83. William Carlos Williams, "Asphodel, That Greeny Flower," in *"Asphodel, That Greeny Flower" and Other Love Poems* (New York: New Directions, 1994), 19. See also Ritchin, *Bending the Frame*, 35–44. John Dewey made the point as well, situating it more directly within democratic theory: "Artists have always been the real purveyors of the news, for it is not the outward happening in itself which is new, but the kindling by it of emotion, perception and appreciation." Dewey, *The Public and Its Problems* (New York: Henry Holt, 1927), 184.
84. Wallace Stevens, *The Necessary Angel: Essays on Reality and the Imagination* (New York: Vintage, 1951), 20.
85. Ibid., 102
86. Joel 2:28, in *The New Oxford Annotated Bible,* New Revised Standard Version (New York: Oxford University Press, 1994). It is important to note that realism does not preclude prophecy. Georg Lukács, a primary exponent of literary realism as a political aesthetic, argued that "'prophetic figures' . . . are to be found exclusively in the works of the important realists" and that prophecy

is an essential feature of "all authentic realism," because the task is to "depict the vital, but not immediately obvious forces at work in objective reality." Lukács, "Realism in the Balance," trans. Rodney Livingston, in *Aesthetics and Politics*, ed. Ronald Taylor (London: Verso, 1977), 46–48.

87. Baudelaire, "The Modern Public and Photography," 154–55.
88. Stevens, *Necessary Angel*, 7.

Chapter Four

1. Alan Trachtenberg, introduction to *Classic Essays on Photography*, ed. Alan Trachtenberg (New Haven, CT: Leete's Island Books, 1980), ix (emphasis in the original).
2. Marvin Heiferman, ed., *Photography Changes Everything* (New York: Aperture/Smithsonian, 2012).
3. Susan Sontag, *On Photography* (New York: Picador, 1977), 24. As we've noted earlier, Sontag was not the first to align photography with the worst features of modernization. That critique runs from Baudelaire through the Frankfort School theorists to mainstream American writers such as Daniel Boorstin. Boorstin's *The Image, or What Happened to the American Dream* (New York: Atheneum, 1962) provides a dual indictment of photography and film; it is still in print as *The Image: A Guide to Pseudo-Events in America*. For a study of midcentury photography that pushes back against this theme, see Blake Stimson, *The Pivot of the World: Photography and the Nation* (Cambridge, MA: MIT Press, 2006).
4. Bruno Latour, *We Have Never Been Modern* (Cambridge, MA: Harvard University Press, 1993).
5. Erwin Panofsky, *Meaning in the Visual Arts: Papers in and on Art History* (New York: Doubleday Anchor, 1955), 12.
6. Ibid., 13–14. The argument is pitched in part against abstract painting, but the distinction applies more broadly even if one does not accept Panofsky's commitment to "balance" between idea and form. Although probably not sufficient to account for the full spectrum of fine art, the distinction acquires special force in respect to most photography precisely because of the strong expectation that the photograph has to include a recognizable subject. One then always can ask about the relationship of the subject matter to the artistic composition of the image—that is, whether the artistry is subdued enough to be merely a vehicle for pragmatic communication or whether it is strong enough to create the additional meaning that becomes the content of an artistic statement.
7. Anne Friedberg supplies an important argument that supports this point: the Albertian perspective that subsequently became coded into photography was "a formula for representation of narrative *historia*, not of empty landscapes

or window-views" (*The Virtual Window: From Alberti to Microsoft* [Cambridge, MA: MIT Press, 2006], 32). The subject matter is placed within a virtual space in order to show a larger pattern of meaning. The Albertian frame is, like the story itself, a rhetorical device for doing cultural work. Friedberg's work also underwrites our argument in chapter 2: the direct copy, literal reference, single meaning (or the lack of meaning), immobile spectator, linear time, and evidentiary status (rather than a capacity for disclosure) are all historically contingent attributions to the photographic image rather than essential features.

8. The photograph is of the dam's spillway, taken during construction. According to the Museum of Modern Art, "This photograph became an icon of the machine age, not only because it was printed as the cover of the first issue of *Life* magazine (November 23, 1936), but also because it showed the power of modern technology to dwarf humankind." Heilbrunn Timeline of Art History, Museum of Modern Art, http://www.metmuseum.org/toah/works-of-art/1987.1100.25.
9. "Franklin Roosevelt's Wild West," *Life*, November 23, 1936, 9–18 (http://books.google.com/books?id=NoEEAAAAMBAJ&q=Franklin+Roosevelt's+Wild+West%2C#v=snippet&q=Franklin%20Roosevelt's%20Wild%20West%2C&f=false).
10. One of the intriguing features of modernism is how it developed strong associations between "high" and "low" arts despite also enforcing those distinctions in aesthetic theory and museum practices. For a model study in this regard, see Lynn Spigel, *TV by Design: Modern Art and the Rise of Network Television* (Chicago: University of Chicago Press, 2008).
11. The classic examples here of course point to the work of Jacob Riis and Lewis Hine, as well as the work by the Farm Security Administration photographers working under the guidance of Roy Stryker. Many of these efforts have been imitated in subsequent reform movements, and the tradition continues, albeit in color, through the work of G. M. B. Akash and many other photographers who are documenting exploitation and deprivation around the globe. See Robert Macieski, *Picturing Class: Lewis W. Hine Photographs Child Labor in New England* (Amherst: University of Massachusetts Press, 2015); Bonnie Yochelson and David Czitrom, *Rediscovering Jacob Riis: Exposure Journalism and Photography in Turn-of-the-Century New York* (New York: New Press, 2007); Miles Orvell, *American Photography* (New York: Oxford University Press, 2003), 71–79; Alan Trachtenberg, *Reading American Photographs: Images as History, Mathew Brady to Walker Evans* (New York: Hill and Wang, 1989), 164–230; Maren Stange, *Symbols of Ideal Life: Social Documentary Photography in America, 1890–1950* (New York: Cambridge University Press, 1989), 47–88; James Guimond, *American Photography and the American Dream* (Chapel Hill: University of North Carolina Press, 1991), 55–148; Cara Finnegan, "Studying Visual Modes

of Public Address: Lewis Hine's Progressive Era Child Labor Rhetoric," in *The Handbook of Rhetoric and Public Address*, ed. J. Michael Hogan and Shawn J. Parry-Giles (London: Blackwell, 2010), 250–70, and *Making Photography Matter: A Viewer's History from the Civil War to the Great Depression* (Champaign: University of Illinois Press, 2015).

12. Robert Hariman and John Louis Lucaites, "The Mushroom Cloud and the Cold War Nuclear Optic," in *Picturing Atrocity: Photography in Crisis*, ed. Geoffrey Batchen, Mark Gidley, Nancy K. Miller, and Jay Prosser (London: Reaktion Books, 2012), 134–45, and "Seeing the Bomb, Imagining the Future: Allegorical Vision in the Post–Cold War Nuclear Optic," *Cahiers ReMix* 1 (2012), http://oic.uqam.ca/en/remix/seeing-the-bomb-imagining-the-future-allegorical-vision-in-the-post-cold-war-nuclear-optic.

13. Catherine A. Lutz and Jane L. Collins, *Reading "National Geographic"* (Chicago: University of Chicago Press, 1993), 125.

14. There is one significant exception, which is in the use of images to create the mythic timelessness of retail advertising and shopping, as has been well documented. For important histories of the role of imagery in advertising and the development of a consumer culture, see Roland Marchand, *Advertising and the American Dream: Making Way for Modernity, 1920–1940* (Berkeley: University of California Press, 1985), 52–88, 117–64; Stuart Ewen, *Captains of Consciousness: Advertising and the Social Roots of Consumer Culture* (New York: McGraw-Hill, 1976); Jackson Lears, *Fables of Abundance: A Cultural History of Advertising in America* (New York: Basic Books, 1994). Guy Debord makes the most sweeping claim, which is that specific temporal fictions of advertising are the universal false consciousness of capitalist societies, necessary to maintain the bourgeoisie as the only agents of history. See *Society of the Spectacle* (Detroit: Black and Red, 1983), paragraph 143.

15. "Modernism" emerged in the nineteenth century as an artistic and intellectual movement and involved complicated responses to the rise of a technology-intensive industrialized civilization. Developments included multiple variants ranging from avid promotion of the machine age to critique of industrialization, from revolutionary politics to technocratic neutrality, and from reconnecting art and everyday life to radical artistic experimentation within a steep hierarchy of high and low arts. By most counts modernism ended in the late 1950s and early 1960s. See Peter Gay, *Modernism: The Lure of Heresy from Baudelaire to Beckett and Beyond* (New York: W. W. Norton, 2010), and Andreas Huyssen, *After the Great Divide: Modernism, Mass Culture, Postmodernism* (Bloomington: Indiana University Press, 1986). That said, modernism has been kept alive in the so-called late modern era as an artistic style or genre, most notably in architecture, literature, painting, sculpture, and dance. The modernism-postmodernism distinction does not provide a neat and consistent basis for distinguishing between conventional critique and our revisionary account.

Although we are critical of modernism, some of those we would place in the new paradigm (e.g., Susie Linfield) are self-defined modernists, and several of those critics who were highly influential in formulating the conventional critique did so in opposition to modernism's use of formalism to keep art and politics in separate spheres, with photography thereby incapacitated by being taken into the museum. Geoffrey Batchen provides a helpful discussion of the debate in *Burning with Desire: The Conception of Photography* (Cambridge, MA: MIT Press, 1997), 2–21, as does Jae Emerling in *Photography: History and Theory* (New York: Routledge, 2012), 1–41. See also the brief summary in Raphaël Pirenne and Alexander Streitberger, eds., introduction to *Heterogeneous Objects: Intermedia and Photography after Modernism* (Louvain, Belgium: Leuven University Press, 2013), vii–xxii. For a volume on behalf of "a politicized postmodernism," see Richard Bolton, ed., *The Contest of Meaning: Critical Histories of Photography* (Cambridge, MA: MIT Press, 1989), xiii. For discussion of the problems of each extreme, see Hal Foster, "The Archive without Museums," *October* 77 (1996): 97–119. One way we split the difference is to argue on behalf of a renewed appreciation of artistic form, but with particular attention to the intertwined practices, mixed media, and political engagement that define public life. In any case, the terms *modernist* and *postmodernist* seem to have longer half-lives in critical practice than they do as working doctrines for photographers. For a brief review of the historical arc of postmodernist photography, see Mary Warner Marien, *Photography: A Cultural History* (London: Lawrence King, 2002), 423–44, 469–73. For a good review of cultural modernism across the arts, see Daniel Joseph Singal, "Towards a Definition of American Modernism," in *Modernist Culture in America*, ed. Daniel Joseph Singal (Belmont, CA: Wadsworth, 1991), 1–27; note, however, our disagreement with Singal's strong distinction between modernism and modernization and his heavy reliance on the premature assessments of postmodernism by Fredric Jameson and Richard Wolin.

16. John Harvey, *Men in Black* (Chicago: University of Chicago Press, 1966).
17. Friedrich Nietzsche, *Beyond Good and Evil*, pt. 4, sec. 146 (1886), translation by Hariman; the original is in *Jenseits von Gut und Böse: Vorspiel einer Philosophie der Zukunft*, from *Digital Critical Edition of the Complete Works and Letters*, based on the critical text by G. Colli and M. Montinari (Berlin: de Gruyter, 1967), ed. Paolo D'Iorio, at Nietzsche Source, http://www.nietzschesource.org/texts/eKGWB/JGB.
18. For a demonstration of how this optic can become a method for cultural history, see Susan Buck-Morss, *Dreamworld and Catastrophe: The Passing of Mass Utopia in East and West* (Cambridge, MA: MIT Press, 2000).
19. For critiques of Brasília as an exemplar of high-modernist city planning, see James C. Scott, *Seeing like a State: How Certain Schemes to Improve the Human Condition Have Failed* (New Haven, CT: Yale University Press, 1998), 117–30,

and James Holston, *The Modernist City: An Anthropological Critique of Brasília* (Chicago: University of Chicago Press, 1989).

20. High modernists, led by the iconoclastic Clement Greenberg, treated art as inherently autonomous and formalist, radically rooted in its medium to the point of eliminating consideration of all content, story, or representation. See Clement Greenberg, "Modernist Painting," in *Forum Lectures* (Washington, DC: Voice of America, 1960) and in *Modern Art and Modernism: A Critical Anthology*, ed. Francis Franscina and Charles Harrison (London: Harper and Row, 1982), 5–10. Such an approach is inherently problematic for photography, of course, which cannot avoid being about something other than itself.
21. Mark Brown, "Alberto Giacometti statue Breaks Auction Record with £65m Sale," *Guardian*, February 3, 2010, http://www.theguardian.com/artanddesign/2010/feb/03/giacometti-statue-breaks-auction-record.
22. For example, Museum of Modern Art director John Szarkowski has been both credited with teaching Americans "how to see" and faulted for channeling the spectator's gaze into a narrow modernism. See John Szarkowski, *The Photographer's Eye* (Garden City, NY: Doubleday, 1966) and *Looking at Photographs: 100 Pictures from the Museum of Modern Art* (Greenwood, CT: New York Graphic Society, 1973).
23. Paul Krugman, *The Great Unraveling: Losing Our Way in the New Century* (New York: W. W. Norton, 2005).
24. We develop this position more fully in a series of online essays published in *Flow* (http://flowtv.org), including "Bad Image / Good Art: Thinking Through Banality" 15, no. 2 (October 2011); "The Banality of Violence," 15, no. 5 (January 2012); and "On the Surface," 15, no. 10 (April 2012).
25. Walter Benjamin, "On the Concept of History," trans. Harry Zohn, in *Walter Benjamin: Selected Writings*, vol. 4, *1938–1940*, ed. Howard Eiland and Michael W. Jennings (Cambridge, MA: Belknap / Harvard University Press, 2003), 392 (emphasis in the original).
26. Changing conceptions of time are fundamental to the differences between various modernities. David Harvey highlights this temporal variable with his notion of "time-space" compression, in which the pace of life has been so accelerated "that the world sometimes seems to collapse inwards upon itself . . . and time horizons shorten to the point where the present is all there is." See Harvey, *The Condition of Postmodernity* (Oxford: Basil Blackwell, 1989), 240. See also Marshall Berman, *All That Is Solid Melts into Air* (New York: Simon and Schuster, 1982), and Fredric Jameson, "Postmodernism, or The Cultural Logic of Late Capitalism," *New Left Review* 146 (1984): 53–92. The visual corollary to time-space compression is marked by Walter Benjamin as a problem of technological "distraction" that subverts contemplation, relies on "habit," and becomes mass culture's characteristic mode of participation. Kevin DeLuca and Jennifer Peeples characterize this as a shift from the (contemplative) "gaze"

to the (hurried and habitual) "glance," marking the later as primary mode of attention in a world dominated by the "public screen"; in addition, they are among those who see possibilities for resistance in breaking with the gaze. See Walter Benjamin, "The Work of Art in the Age of Its Technological Reproducibility, Second Version," trans. Edmund Jephcott and Harry Zohn, in *The Work of Art in the Age of Its Technological Reproducibility, and Other Writings on Media*, ed. Michael W. Jennings, Brigid Doherty, and Thomas Y. Levin (Cambridge, MA: Belknap / Harvard University Press), 39–41; Kevin DeLuca and Jennifer Peeples, "From Public Sphere to Public Screen: Democracy, Activism, and the 'Violence' of Seattle," *Critical Studies in Media Communication* 19 (2002): 125–51. Paul Frosh challenges the critical potential of the glance. In consumer culture, the glance "tends therefore toward a certain *equivalence*: it is that visual dynamic whose momentum partakes of the leveling energy of exchange value, which denies its own duration and the singularity of the object." *The Image Factory: Consumer Culture, Photography and the Visual Content Industry* (Oxford: Berg, 2003), 110 (emphasis in the original). Our method acknowledges these problems of acceleration and comprehension and is an attempt at slowing down perception.

27. Our usage may resonate with the "ordinary time" of the Western Christian liturgical calendar, but the difference should be clear: in the Western tradition of secular modernity, unmodulated linear time is sovereign; there is no liturgical pattern or sacred envelope. See Alfred Gell, *The Anthropology of Time: Cultural Constructions of Temporal Maps and Images* (London: Bloomsbury Academic, 1991), and Carol Greenhouse, *A Moment's Notice: Time Politics across Cultures* (Ithaca, NY: Cornell University Press, 1996).
28. Barbie Zelizer, *About to Die: How News Images Move the Public* (New York: Oxford University Press, 2010).
29. Nancy Martha West, *Kodak and the Lens of Nostalgia* (Charlottesville: University Press of Virginia, 2000). On nostalgia and modernity, see Svetlana Boym, *The Future of Nostalgia* (New York: Basic Books, 2001).
30. Roland Barthes, *Camera Lucida*, trans. Richard Howard (New York: Hill and Wang, 1981).
31. See Paul Connerton, *How Societies Remember* (New York: Cambridge University Press, 1989). For a survey of the relationship between collective and cultural memory and the construction of history, see Astrid Erll and Ansgar Nunning, eds., *A Companion to Cultural Memory Studies* (Berlin: De Gruyter, 2010).
32. For example, Noreen Malone, "The Case against Economic Disaster Porn," *New Republic*, January 22, 2011, http://www.newrepublic.com/article/81954/Detroit-economic-disaster-porn; Whet Moser, "Their City Was Gone: Detroit, Disaster Porn, and the Decline of the Middle Class," *Chicago Magazine*, March 24, 2011, http://www.chicagomag.com/Chicago-Magazine/The-312

/February-2011/Their-City-Was-Gone-Detroit-Disaster-Porn-and-the-Decline-of-the-Middle-Class/; Mark Binelli, "How Detroit Became the World Capital of Staring at Abandoned Old Buildings," *New York Times Sunday Magazine*, November 9, 2012, http://www.nytimes.com/2012/11/11/magazine/how-detroit-became-the-world-capital-of-staring-at-abandoned-old-buildings.html; Peter York, "Detroit: America's Fascination with Disaster Porn and Hero Worship," *Politically Inclined*, October 31, 2013, http://politically-inclined.com/2013/10/detroit-americas-fascination-with-disaster-porn-and-hero-worship/. The discussion was prompted by publications such as Dan Austin and Sean Doerr, *Lost Detroit: Stories behind the Motor City's Majestic Ruins* (Charleston, SC: History Press, 2010); Andrew Moore, *Detroit Disassembled* (Bologna: Damiani / Akron Art Museum, 2010); Yves Marchand and Romain Meffre, *The Ruins of Detroit* (Göttingen, Germany: Steidl, 2011), and similar photo-essays in a number of papers and magazines. A search at Amazon.com will pull up dozens of similar books, including those of Henk van Rensbergen's Abandoned Places project, http://www.abandoned-places.com/. For an important study of the imagery of ruin, see Dora Apel, *Beautiful Terrible Ruins: Detroit and the Anxiety of Decline* (New Brunswick, NJ: Rutgers University Press, 2015). Apel's book arrived too late for incorporation into our work, but we share her interest in moving beyond the aestheticization critique of the medium to confront the catastrophic potential within the social system: "The imagery of ruination challenges us to imagine a society that would eliminate the bankruptcy of cities and the impoverishment of their inhabitants, and to ask how ruin imagery might be harnessed to an emancipatory struggle that would eliminate the constant drive for accumulation, privatization, commodification, and monetization—for to look at Detroit's beautiful terrible ruins and talk about its decline is to talk about everything that is wrong with global capitalism today" (158).

33. John Patrick Leary, "Detroitism," *Guernica*, January 15, 2011, http://www.guernicamag.com/features/leary_1_15_11/.

34. Walter Benjamin identifies ruins and the melancholic mood as important elements of allegory: *The Origin of German Tragic Drama*, trans. John Osborne (London: NLB, 1977), 166, 183–84. We discuss allegory at more length in Robert Hariman, "Allegory and Democratic Public Culture in the Postmodern Era," *Philosophy and Rhetoric* 35 (2002): 267–96, and Hariman and Lucaites, "Seeing the Bomb, Imagining the Future." See also Craig Owens, "The Allegorical Impulse: Toward a Theory of Postmodernism," in *Art after Modernism: Rethinking Representation*, ed. Brian Wallis (New York: New Museum of Contemporary Art, 1984), 203–35. Owens points out "the allegorical potential of photography," which he locates in the tension created by wanting "to fix the transitory, the ephemeral, in a stable and stabilizing image" that at the same time offers "only a fragment, and thus affirms its own arbitrariness and contingency" (207). This is a start, but we find the greater critical potential in photography's

capacity to "arrest narrative in place, substituting a principle of syntagmatic disjunction for one of diegetic combination" (208), and in the "blatant disregard for aesthetic categories . . . in the reciprocity which allegory proposes between the visual and the verbal: words are often treated as purely visual phenomena, while visual images are offered as script to be deciphered. . . . In allegory, the image is a hieroglyph" (208–9).

35. Benjamin, *Origin of German Tragic Drama*, 178.
36. John Roberts, *Photography and Its Violations* (New York: Columbia University Press, 2014), 110–11.
37. Ibid., 110.
38. Note that the continued circulation of images of ruins despite the renovation of the original sites is evidence that their value lies in providing an allegorical optic and melancholic mood for thinking about modernity. The building containing the ruined dentist's office now contains apartments. That is a different story, one of reclamation, and it is easy to imagine stepping from there into the narrative of progress restored. The ruins circulate because other resources continue to be needed, just as disasters will continue to occur.
39. For additional development of this idea, see Robert Hariman and Ralph Cintron, eds., *Culture, Catastrophe, and Rhetoric: The Texture of Political Action* (New York: Berghahn, 2015); Robert Hariman and John Louis Lucaites, *No Caption Needed: Iconic Photographs, Public Culture, and Liberal Democracy* (Chicago: University of Chicago Press, 2007), chap. 8; Buck-Morss, *Dreamworld and Catastrophe.* The theme has been evident at least since Frederic Jameson remarked that "the urgency of the subject demands that we make at least some effort to think the cultural evolution of late capitalism dialectically, as catastrophe and progress all together." *Postmodernism, or The Cultural Logic of Late Capitalism* (Durham, NC: Duke University Press, 1991), 47.
40. Benjamin, "Work of Art in the Age of Its Technological Reproducibility," 42. See also Peter Sloterdijk, *Critique of Cynical Reason* (Minneapolis: University of Minnesota Press, 1988).
41. Walter Benjamin, *The Arcades Project*, trans. Howard Eiland and Kevin McLaughlin (Cambridge, MA: Belknap / Harvard University Press, 1999), 474 (N10, 2).
42. American political discourse has been carefully situated within the idiom of a prophetic tradition from the time of the Puritans forward. See, for example, Sacvan Bercovitch's discussion of the jeremiad as a genre of discourse animated by a righteous tone, the authority of God, and the relationship between chronological and horological temporalities. Sacvan Bercovitch, *The American Jeremiad* (Madison: University of Wisconsin Press, 1978). James Darsey locates the tradition within the context of radical reform and emphasizes the prophetic function over generic form. See James Darsey, *The Prophetic Tradition and Radical Rhetoric in America* (New York: NYU Press, 1997). More recently, see

George Shulman, *American Prophecy: Race and Redemption in American Political Culture* (Minneapolis: University of Minnesota Press, 2008).

43. Michael Walzer, *Interpretation and Social Criticism* (Cambridge, MA: Harvard University Press, 1987), 67–94.

44. Walter Benjamin, "Little History of Photography," trans. Edmund Jephcott and Kingsley Shorter, in *The Work of Art in the Age of Its Technological Reproducibility and Other Writings on Media*, ed. Michael W. Jennings, Brigid Doherty, and Thomas Y. Levin (Cambridge, MA: Belknap / Harvard University Press), 276–77. Elizabeth Abel provides a thoughtful elaboration of this idea in "History at a Standstill: Agency and Gender in the Image of Civil Rights," in *Picturing Atrocity: Photography in Crisis*, ed. Geoffrey Batchen, Mark Gidley, Nancy K. Miller, and Jay Prosser (London: Reaktion Books, 2012), 105–13.

45. The artistic and prophetic significance of the image is underscored by the fact that it is from the evacuation zone for the Fukushima Daini nuclear plant, which is nearby but was not as badly damaged as the Fukushima Daiichi plant and was shut down relatively safely. Both plants were cited in captions—as "a second plant" in the photographer's caption, and in the following manner at a slide show on the aftermath of the quake: "An official in protective gear talks to a woman who is from the evacuation area near the Fukushima Daini nuclear plant in Koriyama March 13. Japanese Chief Cabinet Secretary Yukio Edano confirmed on Saturday there has been an explosion and radiation leakage at Tokyo Electric Power Co's (TEPCO) Fukushima Daiichi nuclear power plant" ("Japan: Earthquake Aftermath," *Big Picture*, March 12, 2011, http://www.boston.com/bigpicture/2011/03/japan_earthquake_aftermath.html). Thus the immediate context for the image is the Daini reactor, but it was associated immediately with the Daiichi reactor and as part of the larger evacuation while "Japan raced to avert a nuclear meltdown" (ibid.). Somewhere along that line, the image shifts from relaying information to providing an evocative depiction of comprehensive danger. Context is variable, then, and the photograph is doing more than reporting on its immediate locale, while its imaginative capability is suited to a broad conception of the news that can include prophetic warnings about dependency on modern technologies. Stated otherwise, one sense of context may be appropriate to articulating the subject matter of the photograph and another to articulating its content, and in some cases such as disasters, those two dimensions may be especially congruent.

46. On the value of "bottom-up" disaster response see "Building Local Capacity and Accelerating Progress: Resilience from the Bottom Up," in National Academies, *Disaster Resilience: A National Imperative* (Washington, DC: National Academies Press, 2012), 117–58.

47. For a fine essay on the role of science fiction in Japanese public culture, see Peter Wynn Kirby, "Japan's Long Nuclear Disaster Film," Opinionator Blog, *New*

York Times, March 14, 2011, http://opinionator.blogs.nytimes.com/2011/03/14/japans-long-nuclear-disaster-film/.

48. Charles Perrow, *Normal Accidents: Living with High-Risk Technologies* (Princeton, NJ: Princeton University Press, 1999).

Chapter Five

1. Henry R. Luce, *Life* prospectus mission statement, 1936, http://life.tumblr.com/post/17551327132/to-see-life-to-see-the-world-to-eyewitness.
2. Susan Sontag, *On Photography* (New York: Picador, 1977), 4, 11, 15, 23.
3. Susan Sontag, *Regarding the Pain of Others* (New York: Picador, 2004), 18.
4. Sontag, *On Photography*, 24 (emphasis in the original).
5. For an earlier statement of this perspective, see Robert Hariman, "Seeing the Stranger in the Mirror: Everyday Life in Magnum's Public World," in *Reading Magnum: A Visual Archive of the Modern World*, ed. Steven Hoelscher (Austin: University of Texas Press, 2013), 247–65.
6. For succinct accounts of the importance of the stranger's becoming the representative figure in modernity and especially of the public sphere, see Paul Frosh, "Telling Presences: Witnessing, Mass Media, and the Imagined Lives of Strangers," in *Media Witnessing: Testimony in the Age of Mass Communication*, ed. Paul Frosh and Amit Pinchevski (London: Palgrave Macmillan, 2009), 49–72; Michael Warner, *Publics and Counterpublics* (New York: Zone Books, 2002), 74–76; and Danielle Allen, *Talking to Strangers: Anxieties of Citizenship since* Brown v. Board of Education (Chicago: University of Chicago Press, 2004).
7. Walter Benjamin grasped this crucial element of photographic meaning in his "Little History of Photography": "For it is another nature that speaks to the camera rather than to the eye . . . photography reveals in this material physiognomic aspects, image worlds, which dwell in the smallest things" (trans. Edmund Jephcott and Harry Zohn, in *The Work of Art in the Age of Its Technological Reproducibility, and Other Writings on Media*, 277–79).
8. The point is illustrated powerfully in Allen's discussion of how the photographs documenting the desegregation of Central High School in Little Rock, Arkansas, in 1957 put the "habits" of citizenship on display (*Talking to Strangers*, 9–12).
9. Affirmations of the idea that philosophy begins in wonder include Plato, *Theaetetus* 155; Aristotle, *Metaphysics* 982b; Thomas Aquinas, *Commentary on Aristotle's Metaphysics* 1.3; Alfred North Whitehead, *Modes of Thought* (Toronto: Macmillan / Free Press, 1938), 168.
10. Jim Dine, *Walking to Boras* (2006), enamel on wood, Crystal Bridges Museum of Art, Bentonville, Arkansas.
11. This claim is made in spite of and in agreement with some of the critiques of museums as ideological institutions and as institutions unsuited to articulat-

ing photography as a public art. See for example Douglas Crimp with Louise Lawler, *On the Museum's Ruins* (Cambridge, MA: MIT Press, 1995). Although they are public institutions, art museums have a very difficult time avoiding the modernist contextualization that overvalues form at the expense of photography's capacity for political engagement, while display practices typically isolate images within zones of empty space that are very different from the mixed-media environment in which the images shape experience. More generally, the museum cannot help but reproduce a fundamental misrecognition of public art when it is seen in a fine arts context. That said, we believe that museum photography plays a vital role in the habitus of photography and that many contemporary curators are producing exhibitions that creatively address these constitutional tensions. Furthermore, and contra Sontag's claim that photography's "main effect is to convert the world into a department store or museum-without-walls in which every subject is depreciated into an article of consumption" (*On Photography*, 110), we hope to demonstrate how the "museum" metaphor is a useful tool for bringing forth the cultural richness and artistic accomplishment of the public image.

12. See Catherine A. Lutz and Jane L. Collins, *Reading "National Geographic"* (Chicago: University of Chicago Press, 1993), especially chaps. 4–5.
13. For more comprehensive discussion of the relationships between ritual performance and mass media production, see Eric W. Rothenbuhler, *Ritual Communication: From Everyday Conversation to Mediated Ceremony* (Thousand Oaks, CA: Sage, 1998), and Daniel Dayan and Elihu Katz, *Media Events: The Live Broadcasting of History* (Cambridge, MA: Harvard University Press, 1992).
14. Phil Bicker, "Pictures of the Week: March 22–March 29," *Time*, Lightbox, March 29, 2013, http://time.com/3798124/pictures-of-the-week-march-22-march-29/.
15. Leading proponents of dramaturgical approaches to social interaction are Erving Goffman in sociology and Kenneth Burke in literary/rhetorical studies. See Kenneth Burke, *A Grammar of Motives* (1945; Berkeley: University of California Press, 1969); Erving Goffman, *The Presentation of Self in Everyday Life* (New York: Doubleday, 1959) and *Frame Analysis* (New York: Harper, 1974). A brief and rather instrumental description is at Dramaturgy (sociology), *Wikipedia*, http://en.wikipedia.org/wiki/Dramaturgy_(sociology).
16. Teju Cole, "A True Picture of Black Skin," *New York Times*, February 18, 2015, http://nyti.ms/1CKSLi2. On the production of whiteness in the cinema, see Richard Dyer, *White: Essays on Race and Culture* (New York: Routledge, 1997).
17. Sontag, *Regarding the Pain of Others*, 81.
18. Lawrence Grossberg, *Caught in the Crossfire: Kids, Politics and America's Future* (Boulder, CO: Paradigm, 2005); Robin Bernstein, *Racial Innocence: Performing American Childhood from Slavery to Civil Rights* (New York: New York University Press, 2011).
19. For more on texture as a methodological concept, see Robert Hariman and

John Louis Lucaites, "Icons, Iconicity, and Cultural Critique," *Sociologica*, no. 1 (2015): 1–32, http://www.sociologica.mulino.it/journal/article/index/Article/Journal:ARTICLE:827/Item/Journal:ARTICLE:827, and Robert Hariman and Ralph Cintron, eds., *Culture, Catastrophe, and Rhetoric: The Texture of Political Action* (New York: Berghahn Books, 2015).

20. Martin Jay, *Downcast Eyes: The Denigration of Vision in Twentieth-Century French Thought* (Berkeley: University of California Press, 1993), 142n219.

21. Danielle Allen suggests that "democratic citizens have a special need for symbols and the world of fantasy precisely because their real political world does not and cannot give them the autonomy, freedom, and sovereignty it promises" (*Talking to Strangers*, 22).

22. "Fighting Intensifies in Syria," slide show, *New York Times*, January 30, 2012, http://www.nytimes.com/slideshow/2012/01/30/world/middleeast/20120131-SYRIA.html?_r=0#16.

23. Apologies to Mr. Luce. Susie Linfield provides a related emphasis: "In approaching photographs with relentless suspicion, critics have made it easy for us to deconstruct images but almost impossible to see them; they have crippled our capacity to grasp what John Berger called 'the *thereness* of the world.' And it is just that—the texture, the fullness of the world outside ourselves—into which we need to delve. Photographs can help us do that." *The Cruel Radiance: Photography and Political Violence* (Chicago: University of Chicago Press, 2010), 30.

24. See Jacques Rancière on "the pensive image," *The Emancipated Spectator* (London: Verso, 2011), 108–32, esp. 116–19.

25. "To the producers, therefore, the social relations between their private labours appear as what they are, i.e., they do not appear as direct social relations between persons in their work, but rather as material [*dinglich*] relations between persons and social relations between things." Karl Marx, *Capital*, trans. Ben Fowkes (New York: Vintage, 1977), vol. 1.4, 165–66.

26. Marx, *Capital*, 167. We should note the importance of this idea to Sontag's critique of photography: her fear of image displacing reality was grounded in the correspondence of photography with the commodity form. Photography was Exhibit A of capitalism's alienating transformation of the lifeworld into phantasmagoria. From our perspective, social reality is more complicated, while the relationship between photography and the commodity form allows the medium to become a means for critical reflection on social processes such as the alienation of labor.

Chapter Six

1. Susan Sontag makes the claim comprehensive: "Needing to have reality confirmed and experience enhanced by photographs is an aesthetic consumer-

ism to which everyone is now addicted." *On Photography* (New York: Picador, 1977), 24.

2. Mark Reinhardt provides an excellent critique of the aestheticization argument in "Picturing Violence: Aesthetics and the Anxiety of Critique," in *Beautiful Suffering: Photography and the Traffic in Pain*, ed. Mark Reinhardt, Holly Edwards, and Erina Duganne (Chicago: University of Chicago Press, 2007). For a strong refutation of the claim that the representation of suffering is pornographic, see Susie Linfield, *The Cruel Radiance: Photography and Political Violence* (Chicago: University of Chicago Press, 2010), 40–42. The pornography charge is another example of shifting the burden of representation: Allan Sekula, Martha Rosler, Sontag, and others making the charge claim that the key to avoiding pornography is to clothe the image in verbal narrative. The problem, of course, is that writing is no less immune to pornography, as is evident from the etymology of the word. See Allan Sekula, "Dismantling Modernism, Reinventing Documentary (Notes on the Politics of Representation)," in *Photography against the Grain: Essays and Photo Works* (Halifax: Press of the Nova Scotia College of Art and Design, 1984), 26, 62–65; Susan Sontag, *Regarding the Pain of Others* (Farrar, Straus and Giroux, 2003), 95. See also Fredric Jameson, *Signatures of the Visible* (London: Routledge, 1992), 1. For an analysis indicative of the paradigm shift on this question, and one that recognizes a much wider range of spectatorship, see Sue Tait, "Pornographies of Violence? Internet Spectatorship on Body Horror," *Critical Studies in Media Communication* 25 (2008): 91–111.
3. See, e.g., Sontag, *Regarding the Pain of Others*, 78–79, 108, and David Levi-Strauss, *Between the Eyes: Essays on Photography and Politics* (New York: Aperture, 2003), 4–7, 42–50.
4. John Taylor provides a careful discussion of press norms regarding the depiction of horror. As opposed to a pornography of violence, he finds that "the press errs on the side of caution in depicting death and destruction." *Body Horror: Photojournalism, Catastrophe and War* (New York: New York University Press, 1998), 193.
5. On the "compassion fatigue" debates see David Campbell, "The Myth of Compassion Fatigue," in *The Violence of the Image: Photography and International Conflict*, ed. Liam Kennedy and Caitlin Patrick (London: I. B. Taurus, 2014), 97–124. For a more theoretical critique of the relationship between compassion, photography, and democratic politics, see James Johnson, "'The Arithmetic of Compassion': Rethinking the Politics of Photography," *British Journal of Political Science* 41 (2011): 621–43. On "helplessness" see Linfield, *Cruel Radiance*, 33–64.
6. On the relationship of photography and the military, see Susan D. Moeller, *Shooting War: Photography and the American Experience of Combat* (New York: Basic Books, 1989); Katy Parry, "Media Visualisation of Conflict: Studying

News Imagery in 21st Century Wars," *Sociology Compass*, 2010, 417–29. On photographs of lynching see Dora Apel, *Imagery of Lynching: Black Men, White Women, and the Mob* (New Brunswick, NJ: Rutgers University Press, 2004), and "Lynching Photographs and the Politics of Public Shaming," in *Lynching Photographs*, ed. Dora Apel and Shawn Michelle Smith (Berkeley: University of California Press, 2008), 42–78; Amy Louise Wood, *Lynching and Spectacle: Witnessing Racial Violence in America, 1890–1940* (Chapel Hill: University of North Carolina Press, 2009), 75–111. On photographs of rape see Ariella Azoulay, "Has Anyone Ever Seen a Photograph of a Rape?" in *The Civil Contract of Photography* (New York: Zone Books, 2008), 217–88; and Wendy S. Hesford, *Spectacular Rhetorics: Human Rights Visions, Recognitions, Feminisms* (Durham, NC: Duke University Press, 2011), 93–124.

7. Peggy Phelan, "Atrocity and Action: The Performative Force of the Abu Ghraib Photographs," in *Picturing Atrocity: Photography in Crisis*, ed. Geoffrey Batchen, Mick Gidley, Nancy K. Miller, and Jay Prosser (London: Reaktion Books, 2012), 55.

8. John Berger claims that "the word *trigger*, applied to rifle and camera, reflects a correspondence which does not stop at the purely mechanical. The image seized by the camera is doubly violent." *About Looking* (1980; New York: Vintage, 1991), 43. Sontag grants that photography doesn't literally kill (quite the concession) but claims "there is an aggression implicit in every use of the camera. . . . A camera is sold as a predatory weapon. . . . To photograph people is to violate them. . . . The act of taking pictures is a semblance of appropriation, a semblance of rape" (*On Photography*, 7, 14, 24). Roland Barthes inadvertently provides the link to the *pharmakon* of classical rhetoric: "The Photograph is violent: not because it shows violent things, but because on each occasion *it fills the sight by force*, and because in it nothing can be refused or transformed (that we can sometimes call it mild does not contradict its violence: many say that sugar is mild, but to me sugar is violent, and I call it so)." *Camera Lucida: Reflections on Photography*, trans. Richard Howard (New York: Hill and Wang, 1981), 91 (emphasis in the original). Rather than wholly deny these analogies, one might consider instead Wallace Stevens's statement that "it is a violence from within that protects us from a violence without. It is the imagination pressing back against the pressure of reality. It seems, in the last analysis, to have something to do with our self-preservation." Wallace Stevens, *The Necessary Angel: Essays on Reality and the Imagination* (New York: Vintage, 1951), 36.

9. Sam Keen, *Faces of the Enemy: Reflections of the Hostile Imagination; The Psychology of Enmity* (San Francisco: Harper and Row, 1986); George H. Roeder Jr., *The Censored War: American Visual Experience during World War II* (New Haven, CT: Yale University Press, 1993); David D. Perlmutter, *Photojournalism and Foreign Policy: Icons of Outrage in International Crises* (Westport, CT: Praeger,

1998); Roger Stahl, *Militainment, Inc.: War, Media, and Popular Culture* (New York: Routledge, 2009); Dora Apel, *War Culture and the Contest of Images* (New Brunswick, NJ: Rutgers University Press, 2012); James R. Ryan, *Picturing Empire: Photography and the Visualization of the British Empire* (Chicago: University of Chicago Press, 1998); Laura Wexler, *Tender Violence: Domestic Visions in the Age of U.S. Imperialism* (Chapel Hill: University of North Carolina Press, 2000); Martin Jay and Sumathi Ramaswamy, eds., *Empires of Vision: A Reader* (Durham, NC: Duke University Press, 2014), esp. 1–46; Liam Kennedy, *Afterimages: Photography and U.S. Foreign Policy* (Chicago: University of Chicago Press, 2016).

10. In *Afterimages* Kennedy features the work of Larry Burrows, Philip Jones Griffiths, David Burnett, Abbas, Gilles Peress, Susan Meiselas, David Turnley, Kenneth Jarecke, Ron Haviv, Gary Knight, Chris Hondros, Ashley Gilbertson, Nina Berman, and Anthony Suau, among others.
11. Particularly influential were Sontag, *On Photography*, and Allan Sekula, "The Traffic in Photographs," in *Modernism and Modernity*, ed. Benjamin H. D. Buchloh, Serge Guilbaut, and David Solkin (Halifax: Nova Scotia College of Art and Design, 1983), 121–54. For additional examples see Linfield, *Cruel Radiance*, 3–32.
12. Linfield, *Cruel Radiance*, 45.
13. Ariella Azoulay, *The Civil Contract of Photography* (New York: Zone Books, 2008), 192.
14. Ibid., 191, 193. Luc Boltanski develops a similar attitude in his discussion of how public opinion created through encounters with distant suffering can function as effective speech. *Distant Suffering: Morality, Media and Politics*, trans. Graham Burchell (Cambridge: Cambridge University Press, 1999), 183–92.
15. Sharon Sliwinski argues that a "passionate aesthetic encounter between spectators and images of distant suffering" played a crucial role in the development of the modern idea of a common humanity. *Human Rights In Camera* (Chicago: University of Chicago Press, 2011), 46. Kevin Rozario argues that there would be no human rights movement without the mass-media apparatus: "modern 'humanitarianism' is in fact a *creation* of a sensationalistic mass culture." Rozario believes this is nothing to bemoan and that relationship was mutually productive: "Humanitarians, then, helped to instill particular ways of seeing and feeling about the sufferings of strangers." "'Delicious Horrors': Mass Culture, the Red Cross, and the Appeal of Modern American Humanitarianism," *American Quarterly* 55 (2003): 417, 425. David Kennedy completes the circle but, in a critique of the bureaucratization of the humanitarian movement, reverses the valuation via the conventional critique of photographic spectatorship: "The human rights intervention is always addressed to an imaginary third eye—the bystander," which "exacts a terrible cost on the habit of using more engaged and open-ended political vocabularies. The result is

professional narcissism guising itself as empathy and hoping to recruit others to solidarity with its bad faith." *The Dark Sides of Virtue: Reassessing International Humanitarianism* (Princeton, NJ: Princeton University Press, 2004), 29. For a synoptic review of humanitarianism and its critics, see Craig Calhoun, "The Imperative to Reduce Suffering: Charity, Progress and Emergencies in the Field of Humanitarian Action," in *Humanitarianism in Question: Politics, Power, Ethics*, ed. Michael Barnett and Thomas G. Weiss (Ithaca, NY: Cornell University Press, 2008), 73–97. For a sophisticated analysis of the contemporary relationship between media aesthetics and humanitarianism, see Lilie Chouliaraki, *The Ironic Spectator: Solidarity in the Age of Post-Humanitarianism* (Cambridge, UK: Polity, 2013).

16. Lawrence H. Keeley, *War before Civilization: The Myth of the Peaceful Savage* (New York: Oxford University Press, 1996); Steven Pinker, *The Better Angels of Our Nature: Why Violence Has Declined* (New York: Viking, 2011). For a data display supporting the argument, see Neil Halloran, dir., "The Fallen of World War II," http://www.fallen.io/ww2/. This is not to deny the appalling rates of rape and domestic abuse, gang warfare, and other forms of violence (that is hardly our intention), but it is notable that sexual and domestic violence have to be hidden, gang violence is contained in specific localities, and state terrorism and other systemic violence are rationalized and denied. For a somewhat more detailed statement of this argument, see Robert Hariman, "Watching War Evolve: Photojournalism and the New Forms of Violence," in *Violence of the Image*, ed. Kennedy and Patrick, 139–49.
17. See Sliwinski, *Human Rights In Camera*; Linfield, *Cruel Radiance*, 33–64; Andrea Noble, "Family Photography and the Global Drama of Human Rights," in *Photography: Theoretical Snapshots*, ed. J. J. Long, Andrea Noble, and Edward Welch (New York: Routledge, 2009), 63–79; David Campbell, "Atrocity, Memory, Photography: Imaging the Concentration Camps of Bosnia—The Case of ITN versus Living Marxism, Part 1," *Journal of Human Rights* 1 (2002): 1–33, "Atrocity, Memory, Photography: Imaging the Concentration Camps of Bosnia—The Case of ITN versus Living Marxism, Part 2," *Journal of Human Rights* 1 (2002): 1–33; Chouliaraki, *Ironic Spectator*, esp. 1–53; Hesford, *Spectacular Rhetorics*, 29–60.
18. Peter Howe, *Shooting under Fire: The World of the War Photographer* (New York: Artisan/Workman, 2002), 186. Cited also in Linfield, *Cruel Radiance*, 60.
19. Linfield, *Cruel Radiance*, 59.
20. Recent scholarship is illuminating some of what was overlooked in the initial critique, although not to undo critical judgment. To survey a range of colonial and postcolonial practices, see Christopher Pinney, *Photography and Anthropology* (London: Reaktion, 2011); and Christopher Pinney and Nicolas Peterson, eds., *Photography's Other Histories* (Durham, NC: Duke University Press, 2003). Earlier work includes Elizabeth Edwards, ed., *Anthropology and Photography, 1860–1920* (New Haven, CT: Yale University Press, 1992).

21. John Louis Lucaites and Jon Simons, eds., *The In/Visibility of America's Twenty-First Century Wars* (New Brunswick, NJ: Rutgers University Press, forthcoming 2017).
22. See John Bodnar, *The "Good War" in American Memory* (Baltimore: Johns Hopkins University Press, 2010).
23. See Robert Hariman and John Louis Lucaites, "The Iconic Image of the Mushroom Cloud and the Cold War Nuclear Optic," in *Picturing Atrocity*, ed. Batchen et al., 135–46; and "Seeing the Bomb, Imagining the Future: Allegorical Vision in the Post–Cold War Nuclear Optic," *Cahiers ReMix* 1 (2012), http://oic.uqam.ca/en/remix/seeing-the-bomb-imagining-the-future-allegorical-vision-in-the-post-cold-war-nuclear-optic.
24. Linfield, *Cruel Radiance*, 133.
25. Ibid., 135.
26. Ibid., 137. Chouliaraki has developed an insightful response to this problem of "solidarity without 'grand narratives,'" in *Ironic Spectator*, 9.
27. Linfield, *Cruel Radiance*, 132.
28. Most notably, Linfield's argument is cut back a notch by the recent example of volunteers migrating from the United States and Europe to join Islamic militias in the Middle East. That ideological solidarity is hard to square with nostalgia for the International Brigades' fight against European fascism. See, e.g., Somini Sengupta, "Nations Trying to Stop Their Citizens from Going to Middle East to Fight for ISIS," *New York Times*, September 12, 2014, http://nyti.ms/1pXCM6W.
29. Jeffrey Gettleman, "Ethnic Violence in Rift Valley Is Tearing Kenya Apart," *New York Times*, January 27, 2008, http://www.nytimes.com/2008/01/27/world/africa/27kenya.html/.
30. For example, six months later the caption became "Violence in Kenya sparked fears of a civil war." Karen Allen, "Kenya: Struggling for Peace," BBC News, August 18, 2008, http://news.bbc.co.uk/2/hi/africa/7568784.stm. Five years later, the photo was captioned "Mr. Odinga's Kibera constituency was hit by violence after the 2007 election." David Okwembah, "Raila Odinga: Third Time Lucky in Kenya?" BBC Africa, March 1, 2013, http://www.bbc.com/news/world-africa-21587054. Situational details are still there, but the photograph stands primarily for violence and fear as expansive, potentially untethered forces.
31. All by Ariella Azoulay: "Regime-Made Disaster: On the Possibility of Nongovernmental Viewing," in *Sensible Politics: The Visual Culture of Nongovernmental Activism*, ed. Meg McLagan and Yates McKee (New York: Zone Books, 2012), 29–41; "A Tour of the Museum of Regime-Made Disasters," *Humanity: An International Journal of Human Rights, Humanitarianism, and Development* 4 (2013): 345–63; *Atto di Stato: Palestina-Israele, 1967–2007*, curated by Maria Nadotti (Milan: Bruno Mondadori, 2008); Ariella Azoulay and Adi Ophir, "The Monster's

Tail," in *Against the Wall: Israel's Barrier to Peace*, ed. Michael Sorkin (NewYork: New Press, 2005), 2–27, reprinted in *Roulotte:05*, http://www.roulottemagazine.com/2011/04/the-monster's-tail-ariella-azoulay-adi-ophir/; see also the bibliography at http://cargocollective.com/AriellaAzoulay.

32. Azoulay, *Civil Contract*, 73. Azoulay borrows the phrase "petty sovereign" from Judith Butler, *Precarious Life: The Powers of Mourning and Violence* (New York: Verso, 2004), 56. Note that the predicament of one's oppression being visually banal may be one reason for seemingly senseless military provocations such as firing rockets that usually are destroyed or do little damage while inducing deadly counterattacks. Even when otherwise ineffective, the provocation will lead to intensified press coverage and dramatic images of the destruction caused by the superior power. For a fine discussion of the importance of attending to the banality of war, see Rebecca A. Adelman and Wendy Kozol, "Discordant Affects: Ambivalence, Banality, and the Ethics of Spectatorship," *Theory and Event* 17 (2014). We provide a précis of our argument in Robert Hariman and John Louis Lucaites, "The Banality of Violence," *Flow* 15, no. 5 (2012), http://flowtv.org/2012/01/banality-of-violence/.
33. Ethan Bronner and Isabel Kershner, "West Bank Settlers Dig In, but Resolve May Have a Limit," *New York Times*, September 14, 2009, A1, A8; "Resolve of West Bank Settlers May Have Limits," *New York Times*, September 13, 2009, http://www.nytimes.com/2009/09/14/world/middleeast/14settlers.html. Note that the caption at the online slide show is more pointed than the paper edition in respect to the actual political situation: "A settler tosses wine at a Palestinian woman on Shuhada Street in Hebron. The approach of some settlers towards neighboring Palestinians, especially around Nablus in the north and Hebron in the south, has often been one of contempt and violence." "Fervent Believers," *New York Times* slide show, http://www.nytimes.com/slideshow/2009/09/13/world/20090913SETTLERS_6.html.
34. Ariella Azoulay, "Potential History: Thinking Through Violence," *Critical Inquiry* 39 (2013): 548–74.
35. Ariella Azoulay, *From Palestine to Israel: A Photographic Record of Destruction and State Formation, 1947–1950* (London: Pluto, 2011), and *Different Ways Not to Say Deportation* (Vancouver, BC: Fillip Editions, 2012).
36. For extensive discussion of how photography is being used to confront and understand the Israeli-Palestinian conflict, see Dora Apel, "Israel/Palestine and the Political Imaginary," in *War Culture and the Contest of Images*, 183–231.
37. Note that street demonstrations loom large in the Global South and may involve processes that are little understood although increasingly characteristic of twenty-first-century politics. Any emergent forms of political organization and identity also may be evident in part in contemporary photojournalism, particularly as they develop their own optics. On the ascendancy of the street, see Dilip Gaonkar, "After the Fictions: Notes towards a Phenomenology of

the Multitude," *e-flux*, October 2014, http://www.e-flux.com/journal/after-the-fictions-notes-towards-a-phenomenology-of-the-multitude/.

38. Dan Jones, "A New Peasants' Revolt, with BlackBerry in Hand," *Evening Standard*, August 11, 2011, http://www.standard.co.uk/news/a-new-peasants-revolt-with-blackberry-in-hand-6431726.html.
39. Sontag, *On Photography*, 51–58.
40. Ibid., 52.
41. T. J. Demos, *The Migrant Image: The Art and Politics of Documentary during Global Crisis* (Durham, NC: Duke University Press, 2013). Demos features film and photography that is reinventing documentary practice by blurring "the divisions between fact and fiction, in order to propose a new politics of truth" that can advance a political alternative to "the current neoliberal world of control, repression, and inequality" (245, 246).
42. For a critique of these images on behalf of restitution of the conventional idealization of documentary witness on behalf of narrative truth, see Donald Weber, "The Rules of Photojournalism Are Keeping Us from the Truth," *Vantage*, https://medium.com/vantage/the-rules-of-photojournalism-are-keeping-us-from-the-truth-52c093bb0436#.36hsrmjk5.
43. Michael Walzer, *Just and Unjust Wars: A Moral Argument with Historical Illustrations* (New York: Harper Collins, 1977), 176–79.
44. Note that like many demonstrations today, medieval popular revolts typically were *not* untethered but represented explicit grievances or, in some cases, ideological fervor. Nor are we implying that the medieval period lacked sophisticated political ideas or practices, or that other forms of revolt (such as those among nobles) were irrelevant. For a collection of source text excerpts that provide vivid documentation of the frequency and character of the uprisings, see Samuel K. Cohn Jr., *Popular Protest in Late-Medieval Europe: Italy, France and Flanders* (Manchester: Manchester University Press, 2004). Popular revolts also vary in respect to the institutional context. Claire Valente argues that popular revolts in England diminished with the rise of more modern institutions that replaced the revolts with parliaments and, ironically, civil wars (*The Theory and Practice of Revolt in Medieval England* [Burlington, VT: Ashgate, 2003]). Thus refeudalization does not mean a direct restoration of medieval social and political practices, and it will develop within the context of existing, and fraying, institutions. By identifying it as a political aesthetic, we recognize that fuller development may be yet to come. We would take seriously, however, such factors as the militarization of the police to create something like a warrior class; the severity of punishments (e.g., beatings, torture, airstrikes) meted out to rebels; the redefinition of the people as a mob and political agency as massed demonstrations; and the restoration of order (rather than reform) becoming a sufficient objective for the use of power.

45. The analogy between war and sport is no doubt facilitated in part by the normalization of the metaphorical relationship between war and argument. See George Lakoff and Mark Johnson, *Metaphors We Live By* (Chicago: University of Chicago Press, 1980), 3–6.
46. See, e.g., Stahl, *Militainment, Inc.*; and Nick Turse, *The Complex: How the Military Invades Our Everyday Lives* (New York: Metropolitan Books, 2008).
47. On the concept of the individuated aggregate, see Robert Hariman and John Louis Lucaites, *No Caption Needed: Iconic Photographs, Public Culture, and Liberal Democracy* (Chicago: University of Chicago Press, 2007), 88–89.
48. For another example see fig. 15 in ibid., 104.
49. See, e.g., William C. Adams, "Whose Lives Count? TV Coverage of Natural Disasters," *Journal of Communication* 36 (Spring 1986): 113–22. On the other hand, Taylor has documented how gruesome images are more likely to be shown of foreign bodies, which in turn affects perception of those areas of the world (*Body Horror*, 129–56).
50. Tim Arango, "Assassinations Grow as Iraqi Elections Near," *New York Times*, April 15, 2013, http://www.nytimes.com/2013/04/16/world/middleeast/killings-grow-as-iraqi-elections-near.html.
51. Michael Schmidt, "Suicide Bombs in Iraq Have Killed 12,000 Civilians, Study Says," *New York Times*, September 2, 2011, http://nyti.ms/1Pqi9zC.
52. Azoulay, *Civil Contract*, 187–215.
53. On the distribution of the sensible, see Jacques Rancière, *The Politics of Aesthetics*, trans. Gabriel Rockhill (New York: Continuum, 2004), and *The Emancipated Spectator*, trans. Gregory Elliott (New York: Verso, 2009). Rancière considers the operation of power through sensation and articulates a need to move beyond conventional ideas of emancipation through critique.
54. For a typical public discussion of the problematic, see Lori Robertson, "Images of War," *American Journalism Review*, October/November 2004, http://ajrarchive.org/Article.asp?id=3759. For more extended analysis see Taylor, *Body Horror*, esp. 1–86.
55. Linfield, *Cruel Radiance*, 60.
56. Azoulay, *Civil Contract*, 122.
57. Michael Herr, *Dispatches* (New York: Avon, 1968), 20.
58. Berger, *About Looking*, 59. Note that Berger draws heavily on Sontag but then moves beyond her position; despite his continued disparagement of any "public" image, his call (61–67) for an "alternative photography" has all the marks of what we refer to as public art.
59. The literature here is long and growing. See Azoulay, *Civil Contract*, 137–86; Jeffrey Edward Green, *The Eyes of the People: Democracy in the Age of Spectatorship* (New York: Oxford University Press, 2010), esp. 32–63; Sliwinski, *Human Rights In Camera*, 17–34; Lillie Chouliaraki, *The Spectatorship of Suffering* (Thousand Oaks, CA: Sage, 2006), and *Ironic Spectator*; Luc Boltanski, *Distant Suffering:*

Morality, Media and Politics, trans. Graham Burchell (London: Cambridge University Press, 1993); and Wendy Hesford, *Spectacular Rhetorics*, esp. 61–124.

60. See Warren P. Strobel, "The CNN Effect," *American Journalism Review*, May 1996, http://ajrarchive.org/Article.asp?id=3572.
61. Andrew Kramer and James Glanz, "U.S. Guards Kill 2 Iraqi Women in New Shooting," *New York Times*, October 10, 2007, http://www.nytimes.com/2007/10/10/world/middleeast/10iraq.html.
62. On the importance of "showing seeing" for the study of visual culture, see W. J. T. Mitchell, *What Do Pictures Want? The Lives and Loves of Images* (Chicago: University of Chicago Press, 2005), 336–56.
63. Elaine Scarry, *The Body in Pain: The Making and Unmaking of the World* (New York: Oxford University Press, 1987), 27–59.
64. Sontag makes this observation the final, emphatic point of *Regarding the Pain of Others*, and virtually all other commentators agree as well. Important differences remain, however. We want to emphasize that images can both hide and expose the distance between representation and reality, and that compassionate response need not wait on full understanding of an inaccessible experience. Too much respect for the authenticity of experience can have the unintended consequence of abandoning victims; the denial of communication is a denial of human community, however flawed the communication may be. Although critical of humanism, John Roberts makes a related argument, claiming that a degree of "representational intolerance" is necessary for photojournalism to have full political efficacy: if we accept that "the effects of violence are unrepresentable and that the inviolability of the rights of the represented is sacrosanct . . . we thereby concede ground to the perpetrators of state violence and the systemic violence of the capitalist system" (*Photography and Its Violations* [New York: Columbia University Press, 2014], 161). Roger Silverstone's thoughtful meditation on this problem features the concept of "proper distance," which "refers to the importance of understanding the more or less precise degree of proximity required in our mediated interrelationships if we are to create and sustain a sense of the other sufficient not just for reciprocity but for a duty of care, obligation and responsibility, as well as understanding. Proper distance preserves the other through difference as well as through shared identity. In other words proper distance is a component, and a precondition of plurality." Roger Silverstone, *Media and Morality: On the Rise of the Mediapolis* (Cambridge, UK: Polity, 2007), 47.
65. Paul Frosh and Amit Pinchevski, "Introduction: Why Media Witnessing? Why Now?" in *Media Witnessing: Testimony in the Age of Mass Communication*, ed. Paul Frosh and Amit Pinchevski (London: Palgrave Mcmillan, 2009), 6–7.
66. To note one of many examples, see Chloe Pantazi, "Susan Sontag Was Right: War Photography Can Anesthetize," *Salon*, January 4, 2014, http://www.salon.com/2014/01/05/war_photography_partner/.

67. Wendy Kozol, *Distant Wars Visible: The Ambivalence of Witnessing* (Minneapolis: University of Minnesota Press, 2014). See also Chouliaraki, *Ironic Spectator*: "The ironic spectator is, in this sense, an impure or ambivalent figure that stands, at once, as skeptical towards any moral appeal to solidary action and, yet, open to doing something about those who suffer" (2).
68. Kozol, *Distant Wars Visible*, 18–19, 94; Linfield, *Cruel Radiance*, 58–59; Chouliaraki, *Ironic Spectator*, 28; Sliwinski, *Human Rights In Camera*, 134–38.
69. Berger, *About Looking*, 43–44 (emphasis in the original).
70. In *Regarding the Pain of Others* Sontag argues, "It is desirable that the account of specific injustices dissolve into a more general understanding that human beings everywhere do terrible things to one another" (115–16). Even so, she closes by emphasizing that "we truly can't imagine what it was like" (125). Thus we are left with a chasm between having to get on with ordinary life in the better places and being forever closed off from those who suffer in the worst places—just as they then are forever closed off from us. Perhaps a better approach would be to use knowledge of human depravity as a basis for an analysis of civilization in any given instance, and to accept the limits of understanding as a reason for reconnecting with others despite our inadequacy and the loss of control that brings.
71. To consider how images can create an opening into engagement with "the great darkness of our time," see Georges Didi-Huberman, *Images in Spite of All: Four Photographs from Auschwitz*, trans. Shane B. Lillis (Chicago: University of Chicago Press, 2008).
72. Kennedy, *Afterimages*, 5–6.
73. Kennedy's *Afterimages* is a discerning study of how photographers have grappled with "the ideological conditions that determine certain ways of seeing, that support practices and representations which establish (in)visibilities and police the relationship between seeing and believing in the American worldview" (4).
74. The photograph was part of the set that received the 2006 Pulitzer Prize for Feature Photography. The photographs can be viewed at http://www.pulitzer.org/works/2006-Feature-Photography. Traditional journalistic renditions of the image reduce the story to a simple consideration of the relationship between "photographer" and "subject," in this case Todd Heisler (the photographer) and Katherine Cathey, the surviving spouse of 2nd Lt. James Cathey, whose body is being transported. See Loup Langton, *Photojournalism and Today's News: Creating Visual Reality* (Malden, MA: Wiley-Blackwell, 2009), 179–87. For reliable tracking of war costs, see http://costsofwar.org.
75. William Ian Miller, *The Anatomy of Disgust* (Cambridge, MA: Harvard University Press, 1997), 184–85.
76. Reuters, "Syria in Ruins," http://www.reuters.com/news/pictures/slideshow?articleId=USRTR3BBJ0.

Chapter Seven

1. Susan Sontag, *On Photography* (New York: Picador, 1977), 24. Sontag's critique probably is influenced by Walter Benjamin's claim that the aura of artistic authenticity was destroyed by the logic of commodity production and its corollary "*desire of the present-day masses to 'get closer' to things, and their equally passionate concern for overcoming each thing's uniqueness . . . by assimilating it as a reproduction*" ("The Work of Art in the Age of Its Technological Reproducibility, Second Version," trans. Edmund Jephcott and Harry Zohn, in *The Work of Art in the Age of Its Technological Reproducibility, and Other Writings on Media*, ed. Michael Jennings, Brigid Doherty, and Thomas Y. Levin [Cambridge, MA: Belknap / Harvard University Press, 2008], 23, emphasis in the original).
2. *Oxford English Dictionary*, www.oed.com, s.v., "excess."
3. Expressions of anxiety about the deluge of images are a convention of contemporary public discourse, even as they reprise statements made through the history of media. Useful discussions include John Edwin Mason, "Déjà Vu All Over Again: James Estrin and 'The Tsunami of Vernacular Photographs,'" *John Edwin Mason: Documentary, Motorsports, Photo History*, September 9, 2012, http://johnedwinmason.typepad.com/john_edwin_mason_photogra/2012/09/estrin-deja-vu.html; David Campbell, "Photographic Anxiety: Should We Worry about Image Abundance," July 12, 2011, http://www.david-campbell.org/2011/07/12/photographic-anxiety-should-we-worry-about-image-abundance/, and "Abundant Photography: The Misleading Metaphor of the Image Flood," September 5, 2013, https://www.david-campbell.org/2013/09/05/abundant-photography-misleading-metaphor-image-flood/; Alexandra Moschovi, Carol McKay, and Arabella Plouviez, "Afterword: Abundant Photography, Discursive Limits and the Work of Images," in *The Versatile Image: Photography, Digital Technologies and the Internet*, ed. Moschovi, McKay, and Plouviez (Louvain, Belgium: Leuven University Press, 2013), 265–72.
4. *Oxford English Dictionary*, www.oed.com, s.v. "abundance."
5. For a more general argument about the relationship between surplus energy and civilization, see Georges Bataille, *The Accursed Share: An Essay on General Economy*, vol. 1, *Consumption* (New York: Zone Books, 1991). Bataille argues that the constant input of the sun's energy creates surpluses in all natural and cultural systems and that consequently "*it is not necessity but its contrary, 'luxury,' that presents living matter and mankind with their fundamental problems*" (12, emphasis in the original). Although not adhering to his argument, we share four of its central claims: that human societies exist amid far more energy than they need; that many forms of scarcity often are artificial; that the encompassing abundance is not adequately recognized or valued; and that there is need for better understanding of the relationship between abundance and scarcity. See also Georges Bataille, *The Accursed Share*, vols. 2 and

3 (bound together), *The History of Eroticism and Sovereignty* (New York: Zone Books, 1993).

6. Facebook, Ericsson, and Qualcomm, *A Focus on Efficiency*, 2013, http://static1.trouw.nl/static/asset/2013/Whitepaper_Facebook_2622.pdf; Stan Horaczek, "How Many Photos Are Uploaded to the Internet Every Minute?" PopPhoto.com, May 27, 2013, http://www.popphoto.com/news/2013/05/how-many-photos-are-uploaded-to-internet-every-minute. All such numbers are lower than actual use, as not all users (including many in China) are being measured. An artistic depiction of the deluge of images was created by Erik Kessels's exhibition *Photography in Abundance*, which is described thus by Anthony Bond: "What If You Printed Out Every Picture Posted on Flickr in Just One Day? Artist's 1m Images Highlight How Much We Share of Our Personal Lives," *Daily Mail*, November 15, 2011, http://www.dailymail.co.uk/sciencetech/article-2061763/Artist-Erik-Kessels-places-1m-Flickr-images-single-room-Foam-gallery-Amsterdam.html. For an earlier installation that features the accumulation of waste, see Thomas Hirschhorn, *Too Too – Much Much*, Museum Dhondt-Dhaenens, Belgium, March-May 2010, http://www.museumdd.be/en/verleden/t4. Apologies to Carl Sagan for "billions and billions": *Billions and Billions: Thoughts on Life and Death at the Brink of the Millennium* (New York: Random House, 1997).
7. These figures come from Silicon Valley analyst Benedict Evans, "The Explosion of Imaging," July 3, 2014, http://ben-evans.com/benedictevans/2014/6/24/imaging. See also Steve Hoffenberg, "Photography Changes and Democratizes Visual Expression," in *Photography Changes Everything*, ed. Marvin Heiferman (New York: Aperture/Smithsonian, 2012), 172–74.
8. Paul Feyerabend, *Conquest of Abundance: A Tale of Abstraction versus the Richness of Being*, ed. Bert Terpstra (Chicago: University of Chicago Press, 1999), 3.
9. Feyerabend, *Conquest of Abundance*, 3–4.
10. George Eliot, *Middlemarch*, ed. David Carroll (Oxford: Clarendon, 1986), 226.
11. Charles Taylor, *Modern Social Imaginaries* (Durham, NC: Duke University Press, 2004), 49. For an excellent synopsis of the Weber/Taylor argument, as well as those by Hans Blumenberg and Simon Critchley, see chap. 4, "Disenchantment Tales," in Jane Bennett, *The Enchantment of Modern Life: Attachments, Crossings, and Ethics* (Princeton, NJ: Princeton University Press, 2001). For additional reconsideration, see Anna Marazuela Kim, "Re-enchantment and Iconoclasm in an Age of Images," *Hedgehog Review* 17, no. 3 (2015): 48–54; this essay is one of seven on reenchantment in that issue of the journal.
12. Paddy Scannell, *Radio, Television and Modern Life* (Oxford: Blackwell, 1996), 170.
13. For a brilliant account of the complex relationships between disenchantment, reanimation, and advertising, see Jackson Lears, *Fables of Abundance: A Cultural History of Advertising in America* (New York: Basic Books, 1994). As Lears

documents, abundance itself has been rationalized and commodified yet never wholly contained. Note also the applicability to the critique of photography of his statement that "nurturing a half-conscious disdain for the things of this world, many participants in the discourse of authenticity unwittingly collaborated in the philosophical project embedded in consumer culture: the construction of a separate, striving subject in a world of alienated objects" (378). Lears affirms an alternative attitude in modern literature: "Their outlook could be characterized as aesthetic rather than ascetic; they delighted in surfaces as well as depths; they saw material artifacts as a mode of making meaning rather than merely concealing it" (378). That doubles as a good statement of our perspective on photography.

14. Don Slater provides an intriguing argument that cuts somewhat across the grain of the alignment of photography with enchantment: "Photography and Modern Vision: The Spectacle of 'Natural Magic,'" in *Visual Culture*, ed. Chris Jenks (New York: Routledge, 1995), 218–37. Slater argues that photography's combination of realism and artistry produces a spectacular experience akin to magic, but it is constitutive of modernity, including the development and public assimilation of modern science. Thus we are the heirs of "a belief in modernity by using its techniques in complete opposition to its own aims and principles: to re-enchant the world through natural magic, rather than to demystify it through objective vision" (236). Of course one could still hold out for complete demystification and objective vision, but that seems merely a variant illusion. Better perhaps to dispense with the idea of "complete" achievement of either mystification or demystification, and instead to recognize that any culture includes processes that can be labeled (and at times misrecognized as) "mystifications" and "spectacles," that living in any culture requires a continual tacking back and forth between the two poles of reason and enchantment, and that photography is tangled up with the various modes of belief across the board.

15. Even this (literalist?) constraint can be challenged: Mel Alexenberg, *Photograph God: Creating a Spiritual Blog of Your Life* (CreateSpace, 2015).

16. The quotations are among thousands of such passages in *The Lotus Sutra*, ed. and trans. Gene Reeves (Boston: Wisdom, 2008).

17. There are many reasons for the falling away from a sense of holy immanence—and many of them are of religious origin, not least in Western Christianity. Part of that falling away may have included writing off images as vehicles of spiritual presence. As W. J. T. Mitchell has noted, there has been an iconoclastic attitude within the secular construction of Western image culture that affects our habits of interpretation. See Mitchell's *Iconology: Image, Text, Ideology* (Chicago: University of Chicago Press, 1987). On secularization, see Charles Taylor, *A Secular Age* (Boston: Belknap / Harvard University Press, 2007).

18. Bennett, *Enchantment of Modern Life*, 4, 76. As in our chapter 2, Bennett extends her argument through Wallace Stevens's contrast between imagination and "the pressure of reality."
19. Martin Jay, "Magical Nominalism: Photography and the Re-enchantment of the World," *Culture, Theory and Critique* 50 (2009): 179, 181.
20. Joshua Landy and Michael Saler, "Introduction: The Varieties of Modern Enchantment," in *The Re-enchantment of the World: Secular Magic in a Rational Age*, ed. Landy and Saler (Stanford, CA: Stanford University Press, 2009), 2 (emphasis in the original). Landy and Saler recommend putting on display "a set of enchantments that are *voluntary*, being chosen (*pace* Adorno) by autonomous agents rather than insidiously imposed by power structures, *respectable*, compatible as they are (*pace* Weber) with secular rationality, and *multiple*, being replacements, each one in its own way, for a polymorphous God" (7, emphasis in the original). See also Michael Saler, "Modernity and Enchantment: A Historiographic Review," *American Historical Review* 111 (2006): 692–716.
21. Ariella Azoulay, *Civil Imagination: A Political Ontology of Photography* (London: Verso, 2012), 26. One might consider also Ernesto Laclau's argument that "if . . . heterogeneity is primordial and irreducible, it will show itself, in the first place, as *excess*." *On Populist Reason* (New York: Verso, 2005), 223 (emphasis in the original).
22. Michael Warner, *Publics and Counterpublics* (New York: Zone Books, 2002), 113.
23. Feyerabend, *Conquest of Abundance*, 3.
24. Relevant scholarship here includes W. J. T. Mitchell, ed., *Landscape and Power*, 2nd ed. (Chicago: University of Chicago Press, 2002); Joan M. Schwartz and James R. Ryan, eds., *Picturing Place: Photography and the Geographical Imagination* (London: I.B. Tauris, 2003); Steven Hoelscher, "Magnum's Geographies: Toward a Progressive Sense of Place," in *Reading Magnum: A Visual Archive of the Modern World*, ed. Steven Hoelscher (Austin: University of Texas Press, 2013), 139–65; Gregory Clark, *Rhetorical Landscapes in America: Variations on a Theme from Kenneth Burke* (Columbia: University of South Carolina Press, 2004). An extensive bibliography of scholarship on the genre in art history and geography is available in the notes to the introductory essay in Schwartz and Ryan, eds., *Picturing Place*. For a fine-grained critique of how the category of landscape photography is itself a construction that misrepresents the nineteenth-century images now included in the history of the genre, see Rosalind Krauss, "Photography's Discursive Spaces," in *The Contest of Meaning: Critical Histories of Photography*, ed. Richard Bolton (Cambridge, MA: MIT Press, 1989), 287–301.
25. Examples now are legion, as with time-lapse photography and satellite imagery being employed to document extreme glacial drawback. See James Balog's *Extreme Ice Survey* at http://extremeicesurvey.org or any number of "before/

after" photo displays such as Katherine Butler's "8 Before-and-After Images of Ice Melt," *Mother Nature Network*, July 12, 2013, http://www.mnn.com/earth-matters/wilderness-resources/stories/8-before-and-after-images-of-ice-melt. For a fuller discussion of the ways in which visual technologies are being mobilized to provide what Nicholas Mirzoeff calls a "countervisuality" to the effects of climate change, see "Visualizing the Anthropocene" in "Visualizing the Environment," a special edition of *Public Culture* 26 (2014): 213–32. For a longer view of the role that photography has played in the environmental movement, see Finis Dunaway, *Seeing Green: The Use and Abuse of American Environmental Images* (Chicago: University of Chicago Press, 2015); Kevin Michael DeLuca and Anne Teresa Demo, "Imaging Nature: Watkins, Yosemite and the Birth of Environmentalism," *Critical Studies in Media Communication* 17 (2000): 241–60, and "Imaging Nature and Erasing Class and Race: Carleton Watkins, John Muir, and the Construction of Wilderness," *Environmental History* 6 (2001): 541–60. See also Jennifer Peeples, "Toxic Sublime: Imaging Contaminated Landscapes," *Environmental Communication: A Journal of Nature and Culture* 5 (2011): 373–92.

26. Sontag, *On Photography*, 51, 138–44, 148–49, and *Regarding the Pain of Others* (New York: Picador, 2003), 27–28.
27. "Brazilian Farmers Offered Cash to Fight Deforestation," slide show, *New York Times*, August 21, 2009, http://www.nytimes.com/slideshow/2009/08/22/world/0822-DEGREES_5.html.
28. Elisabeth Rosenthal, "In Brazil, Paying Farmers to Let the Trees Stand," *New York Times*, August 21, 2009, http://www.nytimes.com/2009/08/22/science/earth/22degrees.html.
29. Azoulay provides a lengthy critique in chapter 2 of *Civil Imagination* of the conventional wisdom that politics and aesthetics should not be mixed together. A major argument for separation involves the inappropriateness and adverse affects of artful depictions of suffering; for critical discussion of this argument, see Mark Reinhardt, Holly Edwards, and Erina Duganne, ed., *Beautiful Suffering: Photography and the Traffic in Pain* (Chicago: University of Chicago Press, 2007), esp. 13–16. See also David Levi Strauss, *Between the Eyes: Essays on Photography and Politics* (New York: Aperture, 2005), 3–11, and *Words Not Spent Today Buy Smaller Images Tomorrow* (New York: Aperture, 2014), 130–35. In *Words Not Spent Today* Strauss includes a discussion of our book *No Caption Needed* and remarks that "the authors . . . are remarkably free of the basic assumptions of the aestheticization-of-suffering discourse" (132). He characterizes that discourse as "dated and overdetermined" and an example of "a period of academic mannerism" (130).
30. For a good synopsis of the critique of consumption, see Don Slater, *Consumer Culture and Modernity* (New York: Polity, 1997).

31. Anne Norton, *Republic of Signs: Liberal Theory and American Popular Culture* (Chicago: University of Chicago Press, 1993), 4.
32. Ibid., 171, 173.
33. "The sages put the abandonment of selfishness and the spirituality of compassion at the top of their agenda. For them, religion *was* the Golden Rule." Karen Armstrong, *The Great Transformation: The Beginning of Our Religious Traditions* (New York: Random House / Anchor, 2006), 468 (emphasis in the original).
34. Feyerabend, *Conquest of Abundance*, 241.
35. Elaine Scarry, *The Body in Pain: The Making and Unmaking of the World* (New York: Oxford University Press, 1985), 27–59.
36. Giorgio Agamben, *Homo Sacer: Sovereign Power and Bare Life*, trans. Daniel Heller-Roazen (Stanford, CA: Stanford University Press, 1998).
37. Lyle Rexer, *The Edge of Vision: The Rise of Abstraction in Photography* (New York: Aperture, 2009), 11–12. Note how his words cut across a statement such as this: "The history of photography could be recapitulated as the struggle between two different imperatives: beautification . . . and truth telling" (Sontag, *On Photography*, 86). Sontag's argument is that beauty and truth telling can be coordinate in a fine art but not in photography, where degraded versions of each impulse fall into a reciprocal cancellation that produces distortion and moral incoherence. Rexer and others now are considering instead how aesthetics can be a mode of discovery that can lead to insight and understanding.
38. Kaja Silverman, *The Miracle of Analogy, or The History of Photography*, pt. 1 (Stanford, CA: Stanford University Press, 2015), 10–11. Silverman's book appeared as we were making the final revisions of this manuscript prior to publication. We look forward to the publication of her second volume.
39. These claims rework an argument made in 1908 by Wilhelm Worringer, *Abstraction and Empathy: A Contribution to the Psychology of Style*, trans. Michael Bullock (1953; Chicago: Elephant Paperbacks, 1997).
40. Henri Focillon, *The Life of Forms in Art*, trans. Charles Beecher Hogan and George Kubler (New York: Zone Books, 1992), 42.
41. Ibid., 35, 41.
42. Hilton Kramer, introduction to ibid., 17.
43. Focillon, *Life of Forms in Art*, 62.
44. Ralph Waldo Emerson, "The American Scholar," 1837, Ralph Waldo Emerson Texts, http://www.emersoncentral.com/amscholar.htm; also at http://digital emerson.wsulibs.wsu.edu/exhibits/show/text/the-american-scholar.
45. Oliver Wendell Holmes, "The Stereoscope and the Stereograph," *Atlantic Monthly*, June 1, 1859, http://www.theatlantic.com/magazine/archive/1859/06 /the-stereoscope-and-the-stereograph/303361/.
46. James C. Scott, *Seeing like a State: How Certain Schemes to Improve the Human Condition Have Failed* (New Haven, CT: Yale University Press, 1998). Scott's in-

sight into the political aesthetic of high modernism still holds: "The carriers of high modernism tended to see rational order in remarkably visual aesthetic terms. For them, an efficient, rationally organized city, village, or farm was a city that *looked* regimented and orderly in a geometrical sense" (4, emphasis in the original).

47. Jay, "Magical Nominalism," 181.

PHOTO CATALOG

Photographic identification in the digital environment is subject to variations regarding sources, captions, and other information. Photographs may be described differently in print, online, at the agency, and at the photographer's website. Copyright information, as provided by those holding the copyright, does not always identify the photographer. The following list is based on information provided by the licensing agents.

Figure 1

Photographer: Suzanne DeChillo

Copyright: Suzanne DeChillo / The New York Times / Redux

Date and place: November 29, 2007, New York City, USA

Caption: "Exterior of the New Museum of Contemporary Art, on the Lower East Side in November 2007. New York is in the cultural doldrums. The city is bursting with gorgeous art exhibitions, where is the raw energy? Where is the new blood, intent on upending the establishment? Today, once-rebellious talents often seem to be wandering lost in the constellation of celebrity, where they soon settle into complacency. Designed by the Japanese firm Sanaa, the New Museum of Contemporary Art, on the Bowery at Prince Street on the Lower East Side, is the kind of building that renews your faith in New York as a place where culture is lived, not just bought and sold."

Figure 2

Photographer: Armend Nimani

Copyright: Armend Nimani / AFP / Getty Images

Date and place: April 9, 2009, Pristina, Kosovo

Caption: "An elderly Kosovan man walks past an advertisement for clothes as he walks in a street of Pristina on April 9, 2009."

Figure 3

Photographer: Andrew Burton

Copyright: Reuters / Andrew Burton

Date and place: September 12, 2012, New York City, USA

Caption: "Audience members watch a model during the J. Mendel Spring/Summer 2013 show at New York Fashion Week, September 12, 2012."

Figure 4

Photographer: Koji Sasahara

Copyright: AP Photo / Koji Sasahara

Date and place: April 24, 2012, Tokyo, Japan

Caption: "People are reflected on a mirror at the shopping center in Tokyo."

Figure 5

Photographer: Aaron Huey

Copyright: Aaron Huey

Date and place: May 28, 2013, Pine Ridge Indian Reservation, South Dakota, USA

Caption: "Mass grave at the site of the 1890 Wounded Knee Massacre."

Figure 6

Photographer: Charlie Riedel

Copyright: AP Photo / Charlie Riedel

Date and place: June 3, 2010, East Grand Terre Island, Louisiana, USA

Caption: "A laughing gull is mired in oil on the beach at East Grand Terre Island along the Louisiana coast after being drenched in oil from the Deepwater Horizon oil spill Thursday, June 3, 2010."

Figure 7

Photographer: Larry Steagall

Copyright: Larry Steagall / Kitsap Sun, Bremerton, Wash.

Date and place: May 11, 2014, Bremerton, Washington, USA

Caption: "Amelia Johnson of Bremerton, plays fetch with her dog Boobah at sunset on the Tracyton boat ramp in Bremerton, Wash., on May 11."

Figure 8

Photographer: Odd Andersen

Copyright: Odd Anderson / AFP / Getty Images

Date and place: May 6, 2014, Berlin, Germany

Caption: "A crow eats it's [*sic*] prey sitting on the roof of the Chancellery in Berlin on May 6, 2014."

Figure 9

Photographer: Margaret Bourke-White

Copyright: Margaret Bourke-White / The LIFE Picture Collection / Getty Images

Date and place: 1936, Fort Peck Dam, Montana, USA

Caption: "The front cover [*Life*, November 23, 1936] is a photograph of a dam at Fort Peck, Montana taken by Margaret Bourke-White."

Figure 10

Photographer: Allen Eyestone

Copyright: Allen Eyestone / Palm Beach Post / ZUMA Press

Date and place: Minneapolis, Minnesota, USA

Caption: "Minneapolis, MN. . [*sic*] Mall of America Field. . [*sic*] Miami Dolphins at Minnesota Vikings . . . A Dolphins fan."

Figure 11

Photographer: Julian Stratenschulte

Copyright: Julian Stratenschulte / DPA / Landov

Date and place: September 24, 2010, Bottrop, North Rhine–Westphalia, Germany

Caption: "A woman eyes works by US abstract artist Ad Reinhardt at Josef Albers Museum Quadrat in Bottrop, Germany, September 24, 2010. The exhibition 'Last Paintings' on Reinhardt is on display from September 26 to January 9, 2011."

Figure 12

Photographer: Bernadett Szabo

Copyright: Reuters / Bernadett Szabo

Date and place: October 5, 2010, Devecser, Hungary

Caption: "Rescue workers clear up toxic sludge in the flooded village of Devecser, 150 km (93 miles) west of Budapest, October 5, 2010. At least two people were killed on Monday when the dam of a sludge reservoir at a big alumina factory burst, flooding parts of three villages, Hungarian news agency MTI quoted Interior Minister Sandor Pinter as saying."

Figure 13

Photographer: Fernando Bizerra Jr.

Copyright: epa / Fernando Bizerra Jr.

Date and place: April 21, 2010, Brasilia, Brazil

Caption: "A man is seen with the morning sun in the background near Brasilia's National Congress at the start of the commemoration of the capital's 50th anniversary, Brasilia, Brazil, 21 April 2010. Brasilia was built from scratch, it was inaugurated on 21 April 1960 and envisioned as the dream city, a transformational project for Latin America's largest nation."

Figure 14

Photographer: Tim Ireland

Copyright: PA Archive / Press Association Images / Tim Ireland

Date and place: February 5, 2010, London, England

Caption: "A Christie's employee poses with Jasper Johns' Flag, 1960–1966, and Femme et fillettes (Woman and Children) by Pablo Picasso, 1961, which is part of the collection of Michael Crichton on display at Christie's in London ahead of its auction on May 11."

Figure 15

Photographer: Louisa Gouliamaki

Copyright: Louisa Gouliamaki / AFP / Getty Images

Date and place: February 1, 2010, Athens, Greece

Caption: "People walk by the Greek Parliament in Athens center on February 1, 2010. Greece's plans to tackle its debt mountain are 'achievable' but the risks involved could require 'additional measures,' the EU Commission said on February 1, 2010 ahead of an official announcement due on February 3."

Figure 16

Photographer: John Moore

Copyright: John Moore / Edit / Getty Images

Date and place: February 2, 2009, Adams County, Colorado, USA

Caption: "Tracy Munch collects some belongings after an eviction team removed the furniture from her foreclosed house on February 2, 2009 in Adams County, Colorado. Smith said she and her fiancé had been renting from an owner, who collected the monthly payments but had stopped paying his mortgage. The bank foreclosed the property and called the Adams County sheriff's department to supervise the eviction. They managed to borrow enough money to rent another house for themselves and their four children, she said, but not in time to avoid eviction."

Figure 17

Photographer: Valentijn Tempels
Copyright: Valentijn Tempels
Date and place: n.d., Stockholm, Sweden
Caption: "Stockholm Subway (Tunnelbana)"

Figure 18

Photographer: Khalil Ashawi
Copyright: Reuters / Khalil Ashawi
Date and place: October 15, 2013, Deir Al Zor, Syria
Caption: "A Free Syrian Army fighter carries his weapon as he takes position inside a house in Deir al-Zor October 1, 2013."

Figure 19

Photographer: Yves Marchand and Romain Meffre
Copyright: Yves Marchand and Romain Meffre
Date and place: 2005, Detroit, Michigan, USA
Caption: "Lawyers, hairdressers, doctors, dentists . . . From then on, life unfolded in tiers in the skyscrapers. The Broderick tower with its 34 stories was one of the multiple vacant skyscrapers downtown. It has been redeveloped into apartments in 2012. 18th FLOOR DENTIST CABINET, BRODERICK TOWER, 2005."

Figure 20

Photographer: Kim Kyung-Hoon
Copyright: Reuters / Kim Kyung-Hoon
Date and place: March 13, 2011, Koriyama, Japan
Caption: "Official in protective gear talks to a woman who is from the evacuation area near the Fukushima Daini nuclear plant in Koriyama March 13, 2011. Japan battled to contain a radiation leak at an earthquake-crippled nuclear plant on Sunday, but faced a fresh threat with the failure of the cooling system in a second reactor."

Figure 21

Photographer: Brad Hunter

Copyright: Brad Hunter / Newspix / Getty Images

Date and place: October 20, 2013, Bilpin, New South Wales

Caption: "Firefighters take part in back burning operations at a property in the Blue Mountains on October 20, 2013 in Bilpin, Australia. At least one man has died and hundreds of properties have been destroyed in bushfires that are devastating the Blue Mountains and Central Coast regions of New South Wales."

Figure 22

Photographer: Steve Hebert

Copyright: Steve Hebert / The New York Times / Redux

Date and place: December 26, 2011, Bentonville, Arkansas, USA

Caption: "Jim Dine's 'Walking to Boras' at the Crystal Bridges Museum of American Art in Arkansas."

Figure 23

Photographer: Manish Swarup

Copyright: AP Photo / Manish Swarup

Date and place: March 22, 2013, Nandgaon, India

Caption: "Indian villagers from Nandgaon wait for the arrival of villagers from Barsana to play Lathmar Holi at the Nandagram temple famous for Lord Krishna and his brother Balram, in Nandgaon 120 kilometers from New Delhi, India, Friday March 22, 2013. During Lathmar Holi the women of Nandgaon, the hometown of Krishna, beat the men from Barsana, the legendary hometown of Radha, consort of Hindu God Krishna, with wooden sticks in response to their teasing as they depart the town."

Figure 24

Photographer: Bruno Barbey

Copyright: Bruno Barbey / Magnum Photos

Date and place: August 18, 2012, Shanghai, China

Caption: "CHINA. Shanghai. In the background, Lujiazui Financial District in Pudong. August 18th, 2012."

Figure 25

Photographer: Ed Ou

Copyright: Ed Ou / The New York Times / Redux

Date and place: February 7, 2011, Tahrir Square, Egypt

Caption: "Feb 7: Egyptian youths use laptops to post video of the protests in Cairo's Tahrir Square on social networking sites like Facebook and Twitter, Feb. 7, 2011. The breath and hum of democracy seemed almost a libidinous thing in parts of the Middle East, but, in truth, the body heat had been simmering for years."

Figure 26

Photographer: Tómas Munita

Copyright: Tómas Munita / The New York Times / Redux

Date and place: January 26, 2012, Syria

Caption: "A portrait of President Bashar Assad hangs on a wall inside a government building in Damascus, Syria, Jan. 26, 2012. As the fighting between Syrian troops and army defectors surged in the nearby suburb of Douma, thousands of backers of Assad rallied in the streets of downtown Damascus in a show of support for his regime."

Figure 27

Photographer: Kevin Bauman

Copyright: Kevin Bauman

Date and place: Detroit, USA, circa 1990

Caption: "100 Abandoned Houses, Frame 64."

Figure 28

Photographer: Kim Kyung-Hoon

Copyright: Reuters / Kim Kyung-Hoon

Date and place: May 21, 2010, Tokyo, Japan

Caption: "Pedestrians are reflected in a stock index board outside of a brokerage in Tokyo May 21, 2010. Japan's Nikkei average slid more than 3 percent and hit a five month low on Friday with exporters hurt after the yen strengthened against the euro on worries about disunity among euro zone leaders on how to address the region's debt crisis."

Figure 29

Photographer: Matthias Schrader

Copyright: AP Photo / Matthias Schrader

Date and place: September 18, 2010, Munich, Germany

Caption: "A visitor sits in front of the main exit of beer tent as waitresses make a brake [*sic*] prior to the opening of the Oktoberfest beer festival in Munich, southern Germany, Saturday 18, 2010. People from around the world are expected at the biggest and most famous beer festival Oktoberfest which runs from Sept 18 until Oct 4 and marks its 200th anniversary this year."

Figure 30

Photographer: Leon Neal

Copyright: Leon Neal / AFP / Getty Images

Date and place: May 24, 2008, Sheffield, United Kingdom

Caption: "US Haley Ishimatsu takes part in the Women's platform semi-final stages of the 2nd FINA Diving World Series in Sheffield on May 24, 2008. Coming three months before the start of the 2008 Olympic Games in Beijing, the FINA event will attract the best divers in the world with competitors set to prove their worth to their national teams."

Figure 31

Photographer: Simon Maina

Copyright: Simon Maina / AFP / Getty Images

Date and place: January 16, 2008, Nairobi, Kenya

Caption: "A man jumps on a burnt vehicle after he and other supporters of Kenya's opposition leader Raila Odinga set barricades on fire on a road in the Kibera slum of Nairobi 16 January 2008. Odinga vowed 16 January 2008 to press with plans to stage nationwide rallies protesting President Mwai Kibaki's re-election despite a police ban. 'Nothing will stop us from mounting such rallies,' Odinga said in a statement, as small groups of protestors started gathering nationwide, heeding his call for three days of rallies."

Figure 32

Photographer: Rina Castelnuovo

Copyright: Rina Castelnuovo / The New York Times / Redux

Date and place: March 10, 2009, West Bank

Caption: "In Hebron, a Jewish settler threw wine at a Palestinian woman in March, 2009. The city is a flashpoint of tensions between settlers and Palestinians."

Figure 33

Photographer: Tara Todras-Whitehill

Copyright: AP Photo / Tara Todras-Whitehill

Date and place: November 20, 2011, Cairo, Egypt

Caption: "A protester throws a gas canister towards Egyptian riot police, not seen, near the interior ministry during clashes in downtown Cairo, Egypt, Sunday, Nov. 20, 2011. Firing tear gas and rubber bullets, Egyptian riot police on Sunday clashed for a second day with thousands of rock-throwing protesters demanding that the ruling military quickly announce a date to hand over power to an elected government."

Figure 34

Photographer: Anatolii Boiko

Copyright: Anatolii Boiko / AFP / Getty Images

Date and place: January 22, 2014, Kiev, Ukraine

Caption: "Riot police officers gather as they clash with protestors in the center of Kiev on January 22, 2014. Ukrainian police today stormed protesters' barricades in Kiev as violent clashes erupted and activists said that one person had been shot dead by the security forces. Total of two activists shot dead during clashing. The move by police increased tensions to a new peak after two months of protests over President Viktor Yanukovych's failure to sign a deal for closer ties with the EU."

Figure 35

Photographer: Ali Ali

Copyright: epa / Ali Ali

Date and place: March 10, 2010, Gaza City

Caption: "Young supporters of the Islamic Jihad movement march during a rally in Gaza City, 10 March 2010, showing solidarity for the Al-Aqsa mosque in Jerusalem."

Figure 36

Photographer: Nati Harnik

Copyright: AP Photo / Nati Harnik

Date and place: November 11, 2009, Omaha, Nebraska, USA

Caption: "An unidentified member on a JROTC honor guard participates in a Veterans Day ceremony in Omaha, Nebraska, Wednesday, Nov. 11, 2009."

Figure 37

Photographer: Ramzi Haidar

Copyright: Ramzi Haidar / AFP / Getty Images

Date and place: May 9, 2008, Beirut, Lebanon

Caption: "A Shiite gunman (R) drinks coffee in the streets of Beirut on May 9, 2008. Hezbollah fighters seized control of rival pro-government strongholds in Beirut today as gunbattles (sic) rocked the Lebanese capital for a third day, edging the nation dangerously close to an all-out civil war. At least 11 people have been killed during sectarian clashes, a security official told AFP."

Figure 38

Photographer: Mohammad Ameen

Copyright: Reuters / Mohammed Ameen

Date and place: April 15, 2013, Baghdad, Iraq

Caption: "Residents gather at the site of a car bomb attack in the Kamaliya district in Baghdad April 15, 2013. Car bombs and attacks on cities across Iraq, including two blasts at a checkpoint at Baghdad international airport, killed at least 20 people and wounded more than 200 on Monday, police said. The wave of attacks in Baghdad, Kirkuk, Tuz Khurmato and other towns to the north to south, came days before Iraqis vote in provincial elections that will test political stability more than a year after US troops left the country."

Figure 39

Photographer: Joao Silva

Copyright: Joao Silva / The New York Times / Redux

Date and place: October 9, 2007, Baghdad, Iraq

Caption: "An Iraqi boy peered Tuesday inside a car that was towed to a Baghdad police station after two women inside were killed."

Figure 40

Photographer: Navesh Chitrakar

Copyright: Reuters / Navesh Chitrakar

Date and place: November 13, 2013, Kathmandu, Nepal

Caption: "A victim, with her eyes wide open, lies on a hospital bed after an attack on a passenger microbus by an unidentified group in Kathmandu."

Figure 41

Photographer: Todd Heisler

Copyright: Todd Heisler / Denver Public Library, Western History Collection

Date and place: 2005, Reno, Nevada, USA

Caption: "When 2nd Lt. James Cathey's body arrived at the Reno Airport, Marines climbed into the cargo hold of the plane and draped the flag over his casket as passengers watched the family gather on the tarmac. During the arrival of another Marine's casket last year at Denver International Airport, Major Steve Beck described the scene as one of the most powerful in the process. 'See the people in the windows? They sit right there in the plane, watching those Marines. You gotta wonder what's going through their minds, knowing that they're on the plane that brought him home,' he said. 'They're going to remember being on that plane for the rest of their lives. And they should.'"

Figure 42

Photographer: Hosam Katan

Copyright: Reuters / Hosam Katan

Date and place: March 7, 2014, Aleppo, Syria

Caption: "People inspect damage at a site hit by what activists said were barrel bombs dropped by forces loyal to Syria's President Bashar al-Assad in Aleppo's district of al-Sukari March 7, 2014."

Figure 43

Photographer: Frans Jo - Imageenation

Copyright: Frans Jo - Imageenation / Getty Images

Date and place: n.d., Chiang Mai, Thailand

Caption: "Loy Kratong Floating Festival in Chiang Mai—Thailand. It started with ceremonies in the morning followed by meditation and prayers."

Figure 44

Photographer: Xinhua

Copyright: Xinhua / Landov

Date and place: April 4, 2013, Donglan, China

Caption: The bird [*sic*] eye view shows paddy fields in golden sunlight at Jiangping Village of Wuzhuan Town in Donglan County, southwest China's Guangxi Zhuang Autonomous Region on April 4, 2013."

Figure 45

Photographer: Damon Winter

Copyright: Damon Winter / The New York Times / Redux

Date and place: August 21, 2009, Querencia, Brazil

Caption: "Small islands of forest dot the landscape of farms and ranches, fulfilling regulations to maintain percentages of native forest on agricultural properties. Driven by profits derived from fertile soil, the region's dense forests have been aggressively cleared over the past decade, and Mato Grosso is now Brazil's leading producer of soy, corn and cattle, exported across the globe by multinational companies."

Figure 46

Photographer: Wojtek Radwanski

Copyright: Wojtek Radwanski / AFP / Getty Images

Date and place: May 13, 2013, Warsaw, Poland

Caption: "The human remains are seen during the exhumation of a Stalinist-era mass grave on the military cemetery in the heart of the Polish capital Warsaw, May 13, 2013. The grave is believed to contain the remains of around 200 victims of a post-war campaign of communist terror."

Figure 47

Photographer: Hiroya Minakuchi

Copyright: Hiroya Minakuchi / Minden Pictures

Date and place: n.d., Channel Islands, California, USA

Caption: "Blue whale (Balaenoptera musculus) surfacing, showing underside of expandable, pleated throat pouch, Channel Islands, California."

Figure 48

Photographer: Lucas Jackson

Copyright: Reuters / Lucas Jackson

Date and place: April 21, 2010, Eyjafjallajökull, Iceland

Caption: "Rocks are reflected in a lake that has been muddied by volcanic ash from Iceland's Eyjafjallajökull volcano April 21, 2010. The Icelandic volcano which grounded air traffic over Europe is still erupting, but it is spewing less ash, the meteorological office and experts said on Wednesday. Close monitoring of the neighboring and potentially more dangerous Katla volcano was also taking place, but there have been no signs it has re-awakened, they added."

INDEX

Page numbers in italics refer to illustrations.